THE WRITINGS • GEORGE WASHINGTON

Publisher's Note

The book descriptions we ask book-sellers to display prominently warn that this is an historic book with numerous typos or missing text; it is not indexed or illustrated.

The book was created using optical character recognition software. The software is 99 percent accurate if the book is in good condition. However, we do understand that even one percent can be an annoying number of typos! And sometimes all or part of a page may be missing from our copy of the book. Or the paper may be so discolored from age that it is difficult to read. We apologize and gratefully acknowledge Google's assistance.

After we re-typeset and design a book, the page numbers change so the old index and table of contents no longer work. Therefore, we often re-move them; otherwise, please ignore them.

We carefully proof read any book that will sell enough copies to pay for the proof reader; unfortunately, many don't. For those we try to let customers download a free copy of the original typo-free book. Simply enter the bar-code number from the back cover of the paperback in the Free Book form at www.RareBooksClub.com. You may also qualify for a free trial membership in our book club to download up to four books for free. Simply enter the barcode number from the back cover onto the membership form on our home page. The book club entitles you to select from more than a million books at no additional charge. Simply enter the title or subject onto the search form to find the books.

If you have any questions, could you please be so kind as to consult our Fre-quently Asked Questions page at www. RareBooksClub.com/faqs.cfm? You are also welcome to contact us there.

General Books LLC™, Memphis, USA, 2012. ISBN: 9781154088700.

❊❊ ❊❊ ❊❊ ❊❊ ❊❊ ❊❊ ❊❊ ❊❊

CORRESPONDENCE AND MISCELLA-NEOUS PAPERS RELATING TO THE AMER-ICAN REVOLUTION. TO MAJOR-GENERAL SCHUYLER.

Head-Quarters, Ramapo, 24 July, 1777.

Dear Sir, Your two favors of the 21st and 22d instant with their enclosures are come to hand. I am sorry to find, that you have not yet been joined by a large number of militia, and that it has been found necessary to dismiss a part even of those, who have come to your assis-tance, though their presence is at this time so urgently wanted. I hope, how-ever, that your situation will soon be far more respectable; as I cannot but think the eastern States, which are so intimately concerned in the matter, will exert themselves to throw in effectual succours to enable you to check the progress of the enemy, and repel a dan-ger, with which they are so immediately threatened. The information of the pris-oners and others, transmitted by you, does not make the numbers of the ene-my to exceed the idea first entertained of them, nor do I see any thing in it to induce a belief, that their progress will be so rapid, as not to give you time to make proper preparations and receive sufficient acces VOL. V. 1 A sions of force to enable you to give them a vig-orous and successful opposition. They do not appear to be much more than five thousand strong, and seem to be un-provided with wagons to transport the immense quantity of baggage and war-like apparatus, without which they can-not pretend to penetrate the country. You mention their having a great num-ber of horses; but they will nevertheless require a considerable number of wag-ons, for there are a great many things that cannot be transported on horses. As they can never think of advancing, with-out securing their rear by leaving gar-risons in the fortresses behind, the force with which they can come against you will be greatly reduced by the detach-ments necessary for the purpose. And as they have to cut out their road, and re-

move the impediments you have put in the,way, this circumstance, with the in-cumbrance they must feel in their bag-gage, will inevitably retard their march a considerable time, and give you leisure and opportunity to prepare a good reception for them. If they con-tinue to act in detachments, you will have it in your power to improve it to very great advantage, by falling vigor-ously upon some one of them with your whole force, which, if you are fortunate enough to succeed in, will be fatal to them.

I have directed General Lincoln to re-pair to you as speedily as the state of his health, which is not very perfect, will permit him. This gentleman has always supported the character of a judicious, brave, active officer, and as he is ex-ceedingly popular and much respected in the State of Massachusetts, to which he belongs, he will have a degree of in-fluence over the militia, which cannot fail of being very advantageous. I have destined him more particularly to the command of them, and I promise my-self it will have a powerful tendency to make them turn out with more cheer-fulness, and to inspire them with perse-verance to remain in the field, and for-titude and spirit to do their duty while in it. The confidence they have in him will certainly go a great way towards producing these desirable ends. You in-timate the propriety of having a body of men stationed somewhere about the Grants. The expediency of such a mea-sure appears to me evident; for it would certainly make General Burgoyne very circumspect in his advances, if it did not totally prevent them. It would keep him in continual anxiety for his rear, and oblige him to leave the posts behind him much stronger than he would oth-erwise do, and would answer many oth-er valuable purposes. General Lincoln could not be more serviceable, than in command of this body, and no person could be more proper for it.

From the view I have of the matter,

I should also think it necessary to send General Arnold, or some other sensible, spirited officer to Fort Schuyler, to take care of that post, keep up the spirits of the inhabitants, and cultivate and improve the favorable disposition of the Indians. This is recommended on the supposition, that any thing formidable should appear in that quarter.

I am, dear Sir, &c.

TO MAJOR-GENERAL PUTNAM.
Head-Quarters, Ramapo, 24 July, 1777.

Dear Sir, I have just received advice of the enemy's fleet having sailed from the Hook; in consequence of which I have to desire, that you will immediately order General Sullivan's and Lord Stirling's divisions to cross the river, and proceed towards Philadelphia. They will have more particular orders on their route. You are to reserve two field-pieces for each brigade that remains behind, except that which is to garrison the forts, and all the rest of the field-artillery is to come on with the before-mentioned divisions. Colonel Crane's battalion is to accompany them, and Colonel Lamb's to supply their place. I am, dear Sir, &c.

TO MAJOR-GENERAL PUTNAM.
Ramapo, 25 July, 1777.

Dear Sir, My letter of yesterday would inform you of the reasons, which occasion the removal of this part of the army towards Philadelphia, and the recall of the divisions under General Sullivan and Lord Stirling. I have now to add, that it is my desire that you should keep as many of the remaining troops, as can possibly be spared from the dejence of the forts and passes of the Highlands, in the most perfect readiness to move, either this way or to the eastward as occasion shall require. I do not pretend to fix upon or ascertain the number, which may be necessary for those defences. You and your officers must determine this point, proportioning your defence to the troops left by General Howe on York Island. If you have not already done if, let the eastern States be immediately advised of the fleet's sailing from the Hook, that they may be in a posture of defence, as no person can with certainty say where the blow will be struck. I am, dear Sir, &c.

P. S. Since writing the above, I have received yours of yesterday's date, enclosing the intercepted letter from General Howe to Burgoyne. To me a stronger proof could not be given, that the former is not going to the eastward, than this letter affords. It was evidently intended to fall into our hands. The complexion of it, the circumstances attending it, evince this beyond a doubt in my mind. I therefore desire, that no time may be lost in sending on General Sullivan and Lord Stirling with their divisions. If it was not too dangerous to hazard their shipping at sea, merely to perform a manoeuvre to deceive, I should think it not unlikely, that the North River might yet be the object, and that they had run out with a view of returning when our troops should be drawn off; but the possibility of a dispersion of their fleet makes so much against this, that I am persuaded more than ever, that Philadelphia is the place of destination, and I therefore hope that no time will be lost in marching the troops already ordered, and preparing as many of the others as can be spared to follow, if my conjectures should prove to be right.

This intercepted letter was in the handwriting of General Howe, and signed by him. It was directed to General Burgoyne. The following is an exact transcript.

" Now York, 30 July, 1777.

" Dear Sir,

" I have received your letter of the 14th of May from Quebec, and shall fully observe the contents. The expedition to B n Boston will take place of that up the North River. If, according to my expectations, we may succeed rapidly in the possession of B, the enemy having no force of consequence there, I shall, without loss of time, proceed to cooperate with you in the defeat of the rebel army opposed to yon. Clinton is sufficiently strong to amuse Washington and Putnam. I am now making demonstration to the southward, which I think will have the full effect in carrying our plan into execution. Success attend you.

" W. Howe."

The young man, who brought out the letter from NeV York, voluntarily sought the American guard, and gave it up. He had been a prisoner in the city, and said he was offered a high reward for carrying this letter to General Burgoyne; that he at first declined taking charge of it, but at last he acceded to the proposal, with the intention to recover hia liberty, and then take the letter to the American camp. Whether this was a true account of the matter, or not, must rest on the testimony of the young man. There can be no question, however, that the letter reached the destination for which it was intended by General Howe.

A» TO WILLIAM FRANKLIN.

Head-Quarters, Ramapo, 25 July, 1777.

Sir, I have this moment received your letter, of the 22d instant, by express. I heartily sympathize with you in your distressing situation; but, however strong may be my inclination to comply with your request, it is by no means in my power to supersede a positive resolution of Congress, under which your present confinement took place. I have enclosed your letter to them, and shall be happy if it may be found consistent with propriety to concur with your wishes in a matter of so delicate and interesting a nature. I sincerely hope a speedy restoration of Mrs. Franklin's health may relieve you from the anxiety you must naturally feel from her present declining condition. I am, with due respect, Sir, &c.

TO THE. PRESIDENT OF CONGRESS.
Ramapo, 25 July, 1777.

Sir, I do myself the honor to transmit to you the enclosed letter from Governor Franklin, which came this minute by express. As Mr. Franklin was confined by order of Congress, I could not think myself at liberty to answer him on the subject of his request, and therefore have referred it to their consideration. At the same time I would observe his situation is distressing, and must interest all our feelings, as I have no doubt of the THE WRITINGS Governor Franklin was a prisoner in Connecticut, where he had remained from the time he was first taken into custody the year before. He was now in Litchfield jaiL OF GEORGE WASHINGTON, VOL. V.

at Morris town, whence it will march southward, if there should be occasion, or northward upon the first advice that the enemy should be throwing any force up the North River. General Howe's in a manner abandoning General Burgoyne is so unaccountable a matter, that, till I am fully assured it is so, I cannot help casting my eyes continually behind me.

As I shall pay no regard to any flying reports of the appearance of the fleet, I shall expect an account of it from you the moment you have ascertained it to your satisfaction; and I desire that, at the same time you advise me of this, you will send an express to Lord Stirling, or the commanding officer at Trenton, to move on with the troops from thence. I am, &c.

TO 'MAJOR-GENERAL PUTNAM.
Coryell'g Ferry, 31 July, 1777.

Dear Sir, I have just received information from Philadelphia, that the enemy's fleet arrived at the Capes of Delaware yesterday. You will therefore please to order the two brigades, which were thrown over the North River, to march immediately towards Philadelphia through Morristown and over Coryell's Ferry, where boats will be ready for them. The troops are to march as expeditiously as possible without injuring the men. I beg you will endeavour to make up your garrison with militia from Connecticut and New York, as soon as possible; and I desire that you will forward this account by express to General Schuyler and to the eastern States. I hope, as they now have nothing to fear from General Howe, that they will turn out their force both Continental and militia to oppose Burgoyne. I am, &.c.

TO GOVERNOR TRUMBULL.
Coryell's Perry, 31 July, 1777.

Sir,

I was just now honored with your letter of the 25th instant. The evacuation of Ticonderoga and Mount Independence was an event so unexpected, that I do not wonder it should produce in the minds of the people, at least the well attached, the effects you mention. I am

entirely in sentiment with you, that the cause, leading to this unhappy measure, should be fully and minutely examined. Public justice, on the one hand, demands it, if it was not the result of prudence and necessity; and, on the other, the reputation of the officers concerned, if they are not blameworthy. Had not Congress considered that as a separate department, appointed the officers in some instances to that command themselves, and been fully possessed of all the facts that I am respecting the events, I should not have doubted a single moment about directing an inquiry. These matters, I say, have laid me under some doubts as to the line I should pursue; but I am persuaded, that an examination will be ordered in a few days, either by the Congress or myself, when I hope the subject will be properly discussed, and that done which is right.

As to sending Continental troops from Peekskill, no more can be detached from thence to the northern army, than are already gone. Two brigades, Nixon's and Glover's, have been ordered from thence to their aid; more than were ever intended in the arrangement of our forces. Not a man more can go, as all the Continental troops at that post, excepting two thousand, are called to join this army. For I have to inform you, that General Howe's object and opera

Vol. y. 2 tions no longer remain a secret. At half after nine o'clock this morning, I received an express from Congress, advising that the enemy's fleet, consisting of two hundred and twenty-eight sail, were at the Capes of Delaware yesterday in the forenoon. This being the case, there can be no doubt but he will make a vigorous push to possess Philadelphia, and we should collect all the force we can to oppose him.

Fearing from report and from the event itself (the abandonment of the northern posts), that distrust, jealousy, and suspicion of the conduct of the officers might arise in the militia, and that degree of confidence in them wanted, which would be necessary to success, and to give a more promising aspect to

our affairs in that quarter, I sent Generals Lincoln and Arnold to assist in that command. These two gentlemen are esteemed good officers, and I think very deservedly. I am persuaded, that nothing their judgments shall direct will be omitted to stop the progress of General Burgoyne's arms, so far as in them lies; and I am equally sure, that their personal exertions and bravery will not be wanting in any instance. Their presence I trust will remove every ground of diffidence and backwardness in the militia, and that they will go on, when and where their services are demanded, with a spirit and resolution becoming freemen and the sacred cause in which they are engaged. As the troops are on their march from hence, I shall not add more, than that I have the most entire confidence in your exertions upon every occasion to advance the common interest; and that I have the honor to be, with great respect, Sir, &,c The appointment of the Marquis de Lafayette as a major-general in the service of the United States, one of the most important events of the revolution, took place on the 31st of July, and is thus recorded in the Journals of Congress.

" Whereas the Marquis de Lafayette, out of his great zeal to the cause of liberty, in which the United States are engaged, has left his family and connexions, and at his own expense come over to offer his service to the United States, without pension or particular allowance, and is anxious to risk his life in our cause; Resolved, that his service be accepted, and that, in consideration of his zeal, his illustrious family, and connexions, he have the rank and commission of major-general in the army of the United States." See Appendix, No. I.

TO MAJOR-GENERAL PUTNAM.
Chester, 1 August, 1777.

Dear Sir,

I have this moment received intelligence by express, that the enemy's fleet yesterday morning about eight o'clock sailed out of the Capes in an eastern course. This surprising event gives me the greatest anxiety, and, unless every possible exertion is made, may be productive of the happiest consequences to the enemy, and the most injurious to us. I have desired General Sullivan's division, and the two brigades that left you last, immediately to return and recross the river, and I shall forward on the rest of the army with all the expedition in my power. I have also written to General Clinton requesting him instantly to reinforce you, with as many militia of the State of New York as he can collect; and you are, on receipt of this, to send on an express to Governor Trumbull, urging it upon him to assist you, with as many of the Connecticut militia as he can get together, and without a moment's loss of time.

The, importance of preventing Mr. Howe's getting possession of the Highlands by a *coup de main* is infinite to America; and, in the present situation of things, every effort that can be thought of must be used. The probability of his going to the eastward is exceedingly small. and the ill effects that might attend such a step inconsiderable in comparison with those, that would inevitably attend a successful stroke upon the Highlands. Connecticut cannot be in more danger through any channel than this, and every motive of its own interest and the general good demands its utmost endeavours to give you effectual assistance. Governor Trumbull will I trust be sensible of this. I am, &c.

TO URIOADIER-GEXERAL DERORRE.

Head-Quarters, Philadelphia, 3 August, 1777.

Sir,

I this day sent you orders by express, to halt wherever my letter should find you, and not to proceed any further towards the Delaware, until you had orders from me for that purpose; nor to return towards Pcekskill, unless you should have certain information, that the enemy's fleet were arrived at the Hook, or had gone further eastward, in which case you were to go back to Peekskill as expeditiously as possible. I have since been favored with yours of the 2d instant from Boundbrook. With respect to the Tory, who was tried and executed by your order, though his crime was heinous enough to deserve the fate he met with, and though I am

convinced you acted in the affair with good intention, yet I cannot but wish it had not happened. In the first place it was a matter, that did not come within the jurisdiction of martial law, and therefore the whole proceeding was irregular and illegal, and will have a tendency to excite discontent, jealousy, and murmurs among the people. In the second place, if the trial could properly have been made by a court-martial, as the division you command is only a detachment from the army, and you cannot have been considered as in a separate department, there is none of our articles of war that will justify your inflicting *capital* punishment, even on a soldier, much less on a citizen. I mention these things for your future government, as what is past cannot be recalled. The temper of the Americans, and the principles on which the present contest turns, will not countenance proceedings of this nature.

I am sorry there is such a difference between Major Mullens and you; but I cannot with propriety consent to your dismissing him without his having had a fair trial, and any charges alleged against him being properly proved. As he is now under arrest, you may order a court-martial to be held for his trial, and report the proceedings to me, on which I shall determine what appears to be just. I am, Sir, &c.

TO THE PRESIDENT OF CONGRESS.

Philadelphia, 3 August, 1777.

Sir, Your favor of this date, with its enclosures, is now before me. At the same time that I express my thanks for the high mark of confidence which Congress have been pleased to repose in me by their resolve, authorizing me to send an officer to command the northern army, I should wish to be excused from making the appointment. For this many reasons might be mentioned, which, I am persuaded, will occur to Congress upon reflection. The northern department in a great measure has been considered as separate, and more peculiarly under their direction; and the officers commanding there always of their nomination. I have never interfered further than merely to advise, and to give

such aids as were in my power, on the requisitions of those officers. The present situation of that depart VOL. V. B mcnt is delicate and critical, and the choice of an officer to the command may involve very interesting and important consequences.

It is certainly necessary, that a body of militia should be immediately called out to reinforce the northern army. In the conference which your committee honored me with yesterday evening, I mentioned the number which I thought sufficient; but my opinion on this point, and the apportioning them to the different States, I wish to submit to Congress, who can best determine the quotas that should come from each. I would only observe, that Connecticut and New York are already, and may be again, called on, to afford succours to the army at Peekskill. I have the honor to be, &c.

Congress had resolved on the 1st of August, that General Schuyler should repair to head-quarters, and that " General Washington should be directed to order such general officer as he should think proper to repair to the northern department to relieve Major-General Schuyler in his command." It was in consequence of this resolve, that the above letter was written. The day after the resolve was passed, General Washington received a letter from the New England delegates in Congress as follows. "sir,

" As Congress have authorized your Excellency to send a proper officer to take the command in the northern department, we take the liberty to signify to your Excellency, that, in our opinion, no man will be more likely to restore harmony, order, and discipline, and retrieve our affairs in that quarter, than Major-General Gates. He has on experience acquired the confidence, and stands high in the esteem, of the eastern States and troops. With confidence in your wisdom we cheerfully submit it to your Excellency's consideration, and have taken this method to communicate our sentiments, judging it would give you less trouble, than a personal application. We are, with great esteem, your Excellency's most obedient and most humble servants."

The original of this paper is in the handwriting of Samuel Adams, and is signed by the following names in the order in which they here stand, John Adams, Nathaniel Folsom, Samuel Adams, Henry Marchant, Elbridge Gerry, Eliphalet Dyer, William Williams. A prejudice existed against General Schuyler among the people of the New England States, which it is not easy now to explain. There was not an individual connected with the revolution;, concerning whom there is more abundant evidence of his patriotism and unwearied services in the cause of his country. But it was his misfortune to command where disasters crowded upon each other, and disappointed public expectation. The failure of the Canada expedition, and recently the loss of Ticonderoga, with the disheartening prospects of a retreating army, were all laid to the charge of the commanding general; and the tjde of popular clamor, strengthened by the party antipathy of a few prominent politicians, was not to be resisted. Even the friends of General Schuyler acquiesced in his being superseded, upon the conviction that the eastern troops would not march to join the army under his command. This point was urged in Congress with great pertinacity by the eastern delegates, but with more zeal than justice, as appears from the fact, that a large reinforcement of troops was then preparing to march from New Hampshire, who. achieved the brilliant victory of Bennington, while General Schuyler was yet at the head of the army. Other particulars on this subject may be seen in Sparks's *Life of Gouvernew Morris,* VoL I. pp. 138-148.

TO GOVERNOR HENRY.

Philadelphia, 4 August, 1777.

Sir, The great expense and loss of time, which has attended the recruiting service in most of the States, and the little advantage derived from it, have induced Congress to recommend to the executive powers of each, to adopt certain new regulations, for promoting this important and essential business, and for taking it entirely out of the hands of the officers of the army. The resolve on this subject, and the regulations recommended, passed on the 31st ultimo; and will, I presume, be transmitted to you by the President.

The plan recommended by Congress was, that each State should be divided into districts, and a person be appointed to raise recruits in each district, the whole to be under the direction of the State authorities. Security was to be taken of every such agent for a faithful discharge of bis duty; and, as a full compensation for his trouble and expense, he was to receive eight dollars for every able-bodied recruit, that he should enlist for three years, or during the war. The same agent was empowered to take up deserters, and allowed five dollars for every deserter he should secure. The recruits were moreover permitted to join any regiment or company, which they vhould choose at the time they enlisted, if such regiment or company was not already full, and in that case they might

I will not urge the expediency of carrying this proceeding into immediate execution. I shall only observe, that the necessity is obvious, and that it demands our most active attention. The principal cause of my troubling you at this lime is, to request that, after the persons recommended are appointed in your State, you would be pleased to transmit to me their names, their places of residence, and those also designed for the rendezvous of recruits and deserters. As soon as I am advised upon these subjects, I shall recall all the officers, who are recruiting, and order them forthwith to join their respective corps. Before I conclude, I would beg leave to mention, that the success of this interesting business, in all its parts, will depend much upon a judicious choice of those, who are to be employed in it, and that, I think, the districts should not be too large and extensive. I have the honor, &,c TO MAJOR-GENERAL GATES.

Head-Quarters, 4 August, 1777.

Sir,

You will perceive by the enclosed copy of a letter.from Congress, that they have destined you to the command of the army in the northern department, and have directed me to order you immediately to repair to that post. I have therefore to desire you will, in pursuance of their intention, proceed to the place of your destination, with all the expedition you can, and take upon you the command of the northern army accordingly. Wishing you success, and that you may speedily be able to restore the face of affairs in that quarter, I am, with great regard, Sir, yours, &c. choose any other. General Washington was directed to call in all the Continental officers then absent on the recruiting service, except such as were necessary to receive recruits, and march them to the army.— *Journals, July 31st.* This letter was likewise sent as a circular to all the States north of Virginia. TO THE COUNCIL OF SAFETY OF NEW YORK., Phfladelphia, 4 August, 1777.

Gentlemen,

The misfortune at Ticonderoga has given a very disagreeable turn to our affairs, and has thrown a gloom upon the prospect, which the campaign, previous to that event, afforded. But I am in great hopes, that the ill consequences of it will not continue long to operate, and that the jealousies and alarms, which. so sudden and unexpected an event has produced in the minds of the people, both in your State and to the eastward, will soon subside, and give place to the more rational dictates of self-preservation, and a regard to the common good. In fact, the worst effect of that event is, that it has served to produce those distrusts and apprehensions; for, if the matter were coolly and dispassionately considered, there would be nothing found so formidable in General Burgoyne and the force under him, with all his successes, as to countenance the least degree of despondency; and experience would show, that even the moderate exertions of the States, more immediately interested, would be sufficient to check his career, and, perhaps, convert the advantages he has gained into his ruin. But while people continue to view what has happened through the medium of suspicion and fear, there is no predicting to what length an enterprising man may push his good fortune. I have the fullest confidence, that no endeavours of the Council

Vol. r. 3 B will be wanted to bring your State (with the distresses of which I am deeply affected) to every effort it is capable of making in its present mutilated situation; and they may rely upon it, that no means in my power shall be unemployed to cooperate with them, in the danger that presses upon the State, and through it threatens the continent. If I do not give so effectual aid as I could wish to the northern army, it is not for want of inclination, nor from being too little impressed with the importance of doing it, but because the state of affairs in this quarter will not possibly admit of it. It would be the height of impolicy to weaken ourselves too much here, in order to increase our strength there; and it must certainly be considered more difficult, as welt as of greater moment, to control the main army of the enemy, than an inferior and I may say dependent one; for it is pretty obvious, that, if General Howe can be kept at bay, and prevented from effecting his principal purposes, the successes of General Burgoyne, whatever they may be, must be partial and temporary.

Nothing that I can do shall be wanting to rouse the eastern States, and excite them to those exertions, which the exigency of our affairs so urgently demands. I lament that they have not yet done more; that so few of their militia have come into the field, and that those few have behaved so inconsistently with the duty they owe their country, at this critical period. But I have nevertheless great reliance upon those States. I know they are capable of powerful efforts, and that their attachment to the cause, notwithstanding they may be a little tardy, will not allow them long to withhold their aid, at a time when their own safety, that also of a sister State, and, in a great measure, the safety of the continent call for their greatest zeal and activity. I flatter myself, that the presence of Generals Lincoln and Arnold, in the northern department, will have a happy effect upon them. Those gentlemen possess much of their confidence, particularly the former, than whom there is perhaps no man from the State of Massachusetts, who enjoys more universal esteem and popularity; and, in addition to that, they may both be considered as very Valuable officers.

You intimate a wish, that some assistance could be drawn from the southern States at this time. But, while things remain in their present posture, and appearances, however illusory they may prove, afford the strongest reason to keep their force at home, to counteract the seeming intentions of General Howe, I could neither ask nor expect them to detach any part of it to the succour of the northern States, which are so well able to defend themselves against the force they now have to oppose.

I hope that an exaggerated idea of the enemy's force may have no injurious influence on our measures. There is no circumstance, with which I am acquainted, that induces me to believe General Burgoyne can have more than six or seven thousand men; and, if the force left in Canada is so considerable, as the information you send me makes it, he cannot have even so many. The representations of prisoners and deserters, in this respect, are of little validity. Their knowledge is always very limited, and their intention, particularly the former, is very often bad. Beyond what regards the state pf their own respective companies, no attention is due to what they say. The number of regiments, which your informant mentions, agrees with other accounts. But as to the number of men in each company, which he gives the establishment, I am persuaded it is not the actual state. The British army in Canada last campaign, though they suffered little by action, must have decreased materially by sickness and other casualties; and if the recruits, both from England and Germany, bore any proportion to those, who have reinforced General Howe, the state of their regiments must be greatly inferior to what your information supposes. Reasoning from analogy, so far as it will apply, I cannot imagine that the British regiments can exceed two hundred and fifty men each, fit for the field, or that the foreign troops can amount to much more than three thousand men.

The appointment of General Clinton to the government of your State is an event, which in itself gives me great pleasure, and very much abates the regret I should otherwise feel for the loss of his services in the military line. That gentieman's character is such, as will make him peculiarly useful at the head of your State, in a situation so alarming and interesting, as it at present experiences. For the future, agreeably to your desire, I shall direct my applications to him.

I have the honor to be, &c.

TO JOHN AUGUSTINE WASHINGTON.

Gerumntown, 5 August, 1777.

Dear Brother, Since General Howe removed from the Jerseys, the troops under my command have been more harassed by marching and countermarching, than by any other thing that has happened to them in the course of the campaign. After he had embarked his troops, the presumption that he would operate upon the North River, to form a junction with General Burgoyne, was so strong, that I removed from Middlebrook to Morristown, and from Morristown to the Clove, a narrow passage leading through the Highlands, about eighteen miles from the river. Indeed, upon some pretty strong presumptive evidence, I threw two divisions over the North River. In this situation we lay till about the 24th ultimo, when receiving certain information, that the fleet had actually sailed from Sandy Hook, and upon the concurring sentiment of every one, though I acknowledge my doubts of it were strong, that Philadelphia was the object, we countermarched and got to Coryell's Ferry on the Delaware, about thirty-three miles above the city, on the 27th, where I lay until I received information from Congress, that the enemy were actually at the Capes of Delaware. This brought us in great haste to this place for the defence of the city. But in less than twenty-four hours after our arrival, we got accounts of the disappearance of the fleet on the 31st; since which, nothing having been heard of them,, we have remained here in a very irksome state of suspense; some imagining that they are gone to the southward, whilst a majority, in whose opinion upon this occasion I concur, are satisfied that they are gone to the eastward. The fatigue, however, and injury which men must sustain by long marches in such extreme heat, as we have felt for the last five days, must keep us quiet till we hear something of the destination of the enemy.

George Clinton was the first governor under the new Constitution of New York. He was chosen in July, and sworn into office at Kingston on the 30th of that month; and although from this date he exercised the civil functions of his station, yet he continued in active command of the militia of the State till after the defeat of Burgoyne.

I congratulate you very sincerely on the happy passage of my sister and the rest of your family through the smallpox. Surely the daily instances, which present themselves, of the amazing benefits of inoculation, must make converts of the most rigid opposers, and bring on a repeal of that most impolitic law, which restrains it.

Our affairs at the northward have taken a turn not more unfortunate than unexpected. The public papers will convey every information that I can on this subject. To these therefore I shall refer, with this addition, that a public inquiry is ordered into the conduct of the general officers in that department, which will give them an opportunity of justifying their conduct, or the public an opportunity of making examples. This however will not retrieve the misfortune; for certain it is, that this affair has cast a dark shade upon a very bright prospect, our accounts from that quarter being very gloomy; but, some reinforcements having been sent up, and some good officers, it is to be hoped that the cloud will be dispelled. It is absolutely necessary, that all the gentlemen in every State should exert themselves to have their quota of troops completed; for, believe me, the whole are most shamefully deficient. I have from the first been among those, who have never built much upon a French war. I ever did and still do think, that they never meant more than to give us a kind of underhand assistance; that is, to supply us with arms and the like for our money and trade. This may, indeed, if Great Britain has spirit and strength enough to resent it, bring on a war; but the declaration, if on either side, must I am convinced come from the last mentioned power.

I have taken Colonel Presly P. Thornton into my family as an extra aid. This, I dare say, his own merit, as well as the great worth of his father, will entitle him to. My love and best wishes are presented to my sister and the rest of your family, and, with sincerest affection, believe and be assured, I am, &c.

It is remarkable, that, as late as the year 1769, a law was passed in Virginia prohibiting inoculation for the smallpox, and imposing a penalty of one thousand pounds on any person, who should import or bring into the colony the infectious matter with a purpose of inoculation.— Hening's *Statutes at Large,* Vol. VIII. p. 371. TO MAJOR-GENERAL PUTNAM.

Germantown, 7 August, 1777.

Dear Sir,

We are yet entirely in the dark as to the destination of the enemy. The fleet has neither been seen nor heard of since they left the Capes of Delaware, on this day week. If they had intended returning to the Hook, we must have heard of their arrival there long before this time, as the winds have been constantly fair. As the sickly season has commenced at the southward, and there is no capital object there, I cannot conceive that they are gone that way. I can therefore only conclude, that they intend to go round Long Island into the Sound, or still farther eastward. If they do either of these, it must be upon a plan of cooperating with General Burgoyne, who, as matters are going on, will find little difficulty in penetrating to Albany; for by the last accounts our army had fallen down to Saratoga.

Congress have thought proper to call down General Schuyler and General St. Clair, to give an account of the causes of our misfortunes to the northward, and General Gates goes up to take the command. General Schuyler urges the necessity of further reinforcements, alleging that he derives no assistance from the militia. Your post is the only one from whence a reinforcement can immediately be sent; but as I would not wish to weaken you, as the enemy seem to bend their course again towards you, I desire that you and the general officers would consider the matter fully, and, if you think you can spare Cortlandt's and Livingston's regiments, that they may be put in readiness to move. I have ordered the heavy baggage of the army to be thrown over the Delaware again, and I hold the men in constant readiness to march the moment we receive any accounts of the enemy. I very much approve of your throwing up redoubts and obstructions at the entrance of the passes near your posts, as these, with the natural strength of the ground, must render the approach of an enemy extremely difficult without considerable loss. I am, &c.

TO THE PRESIDENT OF CONGRESS.

Camp, near Germantown, 9 August, 1777.

Sir, I have been duly honored with your letter of yesterday, and with its enclosures. I shall pay attention to the resolves transmitted; and, as soon as circumstances admit, shall propose to General Howe an exchange between Lieutenant-Colonel Campbell and the Hessian field-officers, and a like number of ours, of equal rank in his hands. I would beg leave to lay before Congress a copy of a report made by a board of general officers, held on the 7th instant, to consult on several matters respecting the army. In the course of their deliberation they took into consideration the subject reported. I shall only add, that this matter has been long complained of by the officers, and the more so as the indulgence they pray for could not nor can be ever attended with the least possible injury to the public, and is what I believe is allowed in most armies. Congress, I am persuaded, will give it their attention, and, if no good objections of a public nature appear against the measure, will grant what the officers wish and the board have recommended. Congress decided that General Prescott, lately captured by Colonel Barton, should be retained as a pledge for the good treatment and release of General Lee, and, as nearly as circumstances would admit, receive the same usage. General Washington was also authorized to negotiate an exchange of prisoners, upon such terms as he should judge expedient, without regard to the previous resolutions of Congress respecting Colonel Campbell and the Hessian field-officers.

The question of General Arnold's rank was brought before Congress, on the 9th of August, and a majority voted against his being restored. Party considerations seem to have mingled in the affair. Seven States were in the negative and four in the affirmative, the latter being New

I perceive by the resolves for recalling Generals Schuyler and St. Clair, that they are directed to repair to head-quarters. I also find that a committee had been resolved on, to digest a mode for inquiring into the reasons for evacuating Ticonderoga and Mount Independence, and into the conduct of the general officers in the northern department at the time of the evacuation. As these gentlemen have received the letter upon this subject by this time, and will probably be down in the course of a few days, I shall be glad to be informed what I am to do with them when they arrive. I may be then at a great distance from this, and, in such case, should be at a loss what to say, or how to conduct myself respecting them, without receiving some directions, which I request to be favored with by the earliest opportunity. I have the honor to be, &c.

Hampshire, Rhode Island, Connecticut, and Georgia. This was the first occasion on which the yeas and nays were entered in the journals of the old Congress. It was often done afterwards, and by the rules of the House it could at any time be required by a single member. — *MS. Letter »f Jama Lovell, August llth.* VOL. V. 4 C TO MAJOR-GENERAL PUTNAM.

Camp, in Bucks County, 11 August, 1777.

Dear Sir, 1 received yours of the 8th instant at this place. I was upon the march with the army to recross the Delaware, upon a supposition that the fleet had certainly gone to the eastward; but I was last night overtaken by an express from Philadelphia, with an account that they had been seen on the 7th instant off Sinepuxent Inlet, about sixteen leagues to the southward of the Capes of Delaware. Upon this I have halted for further intelligence. In the present situation of affairs I can give you no better direction, than to remain at your post and collect all the force, that you possibly can. The season of the year is, to be sure, inconvenient for the militia to be out; but the necessity of the case requires that as many as possible be retained in service; for if General Burgoyne persists in his advance upon our northern army, we must afford it support, or suffer him to make himself master of all the country above.

My last letter to you directed you to consider well, whether you could spare the two New York regiments to General Schuyler's army. If General Clinton is left upon York Island with the number of men you mention, it is undoubtedly for some other reason, than merely to keep the post. It is probably to attack you below, while Burgoyne comes down upon you. It is a matter of great consequence to ascertain that fact. Deserters and people of that class always speak of numbers from report; indeed scarce any person can form a judgment, unless he sees the troops paraded and can count the divisions. But if you can by any means obtain a list of the regiments left upon the Island, we can compute the number of men within a few hundreds, over or under. I beg you will use every method to come at this knowledge. Let your spies also be very particular in their inquiry, whether General Clinton is actually upon the Island, for an officer of his rank and military estimation would scarcely be left to keep garrison only.

It has been reported, that there was a collection of wagons and horses making at Kingsbridge; if so, it can be for no purpose but to move out; and this is another fact of which you should endeavour to know the truth. Till you are fully satisfied in the above particulars, I think you should upon no account keep any more than light parties down towards Kingsbridge; for if there is any design against your post from that quarter, they might by a sudden embarkation, and a favorable wind, get between you and the mountains, should you fall down with any considerable body. I am glad to hear that Governor Clinton has determined to resume the command of Fort Montgomery, for there cannot be a more proper man upon every account. I am, &c.

The British General Clinton had been absent during the past wintei and spring in Great Britain, and had returned to New York on the 5th of July. He was now Sir Henry Clinton, having been invested with the Order of the Bath before his departure from England. He was loft in New York by Sir William Howe, with the command of twenty-two battalions, and-instructed to act on the defensive, or otherwise according to circumstances, always keeping in view the main object of securing New York. — Sir *William Howe' Letter, July 7th.*

General Putnam had proof of Sir Henry Clinton's being on New York Island, August 3d, by his sending up a flag of truce to claim Edmund Palmer, as a lieutenant in the British service. The flag was taken up the river to Verplanck's Point by Captain Montagu in the ship Mercury and thence forwarded to Peekskill. General Putnam sent back the fol lowing reply.

" Heid-Quartera, 7 Aofiut, 1777.

" Edmund Palmer, an officer in the enemy's service, was taken as a spy lurking within our lines; he has been tried as a spy, condemned as a spy, and shall be executed as a spy, and the flag is ordered to depart immediately.

"israel Pctsam."

" P. S. He has been accordingly executed." TO GOVERNOR GEORGE CLINTON, NEW YORK.

Camp, Bucks County, 13 August, 1777.

Dear Sir,

Your vigilance in providing a proper force to oppose the enemy, and the alacrity with which the militia have assembled, afford me great satisfaction. If your efforts are seasonably and skilfully seconded by your eastern neighbours, we may hope, that General Burgoyne will find it equally difficult either to make a further progress, or to effect a retreat. You are the best judge with respect to the length of service to be required from the militia. However, as their assistance is a resource, which must be sparingly employed, I would have them detained no longer than is absolutely necessary. The excuse of want of confidence in the general officers, which has hitherto been alleged by the eastern States, for withholding those reinforcements from the northern army, which were expected from them, will be obviated by the presence of Major-General Gates.

The resolves of Congress, which relate to the recruiting of the army, will have reached you before this time, and you will have acted in consequence. By a resolve of the 3d of August, the commanding officer of the northern department has discretionary power to make requisitions on the States of New Hampshire, Massachusetts Bay, Connecticut, New York, New Jersey, and Pennsylvania. There will, therefore, be a concurrence of authority in yourself and General Gates, which you will arrange between yourselves. I am, with great regard, yours, &c.

TO MAJOR-GENERAL PUTNAM.

Head-Quarters, Bucks County, 16 August, 1777.

Dear Sir, I have your favor of the 14th instant. Just before it came to hand I had received the intelligence, which it contained, from Governor Clinton. The people in the northern army seem so intimidated by the Indians, that I have determined to send up Colonel Morgan's corps of riflemen, who will fight them in their own way. They will march from Trenton to-morrow morning, and reach Peekskill with all expedition. You will please to have sloops ready to transport them, and provisions laid in, that they may not wait a moment. The corps consists of five hundred men. Be pleased to let me have an exact return of your numbers, both Continental and Provin-

cial, that I may form a judgment of the propriety of detaching any more force to the northward. Remark to what time your Provincials are engaged.

I am, dear Sir, your most obedient servant.

TO GOVERNOR CLINTON.

Camp, at Cross Roads, 1C August, 1777.

Dear Sir, I see, with the most sensible pleasure, the exertions of your State, dismembered as it is, and under every discouragement and disadvantage. I lament, that any causes are sufficiently powerful to prevent that effectual aid from your eastern neighbours, which the interest of the public cause, and the immediate safety of your particular State, so pressingly demand at this time. But, though it is dilatory in coming, I cannot but hope it will still come, before it is too late. I imagine one cause, and not the least material, of their delay, is an apprehension of General Howe's army. It were to be wished, that his designs were once reduced to certainty. This I should be in hopes would serve to remove that inactivity and indecision, which I believe proceed in a great measure from suspense and uncertainty. I am however advised, that a body of New Hampshire militia, under General Stark, had joined General Lincoln at Bennington, and that another of Massachusetts militia was partly arrived, and the rest arriving at the same place. A tolerable body of men once collected there would make Genetl Burgoyne anxious for his rear, oblige him to advance circumspectly, and to leave such strong posts behind, as must make his main body very weak, and extremely capable of being repulsed by the force we shall have in front. I should not be very uneasy for the issue, if I could once see our northern army recovered from their present dejection, and restored to a tolerable degree of confidence and animation.

In addition to the two regiments, which are gone from Peekskill, I am forwarding as fast as possible, to join the northern army, Colonel Morgan's, corps of riflemen, amounting to about five hundred. These are all chosen men, selected from the army at large, well ac-

quainted with the use of rifles, and with that mode of fighting, which is necessary to make them a good counterpoise to the Indians; and they have distinguished themselves on a variety of occasions, since the formation of the corps, in skirmishes with the enemy. I expect the most eminent services from them; and I shall be mistaken if their presence does not go far towards producing a general desertion among the savages. I should think it would be well. even before their arrival, to begin to circulate these ideas, with proper embellishmerits, throughout the country and in the army; and to take pains to communicate them to the enemy. It would not be amiss, among other things, to magnify their numbers. I am of opinion, with the Council of Safety, that your presence to the northward might have a very happy influence, and, if it were compatible with the many other calls there are and will be upon you, I could wish to see you with the northern army at the head of the militia of your State.

From some expressions in a letter, which I have seen, written by General Lincoln to General Schuyler, I am led to infer, that it is in contemplation to unite all the militia and Continental troops in one body, and make an opposition wholly in front. If this be really the intention, I should think it a very ineligible plan. An enemy can always act with more vigor and effect, when they have nothing to apprehend for their flanks and rear, than when they have; and it is one of the most approved and most universally practised manoeuvres of war, to keep their fears continually awake on these accounts, and, when circumstances permit, to be actually in condition to give them serious annoyance in those parts. Independent of the inconveniences, that attend a situation, where the rear and flanks are constantly exposed to the insults of light parties, which may at every moment be harassing them; the necessity of never losing sight of the means of a secure retreat, which ought to be the first object of an officer's care, must be exceedingly embarrassing, where there is a force in such a position as to endanger it. If a respectable body of men were to be stationed on the Grants, it would undoubtedly have the effects intimated above, and would render it not a little difficult for General Burgoyne to keep the necessary communication open; and they would frequently afford opportunities of intercepting his convoys. If there should be none there, he might advance with security, leaving small posts behind, and might draw his supplies regularly and without interruption; than which nothing could tend more to facilitate his operations and give them success. These reasons make it clearly my opinion, that a sufficient body of militia should always be reserved in a situation proper to answer those purposes. If there should be more collected, than is requisite for this use, the surplusage may with propriety be added to the main body of the army. I am not, however, so fully acquainted with every circumstance, that ought to be taken into consideration, as to pretend to do any thing more than advise in the matter. Let those on the spot determine and act as appears to them most prudent.

I am, &c.

TO BENJAMIN FRANKLIN, IN PARIS.
Head-Quarters, 17 Auguat, 1777.

Sir, I have been honored with your favor of the 2d of April by Monsieur de Cenis, written in behalf of that gentleman on the credit of Monsieur Turgot's recommendation. I should have been happy, had it been in my power, in deference to your recommendation, founded upon that of so respectable a character as Monsieur Turgot, to afford Monsieur de Cenis the encouragement, to which his zeal and trouble in coming to America to offer his services give him a claim; but such is the situation of things in our army at this time, that I am necessarily deprived of that satisfaction. Our troops being already formed and fully officered, and the number of foreign gentlemen already commissioned and Continually arriving with fresh applications, throw such obstacles in the way of any future appointments, that every new arrival is only a new source of embarrassment to Congress and myself, and of disappointment and chagrin

to the gentlemen, who come over. Had there been only a few to provide for, we might have found employment for them in a way advantageous to the service and honorable to themselves; but, as they have come over in such crowds, we either must not employ them, or we must do it at the expense of one half of the officers of the army; which you must be sensible would be attended with the most ruinous effects, and could not fail to occasion a general discontent. It is impossible for these gentlemen to raise men for themselves; and it would be equally impolitic and unjust to displace others, who have been at all the trouble and at considerable expense in raising corps, in order to give them the command. Even where vacancies happen, there are always those, who have a right of succession by seniority, and who are as tenacious of this right as of the places they actually hold; and in this they are justified by the common principle and practice of all armies, and by resolutions of Congress Were these vacancies to be filled by the foreign officers, it would not only cause the resignation of those, who expect to succeed to them, but it would serve to disgust others, both through friendship to them, and from an apprehension of their being liable to the same inconvenience themselves. This, by rendering the hope of preferment precarious, would remove one of the principal springs of emulation, absolutely necessary to be upheld in an army.

Besides this difficulty, the error we at first fell into, of prodigally bestowing rank upon foreigners, without examining properly their pretensions, having led us VOL. V. 5 to confer high rank upon those who had none, or of a very inferior degree, in their' own country, it now happens, that those who have really good pretensions, who are men of character, abilities, and rank, will not be contented unless they are introduced into some of the highest stations of the army, in which, it needs no arguments to convince you, that it is impossible to gratify them. Hence their dissatisfaction and the difficulty of employing them are increased. These obstacles reduce us to

this dilemma; either we must refuse to commission them at all, and leave all the expense, trouble, and risk, that have attended their coming over, uncompensated; or we must commission them without being able to incorporate or employ them; by which means enjoying the public pay and an unmeaning rank, they must submit to the mortification of being mere ciphers in the army. This last, to some of them, may not be disagreeable; but to men of sentiment, and who are actuated by a principle of honor and a desire to distinguish themselves, it must be humiliating and irksome in the extreme.

From these considerations it would be both prudent and just to discourage their coming over, by candidly opening the difficulties they have to encounter; and if, after that, they will persist in it, they can only blame themselves. I am sensible, Sir, that it is a delicate and perplexing task to refuse applications of persons patronized, as I suppose often happens, by some of the first characters in the kingdom where you are, and whose favor it is of importance to conciliate; but I beg leave to suggest, whether it would not be better to do that, than by compliance to expose them to those mortifications, which they must unavoidably experience, and which they are too apt to impute to other causes than the true ones, and may represent under very disadvantageous colors. Permit me also to observe to you, that even where you do not promise any thing, but simply give a line of recommendation, they draw as strong an assurance of success from that as from a positive engagement, and estimate the hardship of a disappointment nearly the same in the one case as in the other.

I am, &c.

TO BENJAMIN HARRISON, IN CONGRESS.
Neshaminy Bridge, 19 August, 1777.

Dear Sir,'

If I did not misunderstand what you or some other member of Congress said to me, respecting the appointment of the Marquis de Lafayette, he has misconceived the design of his appointment, or Congress did not understand the extent of his views; for certain it is, that I understood him, that he does not conceive his commission is merely honorary, but given with a view to command a division of this army. It is true he has said, that he is young and inexperienced, but at the same time has always accompanied it with a hint, that, so soon as I shall think him fit for the command of a division, he shall be ready to enter upon the duties of it, and in the mean time has offered his service for a smaller command; to which I may add, that he has actually applied to me, by "direction he says from Mr. Hancock, for commissions for his two aids-de-camp.

What the designs of Congress respecting this gentleman were, and what line of conduct I am to pursue to comply with their design and his expectations, I know not, and beg to be instructed. If Congress meant, that this rank should be unaccompanied by command, I wish it had been sufficiently explained to him. If, on the other hand, it was intended to invest him with all the powers of a major-general, why have I been led into a contrary belief, and left in the dark with respect to my own conduct towards him? This difficulty, with the numberless applications for employment by foreigners, under their respective appointments, adds no small embarrassment to a command, which, without it, is abundantly perplexed by the different tempers I have to do with, and different modes which the respective States have pursued in nominating and arranging their officers; the combination of all which is but a too just representation of a great chaos, from whence we are endeavouring, how successfully time only can show, to draw some regularity and order.

I was going to address Congress for instructions in the case of the Marquis de Lafayette, but upon second thought concluded to ask some direction of my conduct in this matter through a member, and therefore have imposed this task upon you. Let me beseech you then, my good Sir, to give me the sentiments of Congress on this matter, that I may endeavour, as far as it is in my power, to comply with them. With respect to commissions for his aids-de-

camp, I told him that I should write to Mr. Hancock about them, and I wish to be instructed. The Marquis is now in Philadelphia, but expected up this day or to-morrow. With sincere regard, I am, &c.

From Mr. Harrison's reply, it appears that Congress considered the appointment of the Marquis dc Lafayette as honorary only, unaccompanied with any pledge, and that General Washington was not bound by the tenor of his commission to give him a command, but was at liberty to follow bis own judgment in this respect. TO MAJOR-GENERAL OATE8.

Head-Quarters, Bucks County, 20 August, 1777.

Sir,

By a letter from General Schuyler of the 13th instant it appears, that you had not reached Stillwater at that time; since which I have not had any accounts from you, but suppose you arrived there soon after that date. From the various representations made to me of the disadvantage the army lay under, particularly the militia, from an apprehension of the Indian mode of fighting, I have despatched Colonel Morgan with his corps of riflemen to your assistance, and.presume they will be with you in eight days from this date. This corps I have great dependence on, and have no doubt but they will be exceedingly useful; as a check given to the savages, and keeping them within proper bounds, will prevent General Burgoyne from getting intelligence as formerly, and animate your other troops from a sense of their being more on an equality with the enemy. Colonel Cortlandt's and Colonel Livingston's regiments are also on their way from Peekskill to join you. They must of course be with you in a very few days. With these reinforcements, besides the militia under General Lincoln, which by this time must be considerable, I am in hopes you will find yourself at least equal to stop the progress of Mr. Burgoyne, and, by cutting off his supplies of provision, to render bis situation very ineligible.

General Gates joined the northern army, and took the command, on the 19th of

August. Although, by an order of Congress, General Schuyler »m directed to repair to head-quarters, yet the time was not fixed, and, with the approbation of Congress and the Commander-in-chief, he remained at Albany till after the capitulation of Burgoyne. In regard to the state of affairs to the westward, Washington wrote to General Schuyler, on the 21st of August; —" I am pleased with the account you transmit of the situation of matters upon the Mohawk River. If the militia keep up their spirits after their late severe skirmish, I am confident they will, with the assistance of the reinforcement under General Arnold, be enabled to raise the siege of Fort Schuyler, which will be a most important matter just at this time." This prediction was verified in its fullest extent, and is one among the innumerable instances of the foresight and sound judgment of the Commander-in-chief. VOL. V. D

Since the enemy's fleet was seen off Sinepuxent, on the 8th instant, we have no accounts from them, which can be depended on. I am now of opinion, that Charleston is the present object of General Howe's attention, though for what sufficient reason, unless he expected to drag this army after him by appearing at different places, and thereby leave the country open for General Clinton to march out and endeavour to form a junction with General Burgoyne, I am at a loss to determine. General Schuyler's sending a reinforcement up to Fort Schuyler I think was absolutely necessary; and I am of opinion, that particular attention should be paid to that quarter, as a successful stroke of the enemy there might be a means of encouraging the whole of the Six Nations to unite against us. I am, Sir, &c.

TO THE PRESIDENT OF CONGRESS.

Neshaminy Camp, 21 August, 1777.

Sir,

From the time which has elapsed since General Howe departed from the Capes of Delaware, there is the strongest reason to conclude, that he is gone far ' either to the eastward or southward, and with a design to execute some determined plan. The danger of the sea, the injury his troops must sustain from being so long confined, the loss of time so late in the campaign, will scarcely admit a supposition that he is merely making a feint, and still intends to return either to the

Delaware or the North River without performing some enterprise first in another quarter. The probability is in favor of a southern expedition, because he has been seen, since his departure from the Capes, off Sinepuxent, steering a southern course; and because, had his destination been to the eastward, his arrival there, from the general state of the winds, must have announced it before this, or his fleet would have been discovered by some of the cruisers on that coast.

If he is gone to the southward, he must be gone far that way; for, had the Chesapeake Bay been his object, he would have been there long since, and the fact well established. Beyond that, there is no place short of Charleston of sufficient importance to engage his attention. The extensive commerce, the vast accumulation of military and other stores in that town and its dependencies, with the eclat it would give his arms if he should unfortunately take it, afford him stronger inducements to direct his operations there, than he could possibly have elsewhere. Matters being thus circumstanced, an important question arises; how this army is to be employed. If his intentions are such as I have supposed them, it appears to me that an attempt to follow him would not only be fruitless, but would be attended with the most ruinous consequences. The distance is so immense, that General Howe might accomplish every purpose he had in view, before we could possibly arrive to oppose him; and so long a march through an unhealthy climate at this season would debilitate and waste a principal part of our force. Added to this, after we had made a considerable progress, he might easily reembark his troops and turn his arms against Philadelphia or elsewhere, as he should think proper, without our being in a condition to give the least aid.

As these, and many other reasons, which will readily occur to Congress, will show the impracticability of our counteracting General Howe in that quarter with any good effect, we have no other alternative left than to remain here idle and inactive, on the remote probability of his returning this way, or to proceed towards Hudson's River, with a view of opposing General Burgoyne, or making an attempt on York Island, as the situation of affairs shall point out. A successful stroke with respect to either would be attended with the most signal advantages, and would be the best compensation we could make for any losses we may sustain at the southward. Besides these considerations, if, after all our conjectures and reasoning upon the subject, General Howe should be gone to the eastward to cooperate with Mr. Burgoyne, the army will be, by the movement proposed, so far on its way, to prevent, I hope, the success of his enterprise.

The above reasons led me to call a council of general officers this morning, to take the subject of removing the troops from hence into consideration; and I am happy to inform Congress, that they were in sentiment with me upon the occasion, as they will perceive by a copy of the proceedings then had, which I do myself the honor of laying before them. Nevertheless, as it is a movement which may involve the most important consequences, I have thought proper to submit it to Congress for their deliberation and decision. If it is deemed expedient, we have perhaps not a moment to lose in carrying it into execution; and, under this persuasion, I have sent Colonel Hamilton, one of my aids, who will have the honor of delivering this, to bring me the result of their opinion. As the northern depart ment has been all along considered separate, and in some measure distinct, and there are special resolves vesting the command in particular persons, — in case it should hereafter appear eligible to unite the two armies, it may perhaps be necessary that Congress should place the matter upon such a footing, as to remove all scruples or difficulties about the command, that could possibly arise on my arrival there.

This I request, from a disposition to harmony, and from my knowing the ill and fetal consequences that have often arisen from such controversies, and not from the most distant apprehension, that one would take place upon such an event. The thing however is possible; and to guard against it can do no injury. I have the honor to be, &.c.

In the council of war it was decided, as the unanimous opinion of the board of officers; first, that the enemy's fleet had most probably

P. S. That I may not appear inconsistent, to advise and to act before I obtain an opinion, I beg leave to mention, that I shall move the army to the Delaware to-morrow morning, to change their ground at any rate, as their present encampment begins to be disagreeable, and would injure their health in a short time. Our forage also begins to grow scarce here.

ailed for Charleston; secondly, that it was not expedient for the army to march southward, as it could not possibly arrive at Charleston in time to afford any succour; thirdly, that the army should move immediately towards the North River. The Marquis de Lafayette took part for the first time in the council of war convened on this occasion, and attended with the rank of major-general. Congress approved this decision, on the same day that the above letter was written; but intelligence arrived the next morning, that the British fleet had been seen far up the Chesapeake Bay, and was communicated to General Washington by President Hancock, in a letter dated August 22d, at half past one o'clock in the afternoon, as follows. "This moment an express arrived from Maryland with an account of near two hundred sail of General Howe's fleet being at anchor in the Chesapeake Bay. In consequence of this advice, Congress have ordered the immediate removal of the stores and prisoners from Lancaster and York in this State to places of greater safety." This intelligence of course immediately changed the plan of operations. VOL. V. 6 J» TO MAJOR-GENERAL PUTNAM.

Bucks County, 22 August, 1777.

Dear Sir, By the enclosed, which has this moment come to hand, you will perceive that the enemy's fleet have at length fairly entered the Chesapeake Bay, Swan Point being at least two hundred miles from the Capes. I desire you will immediately forward this account to Governor Trumbull, to be by him sent on eastward. As there is not now the least danger of General Howe's going to New England, I hope the whole force of that country will turn out, and, by following the great stroke struck by General Stark near Bennington, entirely crush General Burgoyne, who by his letter to Colonel Baum seems to be in want of almost every thing. I hope you will draw in such a force of militia as will effectually secure your post against any attempt from New York. I shall be obliged to draw General Sullivan with his division down to me; for, by General Howe's coming so far up the Chesapeake, he must mean to reach Philadelphia by that route, though to be sure it is a very strange one. I am, &c TO THE PRESIDENT OP CONGRESS.

Camp, at Cross Roads, 22 August, 1777.

Sir, I am honored with your favor containing the intelligence of the enemy's arrival in the Chesapeake Bay, and the resolution of Congress thereupon. I have, in consequence of this account, sent orders to General Nash immediately to embark his brigade and Colonel Procter's corps of artillery, if vessels can be procured for the purpose, and to proceed to Chester; or, if vessels cannot be provided, to hasten towards that place by land with all the despatch he can. I have also directed General Sullivan to join this army with his division as speedily as possible, and I have issued orders for all the troops here to be in motion to-morrow morning very early, with the intention to march them towards Philadelphia and onwards. I am happy to find Congress have ordered the removal of the stores from Lancaster and York to places of greater safety, which is, without doubt, a very proper and necessary measure. With much respect and esteem, I have the honor to be, Sir, your most obedient servant.

To an inquiry by General Putnam respecting the mode of treating deserters from the enemy, General Washington replied, on the 18th of August;—"When any deserters come out from the British army, they have been paid four dollars, and, if they bring out their arms, ten dollars more for them. Be pleased in future to pay those sums, and certify upon their passes that they have been paid, otherwise they claim it again." TO THE PRESIDENT OF CONGRESS. 23 August, 1777.

Sir,

I beg leave to inform you, that the army marched early this morning, and will encamp, I expect, this evening within five or six miles of Philadelphia. To-morrow morning it will move again, and I think to march it through the city, but without halting. I am induced to do this, from the opinion of several of my officers and many friends in Philadelphia, that it may have some influence on the minds of the disaffected there, and those who are dupes to their artifices and opinions. The march will be down Front and up Chesnut street, and I presume about seven o'clock. Notwithstanding the arrival of the enemy's fleet in the Chesapeake Bay, and the seeming probability that General Howe will debark his troops and attempt something, yet I wduld take the liberty to mention, that I think the several works for the defence of the city should be carried on with the usual industry, and that no pains should be omitted to complete them. I would also advise, that the same look-outs for intelligence should be continued at the Capes, and the earliest information communicated of any thing material; for, though the fleet is in the Chesapeake Bay, the enemy may push in a number of vessels with troops, and make an effort to effect some stroke against Philadelphia by surprise. Such an event does not seem probable while they have a larger show of force in a neighbouring State; but it will be prudent to guard against it. I have the honor to be, &c.

TO THE PRESIDENT OF CONGRESS.
Wilmington, six o'clock, P. M., 25 August, 1777.

Sir, The enclosed intelligence has just come to my hands. General Greene's and General Stephen's divisions are within a few miles of this place. I shall order them to march immediately here. The two other divisions halted this day at Derby to refresh themselves; but they will come on as expeditiously as possible. There are about five hundred Pennsylvania militia at Chester and Marcus Hook, that are armed; there is a number more unarmed. I have ordered all the armed immediately down. I do not know what number of militia of this State is yet collected; but I am told they turn out with great alacrity. There is a quantity of public and private stores at the Head of Elk, which I am afraid will fall into the enemy's hands, if they advance quickly; among others, there is a considerable parcel of salt. Every attempt will be made to save that. When I get my force collected, I shall dispose of it in the most advantageous manner in my power. To this end I purpose to view the grounds towards the enemy in the morning. I am yet a stranger to them.

I have the honor to be, &c TO MAJOR-GENERAL ARMSTRONG.

Wilmington, six o'clock, P. M., 25 August, 1777.

Dear Sir, I have just received information, that the enemy began to land this morning about six miles below the Head of Elk, opposite to Cecil Court-House. The informant says he saw two thousand men, but he may be mistaken as to the number. I desire you to send off every man of the militia under your command, that is properly armed, as quick as possible. If they were to begin their march this night while it is cool, it would be the better. They are to proceed to Wilmington, where they will receive orders for their destination. I desire you will immediately send for General Potter, and give him directions to come to me with all possible expedition. You must supply his place in the best manner you can. The first attempts of the enemy will be to seize horses, carriages, and cattle with light parties, and we must endeavour to check them at their outset. Whatever militia are at Philadelphia, and equipped, should be ordered down immediately. I am, &c. Commanding the Pennsylvania militia.

TO THE PRESIDENT OF CONGRESS.

Wilmington, 27 August, 1777.

Sir, I this morning returned from the Head of Elk, which I left last night. In respect to the enemy, I have nothing new to communicate. They remain where they debarked first. I could not find out from inquiry what number is landed, nor form an estimate of it from the distant view I had of their encampment. But few tents were to be seen from Iron Hill and Gray's Hill, which are the only eminences about Elk. I am happy to inform you, that all the public stores are removed from thence, except about seven thousand bushels of corn. This I urged the commissary there to get off as soon as possible, and hope it will be effected in the course of a few days, if the enemy should not prevent it, which their situation gives them but too easy an opportunity of doing. The scarcity of teams in proportion to the demand will render the removal rather tedious, though I have directed the quartermaster to send some from hence to expedite the measure. A part of the Delaware militia is stationed there; and about nine hundred more from Pennsylvania are now on the march that way. I also intended to move part of the army that way to-day, but am under the necessity of deferring it till their arms are put in order, and they are furnished with ammunition, both having been greatly injured by the heavy rains that fell yesterday and last night.

I have the honor to be, &c.

General Rodney commanded the Delaware militia. General Washington wrote to him;—"For the present you can do no more than keep scouts and patrols towards the enemy, to watch their motions; but as soon as you are joined by more force from this State, by the militia of the Eastern Shore of Maryland, and by Richardson's battalion, I would have you move as near the enemy as you can with safety." TO MAJOR-GENERAL SULLIVAN.

Wilmington, 27 August, 1777.

Sir,

I have received your two favors, informing me of the particulars of an expedition you have lately made to Staten Island. It is unfortunate, that an affair, which had so prosperous a beginning, should have terminated so disagreeably, as in a great measure to defeat the good consequences, that might have attended it. I am however glad to hear, that the officers and men distinguished themselves by their good behaviour; and, if there are any, who behaved more remarkably well than others, I should be happy to take all the notice of them consistent with propriety, that their conduct may appear to merit. I am not sufficiently acquainted with circumstances to form a certain judgment of what might have been expected from the expedition; but from the view I have of them, and from your own representation of the matter, the situation of the enemy seems to have been such, as afforded an opportunity of reaping much more decisive advantages than were in fact gained.

As your division must no doubt have been greatly harassed by this movement, their health might be very much injured by pushing them too hard in their march to joi n me. I would therefore wish you to spare them as much as may be necessary to avoid that inconvenience; at the same time there ought to be no 'delay, but what a proper attention to the health and accom modation of the men really demands. I am, &,c.

See a particular account of General Sullivan's expedition to Staten Wind, in Marshall's *Life of Washington,* Vol. III. p. 135. The plan, which was well concerted, and in the beginning well executed, did not succeed according to the expectations of the commander, nor was the result satisfactory to the public. TO THE PRESIDENT OP CONGRESS.

Head-Quarters, Wilmington, 28 August, 1777.

Sir,

Having endeavoured, at the solicitation of Count Pulaski, to think of some mode for employing him in our service, there is none occurs to me liable to so few inconveniences and exceptions, as giving him the command of the horse. This department is still without a head; as I have not, in the present deficiency of brigadiers with the army, thought it advisable to take one from the foot for that command. The nature of the horse service with us being such, that they commonly act in detachments, a general officer with them is less necessary than at the head of the brigades of infantry. In the absence of General Smallwood, who is ordered to put himself at the head of the Maryland militia, we shall have two brigades without general officer.-;. But though the horse will suffer less from the want of a general officer than the foot, a man of real capacity, experience, and knowledge in that service, might be extremely useful. The Count appears, by his recommendations, to have sustained no inconsiderable military character in his own country; and as the principal attention in Poland has been for some time past paid to the cavalry, it is to be presumed this gentleman is not unacquainted with it. I submit it to Congress how far it may be eligible to confer the appointment I have mentioned upon him; they will be sensible of all the objections attending the measure, without my particularizing them, and can determine accordingly.

This gentleman, we are told, has been, like us, engaged in defending the liberty and independence of his country, and has sacrificed his fortune to his zeal for those objects. He derives from hence a title to our respect, that ought to operate in his favor, as far as the good of the service will permit; but it can never be expected we should lose sight of this.

I have the honor to be, &,c TO THE PRESIDENT OF CONGRESS.

Head-Quarters, Wilmington, 29 August, 1777.

Sir, On my return to this place last evening from WhiteClay Creek, I was honored with yours of the 27th, with sundry resolves of Congress, to which I shall pay due attention. The enemy advanced a part of their army yesterday to Gray's Hill, about two miles on this side of Elk, whether with intent to take post there, or to cover while they remove what stores they found in the town, I cannot yet determine. I do not know what quantity of private property remained; but of the public there were several thousand bushels of corn and oats, which might have been removed also, had not most of the teams in the country been employed by private persons in bringing off very valuable goods. Our light parties yesterday took between thirty and forty prisoners. Twelve deserters from the navy and eight from the army have already come in; but they are able to give us very little intelligence. They generally agree, that their troops are healthy, but that their horses suffered very much by the voyage. By a letter from General Gates, which you were pleased to transmit to me yesterday, he requests that commissions may be sent to Brigadiers Glover, Poor, and Paterson, which I beg the favor of you to do by the return express. The two last lost theirs with their baggage at Ticonderoga, and General Glover had none.

Dr. Franklin wrote as follows to General Washington, in a letter dated at Paris, May 29th.

" Count Pulaski of Poland, an officer famous throughout Europe for his bravery and conduct in defence of the liberties of his country against the three great invading powers of Russia, Austria, and Prussia, will have the honor of delivering this into your Excellency's hands. The Court here have encouraged and promoted his voyage, from an opinion, that he may be highly useful in our service. Mr. Deone has written so fully concerning him, that I need not enlarge; and I only add my wishes, that he may find in our armies under your Excellency occasions of distinguishing himself."

Hitherto there had been no officer of cavalry higher than a colonel. The command of that branch of the army was offered by Washington to General Joseph Reed, after he had been appointed a brigadier by Congress, but he declined accepting the commission. In consequence of the above recommendation, Count Pulaski was appointed to the command of the horse, on the 15th of September, with the rank of brigadier-general. VOL. V. 7 E

I have the honor to be, &c.

TO THE PRESIDENT OF CONGRESS.

Wilmington, 30 August, 1777.

Sir,

Since I had the honor of addressing you yesterday, nothing of importance has occurred, and the enemy remain as they then were. I was reconnoitring the country and different roads all yesterday, and am now setting out on the same business again. Sensible of the advantages of light troops, I have formed a corps under the command of a brigadier, by drafting a hundred from each brigade, which is to be constantly near the enemy, and to give them every possible annoyance.

I have the honor to be, &c.

Ten o'clock. — This minute twenty-four British prisoners arrived, taken yesterday by Captain Lee of the light-horse.

TO THE PRESIDENT OF CONGRESS.

Wilmington, 1 September, 1777.

Sir,

The latest and most material intelligence, which I have obtained respecting the enemy, you will find in the enclosed papers, which I do myself the honor of transmitting to you. How far the enemy have it in view to extend themselves in a line from bay to bay, I cannot determine, but the idea has taken place with many; and it is said to be founded on their hints to some persons, who, from accident in some instances, and perhaps choice in others, have had a more familiar intercourse with them. I cannot suppose they have any such design, or, if they have, that it can be more than temporary for procuring supplies of provisions.

General Howe's *Declaration* is agreeable to his constant usage, and is what we might reasonably expect. The only difference is, the present exhibition is styled a " Declaration." It is another effort to seduce the people to give up their rights, and to encourage our soldiery to desert. The facts contained in the deposition of Francis Alexander, which you have also enclosed, seem to be opposed to that regularity and discipline, which are promised by the Declaration. Yesterday there was some skirmishing between one of our advanced parties and one of the enemy's, in which they were obliged to retreat, with the loss of an officer and three men killed, according to report. We had one private wounded. I have received no particular accounts respecting the Maryland Eastern Shore militia; from the best information I have, a great many are well disposed to turn out, but are prevented from giving their aid through the want of arms. Apprehending that the militia there would stand in need of an officer to arrange them, I wrote to General Cadwalader, requesting his good offices, which I am told have been exerted. Colonel Gist is now gone down, and I expect will move on as soon as possible, with such as are armed, towards the enemy. General Smallwood is gone to take the command of those on the Western Shore, of whom I hear many are collecting; but I have no authentic advices on the subject. I have the honor to be, &c.

This Declaration waa issued on the 27th of August, at the Head of Elk, and differed from a Proclamation in nothing but the name. General Howe assured the inhabitants, that the strictest orders had been given for the preservation of regularity and discipline among the soldiers, and that the severest punishment would be inflicted on any one, who should dare to plunder their property or molest their persons. He moreover declared, that security and protection would be extended to all persons, who should remain peaceably at their usual places of abode; and he promised pardon to those, who had taken an active part in the rebellion, provided they should voluntarily return to their allegiance, and surrender themselves to any detachment of the King's forces within a specified time.

TO THE PRESIDENT OF CONGRESS.

Wilmington, eight o'clock, P. M., 3 September, 1777.

Sir, I have this minute returned to head-quarters, where I found your favor of this date, with the resolves respecting General Sullivan, and Colonel Richardson's battalion. I had conversed with General Sullivan upon the subject, and observed to him that it was necessary an inquiry should be had relative to the affair of Staten Island, as his conduct was censured, and much dissatisfaction pre-

but I think, and in this opinion my officers concur, that the service will be injured if any part of the Continental troops were now to be employed about them. If we should be able to oppose General Howe with success in the field, the works will be unnecessary; if not, and he should force us from hence, he will certainly possess himself of them. But, to prevent his attempting it now, I have directed the meadows on Province Island to be overflowed immediately, and any other grounds that may be thought necessary for that purpose. The works have been more particularly made under the direction of Monsieur Ducoudray, and I doubt not he will pay every attention to their completion and security, that the situation of affairs will admit. A part of the militia under General Armstrong will be posted along the Schuylkill, to throw up redoubts at the different fords, which will be occasionally occupied while I move to the other side with the main body of the army. This disposition appears to be most eligible, from a consideration of all circumstances, and better than if any part of our present force was to be employed at the forts. If further reinforcements of the militia should come in, they perhaps may be more properly assigned to that business, than any we now have.

See Appendix, No. L f Appendix, No. II. Your letter respecting General Deborre just now came to hand. I shall transmit to him a copy of it and of the resolutions. There can be no court of inquiry into his conduct at this time. As soon as the state of the army will admit, it will be done.f

I have the honor to be, &c.

TO THE PRESIDENT OF CONGRESS.

Buck Tavern, three o'clock, P. M., 15 September, 1777.

Sir, Your favor of yesterday, with its several enclosures, came to hand last night. Though I would willingly pay every attention to the resolutions of Congress, yet, in the late instance respecting the recall of General Sullivan, I must beg leave to defer giving any order about it, till I hear further from that honorable body. Our situation at this time is critical and delicate; and nothing should

be done to add to its embarrassments. We are now most probably on the point of another action; and to derange the army, by withdrawing so many general officers from it, may and must be attended with many disagreeable if not ruinous consequences. Such a proceeding at another time might not produce any bad effects; but how can the army be possibly conducted with a prospect of success, if the general officers are taken off in the moment of battle? Congress may rely upon it, such a measure will not promote but injure the service.

General Joseph Reed assisted General Armstrong, as a volunteer, in selecting the proper places for redoubts at the fords of the Schuylkill. He was well acquainted with the grounds, and applied himself with his usual promptness and energy in rendering every service in his power. While thus engaged he was appointed a delegate to the Continental Congress from Pennsylvania. t The conduct of General Deborre in the action on the Brandywine was disapproved. He commanded a brigade in General Sullivan's division. By a vote of Congress he was recalled from the army, till the charges against him should be investigated. The next day he waited on the President, and resigned his commission. Being a foreigner he seemed but little acquainted with the habits of the American people, and he had previously committed faults or indiscretions in his military capacity, which subjected him to censure.

It is not my wish to prevent or to delay a proper inquiry into General Sullivan's conduct a single instant, when the circumstances of the army will admit; but now they prohibit it, and, I think, the suspension in his command also. The recall of General St. Clair obliged me to part with General Lincoln, whom I could but ill spare; so that the whole charge of his division is now upon General Wayne, there being no other brigadier in it than himself. The Maryland troops, if General Sullivan is taken away, will not have one general officer, General Smallwood being at the head of the militia coming from that State, and General Deborre suspended. Added to

this, Colonel Gist, who commands one regiment of them, is now absent from it by order. In a word, Sir, whether the charges alleged against General Sullivan are true or false, and whether his conduct has been exceptionable or not, I am satisfied the resolution for his recall at this time was unhappily adopted, and, if carried into execution, will not fail to add new diffi

Vol. v. *r* culties to our present distresses; and I am obliged to observe, in justice to my own character, that I cannot be answerable for the consequences, which may arise from a want of officers to assist me.

It gives me great pleasure to find General Gates is on so respectable a footing; and I hope our affairs in that quarter, in the course of a little time, will be in as prosperous a train as we could reasonably wish.

The main body of the enemy, from the best intelligence I have been able to get, lies near Dilworthtown, not far from the field of action, where they have been busily employed in burying their dead, which, from accounts, amounted to a very considerable number, f We are moving up this road to get between the enemy and Swedes' Ford, and to prevent them from turning our right flank, which they seem to have a violent inclinanation to effect, by all their movements. I would beg leave to recommend in the most earnest manner, that some board or committee be appointed, or some mode adopted, for obtaining supplies of blankets for the troops. Many are now without them, and, the season becoming cold, they will be injured in their health, and unfitted for service, unless they are immediately provided with them. Our supplies in this instance, as well as in every article of clothing, cannot be too great, as there are frequent losses not easily to be avoided. I would also observe, that I think, in point of prudence and sound policy, every species of provisions should be removed from the city, except such as will be necessary to supply the present demands of this army. I have been told there are considerable quantities in private hands, which should not be suffered to remain a moment longer than till they can be conveyed away.

The principal disasters of the battle of Brandy wine happened in the quarter where General Sullivan commanded. Not being a favorite with several members of Congress, these persons censured him severely, and procured a resolve for his recall from the army, till the inquiry before ordered, respecting the affair at Staten Island, should be made. The execution of the resolve was suspended, in consequence of the above letter from the Commander-in-chief. A court of inquiry afterwards honorably acquitted General Sullivan.

The Baron de Kalb was appointed a major-general in the American service on the 15th of September, and his commission was to bear the same date as that of the Marquis de Lafayette.

f The day after the battle of Brandywine, while the enemy were at Dilworthtown, Sir William Howe wrote as follows to General Washington.

" Tho number of wounded officers and men of your army in this neighbourhood, to whom every possible attention has been paid, will nevertheless require your immediate care, as I shall not be so situated as to give them the necessary relief. Any surgeons you may choose to send to their assistance, upon application to me, in consequence of your orders, shall be permitted to attend them. The officers' paroles will be taken, and the men considered as prisoners of war. "

I have the honor to be, &,c.
TO THE PRESIDENT OF CONGRESS.
Yellow Springs, 17 September, 1777.

Sir, I have been honored with your two favors of yesterday, and their enclosures, to which due attention shall be paid. The enemy seem now to be straining every nerve to accomplish their purpose; but I trust, 'whatever present success they may have, they will, ere long, experience a reverse of fortune. If they have four thousand men in the Jerseys, it is probable they have something more serious in view than a mere diversion; but I am in hopes, when General MDougall comes to unite his force with the militia, General Dickinson will be strong enough effectually to make head against them.

General Washington replied; —" The attention, which you are pleased to assure me has been paid to the officers and privates of the army under my command, who were unfortunately wounded in the action on Thursday last, has a claim to my acknowledgments. Agreeably to the permission you offer, I have directed the following gentlemen, Doctors Rush, Leiper, Latimer, and Willet, a mate in the hospital, with their attendants, to wait upon you and take them under their care. The wounded will be considered in the light you place them."

Yesterday the enemy moved from Concord, by the Edgemont towards the Lancaster road, with evident design to gain our right flank. This obliged us to alter our position and march to this place, from whence we intend immediately to proceed to Warwic. We suffered much from the severe weather yesterday and last night, being unavoidably separated from our tents and baggage, which not only endangers the health of the men, but has been very injurious to our arms and ammunition. These, when we arrive at Warwic, we shall endeavour, as soon as possible, to put again into a proper condition; to do which, and to refresh the men, are two principal motives for going there.

Sir Henry Clinton was left in the command at New York; and, as the State of New Jersey became defenceless, when the main army was withdrawn to Pennsylvania, he seized that opportunity for effecting an incursion into the country. His troops landed in four divisions, at Elizabethtowu Point, Schuyler's Landing on Hackinsac River, Fort Lee, and Tappan. Generals Clinton, Vaughan, Campbell, and Skinner accompanied the expedition. The object was to drive off the cattle, and to attack any small party, that might be met with; as it was known that, in the divided state of the American army, no force of much magnitude could at this time be in Jersey. The number of troops engaged in the enterprise amounted to more than two thousand. They penetrated the country from the different points of landing, remained from the 12th to the 10th of September, and then returned to New York with a booty of four hundred cattle, four hundred sheep, and a few horses.

Colonel Malcolm's regiment, then stationed at Ramapo, watched their motions, but was not in force to offer much resistance. A party under Lieutenant-Colonel Aaron Burr, of Malcom's regiment, was sent down to collect intelligence, and prevent the ravages of the enemy's small detachments. There was also skirmishing with the militia. Eight of the enemy were killed, and eighteen wounded, according to Sir Henry Clinton's account; and seventeen were taken prisoners. As soon as General Putnam heard, that the British were in Jersey, he ordered General MDougall to cross the Hudson with fifteen hundred men. The order was obeyed, but not in time to overtake the enemy. This incursion caused alarm in New Jersey, and made it necessary for General Dickinson to station at Elizabethtown and Amboy one thousand of the militia, who were intended to reinforce General Washington. — *Clinton's Lett.er to Sir ffUliam Howe, September 23d. — Dickinson's Letter, September nth.*

I have the honor to be, &.c.
TO THE PRESIDENT OF CONGRESS.
Camp, 19 September, 1777.

Sir, I am much obliged to Congress for the late instance of their confidence, expressed in their resolution of the 17th, and shall be happy if my conduct in discharging the objects they had in view should be such as to meet their approbation. I am now repassing the Schuylkill at Parker's Ford, with the main body of the army, which will be over in an hour or two, though it is deep and rapid. General Wayne, with the division under his command, is on the rear of the enemy, and will be joined to-morrow or next day, I expect, by General Smallwood and Colonel Gist with their corps. As soon as the troops have crossed the river, I shall march them as expeditiously as possible towards Fatland, Swedes', and the other fords, where it is most probable the enemy will attempt to pass. In the prospect of the speedy removal of

Congress from Philadelphia, and the uncertainty as to the time of the next meeting, enlarged powers were delegated to the Commander-in-chief, suited to the exigency of the occasion, and involving a high responsibility.—"Resolved, that General Washington be authorized and directed to suspend all officers who misbehave, and to fill up all vacancies in the American army, un der the rank of brigadiers, until the pleasure of Congress shall be com municated; to take, wherever he may be, all such provisions and other articles as may be necessary for the comfortable subsistence of the army under his command, paying or giving certificates for the same; to remove and secure, for the benefit of the owners, all goods and effects, which may be serviceable to the enemy; provided that the powers hereby vested shall be exercised only in such parts of these States as may be within the circumference of seventy miles of the head-quarters of the American army, and shall continue in force for the space of sixty days, unless sooner revoked by Congress." — *Journals, September 17th.* VOL. V. 9 F

When I left Germantown with the army, I hoped I should have an opportunity of attacking them, either in front or on their flank, with a prospect of success; but unhappily a variety of causes concurred to prevent it. Our march, in the first place, was greatly impeded through want of provisions, which delayed us so long that the enemy were apprized of our motions, and gamed the grounds near the White Horse Tavern, with a part of their army turning our right flank, whilst another part, composing the main body, were more advanced towards our left. We should have disappointed them in their design by getting on their left; but the heavy rain, which fell on Tuesday evening and in the course of that night, totally unfitted our guns for service and nearly the whole of the ammunition with which the army had been completed a day or two before, being forty rounds a man. At first I expected that the loss was by no means so considerable, and intended only to file off with the troops a few miles to

replace it and clean the arms, and then to proceed on my original plan; but on examination I found it as I have mentioned, and that we had not a sufficient supply with us to furnish the men with the necessary complement. In this situation it was judged necessary, that we should proceed as far as Reading Furnace for the security of the army. On these accounts, particularly the latter, matters have General Smallwood was coming forward with eleven hundred and fifty Maryland militia, and Colonel Gist with seven hundred.

not been conducted as I intended and wished, and the enemy have had an opportunity of making their advances without being attacked. I yet hope, from the present state of the river, that I shall be down in time to give them a meeting, and, if unfortunately they should gain Philadelphia, that it will not be without loss.

I have the honor to be, &c.

TO LIEUTENANT-COLONEL ALEXANDER HAMILTON.

Camp, 22 September, 1777.

Sir,

The distressed situation of the army for want of blankets, and many necessary articles of clothing, is truly deplorable; and must inevitably be destructive to it, unless a speedy remedy be applied. Without a better supply than they at present have, it will be impossible for the men to support the fatigues of the campaign in the further progress of the approaching inclement season. This you well know to be a melancholy truth. It is equally the dictate of common sense and the opinion of the physicians of the army, as well as of every officer in it. No supply can be drawn from the public magazines. We have therefore no resource but the private stock of individuals. I feel. and I lament, the absolute necessity of requiring the inhabitants to contribute to those wants, which we have no other means of satisfying, and which if not removed would involve the ruin of the army, and perhaps the ruin of America. Painful as it is to me to order and as it will be to you to execute the measure, I am compelled to desire you immediately to proceed

to Philadelphia, and there procure from the inhabitants contributions of blankets and clothing, and materials to answer the purposes of both, in proportion to the ability of each. This you will do with as much delicacy and discretion, as the nature of the business demands; and I trust the necessity will justify the proceeding in the eyes of every person well affected to the American cause, and that all good citizens will cheerfully afford their assistance to soldiers, whose sufferings they are bound to commiserate, and who are eminently exposed to danger and distress, in defence of every thing they ought to hold dear.

As "there is also a number of horses in Philadelphia both of public and private property, which would be a valuable acquisition to the enemy, should the city by any accident fall into their hands, you are hereby authorized and commanded to remove them thence into the country to some place of greater security, and more remote from the operations of the enemy. You will stand in need of assistance from others to execute this commission with despatch and propriety, and you are therefore empowered to employ such persons as you shall think proper to aid you therein. I am, Sir, &c.

TO BARON D'arendt.

Camp, 23 September, 1777.

Sir, It is of the utmost importance to prevent the enemy's land forces and fleet from forming a junction, which it is almost morally certain they will attempt, by seizing on Fort Island below Philadelphia, if it is possible, and thereby gain the navigation of the Delaware by weighing and removing the *chevaux-de-frise,* which have been sunk for that purpose. This post (Fort Island), if maintained, will be of the last consequence, and will effectually hinder them from union. I therefore appoint you to the command of it, and desire that you will repair thither immediately. The defence is extremely interesting to the United States, and I am hopeful will be attended with much honor to yourself and advantage to them. Troops are there now, and a detachment to reinforce them will immediately march from this army. I have nothing further to add, than my wishes for your success, and to assure you, that I am, with esteem, Sir, &c.

TO THE PRESIDENT OP CONGRESS.

Camp, near Pottsgrove, 23 September, 1777.

Sir, I have not had the honor of addressing you since your adjournment to Lancaster, and I sincerely wish that my first letter was upon a more agreeable subject. The enemy, by a variety of perplexing manoeuvres through a country from which I could not derive the least intelligence (being to a man disaffected), contrived to pass the Schuylkill last night at the Fatland and other fords in the neighbourhood of it. They marched immediately towards Philadelphia, and I imagine their advanced parties will be near that city to-night. They had so far got the start before I received certain intelligence that any considerable number had crossed, that I found it in vain to think of overtaking their rear, with troops harassed as ours had been with constant marching since the battle of Brandy wine; and therefore concluded, by the advice of all the general officers, to march from this place to-morrow morning towards Philadelphia, and on the way endeavour to form a junction with the Continental troops under General MDougall, from Peekskill, and the Jersey militia under General Dickinson, both of whom are, I hope, on this side of the Delaware. I am also obliged to wait for General Wayne and General Smalhvood, who were left upon the other side of the Schuylkill, in hopes of falling upon the enemy's rear; but they have eluded them as well as us.

When the enemy approached Philadelphia, September 18th, Congress adjourned to Lancaster, in Pennsylvania, where they assembled on the 27th. The same day they adjourned to York beyond the Susquehanna, in which place they met on the 30th, and continued there till the British evacuated Philadelphia.

When I last recrossed the Schuylkill, it was with a firm intent of giving the enemy battle wherever I should meet them; and accordingly I advanced as far as the Warren Tavern upon the Lancaster road, near which place the two armies were upon the point of coming to a general engagement, but were prevented by a most violent flood of rain, which continued all the day and following night. When it held up, we had the mortification to find that our ammunition, which had been completed to forty rounds a man, was entirely ruined; and in that situation we had nothing left for it but to find out a strong piece of ground, which we could easily maintain till we could get the arms put in order, and a recruit of ammunition. Before this could be fully effected, the enemy marched from their position near the White Horse Tavern, down the road leading to the Swedes' Ford. I immediately crossed the Schuylkill above them, and threw myself full in their front, hoping to meet them in their passage, or soon after they had passed the river. The day before yesterday they were again in motion, and marched rapidly up the road leading towards Reading. This induced me to believe that they had two objects in view, one to get round the right of the army, the other perhaps to detach parties to Reading, where we had considerable quantities of military stores. To frustrate those intentions, I moved the army up on this side of the river to this place, determined to keep pace with them; but early this morning I received intelligence, that they had crossed the fords below. Why I did not follow immediately, I have mentioned in the former part of my letter; but the strongest reason against being able to make a forced march is the want of shoes. Messieurs Carroll, Chase, and Penn, who were some days with the army, can inform Congress in how deplorable a situation the troops are, for want of that necessary article. At least one thousand men are bare-footed, and have performed the marches in that condition. I was told of a great number of shoes in the hands of private people in Philadelphia, and sent down to secure them; but I doubt the approach of the enemy will prevent it.

I have planned a method of throwing a garrison into Fort Mifflin. If it suc-ceeds, and they, with the assistance of the ships and galleys, should keep the obstructions in the river, General Howe's situation in Philadelphia will not be the most agreeable; for if his supplies can be stopped by water, it may be easily done by land. To do both shall be my utmost endeavour; and I am not yet without hope, that the acquisition of Philadelphia may, instead of his good fortune, prove his ruin. General St. Clair, who has been constantly with the army for some time past, can give you many pieces of information, which may have escaped me, and therefore I refer you to him for many particulars.

If there are any shoes and blankets to be had in Lancaster or that part of the country, I earnestly entreat you to have them taken up for the use of the army. I have been informed, that there are large pareels of shoes in particular there. Finding that the enclosed came from Colonel Gibson, I took the liberty of opening it, as I wanted much to know what route he was taking. I have ordered all the Virginia militia, who are tolerably armed, to come forward, and join the army. Those who have no arms are to wait at Fredericktown in Maryland, till they hear whether any can be provided for them at Lancaster. You will therefore be pleased to make inquiry what number can be procured there, and send an express to Fredericktown with orders for as many men to come forward, as there are arms. I have the honor to be, &c.

TO MAJOR-GENERAL PUTNAM.

Camp, 23 September, 1777.

Dear Sir, The situation of our affairs in this quarter calls for every aid and for every effort. General Howe, by various manoeuvres and marching high up the Schuylkill, as if he meant to turn our right flank, found means by countermarching to pass the river, several miles below us, last night, which is fordable almost in every part, and he is now fast advancing towards Philadelphia. I therefore desire, that, without a moment's loss of time, you will detach as many effective rank and file, under proper generals and other officers, as will make the whole number, including those with General MDougalL amount to twenty-five hundred privates and noncommissioned fit for duty. The corps under General MDougalL to my great surprise, by a letter from him some days ago, consisted only of nine hundred and eleven. You will direct the officers, commanding the detachment now ordered, to proceed as expeditiously as they can to reinforce me. The route through Morristown and over Coryell's Ferry will be best for them to pursue. Before they arrive at the ferry, they will hear where I am; but that they may know their destination, when they are within two days' march of it, they are to advise me by express, and I will write on the subject.

I must urge you, by every motive, to send on this detachment without the least possible delay. No considerations are to prevent it. It is our first object to defeat, if possible, the army now opposed to us here. That the passes in the Highlands may be perfectly secure, you will immediately call in all your forces now on command at outposts. You must not think of covering a whole country by dividing them; and when they are ordered in and drawn together, they will be fully competent to repel any attempt, that can be made by the enemy from below in their present situation. Besides, if you are threatened with an attack, you must get what aid you can from the militia. The detachment will bring their baggage, but I wish them to come with no more than will be absolutely necessary. That you may not hesitate about complying with this order, you are to consider it as peremptory and not to be dispensed with. Colonel Malcom's regiment will form a part of the detachment. I am, dear Sir, &c.

General Putnam had formed a plan for a separate attack on the enemy at Staten Island, Paulus Hook, York Island, and Long Island, at the same time. He had obtained accurate knowledge of the enemy's strength, and Governor Trumbull had encouraged him to expect large reinforcements of militia from Connecticut for this purpose, which, with the Continental forces under his command, and the aids he might procure from New York and New Jersey, he believed would enable him to execute his design. —MS. Letter, September 13th. The above order from General Washington put an end to the project. VOL. V. 10 O

TO MAJOR-GENERAL GATES.

Camp, near Pottsgrove, 24 September, 1777.

Sir,

This army has not been able to oppose General Howe's with the success that was wished, and needs a reinforcement. I therefore request, if you have been so fortunate as to oblige General Burgoyne to retreat to Ticonderoga, or if you have not and circumstances will admit, that you will order Colonel Morgan to join me again with his corps. I sent him up when I thought you materially wanted him; and if his services can be dispensed with now, you will direct his immediate return. You will perceive, I do not mention this by way of command, but leave you to determine upon it according to your situation. If they come, they should proceed by water from Albany, as low down as Peekskill. In such case you will give Colonel Morgan the necessary orders to join me with despatch. I am, &c TO THE PRESIDENT OF CONGRESS.

Camp, Pennibecker's Mill, 29 September, 1777.

Sir, Lieutenant-Colonel Smith must have arrived at Fort Mifflin two days ago, as I heard from him at Ancocus Creek in the Jerseys. Colonel Nicola was in the fort with about sixty of his regiment of Invalids, and two companies of artillery, of thirty each; and I advised him to withdraw what force was at Billingsport, and to remove the few stores from thence to Fort Mifflin. He intended to call on Governor Livingston for a reinforcement of Jersey militia. General Smallwood joined me yesterday with the Maryland militia, but much reduced by desertion. I question whether they will exceed one thousand rank and file. General Forman will fall in with the army to-day, with between eight and nine hundred militia and Continental troops from Jersey. There are but few of the latter, being only small detachments picked up on his march.

To this letter General Gates replied; — "Since the action of the 19th ultimo, the enemy have kept the ground they occupied the morning of that day, and fortified their camp. The advanced sentries of my pickets are posted within shot, and opposite the enemy's. Neither side has given ground an inch. In this situation your Excellency would not wish me to 'part with the corps the army of General Burgoyne are most afraid of." — Dated October 5th. This letter was written only two days before the decisive action against Burgoyne, and yet, after that event, General Gates complied tardily with General Washington's request. Morgan was detained till after the capitulation, when the troops were no longer wanted in the northern department.

I shall move the army four or five miles lower down to-day, from whence we may reconnoitre and fix upon a proper situation, at such distance from the enemy as will enable us to make an attack, should we see a proper opening, or stand upon the defensive till we obtain further reinforcements. This was the opinion of a majority of a council of general officers, which I called yesterday. I congratulate you upon the success of our arms to the northward, and if some accident does not put them out of their present train, I think we may count upon the total ruin of Burgoyne.

I have the honor to be, &c.

TO GOVERNOR TRUMBULL.

Head-Quarters, 1 October, 1777.

Sir,

The prosperous situation of our northern affairs is a very pleasing and important circumstance. It is to be hoped, that they may continue in the same train, and have as happy an issue, as they seem now to promise. If they should, besides the advantage of disappointing the views of the enemy in that quarter, it will necessarily have a very desirable influence upon our operations here. You will hear before this gets to hand, that the enemy have, at length, gained possession of Philadelphia. Many unavoidable difficulties and unlucky accidents, which we had to encounter, helped to promote this success.

This is an event, which we have reason to wish had not happened, and which will be attended with several ill consequences; but I hope it will not be so detrimental as many apprehend, and that a little time and perseverance will give us some favorable opportunity of recovering our loss, and of putting our affairs in a more flourishing condition. Our army has now had the rest and refreshment it stood in need of, and our soldiers are in very good spirits. With great regard and esteem, I am, &c.

TO THE PRESIDENT OF CONGRESS.

Camp, Twenty Miles from Philadelphia, 3 October, 1777.

Sir, Yesterday afternoon I had the honor to receive your favors of the 30th ultimo, with their enclosures. I was much obliged by the accounts from the northern army, though in general they had reached me before; and I flatter myself we shall soon hear that they have been succeeded by other fortunate and interesting events, as the two armies, by General Gates's letter, were encamped near each other. I shall pay due attention to the resolution you refer me to; and no exertions on my part shall be wanting to collect what necessaries I can for the army. This, I am persuaded, will be equally attended to by the honorable Board of War; and I hope, by care and industry, many supplies may be obtained to relieve our distresses, which, in the articles of shoes, stockings, and blankets, are extremely great.

Since my letter of the 29 th, no favorable change has taken place-in our affairs; on the contrary, we have sustained an additional loss in the capture of the Delaware. She fell into the enemy's hands in a day or two after they were in possession of the city, and in a manner not yet well understood. Some have supposed.the crew mutinied, while another report is, that she was disabled in her rudder by a shot, and driven on shore. This misfortune takes off the success of Captain Biddie's cruise. I will not dwell longer on the subject. Congress may rest assured, all the means in my power' shall be employed to put our affairs in a more agreeable train, and to accomplish the end they so earnestly wish.

I have the honor to be, &c.

As soon as the British had taken possession of Philadelphia, they erected three batteries near the river to protect the city against such American shipping and craft, as might approach the town. On the 26th of September, before the batteries were finished, Commodore Hazelwood, by the advice of a council of officers, ordered two frigates, the Delaware and Montgomery, each of twenty-four guns, the sloop Fly, and several galleys and gondolas, to move up to Philadelphia, and commence a cannonade on the town, should the enemy persist in erecting fortifications. The Delaware anchored within five hundred yards of the batteries, and the other vessels took such stations as were suited to their object. At ten o'clock on the morning of the 27th the cannonade began, but on the falling of the tide the Delaware grounded. In this disabled condition the guns from the batteries soon compelled her colors to be struck, and she was taken by the enemy. A schooner was likewise driven on shore, but the other frigate and small craft returned to their former station near the fort. The suspicion, that the crew mutinied, was never confirmed, nor was there any such hint in the British commander's despatch describing the event. — *Commodore HazelicoocTs Instructions to Captain Alexander, September 26JA.*— Sir *A'tUiam Howe's Letter to Lord George Germain, October 10th.*

G TO THE PRESIDENT OF CONGRESS.

Camp, near Pennibeckcrt Mill, 5 October, 1777.

Sir,

Having received intelligence through two intercepted letters, that General Howe had detached a part of his force for the purpose of reducing Billingsport and the forts on the Delaware, I communicated the accounts to my general officers, who were unanimously of opinion that a favorable opportunity offered to make an attack upon the troops, which were at and near Germantown. It was accordingly agreed that it should take place yesterday morning, and the following dispositions were made.

The divisions of Sullivan and Wayne, flanked by Conway's brigade, were to enter the town by the way of Chesnut Hill, while General Armstrong with the Pennsylvania militia should fall down the Manatawny road by Vandeering's Mill, and get upon the enemy's left and rear. The divisions of Greene and Stephen, flanked by MDougall's brigade, were to enter, by taking a circuit by way of the Lime-kiln road, at the Market-house, and to attack their right wing; and the militia of Maryland and Jersey, under Generals Smallwood and Forman, were to march by the old York road, and fall upon the rear of their right. Lord Stirling, with Nash's and Maxwell's brigades, was to form a *corps de reserve.*

We marched about seven o'clock the preceding evening, and General Sullivan's advanced party, drawn from Conway's brigade, attacked their picket at Mount Airy, or Mr. Allen's house, about sunrise the next morning, which presently gave way; and his main body, consisting of the right wing, following soon, engaged the light infantry and other troops encamped near the picket, which they forced from their ground. Leaving their baggage, they retreated a considerable distance, having previously thrown a party into Mr. Chew's house, who were in a situation not to be easily forced, and had it in their power, from the windows, to give us no small annoyance, and in a great measure to obstruct our advance.

The attack from our left column, under General Greene, began about three quarters of an hour after that from the right, and was for some time equally successful. But I cannot enter upon the particulars of what happened in that quarter, as I am not yet informed of them with sufficient certainty and precision. The morning was extremely foggy, which prevented our improving the advantages we gained, so well as we should otherwise have done. This circumstance, by concealing from us the true situation of the enemy, obliged us to act with more caution and less expedition than we could have wished; and gave the enemy time to recover from the effects of our first impression; and, what was still more unfortunate, it served to keep our different parties in ignorance of each other's movements and hinder their acting in concert. It also occasioned them to mistake one another for the enemy, which I believe more than any thing else contributed to the misfortune that ensued. In the midst of the most promising appearances, when every thing gave the most flattering hopes of victory, the troops began suddenly to retreat, and entirely left the field, in spite of every effort that could be made to rally them.

Upon the whole, it may be said the day was rather unfortunate than injurious. We sustained no material loss of men, and brought off all our artillery, except one piece which was dismounted. The enemy are nothing the better by the event; and our troops, who are not in the least dispirited by it, have gained what all young troops gain by being in actions. We have had however several valuable officers killed and wounded, particularly the latter. General Nash is among the wounded, and his life is despaired of. As soon as it is possible to obtain a return of our loss, I will transmit it. In justice to General Sullivan and the whole right wing of the army, whose conduct I had an opportunity of observing, as they acted immediately under my eye, I have the pleasure to inform you, that both officers and men behaved with a degree of gallantry that did them the highest honor. I have the honor to be, &c.

P. S. As I have observed, I have not received a return of our loss; but, from what I have just now learned from General Greene, I fear it is more considerable than I at first apprehended, in men. The cannon, mentioned above, is said to have been brought off in a wagon.

TO SIR WILLIAM HOWE.

Head-Quartets, 6 October, 1777.

Sir,

I cannot forbear assuring you, that I am somewhat at a loss to understand the design of your letter of the 3d instant. I can hardly believe you to be serious in remonstrating against a procedure fully authorized by the common practice of armies, countenanced by your own troops at Trenton, and obviously calculated to answer a purpose very different from that of distressing the inhabitants and increasing the common calamities incident to a state of war. If this is a consequence of it, it is an unavoidable one, and had no part in producing the measure. I flatter myself the public is sufficiently sensible, that it is not my wish nor aim to distress, but to protect the inhabitants, and know how to interpret any thing, that, with respect to individuals, may seem to deviate from this end. Nor will they be easily persuaded to consider it as any injustice or cruelty to them, that my parties should have rendered useless, for a time, a few mills in the neighbourhood of your army, which were so situated as to be capable of affording them no inconsiderable advantages.

The letter from General Howe, to which this is an answer, was in the following words.

" Hetd-Clauten, 3 October, 1777.

"sir,

" Your parties having destroyed several mills in the adjacent country, which can only distress the peaceable inhabitants residing in their houses,

I am constrained from a regard to their sufferings, and a sense of the duty I owe to the public, to forewarn you of the calamities which may ensue, and to express my abhorrence of such a proceeding. At the same time I am inclined to believe, that the outrages already committed have not been in consequence of your orders, and that this early notice will engage you to put an effectual stop to them. If not, I do in the most direct terms disclaim any share in creating the general scene of distress among the inhabitants, which such destruction must inevitably cause. With due respect, I am, &c.

I am happy to find that you express so much sensibility to the sufferings of the inhabitants, as it gives room to hope, that those wanton and unnecessary depredations, which have heretofore, in too many instances, marked the conduct of your army, will be discontinued for the future. The instances I allude to need not be enumerated; your own memory will suggest them to your imagination, from the destruction of Charlestown, in Massachusetts, down to the more recent burning of mills, barns, and houses at the Head of Elk, and in the vicinity of the Schuylkill. I am, &c

"W. Howe." It is interesting to observe, that, in the midst of solemn and important affairs, and the forms of official station, there was room for courtesy VOL. V. 11 TO THE PRESIDENT OF CONGRESS.

Camp, near Pennibecker'a Mill, 7 October, 1777.

Sir,

Since I had the honor of addressing you on the 5th, I have obtained a return of our loss in the action on Saturday, by which it appears to be much more considerable than I at first apprehended, though I always imagined myself that it was greater than it was generally supposed to be. The copy of the return enclosed will show the amount as it now stands; but I hope many of those who are missing will yet come in. I fear however there are several under that denomination to be added to the number of the slain, as the action was warm in every quarter, from the information of the officers who commanded the different attacks. What loss the, enemy sustained, I am not able precisely to ascertain; but from a variety of corresponding accounts of persons, who left the city since, and those of a deserter, it was very considerable. The deserter, who is intelligent, says General Agnew was killed, Sir William Erskine wounded in the head and leg, and that their general loss, in killed and wounded, amounted to near eight hundred. Several reputable persons from the city corroborate this, particularly with respect to General Agnew's death; some say upwards of two hundred wagons with wounded were carried in after the action, and before they came out; and that it was the common belief there, that the enemy had been severely handled.

and civil acta in small things. The following note was sent on the same day that the above letter was written, and they probably were both forwarded with the same flag.

"General Washington's compliments to General Howe, — does himself the pleasure to return to him a dog, which accidentally fell into his hands, and, by the inscription on the collar, appears to belong to General Howe.

It is with much chagrin and mortification I add, that every account confirms the opinion I at first entertained, that our troops retreated at the instant when victory was declaring herself in our favor. The tumult, disorder, and even despair, which, it seems, had taken place in the British army, were scarcely to be paralleled; and it is said, so strongly did the ideas of a retreat prevail, that Chester was fixed on as their rendezvous. I can discover no other cause for not improving this happy opportunity, than the extreme haziness of the weather.

My intention is to encamp the army at some suitable place to rest and refresh the men, and recover them from the still remaining effects of that disorder naturally attendant on a retreat. We shall here wait for the reinforcements coming on, and shall then act according to circumstances. General Varnum, with the detachment from Peek skill amounting to about twelve hundred, including officers, would be last night at Coryell's Ferry. About five hundred militia from Virginia, and two hundred from Maryland, together with Colonel Gibson's State regiment consisting of two hundred and twentysix effectives, have already joined the army. Since the action, General Forman's brigade of Jersey militia has quitted us. The men began to be uneasy at their situation, and desirous to return home; and as, by some intelligence received from General Dickinson, there was reason to imagine there might be a call for their services in the Jerseys, it was thought expedient to gratify their desire.

General Washington wrote at the same time to Governor Trumbull; — " Having obtained information of the situation of the enemy, we determined to endeavour to do something by way of surprise. We accordingly marched all night, and reached the town by break of day. We attacked them upon two quarters, in both of which we were successful. But the morning was so excessively foggy, that we could not see the confusion the enemy were in, and the advantage we had gained; and, fearing to push too far through a strong village, we retired, after an engagement of two hours, bringing off all our artillery with us. We did not know, till after the affair was over, how near we were to gaining a complete victory; but we have since learnt from deserters and others, who have come out, that preparations were making to retreat to Chester. While the action lasted, it was pretty severe. Our loss will amount, in killed and wounded, to upwards of three hundred." This estimate of the loss was founded on loose returns. In writing to his brother, on the 17th of October, General Washington described the loss as being about one thousand men, in killed, wounded, and missing. General Howe, in his official despatch, stated the American loss to be between two and three hundred killed, about six hundred wounded, and upwards of four hundred taken. This is doubtless an exaggeration. For other particulars relating to the battle of Germantown, and the letter of approbation and thanks from Congress to General Washington in reference to it, see Appendix, No. III.

The state of our water defence on the Delaware is far from being as flattering as could be wished. After some slight opposition from the Jersey militia under General Newcomb, a detachment of the enemy took possession of BillingsporL This perhaps is an event of no material consequence; but it is to be lamented, that many of the officers and seamen on board the galleys have manifested a disposition that does them little honor. Looking upon their situation as desperate, or probably from worse motives, they have been guilty of the most alarming desertions. Two whole crews, including the officers, have deserted to the enemy. I learn however by Captain Brewer, who is this moment arrived here from the fleet, that the accounts they have received from the city, of our late attack, were such as to have produced a favorable change, and to have inspired them with more confidence. I would here observe, that the charge of bad conduct was by no means applicable to the whole; far from it. He further adds, that four of the enemy's ships made an attempt yesterday morning to weigh the chevaux-de-frise opposite to Billingsport, but were repulsed by our galleys: which has also contributed to raise the spirits of the seamen. Our garrison on Fort Island, consisting of little more than two hundred Continental troops under Lieutenant-Colonel Smith, appear determined to maintain their post to the last extremity.

I beg leave to mention to Congress, that there is a great deficiency of general officers in this army. When the detachment coming from Peekskill joins us, we shall have thirteen brigades. These require as many brigadiers, and six major-generals. Instead of these, we shall have only four major-generals and eleven brigadiers; and the deficiency will be still increased by the death of General Nash, which, from every appearance, is momentarily to be expected. General Woodford's absence, occasioned by his wound, adds to our embarrassments, though it will be but for a time. Under these circumstances, Congress will be sensible that the government of the army cannot go on with that energy, which is essential to its well-being and success. Neither officers nor men will transfer the respect and obedience they pay to a general officer, to a colonel who happens to be appointed to the temporary command of a brigade; nor will he, knowing his authority to be only temporary, be as solicitous to enforce it, as one who is conscious he is to continue in the station he fills. Want of leisure prevents my being more particular at this time; but I shall take the liberty, in a day or two, to point out the troops that are in want of general officers, with my observations on the subject.

I cannot however omit this opportunity of recommending General MDougall to their notice. This gentleman, from the time of his appointment as brigadier, from his abilities, military knowledge, and approved bravery, has every claim to promotion. If I mistake *YOU* V. H t not, he was passed over in the last appointments of major-generals, and younger officers preferred before him; but his disinterested attachment to the service prevented his acting in the manner, that is customary in like circumstances. This, I think, gives him a peculiar title to esteem, and concurs with the opinion I have of his value as an officer, to make me wish it may appear advisable to Congress to promote him to one of the vacancies. It would be well if the intended inquiry into the conduct of General St. Clair could be brought to a speedy issue; and, if he is acquitted to the satisfaction of Congress, that, as his general character as an officer is good, he may be again restored to the service.

By a letter this evening received from Colonel Hawkes Hay of Haverstraw, dated the 5th, at four o'clock in the afternoon, four ships of war, a considerable number of armed vessels, eight transports, and forty flat-bottomed boats, arrived that morning in the bay opposite that place, and were landing troops at Verplanck's Point. Their number and design were not known.

I have the honor to be, &c TO COLONEL CHRISTOPHER GREENE.

Instructions. Sir, I have directed General Varnum to send your regiment and that of Colonel Angell to Red Bank, by a route which has been marked out to him. The command of that detachment will of course devolve upon you, with which you will proceed with all expedition, and throw yourself into that place. When you arrive there, you will immediately communicate your arrival er.

to Colonel Smith, commander of the garrison at Fort Mifflin, and Commodore Hazelwood, commander of the fleet in the 'river. You are to cooperate with them in every measure necessary for the defence of the obstructions in the river, and to counteract every attempt the enemy may make for their removal. You will find a very good fortification at Red Bank; but if any thing should be requisite to render it stronger, or proportion it to the size of your garrison, you will have it done. The cannon you

will stand in need of, as much as can be spared, will be furnished from the galleys and Fort Mifflin, from whence also you will derive supplies of military stores.

I have sent Captain Duplessis,f with some officers and men, to take the immediate direction of the artillery, for your garrison. He is also to superintend any works that may be wanted. If there should be any deficiency of men for the artillery, the security of the garrison will require you to assist him with a few additional ones from your detachment. You should not lose a moment's time in getting to the place of your destination, and making every proper preparation for its defence. Any delay might give the enemy an opportunity of getting there before you, which could not fail of being most fatal in its consequences. If in the progress of your march you should fall in with any detachment of the enemy, bending towards the same object, and likely to gain it before you, and from intelligence should have reason to think yourself equal to the task, you will by all means attack them, and endeavour by that means to disappoint their design. I have written to General Newcomb, of the Jersey militia, to give you all the aid in his power, for which you will accordingly apply when necessary.

Commodore Hazelwood acted under a commission from Pennsylvania, and originally commanded only the armed vessels belonging to that State. But the Continental shipping in the Delaware was now likewise put under his command. This caused some uneasiness on the part of the Continental navy officers, and occasional want of harmony. f A young French officer of great merit, appointed by Congress a captain of artillery in the American service.

Upon the whole, Sir, you will be pleased to remember, that the post with which you are now intrusted is of the utmost importance to America, and demands every exertion of which you are capable for its security and defence. The whole defence of the Delaware absolutely depends upon it, and consequently all the enemy's hopes of keep-

ing Philadelphia, and finally succeeding in the object of the present campaign. Influenced by these considerations, I doubt not your regard to the service, and your own reputation, will prompt you to every possible effort to accomplish the important end of your trust, and frustrate the intentions of the enemy. Given at Head-Quarters, this 7th day of October, 1777.

TO GOVERNOR LIVINGSTON.

Head-Quarters, 8 October, 1777.

Sir, I yesterday received certain intelligence, that the enemy had proceeded up Hudson's River from New York, and landed a body of men at Verplanck's Point, a few miles below Peekskill. This movement fully explains those appearances, which lately induced General Dickinson to apprehend a second incursion into the Jerseys; and gives reason to believe, that, instead of that, the enemy meditate a serious blow against our posts in the Highlands. This circumstance is somewhat alarming, as the situation of our affairs this way has obliged us to draw off so large a part of our force from Peekskill, that what now remains there may perhaps prove inadequate to the defence of it. Should any disaster happen, it is easy to foresee the most unhappy consequences. The loss of the Highland passes would be likely to involve the reduction of the forts. This would open the navigation of the river, and enable the enemy with facility to throw their force into Albany, get into the rear of General Gates, and either oblige him to retreat, or put him between two fires. The success of the present attempt upon Peekskill may, in its consequences, entirely change the face of our northern affairs, and throw them into a very disagreeable and unfavorable train.

From the Orderly Book, October 70u " The situation of the army frequently not admitting of the regular performance of divine service on Sundays, the chaplains of the army are forthwith to meet together and agree on some method of performing it at other times, which method they will make known to the Commander-in-chief."

I am confident, that no arguments need

be used to dispose you to contribute every effort in your power, to obviate an evil of so great magnitude; and as I do not conceive, that there can be now any danger of your militia being wanted at home, for the internal security of your State, I am persuaded you will readily consent to my request, that as large a part of them, as can be prevailed upon to go, may immediately march with all expedition to the aid of General Putnam. At this distance, unacquainted as I am with what may have taken place, I cannot give any particular directions to regulate their march; they must govern themselves by circumstances, and act according to the intelligence and orders they may receive from General Putnam.

I have the honor to be, &c.

TOUT. 12 H« TO LIEUTENANT-COLONEL SAMUEL SMITH.

Skippack Camp, 11 October, 1777.

Sir, I received yours of the 9th, informing me of the occasion of the late firing. I imagine the enemy still persist in their attempt, as the firing has continued at intervals ever since. As the rear of the fort is only defended by a picket work, I think you ought to lose no time in throwing up a bank against the picket, which would strengthen it and make it defensible against shot. If some blinds were thrown up, within the area of the fort, they would be a security against shells, of which I think you are in more danger than from shot. You seem apprehensive, if the enemy should possess Province Island, that your men must quit their barracks. In that case you should think of finding out some more secure place for sheltering them. I cannot at present think of any place better than between the east face of the Stone Fort and the lower battery; they will at least be safe there until an attack begins from the water. I desired Captain Brewer, who went from hence yesterday, to caution the Commodore against an unnecessary expenditure of ammunition, and I beg that you will also be careful in that point; for should the enemy cut off your intercourse with us, you will find the want of it. I am, &c.

The enemy erected a battery, on the 9th of September, at the mouth of the Schuylkill, to secure the passage at Webb's Ferry. Commodore Hazelwood sent several galleys to attack the battery, which was silenced in a short time. In the night of the 10th the enemy crossed Webb's Ferry and erected a redoubt opposite the fort, within two musket shots of the blockhouse. As soon as the redoubt was discovered in the morning, the Commodore despatched three galleys and a floating battery to attack it; which was so well executed, that one lieutenant, one ensign, and fifty-six privates were compelled to surrender themselves prisoners of war.— *HazdwooeTs MS. Letter, October 11th.*

In speaking of the probability, that the enemy would bring their cannon to bear upon the fort from the opposite shore, Colonel Smith wrote; — "I shall in that case be obliged to cover my men; and should they keep up their fire in the night, it will compel us to sleep in the open air, which will soon destroy my small party. I have already sent away six men and one officer sick. Besides this, we have seven more in garrison unfit for duty; however, if they keep their men in the marshes two or three days, they must in this weather become equally sickly. From the number of the enemy we saw on the shore, I am of the opinion that they have at least seven hundred and fifty men, perhaps a thousand. I have now two hundred effective men in garrison. The number of wounded in last Saturday's engagement at Germantown, by every account we can get from the city, exceeds twelve hundred."—*MS. Letter, October 96k.*

P. S. It is my wish that Colonel Greene and you, in concert with the gentlemen of the navy, would turn your attention to every place, which will contribute to the defence of the water obstructions, and, if it is in my power to afford assistance, I will do it.

TO GOVERNOR GEORGE CLINTON.

Head-Quarters, 15 October, 1777.

Dear Sir, I was this day honored with yours of the 9th, containing a full account of the storm of Forts Montgomery and Clinton. General Putnam had given me information of the loss two days before, but not in so full and ample a manner. It is to be regretted, that so brave a resistance did not meet with a suitable reward. You have however the satisfaction of knowing, that every thing was done, that could possibly be done by a handful against a far superior force. This I am convinced was the case. This affair might have been attended with fatal consequences, had not there been a most providential intervention in favor of General Gates's arms on the 7th instant; but I am fully of opinion, that

Sir Henry Clinton will not advance much farther up the river, upon hearing of Burgoyne's defeat and retreat. Nothing but an absolute necessity could have induced me to withdraw any further part of the troops allotted for the defence of the posts up the North River; but such was the reduced state of our Continental regiments, after the battle of Brandy wine, and such the difficulty of procuring reinforcements of militia from the southward, that without the troops from Peekskill we should scarcely have been able to keep the field against General Howe. I had the greatest hopes, that General Putnam would draw in as many Connecticut militia, as would replace the Continental troops, and I make no doubt but he did all in his power to obtain them in time. I am sorry that you were under the necessity of destroying the frigates. The only consolation is, that if we had not done it ourselves, the enemy would either have done it for us, or have carried them down for their own use.

Since the battle of Germantown, the two armies have remained in a manner quiet. The enemy have made several attempts to remove the obstructions in the Delaware, but hitherto without effect. They are now making preparations to raise batteries in the rear of Fort Mifflin, which commands the uppermost chevauxde-frise. If we can maintain that post, and one opposite upon the Jersey shore, I hope our ships, galleys, and floating batteries, will be able to keep their stations and repel any force, that can be brought by water directly in front. I most earnestly wait for further news from the northward, which I hope will bring us accounts of the total ruin of Burgoyne's army.

For other particulars respecting the capture of Forts Montgomery and Clinton, see Appendix, No. IV.

It is not unlikely, that one of Sir Henry Clinton's objects will be to destroy the boats and small craft in *the* North River. Should this be the case, and he succeed, I think it will be advisable to set a number of workmen to building flat-bottomed boats at some secure places within three or four miles of the water, from which they may be easily hauled. They are so exceedingly useful, and so frequently wanted, that I think the business cannot, in such case, be too soon begun or carried on with too much expedition. I have written to General Putnam upon the same subject.

I am, dear Sir, &c.

TO THE PRESIDENT OF CONGRESS.

Head-Quarters, at Peter Wintz's, 16 October, 1777.

Sir, In respect to the resolution, directing a flag to be sent to General Howe, I am inclined to think, that the information upon which it was framed was without foundation. The letters, which have come from our officers, who have been lately taken, generally mention that their treatment has been tolerably good; and such privates as have escaped have said nothing, in the course of their examination, of their having been compelled to work. For these reasons I have taken the liberty to decline sending the flag. At the same time Congress may be assured, if our prisoners suffer any wrongs, I shall take every means in my power to have them redressed as soon as I am apprized of them.

Information bad at different times been conveyed to Congress, that the prisoners in Philadelphia were compelled to labor, and were employed in throwing up works in the neighbourhood of the city. Congress thought it incumbent on them to inquire into the truth of the report, and directed that a flag should be immediately despatched to General Howe for that purpose. — *President Hancock's Letter, October 12th.*

It is with the highest satisfaction I congratulate Congress on the success of our arms at the northward in the action of the 7th, an event of the most interesting importance at this critical juncture. From the happy tram in which things then were, I hope we shall soon hear of the most decisive advantages. We moved this morning from the encampment at which we had been for six or seven days past, and are just arrived at the grounds we occupied before the action ofthe 4th. One motive for coming here is to divert the enemy's attention and force from the forts. These they seem to consider as capital objects, and, from their operations, mean to reduce if possible. At present their designs are directed against Fort Mifflin and the chevaux-defrise. I have therefore detached a further reinforcement to the garrison.

I yesterday, through the hands of Mrs. Ferguson of Graham Park, received a letter of a very curious and extraordinary nature from Mr. Duche, which I have thought proper to transmit to Congress. To this ridiculous, illiberal performance, I made a short reply, by desiring the bearer of it, if she should hereafter by any accident meet with Mr. Duche, to tell him I should have returned it unopened, if I had had any idea of the contents; observing at the same time, that I highly disapproved the intercourse she seemed to have been carrying on, and expected it would be discontinued. Notwithstanding the author's assertion, I cannot but suspect that the measure did not originate with him; and that he was induced to it by the hope of establishing his interest and peace more effectually with the enemy.

I have the honor to be, &c Concerning Duche's letter to General Washington, see Appendix. No. V.

TO THOMAS WHARTON, PRESIDENT OF PENN-

SYLVANIA.

Head-Quarters, 17 October, 1777.

Sir,

As the term of service of a great number of the militia of this State, who were called out some time ago, has expired, and their places have been by no means punctually filled up by succeeding classes, I am constrained to call upon you, in the most pressing manner, to exert the powers of government, not only to keep up the number of four thousand men demanded by Congress, but of a much greater number, if they can possibly be armed and accoutred. When the capital of your State is in the enemy's hands, and when they can only be dislodged from thence by a powerful reinforcement of militia, in aid of Continental troops, there should not be a moment's hesitation, whether one or two classes should be commanded to appear; but at least one half of the men, capable of bearing arms, should be called into the field. By exertions of this kind, New York, though sorely oppressed by our avowed enemies, and more so by our internal foes, has made a noble resistance; and New Jersey has kept the enemy out of her limits, except now and then a hasty descent, without a Continental regiment. Besides doing this, she has sent and is now sending reinforcements to this and the northern army. It will not be long, before the militia from Maryland and Virginia will have performed their tour of duty; and from the distance, which most of them have to travel before they reach the army, I cannot expect much more assistance from those quarters, in the course of the remaining part of the campaign.

I assure you, Sir, it is matter ol astonishment to every part of the continent, to hear that Pennsylvania, the most opulent and populous of all the States, has but twelve hundred militia in the field, at a time when the enemy are endeavouring to make themselves completely masters of, and to fix their winter quarters in, her capital. Without the free navigation of the Delaware I am confident, that General Howe will never remain in Philadelphia, and I am as confident, that, had I a sufficient force to afford as much assistance to the forts upon the Delaware as their importance deserves, he would not be able to possess them. I have spared as many of the Continental troops as I possibly can, without endangering the safety of the army, and I shall still continue to afford every further relief in my power. From this state of facts, I hope that you will not lose a moment, in calling upon and endeavouring to rouse the people of this State to a manly and effectual opposition; and I know of no means so likely to answer this end, as not to confine the demand to any particular number, but to call upon every man to come forth. The county lieutenants should be particularly careful to see, that all those, who have arms and accoutrements of their own, bring them out; for they have a very mistaken notion, that there are full supplies in the Continental stores. Many even come out without blankets, expecting to find them.

There is another matter, which I beg leave to recommend to the serious consideration of the legislature of your State; that is, the adopting of some mode of completing and keeping up the quota of your Continental regiments. Upon an average, your battalions have never been above one third full; and now many of them are far below even that. From the extravagant prices given to substitutes in the militia, in the different States, it has become impossible to recruit more upon the bounty allowed by Congress. The New England States and Virginia have begun to adopt the mode of drafting, and, I am informed, they have succeeded very well. I am convinced, that this will be found the only method of raising Continental troops; and, if the measure were to become general throughout the States, it would not be deemed a hardship. I mention this matter to you at this time, in the hope that you will as soon as possible fall upon this, or some other mode, to recruit your regiments in the course of this fall and winter j and, as it is more than probable, that our opposition will not end with this campaign, we ought to endeavour to have a respectable army in the field in the spring, before the enemy can receive, further reinforcements from Europe. I have the honor to be, &c.

TO RICHARD HENRY LEE, IN CONGRESS.

Matuchen Hill, 17 October, 1777.

Dear Sir,

Your favor of the 5th instant, as also that of the 11th by Baron de Kalb, are both at hand. It is not in my power at present to answer your query respecting the appointment of this gentleman. But, Sir, if there is any thing in a report, that Congress have appointed, or as others say are about to appoint, Brigadier Conway a major-general in this army, it will be as unfortunate a measure as ever was adopted. I may add, and I think with truth, that it will give a fatal blow to the existence of the army. Upon so interesting a subject, I must speak plainly. The duty I owe my country, the ardent desire I have to promote its true interests, and justice to individuals, require this of me. General Conway's merit, then, as an officer, and his importance

Vol. v. 13 I in this army, exist more in his own imagination, than in reality. For it is a maxim with him, to leave no service of his own untold, nor to want any thing, which is to be obtained by importunity.

But as I do not mean to detract from him any merit he possesses, and only wish to have the matter taken upon its true ground, after allowing him every thing that his warmest friends would contend for, I would ask, why the youngest brigadier in the service (for I believe he is so) should be put over the heads of all the eldest, and thereby take rank of, and command gentlemen, who but yesterday were his seniors; gentlemen, who, I will be bold to say, in behalf of some of them at least, are of sound judgment and unquestionable bravery? If there was a degree of conspicuous merit in General Conway, unpossessed by any of his seniors, the confusion, which might be occasioned by it, would stand warranted upon the principles of sound policy; for I readily agree, that this is no time for trilling; but, at the same time that I cannot subscribe to the fact, this truth I am very well assured of (though I have not directly, nor indirectly, exchanged a word with any one of the brigadiers on the subject, nor am I certain that any one has heard of the appointment), that they will not serve under him. I leave you to guess, therefore, at the situation this army would be in at so important a crisis, if this event should take place. These gentlemen have feelings as officers; and though they do not dispute the authority of Congress to make appointments, they will judge of the propriety of acting under them.

In a word, the service is so difficult, and every necessary so expensive, that almost all our officers are tired out. Do not, therefore, afford them good pretexts for retiring. No day passes over my head without application for leave to resign. Within the last six days, I am certain, twenty commissions at least have been tendered to me. I must, therefore, conjure you to conjure Congress to consider this matter well, and not, by a real act of injustice, compel some good officers to leave the service, and thereby incur a train of evils unforeseen and irremediable. To sum up the whole, I have been a slave to the service; I have undergone more than most men are aware of, to harmonize so many discordant parts; but it will be impossible for me to be of any further service, if such insuperable difficulties are thrown in my way. You may believe me, my good Sir, that I have no earthly views, but the public good, in what I have said. I have no prejudice against General Conway, nor desire to serve any other brigadier, further than I think the cause will be benefited by it; to bring which to a speedy and happy conclusion, is the most fervent wish of my soul.

Mr. Lee replied; — "I was a good deal surprised to find you had been told Congress had appointed General Conway a major-general. No such appointment has been made, nor do I believe it will, whilst it *is* likely to produce the evil consequences you suggest. It is very true, that, both within and without doors, there have been advocates for the measure, and it has been affirmed, that it would be very agreeable to the army, whose favorite Mr. Conway was asserted to be. My judgment on this business was not formed until I received your letter. I am very sure Congress would not take any step that might injure the army, or even have a tendency that way; and I verily believe they wish to lessen your difficulties by every means in their power, from an entire conviction that the purest motives of public good direct your actions.

" The business of a Board of War is so extensive, so important, and demanding such constant attention, that Congress see clearly the necessity of constituting a new board, out of Congress, whose time shall be entirely devoted to that essential department. It is by some warmly proposed, that this board shall be filled by the three following gentlemen, Colonel Reed, Colonel Pickering, the present adjutant-general, and Colonel Harrison, your secretary; and that General Conway be appointed adjutant-general in the room of Colonel Pickering. It is my wish, and I am sure it is so of many others, to know your full and candid sentiments on this subject. For my own part, I cannot be satisfied with giving any opinion on the point, until I am favored with your sentiments, which I shall be much obliged to you for, Sir, as soon as your time will permit.

With respect to the wants of the militia, in the articles of clothing, you must be well convinced, that it is not in my power to supply them in the smallest degree, when near one half of our own men are rendered unfit for service for want of these things. I can add no more at present, than that I am, dear Sir, &c.
TO BARON D'ARENDT.

Head-Quarters, 18 October, 1777.

Sir, Being recovered from the indisposition under which you lately labored, you are to proceed immediately to Fort Mifilin on Mud Island and take the command of the troops there, and those which may be sent. I shall not prescribe any particular line for your conduct, because I repose the utmost confidence in your bravery, knowledge, and judgment; and because the mode of defence must depend on a variety of circumstances, which will be best known to those, who are on the spot. I will add, that the maintenance of this post is of the last importance to the States of America, and that preventing the enemy from obtaining possession of it, under the smiles of Heaven, will be the means of our defeating the army to which we are now opposed; or of obliging them disgracefully to abandon the city of Philadelphia, which is now in their hands. TO JOHN AUGUSTINE WASHING-TON.

" It has been affirmed, that General Conway would quit the service, if he were not made a major-general. But I have been told in confidence, that he would leave it at the end of this campaign if he *was* appointed, unless his word of honor were taken to continue for any fixed tune. And it is a question with me, whether the advocates for Genera! Conway will not miss their aim, if he should be appointed adjutant-general, unless he has the rank of major-general also. My reason for thinking so is, that I have been informed General Conway desires to retire to his family, provided he can carry from this country home with him a rank that will raise him in France. It is very certain that the public good demands a speedy erecting and the judicious filling of the new Board of War, and I sincerely wish it may be done in the most proper manner. I do not imagine Congress would appoint Colonel Harrison, without first knowing whether you could spare him; nor do I think that so important an office, as that of adjutant-general, should be touched without the maturest consideration." — *MS. Letter, October* 20tt

Notwithstanding the strong representations of General Washington w the above letter to Mr. Lee, and the decided opinions expressed in Mr. Lee's reply, General Conway was appointed by Congress a few weeks afterwards inspector-general of the army, and raised to the rank of major-general over several older brigadier-generals.—*Journal, December* 13/A.

I have detached to-day a further reinforcement to the garrison, and have instructed Colonel Greene, who commands at Red Bank, to cooperate with you, and to render you every assistance in his power. You will maintain with him, and with Commodore Hazelwood, who commands our fleet, a good understanding and the strictest harmony. These will be essential; and, by mutually aiding each other, I shall look forward for the most happy events. You will be particularly attentive to the state of your ammunition and provision, advising me of the same from time to time, and of

such supplies as you may judge necessary to be sent to you. You will also report to me the situation of the garrison, as often as it shall be requisite, and will not fail to transmit to me frequent and the most early intelligence of every important occurrence. I recommend your utmost despatch to arrive at the garrison; and you have my warmest wishes, that the command may prove honorable to yourself and beneficial to America. I am, &c The Baron d'Arcndt was a colonel in the Continental service, and had been appointed on the 19th of March to the command of the German Battalion.

Philadelphia County, 18 October, 1777.

Dear Brother,

When my last to you was dated I know not; for truly I can say, that my whole time is so much engrossed, that I have scarcely a moment, but sleeping ones, for relaxation, or to indulge myself in writing to a friend. The anxiety you have been under, on account of this army, I can easily conceive. Would to God there had been less cause for it; or that our situation at present was such as to promise much. The enemy crossed the Schuylkill (which, by the by, above the Falls is as easily crossed in any place as Potomac Run, Aquia, or any other broad, shallow water) rather by stratagem; though I do not know, that it was in our power to prevent it, as their manoeuvres made it necessary for us to attend to our stores, which lay at Reading, towards which they seemed bending their course, and the loss of which must have proved our ruin. After they had crossed, we took the first favorable opportunity of attacking them.

This was attempted by a night's march of fourteen miles to surprise them, which we effectually did, so far as to reach their guards before they had notice of our coming; and if it had not been for a thick fog, which rendered it so dark at times that we were not able to distinguish friend from foe at the distance of thirty yards, we should, I believe, have made a decisive and glorious day of it. But Providence designed it otherwise; for after we had driven the enemy a mile or two, after they were in the utmost confusion and flying before us in most places, after we were upon the point, as it appeared to every body, of grasping a complete victory, our own troops took fright and fled with precipitation and disorder. How to account for this, I know not; unless, as I before observed, the fog represented their own friends to them for a reinforcement of the enemy, as we attacked in different quarters at the same time, and were about closing the wings of our army when this happened. One thing, indeed, contributed not a little to our misfortune, and that was a want of ammunition on the right wing, which began the engagement, and in the course of two hours and forty minutes, which time it lasted, had, many of them, expended the forty rounds, that they took into the field. After the engagement we removed to a place about twenty miles from the enemy, to collect our forces together, to take care of our wounded, get furnished with necessaries again, and be in a better posture, either for offensive or defensive operations. We are now advancing towards the enemy again, being at this time within twelve miles of them.

Our loss in the late action was, in killed, wounded, and missing, about one thousand men, but of the missing, many, I dare say, took advantage of the times, and deserted. General Nash of North Carolina was wounded, and died two or three days after. Many valuable officers of ours were also wounded, and some killed. In a word, it was a bloody day. Would to Heaven I could add, that it had been a more fortunate one for us.

I very sincerely congratulate you on the change in your family. Tell the young couple, after wishing them joy of their union, that it is my sincere hope, that it will be as happy and lasting as their present joys are boundless. The enclosed letter of thanks to my sister for her elegant present, you will please to deliver; and, with sincere affection for you all, I am, &c In this letter General Washington enclosed to his brother the copy of a brief despatch, which he received after the letter was written, from Governor Clinton, announcing the ca-

pitulation of Burgoyne's army at Saratoga. He added in a postscript; —" I most devoutly congratulate my country, and every well-wisher to the cause, on this signal stroke of Providence.

TO MAJOR-GENERAL PUTNAM.

Camp, 19 October, 1777.

Dear Sir, Your favor of the 16th I received yesterday morning, and was much obliged by the interesting contents. The defeat of General Burgoyne is a most important event, and such as must afford the highest satisfaction to every well-affected American. Should Providence be pleased to crown our arms in the course of the campaign with one more fortunate stroke, I think we shall have no great cause for anxiety respecting the future designs of Britain. I trust all will be well in His good time. The obvious intention of Sir Henry Clinton was to relieve General Burgoyne, and being disappointed in that by his surrender, I presume he will make an expeditious return. I am happy to find you at the head of so respectable a force, and flatter myself, if he should land with a view to action, though I do not expect it, you will give us a happy account of him. I believe, from the bravery of the garrison of Fort Montgomery, he purchased victory at no inconsiderable expense. General Campbell was certainly killed. This they mention in their own printed account, but call him lieutenant-colonel of the fifty-second regiment. He was a general on the American establishment, so declared in one of the orderly books, which fell into our hands.

After the British had captured Fort Montgomery, and the other posts on the Hudson, General Putnam retreated from Peekskill, and established his headquarters at Fishkill beyond the Highlands. He wrote to General Washington from Fishkill; — "Last Monday General Parsons, with about two thousand troops, marched down and took possession of Peekskill, and the passes in the Highlands. He has taken a number of cattle, horses, and sheep, which were collected by the enemy. They had burnt the buildings and barracks at the Continental Village, and several dwelling-

houses and other buildings at Peekskill. They have demolished Forts Montgomery and Constitution, and are repairing Fort Clinton. Yesterday about forty sail passed up the river crowded with troops, and are at anchor above Poughkeepsie, the wind not favoring. We were on our march after them, when I met the agreeable intelligence of the surrender of General Burgoyne and his army as prisoners of war, a copy of which is enclosed. I thereupon most sincerely congratulate your Excellency. I have halted my troops, and am now considering what ought to be my movement; I have sent to Governor Clinton for his opinion, and ordered General Parsons to spare no pains to find out the situation and strength of the garrison at Kingsbridge, in order to direct my future operations most advantageously. I have about six thousand troops, who are chiefly militia. I understand that General Campbell was killed at Fort Montgomery, and several field-officers and others of inferior rank. The two Continental frigates and the row-galley were burnt, to prevent their falling into the hands of the enemy, for which I am very sorry, as one of them I believe might have been saved." — MS. Letter, October 16th.

I have but little to add respecting the situation of affairs here. They remain much as they were, when I wrote to you last. To remove the obstructions in the river, seems to be a capital object with the enemy. Their attempts hitherto have not succeeded, and I hope they will not. I am extremely sorry for the death of Mrs. Putnam, and sympathize with you upon the occasion. Remembering that all must die, and that she had lived to an honorable age, I hope you will bear the misfortune with that fortitude and complacency of mind, that become a man and a Christian. I am, dear Sir, with great esteem, yours, &c.

There is probably an error here, in regard to the identity of the persona. Sir Henry Clinton, in his official return of the killed and wounded, gives the name of " Lieutenant-Colonel Campbell of the fiftysecond regiment." There was a General Campbell in the British army at that time; but General Dickinson, in a letter dated November 18th, states that he was then on Staten Island. Whence it would follow, that he could not have been the same person, that was killed at Fort Montgomery. VOL. V. 14 fO THE PRESIDENT OF CONGRESS.

Head-Quarters, 22 October, 1777.

Dear Sir,

It gives me real pain to learn, that the declining state of your health, owing to your unwearied attention to public business, and the situation of your private affairs, oblige you to relinquish a station, though but for a time, which you have so long filled with acknowledged propriety. Motives as well of a personal as of a general concern make me regret the necessity that compels you to retire, and to wish your absence from office may be of as short a duration as possible. In the progress of that intercourse, which has necessarily subsisted between us, the manner in which you have conducted it on your part, accompanied with every expression of politeness and regard to me, gives you a claim to my warmest acknowledgments.

I am not so well informed of the situation of things up the North River, as to be able to give you any satisfactory advice about your route. I should rather apprehend it might be unsafe for you to travel that way at this time, and would recommend, if you can do it without any material inconvenience, that you should defer your journey till there is some change in affairs there, or till they have taken a more settled form. If you should, however, resolve to proceed immediately, and will be pleased to signify the time, an escort of horse will meet you at Bethlehem, to accompany you to General Putnam's camp, where you will be furnished with another escort in the further prosecution of your journey.

This letter was in reply to one from President Hancock, containing a notice of bis intention to retire from Congress. " It is now above two years," he wrote, " since I have had the honor of presiding in Congress, and I should esteem myself happy to have it in my power to render further service to my country in that department; but the decline of health, oc-

casioned by so long and unremitted an application to the duties of my office, both in Congress and out of Congress, joined to the situation of my own private affairs, has at length taught me to think of retiring for two or three months; and I have determined to take my leave the ensuing week, and set out immediately for Boston after Una express returns. As the Congress will doubtless proceed to appoint a successor in my stead, on him therefore will devolve the business of the chair. The politeness and attention I havo ever experienced from you, in the coarse of our correspondence, will always be a source of the I pleasing satisfaction to me."— *MS. Letter, October 171k.*

I am extremely obliged to you for your polite tender of services during your intended residence at Boston, and shall always be happy, when leisure and opportunity permit, if you will give me the pleasure of hearing from you. I have the honor to be, &c.

TO LIEUTENANT-COLONEL SAMUEL SMITH.

Head-Quarters, 22 October, 1777.

Sir,

Your letter of the 18th instant I received last night, wherein you express a desire to be recalled from Fort Mifflin to join your corps. I found it absolutely necessary to reinforce your garrison, and that it was impracticable to do it consistently, without superseding you. This determined me to send the Baron d'Arendt, as the person originally mentioned to you to command there; but I would have omitted it, after you had remained some time in command, had not the additional detachment been judged expedient for the defence of so important a post. This I mention, that you may be satisfied of the real motives in this transaction, and that a desire to supersede you had no influence in it; on the contrary, your conduct and exertions, since the commencement of your command there, have been such as merit my approbation and thanks. I now leave it to your own option, whether to rejoin your corps, or continue where you are are; and I have no doubt but you will determine upon that, which, in your opin-

ion, is most serviceable and consistent with the character of an officer.

There should be no hesitation in burning the barrackmaster's house, if it is found in the least to impede an opposition, or cover the enemy in advance. I am, Sir, with much regard, &,c.

TO MAJOR-GENERAL SULLIVAN.

Head-Quarters, 24 October, 1777.

Dear Sir, It ever has been, apd I hope ever will be a ruling principle with me, to endeavour to do impartial justice to every officer, over whom I have the honor to preside. I shall therefore in answer to the queries, contained in your letter of this date, readily declare, that, although I ascribed the misfortune, which happened to us on the 11th of September, principally to the information of Major Spear, transmitted to me by you, yet I never blamed you for conveying that intelligence. On the contrary, considering from whom and in what manner it came to you, I should have thought you culpable in concealing it. The Major's rank, reputation, and knowledge of the country, gave him a full claim to credit and attention. His intelligence was no doubt a most unfortunate circumstance, as it served to derange the disposition that had been determined on, in consequence of prior information of the enemy's attempt to turn and attack our right flank; which ultimately proving true, too little time was left us, after discovering its certainty, to form a new plan, and make adequate arrangements to prevent its success. Hence arose that hurry and consequent confusion, which afterwards ensued. But it was not your fault, that the intelligence was eventually found to be erroneous.

The Baron d'Arendt had been prevented by illness from taking the command at Fort Mifflin. On his partial recovery he was ordered again to the same station. As Lieutenant-Colonel Smith had sustained the post from the beginning, and acquitted himself with much honor, he was not pleased with being, as he thought, superseded, and he asked to be withdrawn. The above full explanation of the matter, however, from General Washington, was satisfactory, and he remained. It happened, that the Baron d'Arendt's illness returned soon after he arrived at the fort, and he was obliged to go over to the main land near Red Bank. The fort was thus left again in the charge of Lieutenant-Colonel Smith, and he defended it with the greatest credit to himself, till he was disabled by his wounds.

With respect to your other query, whether your being posted on the right was to guard that flank, and if you had neglected it, I can only observe, that the obvious if not declared purpose of your being there implied every necessary precaution for the security of that flank. But it is at the same time to be remarked, that all the fords above Chad's, from which we were taught to apprehend danger, were guarded by detachments from your division; and that we were led to believe, by those whom we had reason to think. well acquainted with the country, that no ford above our pickets could be passed, without making a very circuitous march.

Upon the whole, then, no part of your conduct, preceding the action, was in my judgment reprehensible. What happened on your march to the field of battle, your disposition there, and behaviour during the action, I can say nothing about, no part till the retreat commenced having come under my immediate observation. I can only add, therefore, that the whole tenor of your VOL. V. J conduct, so far as I have had opportunities of judging, has been spirited and active. I am, dear Sir, your most obedient servant.

TO THE PRESIDENT OF CONGRESS.

Head-Quarters, 34 October, 1777.

Sir,

I do myself the honor of transmitting to Congress the enclosed copies of sundry letters just now received, and congratulate them most sincerely on the important intelligence which they contain. The damage the enemy have sustained in their ships, I hope, will prevent their future attempts to gain the passage of the river; and the repulse of the troops under Count Donop, and his captivity, I flatter myself, will also be attended with the most happy consequences. At the time these actions happened, a supply of ammunition was on the way to the forts; and I have also ordered a further quantity to be immediately sent. By Colonel Blaine, one of the issuing commissaries, who left Red Bank the morning before the action, I am happily informed that he had thrown considerable supplies of provision into both garrisons. He also adds, that he came from Jersey this morning, and that the enemy had recrossed the Delaware and returned to Philadelphia. I have written to Colonel Greene, that the prisoners must be immediately sent from his post; and Mr. Clymer, a deputy under Mr. Boudinot, will set out to-morrow morning to make a proper disposition of them.

It gives me great concern to inform Congress, that, after all my exertions, we are still in a distressed situation for want of blankets and shoes. At this time no inconsiderable part of our force is incapable of acting, through the deficiency of the latter; and I fear, unless we can be relieved, it will be the case with two-thirds of the army in the course of a few days. I am and have been waiting with the most anxious impatience for a confirmation of General Burgoyne's surrender. I have received no further intelligence respecting it, except vague report, than the first account, which came to hand so long ago as Saturday morning. If Congress have had authentic advices about it, I wish to be favored with them. I have the honor to be, &c.

See Appooiz, No. II. TO COLONEL CHRISTOPHER GREENE.

Head-Quarters, 24 October, 1777.

Sir,

I have just received a letter from Major Ward, written by your desire, giving an account of your success over the enemy on the 22d instant. I heartily congratulate you upon this happy event, and beg you will accept my most particular thanks, and present the same to your whole garrison, both officers and men. Assure them, that their gallantry and good behaviour meet my wannest approbation. All the prisoners should be immediately removed to a distance from your post, to some convenient and safe place. I am sorry you have thought of sending the officers to Burlington, as they would be in no kind of security at that place, but might be taken and carried off by the enemy with the greatest ease. Immediately on the receipt of this, you will be pleased to have all the prisoners both officers and men conveyed to Morristown. The wounded can be accommodated in the hospitals there and in its neighbourhood. Count Donop in particular is a man of importance, and ought by all means to be taken care of.

With respect to the arms you have taken, as they are no doubt good, it will be well to exchange all the indifferent arms you may have for them; but after that is done, I would recommend to you to send all your superfluous arms away. They can be put in the wagons, that are on the way to you with ammunition.

I am, Sir, &c Major Ward's letter was dated, October 23d.—"By the desire of Colonel Greene," he wrote, " I congratulate your Excellency on the Buccess of the troops under his command yesterday. On the 21st instant, four battalions of Germans, amounting to about twelve hundred men, commanded by Count Donop, landed at Cooper's Ferry, and marched the same evening to Haddonfield. At three o'clock yesterday morning they marched for this place. When the guard at Timber Creek Bridge were informed of their approach, they took up that bridge, and the enemy filed off to the left and crossed a bridge four miles above. Their advanced parties were discovered within four miles of the fort at twelve o'clock. At half after four in the afternoon they sent a flag to summon the fort. The reply was, that it should never be surrendered. At three quarters past four they began a brisk cannonade, and seon after advanced in two columns to the attack. They passed the *abatis,* gained the ditch, and some few got over the pickets; but the fire was so heavy, that they were soon driven out again, with considerable loss; and they retreated precipitately towards Haddonfield. The enemy's loss amounts to one lieutenant-colonel, three captains, four lieutenants, and near seventy killed; and Count Donop, his brigade-major, a captain, lieutenant, and upwards of seventy non-commissioned officers and privates wounded and taken prisoners. We are also informed, that several wagons are taken. The Colonel proposes to send the wounded officers to Burlington. He also enjoins me to tell your Excellency, that both officers and men behaved with the greatest bravery. The action lasted forty minutes."

The loss of the enemy here stated is considerably less, than it has usually been represented. Judge Marshall says, that, according to the best information, it was about four hundred men. It is to be observed, indeed, that Major Ward does not profess to speak with precision; and it is probable, that exact returns had not then been obtained. Colonel Greene's loss in the fort was eight men killed, twenty-nine wounded, and a captain taken prisoner while reconnoitring.

Count Donop died of his wounds three days after the action, at a house near the fort. A short time before his death, he said to Monsieur Duplessis, a French officer, who constantly attended him in his illness, " It is finishing a noble career early; I die the victim of my ambition and of the avarice of my sovereign." — Chastellux's *Tmrdt*, TO MAJOR-GENERAL PUTNAM.

Head-Quarters, 25 October, 1777.

Dear Sir, I have your favor of the 20th, enclosing a copy of General Burgoyne's capitulation, which was the first authentic intelligence I received of the affair. Indeed I began to grow uneasy and almost to suspect that the first accounts you transmitted to me were premature. As I have not received a single line from General Gates,

Vol. I. p. 266. This was told to Chastellux and Lafayette by Duplessis himself, when they afterwards visited the spot together. Count Donop was considered a gallant and valuable officer. The fortification at Red Bank was called Fort Mercer.

The naval part of the action is thus described by Commodore Hazelwood. " While the fort at Red Bank was attacked, the Augusta of sixty-four guns, the Roebuck of forty-four, two frigates, the Merlin of eighteen guns, and a galley, came up through the lower chevaux-defrise, and were attacked by our floating batteries and some of the galleys, while the rest of the galleys were flanking the enemy, that were attacking the fort. These galleys did much execution. As soon as the enemy were repulsed at the fort, the ships October 23d, finding so hot a fire, endeavoured to fall down, but the Augusta and Merlin were grounded. Early the galleys and floating batteries attacked them, and an incessant fire was kept up. About eleven o'clock I believe one of our shot set the Augusta on fire, and at twelve she blew up, being aground. The engagement continued with the other ships, and at three in the afternoon the Merlin we think also took fire and blew up. Then the firing ceased on both sides. The Roebuck dropped down to the lower chevaux-de-frise and went through. Yesterday I went down to the wrecks, and found that the guns of both ships might be got out, if the enemy's ships can be kept at a proper distance. We brought off two twenty-four pounders, and as soon as possible I shall endeavour to get the rest." — MS. Letter, October 26tt.

Commodore Hazelwood also complained of his deficiency of men. " The fleet is now so poorly manned," he said, " (and the constant cry from Fort Mifflin is to guard that post,) that I know not how to act without more assistance. " There had been numerous desertions from the fleet, particularly from the vessels belonging to Pennsylvania. Colonel Smith had written some time before; — "So general a discontent and panic run through that part of the fleet, that neither officers nor men can be confided in. They conceive the river is lost, if the enemy gets VOL. V. 15 J»

I do not know what steps he is taking with the army under his command, and therefore cannot advise what is most proper to be done in your quarter. But I should think, if a junction of your forces was formed, part to proceed down upon one side of the river and part upon the other, that Sir Henry Clinton would be obliged to retreat immediately before you; or, if he suffered you to get between him and New York, you might perhaps in its weak state enter the city. I mention this merely as a matter of opinion, taking it for granted you will pursue the most proper and efficacious measure. Whatever may be determined upon, I beg it may be constantly communicated to me, as the operations of this army may depend much upon the situation of yours. I am, dear Sir, &c possession of BHlingsport. Nothing can convince them of the contrary, and I am persuaded, that, as soon as that fort is taken, almost all the fleet will desert. Indeed, from their disposition I am induced to believe they will openly avow themselves and desert, officers with their crews, and perhaps with their galleys, which has been the case with two. " — *October 2d*. This spirit, Colonel Smith says, was promoted by the representations of the relatives and friends of the officers and men, who remained in the city when it was entered by the British.

Colonel Wilkinson, adjutant-general in Gates's army, was made by him the bearer of despatches to Congress communicating the official intelligence of the surrender of Burgoyne, and the articles of capitulation. Wilkinson arrived at Easton, in Pennsylvania, on the 24th of October, and wrote from that place a line to General Washington, merely stating the fact of the surrender, the number of prisoners taken, and the nature of his errand to Congress, but not intimating that he had any authority from General Gates to make this communication to the Commander-in-chief, nor enclosing a copy of the articles. Wilkinson did not reach the seat of Congress till the 31st of October, fifteen days after the convention of Saratoga was signed, and then it took him three days to put the papers in order, which he was to lay before Congress. It was on this occasion, that one of the members made a motion in Congress, that they should compliment Colonel Wilkinson with the gift of a pair of spun. TO MAJOR-GENERAL LINCOLN.

Head-Quarters, 25 October, 1777.

Dear Sir, It gives me great pleasure

to find by yours of the 20th, that you are likely to save your leg, and that you think you will be able to take the field in the spring, should there be occasion. I congratulate you upon the glorious termination of the campaign against General Burgoyne, which I hope in its consequences will free us from all our oppressors. Ever since the enemy got possession of Philadelphia, their whole attention has been paid to reducing the forts upon the Delaware, and endeavouring to remove the chevaux-defrise. After nearly a month's work they removed two of the lower chevaux-defrise, through which opening six of their ships of war passed on the morning of the 22d, and began a most furious cannonade upon Fort Mifflin, and our ships and galleys at the upper chevauxdefrise; but they were so warmly opposed, that they were obliged to sheer off. In going down, a sixtyfour gun ship ran aground; she took fire and blew up. Our galleys overtook and destroyed a frigate. The remainder made the best of their way down. The day following, Count Donop, with about twelve hundred men, attempted to carry our fort at Red Bank on the Jersey shore by storm; he was repulsed, with the loss of about four hundred killed and wounded, among the latter the Count himself, who is a prisoner. Since this they have remained tolerably quiet by land and water. General Howe has withdrawn himself within his lines thrown round Philadelphia.

The day after die second battle of Behmus's Heights, which decided the fate of Burgoyne's army, General Lincoln was badly wounded in the -g by random shot, while riding near the enemy's lines.

I observe by the terms of General Burgoyne's capitulation, that an exchange of prisoners may probably take place; if so, the number of officers taken in his army will liberate all ours. In that case, Mr. Douglass, your aid-de-camp, will soon be redeemed. But if this exchange should not take place, you may depend that Mr. Douglass shall be called for as soon as it comes bis turn; for I have made it an invariable rule to

give a preference to those, who have been longest in captivity. I most sincerely wish you a speedy and effectual cure, as I am, with great regard, dear Sir, &c TO FRANCIS HOPKINSON AND JOHN WHARTON, OF THE NAVY BOARD.

Skippeck Road, 27 October, 1777.

Gentlemen, The more I reflect upon the evil, that may arise from the enemy's possessing themselves of our unfinished frigates up the Delaware, the more convinced I am of the indispensable obligation we are under to prevent it effectually. If no other method could be devised, I should be for absolutely burning them; but scuttling and sinking them, with or without ballast, as they, who are best acquainted with the difficulties of raising them in either state at this season, may determine, will in my judgment answer the end. We all know that the enemy have made one vigorous though unsuccessful effort to dispossess us of our forts, and drive off our vessels, which defend the chevaux-de-frise in the river; we know, also, that, besides having the Delaware frigate, they are busily employed in preparing two other large armed vessels at the city. If, in addition to these, they should by surprise or force obtain the frigates above Bordentown, and bring the whole in aid of their ships in a general attack upon our little fleet thus surrounded, we may, without the spirit of divination, but too easily foretell the consequences. Their destruction will be certain and inevitable.

When the Congress retired from Philadelphia to York, the Navy Board remained behind, and continued chiefly at Bordentown in New Jersey, where their services could be more immediately rendered in managing the concerns of the Continental shipping in the Delaware.

At present these frigates are of no use to us, while the crews are greatly wanted. Considered therefore in this point of view simply, the measure proposed, in my opinion, is highly expedient; and under the prevailing sentiment, that the enemy cannot hold Philadelphia, unless their shipping get up, it appears absolutely necessary. The fatal conse-

quences, that may result from suffering those frigates to fall into the enemy's hands, are too obvious to need more arguments to prove them; and when it is considered of how little importance they are to us in their present situation, prudence requires that they should be so disposed of as to be hereafter useful, and put out of the way of being destroyed by the enemy or being rendered serviceable to them.

Upon the whole, I take the liberty of delivering it as my clear opinion, that the frigates ought to be immediately and with the utmost secrecy sunk, either with or without ballast, so as to make it next to impossible to raise them, without men's diving either to unlade them or fix their purchases, and that their crews should be sent down to the fleet below, where sailors are exceedingly wanted. If I have stepped out'of the line of my duty to make this request, I am persuaded you will excuse it when I add, that the good of the service, not only in my judgment but in that of others, absolutely requires it to be carried into execution.

When the Navy Board was first established at Bordentown, and the frigates were taken up the river to that place, a plan was formed to defend them by a battery on the shore, and this plan was approved by Congress. But as soon as the Board received the above letter from the Commander-in-chief, his instructions were complied with, and the frigates were sunk. All the other vessels, great and small, which were in the river above Philadelphia, were forced up with much labor into Croswicks Creek, where they lay aground. — *MS. Letter from the .Vary Board, November* 10ft.

I have the honor to be, &c.

TO LANDON CARTER.

Philadelphia County, 27 October, 1777.

Dear Sir,

Accept my sincere thanks for your solicitude on my account, and for the good advice contained in your little paper. At the same time I assure you, that it k mot my wish to avoid any danger, which duty requires me to encounter, I can as confidently add, that it is not my intention to run unnecessary risks.

In the instance given by you, I was acting precisely in the line of my duty, but not in the dangerous situation you have been led to believe. I was reconnoitring, but I had a strong party of horse with me. I was, as I afterwards found, in a disaffected house, at the Head of Elk, but I was equally guarded against friend and foe; the information of danger, then, came not from me.

So many accounts have been published of the battle of Brand) w ine, that nothing more can be said of it. The subsequent engagement on the 4th instant had every appearance of a glorious result, after a hot contest of two hours and forty minutes; but, after driving the enemy from their encampment, possessing their ground, and being, as we thought, upon the point of grasping victory, it was snatched from us by means altogether unaccountable; excepting that a very heavy atmosphere, aided by the smoke of four field-pieces and small arms, rendered it impossible at times to distinguish friend from foe at the distance of thirty yards; which caused our men, I believe, to take fright at each other. Since that, the enemy have retired to Philadelphia, where they have been strengthening themselves as much as possible, whilst we hover around to cut off their supplies.

The galleys and other craft, which escaped, on the reduction of Forts Mifflin and Mercer, passed up the river under Commodore Hazclwood, and wintered there, but were not sunk.

The great and important event to the northward, of which no doubt you have heard, must be attended with the most fortunate consequences. It has caused Sir Henry Clinton's expedition from New York, in aid of Burgoyne, to end in (something more than smoke indeed) the burning of mills, gentlemen's seats, and the villages near the water, an evident proof of their despair of carrying their diabolical designs into execution. My inclination leads me to give you a more minute detail of the situation of our army; but prudence forbids, as letters are subject to too many miscarriages. My best respects attend the good family at Sabine Hall, and neighbours at Mount Airy. With affectionate regard, I remain, dear Sir, &c.

P. S. I have this instant received an account of the prisoners taken by the northern army (including Tories in arms against us), in the course of the campaign. This singular instance of Providence, and of our good fortune under it, exhibits a striking proof of the advantages, which result from unanimity and a spirited conduct in the militia. The northern army, before the surrender of General Burgoyne, was reinforced by upwards of twelve hundred militia, who shut the only door by which Burgoyne could retreat, and cut off all his supplies. How different our case! The disaffection of a great part of the inhabitants of this State, the languor of others, and the internal distraction of the whole, have been among the great and insuperable difficulties, which I have met with, and have contributed not a little to my embarrassments this campaign. But enough; I do not mean to complain. I flatter myself, that a superintending Providence is ordering every thing for the best, and that, in due time, all will end well. That it may do so, and soon, is the most fervent wish of yours.

TO LIEUTENANT-COLONEL SAMUEL SMITH.

Head-Quarters, 28 October, 1777.

Sir, As there seems to be a doubt of the priority of the date of your and Lieutenant-Colonel Green's commissions, I have in a letter of this date desired him to wave the matter in dispute for the present, and act under your command, as you have been in the fort from the beginning, and must be better acquainted with the nature of the defences than a stranger. I have ordered a very handsome detachment for the reinforcement of Forts Mifflin and Mercer, and the galleys. They have been ready since yesterday, but the weather has been such, that they could not march. When they arrive, the duty will not be so severe; and, if the men that you took down at first can possibly be spared, they shall be relieved. I will send them down necessaries out of the first that arrive from Lancaster.

Lieutenant-Colonel John Green, of the 6rst Virginia regiment, who had been sent to Fort Mifflin with a reinforcement of two hundred men. Colonel Christopher Greene, of Rhode Island, commanded at Red Bank.

You seem to have mistaken the Commodore's meaning. From his letter I understand, that he will always assist you whenever it is in his power. He tells you, that in rough weather his galleys and armed boats cannot live, and therefore guards you against expecting much assistance from them at such times. I beg you of all things not to suffer any jealousies between the land and sea service to take place. Consider that your mutual security depends upon acting perfectly in concert. I have written to Colonel Greene to afford you every possible assistance from ited Bank, till the reinforcement gets down. I have the greatest hopes that this storm of rain and wind at northeast will overflow all the enemy's works at Province Island, and ruin the new roads they have been making. I recommend to you every attention, and I hope a glorious success will reward your exertions. I am, Sir, &,c.

P. S. Keep the banks of Province Island constantly cut, and you will embarrass the enemy excessively. Do not mention any thing of the expectation of a reinforcement, lest the enemy should take means to intercept them.

TO LIEUTENANT-COLONEL ALEXANDER HAMILTON.

Head-Quarters, 30 October, 1777.

Dear Sir, It having been judged expedient by the members of a council of war held yesterday, that one of the gentlemen of my family should be sent to General Gates, VOL. V. 16 K in order to lay before him the state of this army and the situation of the enemy, and to point out to him the many happy consequences, that will accrue from an immediate reinforcement being sent from the northern army, I have thought proper to appoint you to that duty, and desire that you will immediately set out for Albany, at which place or in the neighbourhood, I imagine you will find General Gates.

You are so fully acquainted with the two principal points on which you are sent, namely, the state of our army and the situation of the enemy, that I shall not enlarge on these heads. What you are chiefly to attend to is, to point out in the clearest manner to General Gates the absolute necessity that there is for his detaching a very considerable part of the army, at present under his command, to the reinforcement of this; a measure that will in all probability reduce General Howe to the same situation in which General Burgoyne now is, should he attempt to remain in Philadelphia without being able to remove the obstructions in the Delaware, and open a free communication with his shipping.

The force, which the members of the council of war judged it safe and expedient to draw down at present, is the three New Hampshire and fifteen Massachusetts regiments, with Lee's and Jackson's, of the sixteen additional regiments. But it is more than probable, that General Gates may have destined part of these troops to the reduction of Ticonderoga, should the enemy not have evacuated it, or to the garrisoning of it, if they should. In that case, the reinforcement will vary according to circumstances; but if possible let it be made up to the same number out of other corps. If, upon your meeting with General Gates, you should find that he intends, in consequence of his success, to employ the troops under his command upon some expedition, by the prosecution of which the common cause will be more benefited than by their being sent down to reinforce this army, it is not my wish to give any interruption to the plan. But if he should have nothing more in contemplation, than those particular objects, which I have mentioned to you, and which it is unnecessary to commit to paper, in that case you are to inform him, that it is my desire that the reinforcements before mentioned, or such part of them as can be safely spared, be immediately put in march to join this army.

To the council of war General Washington made the following report, as to the strength of the two armies, namely, that the troops under Sir William Howe present and fit for duty amounted, according to the best intelligence he could obtain, to ten thousand rank and file, stationed at Philadelphia and in its immediate vicinity; and that the force under his command, present and fit for duty, was eight thousand three hundred and thirteen Continental troops, and two thousand seven hundred and seventeen militia. There were, in addition, seven hundred and fifty Continental troops at Red Bank and Fort Mifflin, and a detachment of three hundred militia on their way to reinforce those posts. A body of five hundred militia under General Potter was likewise on the other side of the Schuylkill. This was his whole force, and it was likely soon to suffer a diminution of nineteen hundred and eighty six militia, by the expiration of the term of service for which those from Maryland and Virginia had been engaged. — *Minutet of Oue Council of War, October* 296L

I have understood, that General Gates has already detached Nixon's and Glover's brigades to join General Putnam; and General Dickinson informs me, that by intelligence, which he thinks may be depended upon, Sir Henry Clinton has come down the river with his whole force. If this be a fact, you are to desire General Putnam to send the two brigades forward with the greatest expedition, as there can be no occasion for them there. I expect you will meet Colonel Morgan's corps upon their way down; if you do, let them know how essential their services are to us, and desire the Colonel, or commanding officer, to hasten his march, as much as is consistent with the health of the men after their late fatigues. Let me hear from you when you reach the North River, and upon your arrival at Albany. I wish you a pleasant journey, and am, dear Sir, &c.

The British evacuated Forts Montgomery and Clinton, on the 36th of October, and the same day proceeded down the river with their whole force both of troops and shipping. In a letter from General Putnam to the TO MAJOR-GENERAL GATES.

Head-Quarters, near Whitemarsh, October 30,1777.

Sir, By this opportunity I do myself the pleasure to congratulate you on the signal success of the army under your command, in compelling General Burgoyne and his whole force to surrender themselves prisoners of

Commander-in-chief, dated at Fishkill, October 31st, he stated that Poor's, Warner's, Learned's, and Paterson's brigades, Colonel Van Schakk's regiment, and Morgan's riflemen, were on their way from the northward to join him, amounting in the whole to five thousand seven hundred men, which number, added to those already with him, would make his whole force about nine thousand strong, exclusive of Morgan's corps, the artillery-men, and the militia from Connecticut and New York. The militia had been mostly discharged. General Warner's brigade consisted of sixteen hundred Massachusetts militia, whose time of service was to expire at the end of November.

On the same day that the above intelligence was communicated, General Putnam called a council of his principal officers, whose unanimous advice it was, that four thousand men should move down the west side of the Hudson and take post near Haverstraw; that one thousand should be retained in the Highlands to guard the country and repair the works; and that the remainder should march down on the east side of the river towards Kingsbridge, except Morgan's corps, which was ordered immediately to join the Commander-in-chief. The object proposed by this disposition of the forces was to cause a diversion of the enemy in New York, and prevent a reinforcement from being sent to General Howe; and it was doubtless an ulterior purpose to attack the city, should a favorable opportunity present itself. — *Minutes of the Council, October* 314.

war; an event that does the highest honor to the American arms, and which, I hope, will be attended with the most extensive and happy consequences. At the same time, 1 cannot but regret, that a matter of such magnitude, and so interesting to our general operations, should have reached me by report only, or through the channel of letters, not bearing that authenticity, which the importance of it required, and which it would have received by a line under your signature, stating the simple fact.

Our affairs having happily terminated at the northward, I have by the advice of my general officers sent Colonel Hamilton, one of my aids, to lay before you a full state of our situation, and that of the enemy in this quarter. He is well informed upon the subject, and will deliver my sentiments upon the plan of operations, that is become necessary to be pursued. I think it improper to enter into a particular detail, not being well advised how matters are circumstanced on the North River, and fearing that by some accident my letter might miscarry. From Colonel Hamilton you will have a clear and comprehensive view of things, and I persuade myself you will do all in your power to facilitate the objects I have in contemplation.

I am, Sir, your most obedient servant. General Gates wrote a very short letter to Washington, on the 2d of November, and of course before this could have reached him, giving notice that Morgan's corps had been sent to the southward. He added, apparently as a matter of secondary consequence; " Congress having been requested immediately to transmit copies of all my despatches to them, I am confident your Excellency has long ago received all the good newa from this quarter." These words contain the only intelligence, which was transmitted to the Commander-in-chief by General Gates, respecting the defeat of Burgoyne, and the convention of Saratoga. TO THE PRESIDENT OF CONGRESS.

Head-Quarters, near Whitemarsh, 1 November, 1777.

Sir,

After the action of the 4th ultimo at Germantown, I hoped we should have been in a situation to attack the enemy again on those grounds, and with more success than in the former instance; but this I was not able to effect. The severe rain on the 16th of September, the action on the 4th, the removal of our stores, and having to form a new lab-

oratory, added to the small number of hands engaged in the business of it, laid us under difficulties in the capital and essential article of ammunition, that could not be surmounted. Every exertion was directed to obtain supplies; but, notwithstanding, they were inadequate, too scanty, and insufficient to attempt any thing on a large and general scale, before the enemy withdrew themselves. With what we had, in case an experiment had been made, fortune might have decided in our favor for the present; but we should not have been afterwards in a situation to maintain the advantage we might have gained; and, if a repulse had taken place, and the enemy been pursued, we might for want of a reserve have been exposed to the most imminent danger of being ruined. The distress of the soldiers for want of shoes was also a powerful obstacle to the measure.

I could wish that our circumstances were now such as to authorize a general attack for dislodging them from the city; but I think they are not. This also is the opinion of my general officers, upon a full and comprehensive view of matters, as Congress will perceive by the enclosed copy of the minutes of council on the 29th ultimo, which I have taken the liberty to transmit and lay before them. The superiority of numbers on the part of the enemy, in respect to regular troops; their superior discipline, and the redoubts and lines which they have thrown up between the two rivers and about the city; the happy state of our affairs at the northward, and the practicability of drawing succours from thence; the consequences of a defeat;—these were all motives, which led to a decision against an attack at this time. I have sent Colonel Hamilton, one of my aids, to General Gates, to give him a just representation of things, and to explain to him the expediency of our receiving the reinforcements, which have been determined necessary, if they will not interfere with and frustrate any important plans he may have formed. Indeed I cannot conceive that there is any object now remaining, that demands our attention and most vigorous efforts so

much, as the destruction of the army in this quarter. Should we be able to effect this, we shall have little to fear in future.

General Howe's force, according to the statement now made, is more considerable than it was generally supposed to be. I did not think it quite so great myself, but always imagined the common estimate much too low; nor can I positively say what it really is. However, there are strong reasons to believe that it is not overrated. After the evacuation of Germantown, an almost infinite number of scraps and bits of paper were found, which, being separated and arranged with great industry and care, bear the marks of genuine and authentic returns at different periods. The manner in which they were destroyed and disposed of gives no room to suspect that it was the effect of design. In addition to this, I am informed by General Putnam that he had heard a reinforcement of four regiments was coming round to Delaware from New York. The enclosed return will give Congress a general view of the strength of this army when it was made, and a particular one of the forces of each State which compose it. By this they will perceive how greatly deficient the whole are in furnishing their just quotas. The militia from Maryland and Virginia are no longer to be counted on. All the former, except about two hundred, are already gone; and a few days, I expect, will produce the departure of the whole or a chief part of the latter, from the importunate applications which some of them have made. Besides this diminution, I am apprehensive we shall have several men added to the sick list, by reason of the late excessive rain and want of clothes. We have not yet come to any determination respecting the disposition of our troops for the winter; supposing it a matter of great importance, and that for the present we should be silent upon it. The reasons will readily occur. By continuing the campaign, perhaps many salutary if not decisive advantages may be derived; but it appears to me that this must depend upon the supplies of clothing which the men receive. If they cannot be accommodated in this instance, it will be difficult if not impossible to do it without effecting their destruction.

I would take the liberty to mention, that I feel myself in a delicate situation with respect to the Marquis de Lafayette. He is extremely solicitous of having a command equal to his rank, and professes very different ideas, as to the purposes of his appointment, from those Congress have mentioned to me. He certainly did not understand them. I do not know in what light they will view the matter; but it appears to me, from a consideration of his illustrious and important connexions, the attachment which he has manifested for our cause, and the consequences which his return in disgust might produce, that it will be advisable to gratify him in his wishes; and the more so, as several gentlemen from France, who came over under some assurances, have gone back disappointed in their expectations. His conduct, with respect to them, stands in a favorable point of view, he having interested himself to remove their uneasiness, and urged the impropriety of their making any unfavorable representations upon their arrival at home; and in all his letters he has placed our affairs in the best situation he could. Besides, he is sensible, discreet in his manners, has made great proficiency in our language, and, from the disposition he discovered at the battle of Brandy wine, possesses a large share of bravery and military ardor. There is a French gentleman here, Monsieur Vrigny, in whose favor the Marquis seems much interested. He assures me he b an officer of great merit, and, from that motive and a regard to the service, wishes to see him promoted. The rank he holds in France, and his present expectations, are contained in the enclosed copy of a paper given me by the Marquis. Monsieur Vrigny also has honorable certificates of his services, nearly corresponding with the Marquis's account of them. If Congress are pleased to honor him with a commission in the army of the States, I must try to employ him.

This topic had been discussed in the late, council of war, but it' deferred without any decision.

At the request of Governor Clinton, I have transmitted a copy of his letter to me, giving an account of General Vaughan's expedition up the North River after the capture of Fort Montgomery, and of the destruction committed by his troops in burning Kingston and the houses and mills on the river. According to the latest advices they have returned again; and it is reported,

Vol. v. 17 that they have destroyed the barracks and forts, and gone to New York; but this is not confirmed.

A few days ago Mr. Franks of Philadelphia, agent for the British prisoners, sent out six thousand Continental dollars to Mr. Richard Graham of Virginia, for the subsistence of the Hessians and other prisoners in that State. The policy of suffering the enemy to support their prisoners with money, which they refuse themselves, and which they attempt to depreciate in every instance they possibly can, appears to me very questionable, and the more so, as it may be counterfeited. Besides, they have laid us under every difficulty they can devise, as to our prisoners in their hands. Nothing will do for their support but hard money. If the enemy were obliged to furnish the same, the quantity with us would be greater, and of course the means of relieving ours easier. I do not know what consequences a prohibition against receiving Continental money or the currency of any State from them might involve; I think the subject is worthy of the consideration of Congress, and for that reason I have mentioned it. I am, &c.

After the British had removed the chev &ux-de-frise at Fort Montgomery and Fort Constitution, they passed up the river with several armed vessels commanded by Sir James Wallace, and a body of troops under General Vaughan. They burnt such shipping as they found in the river, and also houses and mills on the shore. At Esopus, on the 15th of October, a party landed, led on by General Vaughan himself, and burnt the village of Kingston. So complete was the destruction, that not more than one house escaped the flames. The reason he gave for this act was, that the people

fired from the houses upon his men. He then went on board, and passed up as high as Livingston's Manor, where he likewise burnt several private dwellings and mills. Gordon says, that the people of Kingston did not fire from their houses upon the British troops. — *History,* Vol. II. p. 579. It had been agreed between General Putnam and Governor Clinton, that, during these operations of the enemy, they should move up the river with their respective forces, the former on the east side and the latter on the west, to prevent their landing and committing ravages in the country; and also to be at hand to fall upon their rear, in case they should proceed to Albany, and attempt to succour Burgoyne. When the news of the Convention of Saratoga reached General Vaughan, he retreated down the river, and soon after to New York. General Putnam had advanced with his anny as far as Red Hook, but immediately returned to Fishkill. He appears to have had a strong tendency towards New York, even after the enemy had ascended above the Highlands, and wrote in that temper to General Gates, who replied; —

" It is certainly right to collect your whole force, and push up the east aide of the river after the enemy. You may be sure they have nothing they care for in New York. Then why should you attack an empty town, which you know to be untenable the moment they bring their men of war against it? Yesterday General Burgoyne proposed to surrender upon the enclosed terms. The capitulation will, I believe, be settled today, when I shall have nothing but General Clinton to think of. If you keep pace with him on one side, the Governor on the other, and I in his front, I cannot see how he is to get home again."—*MS. Letter, October* 15M.

TO BRIGADIER-GENERAL VARNUM.

Head-Quarters, 1 November, 1777.

Sir,

I hope this will find you arrived safe at Red Bank with your detachment. By letters from the Baron d'Arendt, who has retired for a few days to the Jersey side, for the benefit of his health, I understand that what they principally fear at Fort Mifflin is a surprise by night, or a lodgment upon the upper end of the Island, by which they may cover themselves before morning and open a battery upon the rear of the fort, which is only secured by palisadoes. The only method of guarding effectually against this, is by keeping boats stationed by night between Fort and Province Islands, to give an immediate alarm; and when the weather is calm, if the galleys were to lie near the Island to be ready to begin to fire, upon the first landing of the enemy, it would harass and retard them much in their operations.

Four days after the capture of Fort Montgomery, a spy was brought to Governor Clinton, then at New Windsor, who was seen to swallow a silver bullet. It was recovered by a prescription of tartar emetic, and found to be hollow, and to contain within its cavity the following brief message from Sir Henry Clinton to Burgoyne, dated at Fort Mongomery, October 8th.

".You *y void,* and nothing now between us but Gates. I sincerely hope this little success of ours may facilitate your operations. In answer to your letter of the 28th of September by C. C. I shall only say, I cannot presume to order, or even advise, for reasons obvious. I heartily wish you success. Faithfully yours.

" H. Clinton."

Fort Montgomery was denominated *Fort Vaughan* by the British, during the twenty days that it was in their possession.

I am afraid that matters do not go on smoothly be tween the Commandant at Fort Mifflin and the Commodore, as there are every now and then complaints of inattention in the Commodore; but I do not know whether with just grounds. I beg you will do all in your power to reconcile any differences, that may have arisen, not by taking notice of them in a direct manner, but by recommending unanimity and demonstrating the manifest advantages of it. As the Commodore will have a considerable reinforcement after you arrive, I hope he will be able to afford more assistance than he has hitherto done.

You will have an opportunity of seeing and conversing with the Baron d'Arendt, and I must beg you will lay such plans, as will most effectually contribute to the mutual support and defence of your posts; for you are to consider, if one falls, the other goes of course. As soon as you have looked about you, and taken a survey of the ground, I shall be glad to have your opinion of matters. I am, &c.

TO JOHN HANCOCK.

Head-Quarters, 2 November, 1777.

Sir,

Your favor of the 25 th I received on Monday afternoon. You have my warmest wishes for your recovery, and I shall be happy if your recess should be attended with benefits, superior to your most sanguine expectations. Your exertions to promote the general interest I am well convinced will be unceasing, and that every measure, which the situation of your health will permit you to pursue, will be employed to that end, whether you are in Congress or obliged to remain in the State of Massachusetts. I have ordered Cornet Buckmer, with twelve dragoons, to attend you as an escort, and to receive your commands. For this purpose you will be pleased to retain them, as long as you may consider their attendance necessary. I would willingly have directed a larger number, but the severe duty the horse have been obliged to perform, for a long time past, has rendered many of them unfit for service; to which I must add, that we are under a necessity of keeping several considerable patrols of them constantly along the enemy's lines. These reasons, I trust, will apologize for the escort being so small.

I have taken the liberty to trouble you with the enclosed letters, containing a proclamation respecting deserters, which I must request the favor of you to put into some safe channel of conveyance to the printers. That for Mr. Loudon I imagine will get to hand by delivering it to Governor Clinton or General Putnam. Those for Rhode Island and New Hampshire will go safe from the postoffice at New Haven or Hartford. I have nothing further to add,

than to wish you an agreeable journey and a happy meeting with your lady and friends, and to assure you, that I am, dear Sir, &c " Proclamation by his Excellency George Washington, Commanderin-chief of the Forces of the United States of America. — Whereas sundry soldiers belonging to the armies of the said States have deserted from the same; these are to make known to all those, who have so offended, and who shall return to their respective corps, or surrender themselves to the officers appointed to receive recruits and deserters in their several States, or to any Continental commissioned officer, before

VOL. V. L TO MAJOR-GENERAL DICKINSON.

Head-Quarters, Whitemarsk, 4 November, 1777.

Dear Sir, I have received your letter of the 1st instant, informing me of the delay of the governor and council in giving an answer on the subject of my last to you, and the reluctance of the eastern militia to abandon Elizabethtown. To compensate for the backwardness of the latter in obeying orders, which they themselves do not absolutely approve, and make the best of their thwarting disposition, you propose a plan of operations, which you think would be so perfectly coincident with the desires of the militia, as greatly to increase their numbers, and which at the same time might be productive of important good consequences. I should perfectly agree with you and press the executive, if the advanced season and the consequent difficulty of breaking ground, and the great danger of having troops cut off, that might be landed on Long Island, did not present themselves to me as obstacles, which render the enterprise ineligible.

the first day of January next, that they shall obtain a full and free pardon;— And I do further declare to all such obstinate offenders aa do not avail themselves of the indulgence hereby offered, that they may depend, when apprehended, on being prosecuted with the utmost rigor, and suffering the punishment justly due to crimes of such enormity. Lest the hope of escaping punishment, by remaining undiscovered, should tempt any to reject the terms now held out to them, they may be assured, that the most effectual measures will be pursued in every State for apprehending and bringing them to a speedy trial."—*Dated Cktokr34tt.*

Your idea of counteracting the intended reinforcements for Mr. Howe's army, by a demonstration of designs upon New York, I think an exceedingly good one, and I am very desirous that you should improve and mature it for immediate execution. A great show of preparatives on your side, boats collected, troops assembled, your expectation of the approach of Generals Gates and Putnam intrusted as a secret to persons, who you are sure will divulge and disseminate it in New York; in a word, such measures taken for effectually striking an alarm in that city, as it is altotogether unnecessary for me minutely to describe to you, I am in great hopes will effect the valuable purpose which you expect. I am, dear Sir, &,c TO LIEUTENANT-COLONEL SAMUEL SMITH.

Head-Quarters, 4 November, 1777

Sir, I have received your letter dated yesterday giving an account of the reinforcement, which you expect from General Varnum, and the supplies of clothing from General Forman. It gives me pain to learn, that the latter are likely to be so inadequate to your wants; but I hope, that by taking proper measures, the contributions of the inhabitants will not prove so poor a resource as you seem to fear. Enclosed is a letter to Major Fleury, whom I ordered to Fort Mifflin to serve in quality of engineer. As he is a young man of talents, and has made this branch of military service his particular study, I place a confidence in him. You will therefore make the best arrangement for enabling him to carry such plans into execution, as come within his department. His authority, at the same time that it is subordinate to yours, must be sufficient for putting into practice what his knowledge of fortification points out as necessary for defending the post; and his department, though inferior, being of a distinct and separate nature, requires that his orders

should be in a great degree discretionary, and that he should be suffered to exercise his judgment. Persuaded that you will concur with him in every measure, which the good of the service may require, I remain, Sir, &,c.

General Dickinson had proposed, that Generals Gates and Putnam abould collect such militia as they could, and march down and make an attack on Long Island and New York, while he at the some time with the New Jersey militia should make a descent upon Staten Island. He had now six hundred men, and he thought he could increase his number to twelve hundred; and he had already boats enough to transport five hundred men across the water from Elizabethtown to the Island His opinion was, that, if these attacks did not all succeed, they would effect the important purpose of delaying, and perhaps of detaining, the reinforcements, which were evidently in preparation for being sent to General Howe. TO SIR WILLIAM HOWE.

Head-Quarters, 4 November, 1777.

Sir, I have been informed by Lieutenant-Colonel Frazer, who is now a prisoner in your possession, that Major Balfour, one of your aids, had assured him, that it was your earnest desire, that a general exchange of prisoners should take place on equitable terms, or, if this could not be effected, that the officers on both sides should be released on parole. This, I have no doubt, was done by your authority, and with an intention, that it should be communicated to me. I assure you, Sir, nothing would afford me more satisfaction, than to carry the first proposition into execution. But, lest we should still unhappily disagree about the privates to be accounted for, and that this may not operate to the prejudice of the officers, it is my wish, for their mutual relief, that their exchange may immediately take place, so far as circumstances of rank and number will apply; and if any should then remain, that they may return to their friends on parole. I am induced to mention an exchange, in preference to the other mode of release, supposing that it would be more agreeable to both parties.

While we are on this subject, I would take the liberty to suggest, that on the footing of our present agreement the colonels, who are your prisoners, cannot be exchanged, there being no officers of the like rank in your army prisoners with us. From this consideration, I am led to inquire, whether an equivalent cannot be fixed on to effect it, as has been practised in similar cases. I have the honor to be, &c.

TO JEREMIAH POWELL, PRESIDENT OF THE COUNCIL OF MASSACHUSETTS.

A Camp, at Whitemarsh, 5 November, 1777.

Sir,

I have been duly honored with your favor of the 25th ultimo, and join your honorable Board most heartily in congratulations on our success in the surrender of General Burgoyne and his army; an event of great importance, and which reflects the highest honor upon our arms. In respect to the embarkation of the prisoners, VOL. V. 18 L«

I take it for granted, that the beneficial consequences, which the British nation would derive from their arrival in England will be sufficient motives for General Howe to use every possible exertion to get them away, and that no application for that end will be necessary. For, as soon as they arrive, they will enable the ministry to send an equal number of other troops from their different garrisons to join him here, or upon any other service against the American States. I shall be sorry, if their remaining should subject you to the inconveniences, which you seem to apprehend; and, if they can be accommodated, I think, in point of policy, we should not be anxious for their early departure. As to the transports, if General Howe is in a situation to send them, it is to be presumed, that they will be properly appointed with provisions and wood, the terms of convention not obliging us to furnish their prisoners for a longer time, than their continuance in our hands. I do not apprehend, that there will be any thing to fear from the vessels assigned for their transportation. The con- dition, upon which they are to be allowed an entry, imports a time, and no stipulations that can be made will be more obligatory. Nevertheless, prudence and the usage of nations do not only justify, but require, that every precaution should be had, previous to their being admitted into port, to prevent an infraction of treaty and any act incompatible with the design of their coming. What these precautions ought to be will naturally occur.

In fine, Sir, I do not know how far I should advise in this business, and suppose it probable, that Congress will give you their sentiments fully upon it, they being possessed of all the circumstances, by a statement from General Gates, and also from General Heath. I have the honor to be, &c.

TO BRIGADIER-GENERAL CONWAY. 9 November, 1777.

Sir, A letter, which I received last night, contained the following paragraph.

" In a letter from General Conway to General Gates he says, *Heaven has been determined to save your country, or a weak General and bad counsellors icould have ruined it.'*"

I am, Sir, your humble servant.

TO HENRY LAURENS, PRESIDENT OF CONGRESS.f Camp, at Whitemarsh, 10 November, 1777.

Sir,

I have been duly honored with your favors of the 4th and 5th instant, with their several enclosures. Among those of the former, I found the resolution you are pleased to allude to, respecting your appointment as president. Permit me, Sir, to congratulate you upon this event, and to assure you I have the most entire confidence, that I shall experience in you during your presidency the same politeness, and attention to the interests of the States, that marked the conduct of your worthy predecessor.

With respect to the views of the Navy Board for securing the frigates, the situation of the army would not admit of a compliance with them, supposing they would answer the end. I have therefore written to the Board, in the most pressing terms, to have the frigates scuttled in such a way, that they may be raised when it shall be necessary, and that in the mean time they may not be liable to injury from floating ice. I see no measure so likely to secure them to us, and against the enemy's attempts. I have been extremely fearful they would have possessed and employed them, with the Delaware and their batteries, on the rear of the galleys and the fort, while the ships below attacked in front. I need not point out the probable consequences of such an event; they are too obvious. The resolves, which you request to be communicated to the army, shall be published in general orders. The letters for Commodore Hazelwood have been put in a proper channel of conveyance.

See Appendix, No. VI. Henry Laurens was chosen President of Congress on the 1st of No, as the successor of President Hancock.

As to the disposition of part of the northern army, my letter of the 1st contains my ideas upon the subject, and those of my general officers. I shall be sorry if the measures I have taken on this head should interfere with, or materially vary from, any plans Congress might have had in view. Their proceedings of the 5th, I presume, were founded on a supposition, that the enemy were still up the North River, and garrisoning the forts they had taken. This not being the case, and all accounts agreeing that reinforcements to General Howe are coming from York, I hope the aids I have required will be considered expedient and proper. Independent of the latter consideration, I think our exertions and force should be directed to effect General Howe's destruction, if it is possible.

Among' the various difficulties attending the army, the adjustment of rank is not the least. This, owing to the several modes, the several principles, that have prevailed in granting commissions, is involved in great perplexity. The officers of the Pennsylvania troops are in much confusion about it. In many instances, those who were junior in rank, from local and other circumstances, have obtained commissions older in date than those which were granted afterwards to officers, their superiors before. This, with many other irregularities, has been and is the cause of great uneasiness; and, though precedency of rank so claimed should not be supported in justice or upon any principle, we find all, having the least pretext for the title, strenuous to support it, and willing to hold a superiority. I was therefore induced to order a board of officers to take the matter under consideration. The result, respecting the field-officers of this State, I now enclose, and wish Congress to adopt the regulation, which the Board have made, and transmit to me, by the earliest opportunity, commissions dated according to their arrangement. At the same time it may be proper, that there should be a resolve vacating the commissions they now have, and directing them to be delivered to me. Their attention to this business, I trust, will be immediate; the disputes and jealousies with the officers require it.

I have enclosed the memorial of Colonel Duportail and the other engineers for their promotion, referred to me by the Board of War for my sentiments. As to the terms these gentlemen mentioned to have been proposed and agreed to when they first arrived, I know nothing of them further than the memorial states. In respect to their abilities and knowledge in their profes- sion, I must observe they have had no great opportunity of proving them since they were in our service. However, I have reason to believe, that they have been regularly bred in this important branch of war, and that their talents, which have been hitherto, as it were, dormant, want only a proper occasion to call them forth; in which case, I have no doubt they would do themselves honor, and the States essential service. It is of great importance, too, to consider the practicability of replacing these gentlemen with persons equally quali fied, if they should quit the service; and how indispensable men of skill in this branch of military science are to every army. While I am on this subject, I would take the liberty to mention, that I have been well informed, that the engineer in the northern army (Kosciuszko I think his name is) is a gentleman of science and merit. From the character I have had of him, he is deserving of notice too.

I would beg leave to mention, that we are in great distress for want of money. This will be more urgent every day; and it is probable there will be a good deal of pay due to the troops coming to reinforce us. General Putnam writes pressingly for a supply, and says, he is in a most disagreeable situation for want of it. I must request the attention of Congress to this subject.

Tour favor of the 7th came to hand this morning. I shall pay proper attention to the enclosures. The rank of the officers of cavalry I will attempt to have settled as soon as circumstances will admit. I have nothing very interesting to communicate. The enemy have lost one of their new floating batteries; it sunk in a little time after it was launched. There has been a cannonade to-day; it still continues. I do not know the occasion, but imagine that it is between the ships and galleys.

November Wth.—By advices just received, thirtyeight transports have arrived in the Delaware with troops. They were as high up as Reedy Island yesterday. I suppose they are from New York. I am, &c Kosciuszko was appointed an engineer in the Continental service, October 18th, 1776, and had been constantly employed in the northern department, first at Ticondoroga and Mount Independence, and afterward in the army of Generals Schuyler and Gates. He planned the encampment for the American army at Behmus's Heights; and he wu afterwards the principal engineer in executing the military works at West Point. TO LIEUTENANT-COLONEL SAMUEL SMITH.

Head-Quarters, 12 November, 1777.

Snt,

I last night received your favor of the 10th instant, and am sorry to find the enemy's batteries had played with such success against our works. Nevertheless, I hope they will not oblige you to evacuate them. They are of the greatest importance, and I trust they will be maintained to the last extremity. I have written to General Varnum to afford you immediate succour, by sending fresh troops to relieve those now in the

garrison, and also such numbers of militia, as he may be able to prevail on to go to your assistance. With these, every exertion should be used for repairing in the night whatever damage the works may sustain in the day. The militia are principally designed for this end, and they are to be permitted every morning to return to Red Bank, if such shall be their choice. General Varnum will furnish all the fascines and palisadoes he can. You may rest assured, that I will adopt every means, which our situation will admit, to give you relief. I am, Sir, &c.

TO MAJOR-GENERAL HEATH.

Head-Quarters, 13 November, 1777.

Dear Sir, In my letter of the 5th in answer to yours of the 22d ultimo I mentioned, that it was not our interest to expedite the passage of the prisoners to England. Upon a review of the matter, I am more and more convinced of the propriety of the observation. The most scrupulous adherence, on the part of the enemy, to the convention of Saratoga will justify their placing the prisoners in garrisons, as soon as they arrive in Britain, and will enable the ministry to send out an equal number of troops to reinforce General Howe, or upon any other service against these States. This being the case, policy and a regard to our own interest are strongly opposed to our adopting or pursuing any measures, to facilitate their embarkation and passage home, which are not required of us by the capitulation. If by our exertions these ends are promoted, our generosity will be rewarded, in the arrival of as large a force by the end of March, or early in April, for the purposes suggested above.

These considerations lead me to observe, that it is extremely probable General Burgoyne will apply to you, or perhaps to the council of the State, to dispense with the articles of convention, so far as they respect the port for their embarkation, and to change it from Boston to some place in Rhode Island or the Sound. I know he has received a hint upon the subject from General Howe. Should such a requisition be made, it ought not to be complied with upon any

principles whatever. It cannot be asked as a matter of right, because by the articles Boston is assigned as the port. It should not be granted as a matter of favor, because the indulgence will be attended with most obvious and capital disadvantages to us. Besides the delay, which will necessarily arise from confining them to Boston, as the place of departure, their transports in a voyage round at this season may probably suffer considerable injury, and many of them may be blown as far as the West Indies. These considerations, and others needless to be added, have struck me in so important a point of view, that I have thought it expedient to write to you by express. Lieutenant Vallancey, who came with General Burgoyne's despatches, left this on his return yesterday morning, and I make no doubt, in a little time after his arrival, General Burgoyne will request the port of embarkation to be altered. Independently of the impolicy of granting the requisition, it appears to me, that no one has authority to do it but Congress. I am, dear Sir, with great respect, &,c TO PATRICK HENRY, GOVERNOR OF VIRGINIA.

Whitemarsh, 13 November, 1777.

Dear Sir, I shall beg leave to refer you to a letter of mine, which accompanies this, and of the same date, for a general account of our situation and wants. The design of this is only to inform you, and with great truth I can do it, strange as it may seem, that the army which I have had under my immediate command, has not, at any one time since General Howe's landing at the Head of Elk, been equal in point of numbers to his. In ascertaining this, I do not confine myself to Continental troops, but comprehend militia.

General Burgoyne resolved to adhere rigidly to the articles of the convention, as appears by General Heath's letter in reply to the above. Congress had directed that the name and rank of every commissioned officer included in the convention should be recorded; and also the name, former place of abode, size, age, and description of every non-commissioned officer and soldier. With this latter clause of the direction General Burgoyne refused to comply, any further than to give the names. " He asserted," says General Heath, " that no precedent could be produced in military history of more being given; that the public faith is to be the security; that, if the convention was short in any article, additions cannot now be made; for, if it were to be admitted in one article, amendments may be proposed in the whole." This reasoning might be used with equal force against assenting to a different port of embarkation from the one originally stipulated, in addition to the policy and strict justice of conforming to the articles in this respect.

At the close of his letter General Heath wrote, " General Burgoyne is much pleased with your treatment of Lieutenant Vallancey, which he says was polite and noble." VOL. V. 19 M

The disaffected and lukewarm in this State, in whom unhappily it too much abounds, taking advantage of the distraction in the government, prevented those vigorous exertions, which an invaded State ought to have yielded; and the short term, for which their militia was drawn out, expiring before others could be got in, and before the Maryland militia (which, by the by, were few in number, and did not join till after the battle of Brandywine,) came up, our numbers kept nearly at a stand, and I was left to fight two battles, in order if possible to save Philadelphia, with less numbers than composed the army of my antagonist, whilst the world has given us at least double. This impression, though mortifying in some points of view, I have been obliged to encourage, because, next to being strong, it is best to be thought so by the enemy; and to this cause principally I think is to be attributed the slow movements of General Howe.

How different the case in the northern department! There the States of New York and New England, resolving to crush Burgoyne, continued pouring in their troops, till the surrender of that army; at which time not less than fourteen thousand militia, as I have been informed, were actually in General Gates's camp, and those composed, for the most part, of the best yeomanry in the country, well armed, and in many instances supplied with provisions of their own carrying. Had the same spirit pervaded the people of this and the neighbouring States, we might before this time have had General Howe nearly in the situation of General Burgoyne, with this difference, that the former would never have been out of reach of his ships, whilst the latter increased his danger every step he took, having but one retreat in case of a disaster, and that blocked up by a respectable force.

My own difficulties, in the course of the campaign, have been not a little increased by the extra aid of Continental troops, which the gloomy prospect of our affairs in the north, immediately after the reduction of Ticonderoga, induced me to spare from this army. But it is to be hoped, that all will yet end well. If the cause is advanced, indifferent is it to me where or in what quarter it happens. The winter season, with the aid of our neighbours, may possibly bring some important event to pass.

I am, sincerely and respectfully, dear Sir, &,c.

TO SIR WILLIAM HOWE.

Head-Quarters, 14 November, 1777.

Sir, I am sorry to find, by the tenor of your letter of the 6th instant, that we still unhappily differ in our ideas of those just and reasonable terms, upon which a general exchange of prisoners might take place, and that an event so desirable is probably yet at a distance. This being the case, that relief to the unhappy, where it is practicable, may no longer be delayed, I am induced to accede to your proposition, made through LieutenantColonel Frazer, " that the officers, who are prisoners of war, on both sides should be released, and have liberty to return among their friends on parole." I shall expect your answer as soon as possible upon this subject; after which I shall give the necessary orders for the return of your officers to such places as you may appoint. At the same time, I wish that their exchange may appear to you, as it does to me, the more eligible mode of release. Notwithstanding what I have said, if the interpreta-

tion I have given your letter does not correspond with your own meaning, and you are disposed to proceed to an exchange of all the prisoners in your possession, for an equal number of those in my hands, without regard to the dispute subsisting between us, I shall be happy to adopt the measure. I therefore request an explanation of the third paragraph of your letter, where you say, —" Those at present prisoners with me are ready to be delivered on the shortest notice, and it rests solely with you to justify me in doing it."

In respect to the charge against Mr. Boudinot, the enclosed paper will show he has not failed to represent to Mr. Loring the wants of the prisoners in our hands. That these may be supplied, I shall upon your application grant passports to such persons, not above the rank of a regimental quartermaster, as you may send out with necessaries for them.

You call upon me to redress the grievances of several of your officers and men, who, you are pleased to say, "you are well informed are most injuriously and unjustifiably loaded with irons." If there is a single instance of a prisoner of war being in irons, I am ignorant of it; nor can I find on the most minute inquiry, that there is the least foundation for the charge. On the contrary, I have every reason to believe, that your officers and men, who are prisoners with us, are experiencing a very different treatment. I wish you to particularize the cases you allude to, that relief may be had, if the complaints are well founded, and the character and conduct of the persons shall not forbid it.

Now we are upon the subject of grievances, I am constrained to observe, that I have a variety of accounts, not only from prisoners who have made their escape, but from persons who have left Philadelphia, that our private soldiers in your hands are treated in a manner shocking to humanity, and that many of them must have perished through hunger, had it not been for the charitable contributions of the inhabitants. It is added in aggravation, that this treatment is to oblige them to enlist in the corps you are raising. The friends of these unhappy men call daily upon me for their relief, and the people at large insist on retaliating upon those in our possession. Justice demands it. However, before I could proceed to a measure my feelings recoil at, I thought it right to mention the facts to you; and I would propose, that I may be allowed to send a suitable person into the city under the usual restrictions, to examine into the truth of them.

I must also remonstrate against the cruel treatment and confinement of our officers. This, I am informed, is not only the case of those in Philadelphia, but of many in New York. Whatever plausible pretences may be urged to authorize the condition of the former, it is certain but few circumstances can arise to justify that of the latter. I appeal to you to redress these several wrongs; and you will remember, whatever hardships the prisoners with us may be subjected to will be chargeable to you. At the same time it is but justice to observe, that many of the cruelties exercised towards prisoners are said to proceed from the inhumanity of Mr. Cunningham, provost-martial, without your knowledge or approbation. I am, Sir, with due respect, &c.

P. S. Just as I was about to close my letter, two persons, men of reputation, came from Philadelphia. 1 transmit to you their depositions respecting the treatment they received while they were your prisoners.

I will not comment upon the subject. It is too painful.

TO BRIGADIER-GENERAL CONWAY.
Head-Quarters, 16 November, 1777.

Sir, In answer to your favor of this date, it remains with Congress alone to accept your resignation. This being the case, I cannot permit you to leave the army, till you have obtained their consent. When that is done, I shall not object to your departure, since it is your inclination. I thank you much for your wishes for the liberty of America, and the success of our arms, and have only to add, that, in case you are permitted to return by Congress, you will have

my hopes for a favorable passage, and a happy meeting with your family and friends. I am, Sir, &c.f See the Answer to the above, and also Sir William Howe's letter of November 6th, in the Appendix, No. VII.

t General Conway had the day before sent his commission to Congress, and he gave as a reason to General Washington, that a longer stay in America would endanger his rank and hopes of promotion in France, adding,— "Although I leave the continent, I shall ever cherish the cause for which I fought; and, if the plan I sent to Congress is accepted, I hope I shall serve the cause more effectually in another part of the world." What this plan was he does not intimate; nor is it apparent from the journals, that Congress accepted his resignation, though it would seem that he retired from the army. He wrote at the same time a long, complaining, boastful, and somewhat impudent letter to Mr. Charles Carroll, which was meant for Congress, and was accordingly read in that assembly. In that letter he said, " Seven weeks ago several gentlemen wrote to me from the seat of Congress, mentioning the very extraordinary discourses held by you, Sir, by Mr. Lovell, Mr. Duer, and some other members, on account of my applying for the rank of major-general. If I had hearkened to well grounded resentment, I should undoubtedly have left the army instantly." TO THE PRESIDENT OF CONGRESS.

Whitemarsh, 17 November, 1777.

Sir,

I am sorry to inform you that Fort Mifflin was evacuated the night before last, after a defence which does credit to the American arms, and will ever reflect the highest honor upon the officers and men of the garrison. The works were entirely beat down; every piece of cannon dismounted, and one of the enemy's ships so near, that she threw grenades into the fort, and killed men upon the platforms, from her tops, before they quitted the Island. This ship had been cut down for the purpose, and so constructed that she made but a small draft of water, and by these means

warped in between Fort Mifflin and Province Island. Some complaints are made, that the captains of the galleys did not sufficiently exert themselves to drive this vessel from her station; but I shall not determine any thing upon the matter till a proper inquiry is made.

Nothing in the course of this campaign has taken up so much of the attention and consideration of myself and all the general officers, as the possibility of giving a further relief to Fort Mifflin, than what we had already afforded. Such a garrison was thrown into it, as has been found by experience capable of defending it to the last extremity; and Red Bank, which was deemed essentially necessary, not only for the purpose of keeping open the communication, but of annoying the enemy's ships and covering our own fleet, has been possessed by a considerable detachment from this army. The only remaining and practicable mode of giving relief to the fort was by dislodging the enemy from Province Island, from whence they kept up an incessant fire. But this, from the situation of the ground, was not to be attempted with any degree of safety to the attacking party, unless the whole or a considerable part of the army should be removed to the west side of the Schuylkill to support and cover it.

To account for this, you must be made acquainted with the nature of the ground. In order to have made the attack upon Province Island, the party destined for that service, which should have been at least fifteen hundred, must have marched down the Chester road as far as the Bell Inn near Derby, and thence, turning towards the Delaware, must have proceeded about four miles further through a neck of land to the Island. The enemy have a bridge at the Middle Ferry upon the Schuylkill, which is but four miles from the Bell Inn; consequently, by throwing a body of men over that bridge upon the first discovery of our design, and marching down to the Bell, they would have effectually cut off our detachment upon their return. It is true, the covering party might have consisted of a less number than the whole army; but then those remaining upon this side of the river would have been too few to be intrusted with all the artillery and stores of the army, within twelve miles of the enemy.

There were many and very forcible reasons against a total remove to the west side of the Schuylkill. Leaving all our stores at Easton, Bethlehem, and Allentown uncovered, and abandoning several of our hospitals within reach of the enemy, first presented themselves. Another, and in my opinion a more weighty reason than either of the preceding, was the importance of supporting the post at Red Bank, upon which that at Fort Mifflin in a great measure depended, as through it we sent in great supplies of men, provision, and ammunition. The enemy, sensible of this, endeavoured to dislodge us from Red Bank on the 22d of last month; which, as Congress have been informed, cost them four hundred men.

Now had our army been on the west side of the Schuylkill, they might, without any danger of an attack upon their lines, have thrown over so considerable a force into Jersey, that they might have overpowered the garrison, and, by making themselves masters of it, have reduced Fort Mifflin by famine or want of ammunition. Thus we should in all probability have lost both posts by one stroke. They might also, by taking possession of the fords upon the Schuylkill, have rendered the junction of our northern reinforcements with us a very difficult, if not an impracticable matter; and, should any accident have happened to them, we should have stood a very poor chance of looking General Howe in the face through the winter, with an inferior army. We should finally have thrown the army into such a situation, that we must inevitably have drawn on a general engagement before our reinforcements arrived; which, considering our disparity of numbers, would probably have ended with the most disagreeable consequences.

It was therefore determined a few days ago to wait the arrival of the reinforcement from the northward, before any alteration could safely be made in the disposition of the army; and I was

not without hopes, that the fort would have held out till that time. That we might then have moved without endangering the stores, I had given orders for the removal of them, from the places before mentioned, to Lebanon and other places in Lancaster county, which is at any rate more safe and convenient than where they were.

As the keeping possession of Red Bank, and thereby still preventing the enemy from weighing the chevauxdefrise before the frost obliges their ships to quit the river, has become a matter of the greatest importance,

Vol. v. 20

I have determined to send down General St. Clair, General Knox, and Baron de Kalb, to take a view of the ground, and to endeavour to form a judgment of the most probable means of securing it. They will at the same time see how far it is possible for our fleet to keep their station since the loss of Fort Mifflin, and also make the proper inquiry into the conduct of the captains of the galleys mentioned in the former part of this letter. J For six days preceding the evacuation of Fort Mifflin, the fire from the enemy's batteries and shipping had been incessant. Major Fleury kept a journal of events, which was daily forwarded to General Washington, and from which the following are extracts. —" *November 10th, at noon.* I am interrupted by the bombs and balls, which fall thickly. The firing increases, but not the effect; our barracks alone suffer. *Tiro o'clock;* the direction of the fire is changed; our palisades suffer; a dozen of them are broken down; one of our cannon is damaged; I am afraid it will not fire straight. *Eleven o'clock at night;* the enemy keep up a firing every half hour. Our garrison diminishes; our soldiers are overwhelmed with fatigue. — *lUh.* The enemy keep up a heavy fire; they have changed the direction of their embrasures, and instead of battering our palisades in front, they take them obliquely and do great injury to our north side. *Jit night;* the enemy fire and interrupt our works Three vessels have passed up between us and Province Island without any molestation from the galleys.

Colonel Smith, Captain George, and myself wounded. Those two gentlemen passed immediately to Red Bank. — 12M. Heavy firing; our two eighteen-pounders at the northern battery dismounted. *At night;* the enemy throw shells, and we are alarmed by thirty boats. — *13th.* The enemy have opened a battery on the old Ferry Wharf; the walk of our rounds is destroyed, the blockhouses ruined. Our garrison is exhausted with fatigue and ill health. — 14/A. The enemy have kept up a firing upon us part of the night. Daylight discovers to us a floating battery placed a little above their grand battery and near the shore. *Seven o'clock;* the enemy keep up a great fire from their floating battery and the shore; our blockhouses are in a pitiful condition. *It noon;* we have silenced the floating battery. A boat, which this day deserted from the fleet, will have given the enemy sufficient intimation of our weakness; they will probably attempt a lodgment on the Island, which we cannot prevent with our present strength."

Colonel Smith was wounded on the 11th. He had gone into the barracks to answer a letter to General Vamum. A ball passed through the chimney; he was struck by the scattered bricks, and for a time remained senseless. He retired the same day to Red Bank, and the command devolved on Lieutenant-Colonel Russell, of the Connecticut line. Exhausted with fatigue and ill health, he desired soon after to be recalled. Major Thayer, of the Rhode Island line, then volunteered to take the command, which he retained from the 12th till the morning of the 16th. General Vamum wrote on the 15th, at six o'clock in the afternoon,— "The fire is universal from the shipping and batteries. We have lost a great many men to-day; a great many officers are killed and wounded. BIy fine company of artillery is almost destroyed. We shall be obliged to evacuate the fort this night. Major Talbut is badly wounded. Major Fleury is wounded also. It is impossible for an officer to possess more merit, than Colonel Thayer, who commands the brave little garrison. " Again, on the 16th. —" We were obliged to evacuate Fort Mifflin last evening. Major Thayer returned from thence a little after two this morning. Every thing was got off, that possibly could be. The cannon could not be removed without making too great a sacrifice of men, as the Vigilant lay within one hundred yards of the southern part of the works, and with her incessant fire, hand-grenades, and musketry from the round-top, killed every man that appeared upon the platforms." — *MS. Letters.*

I am informed that it is matter of amazement, and that reflections have been thrown out against this army, for not being more active and enterprising than, in the opinion of some, they ought to have been. If the charge is just, the best way to account for it will be to refer you to the returns of our strength, and those which I can produce of the enemy, and to the enclosed abstract of the clothing now actually wanting for the army; and then I think the wonder will be, how they keep the field at all in tents at this season of the year. What stock the clothier-general has to supply this demand, or what are his prospects, he himself will inform you, as I have directed him to go to York Town to lay these matters before Congress. There are, besides, most of those in the hospitals more bare than those in the field; many remain there for want of clothes only.

After the affair of Red Bank, Congress resolved, that a sword should be presented to Colonel Greene, and also to Colonel Smith, and Commodore Hazelwood, as a reward of their gallantry. The management of the fleet, however, had not been thought such, as to justify an honor of this kind to its commander. Fleury was promoted to the rank of lieutenant-colonel in the army. He had already received from Congress the gift of a horse, as a testimonial of their sense of his merit at the battle of Brandy wine, where a horse was shot under him. — *Journals, September 13th; November Ath,* 26WL

Several general officers, unable to procure clothing in the common line, have employed agents to purchase up what could be found in different parts of the country. General Wayne, among others, has employed Mr. Zantzinger of Lancaster, who has purchased to the amount of four thousand five hundred pounds, for which he desires a draft upon the Treasury Board. Enclosed you have a copy of his letter. I am not clear whether this application should properly be made to the treasury, or to the clothier-general, who should charge the money to the regiments for whom the clothes are designed, as so much advanced to them. If the latter should appear the most proper mode, I will order it to be done. I am anxiously waiting the arrival of the troops from the northward, who ought, from the time they have had my orders, to have been here before this. Colonel Hamilton, one of my aids, is up the North River, doing all he can to push them forward; but he writes me word, that he finds many unaccountable delays thrown in his way. However, I am in hopes that many days will not elapse before a brigade or two at least will arrive. The want of these troops has embarrassed all my measures exceedingly. I have the honor to be, &c.

TO BRIGADIER-GENERAL VARNU'M.
Head-Quarters, ten o'clock, P. M., 18 November, 1777.

Dear Sir, A body of the enemy marched last night from Philadelphia across the bridge at the Middle Ferry, and proceeded to Chester. Their number is variously reported, being from fifteen hundred to three thousand; but I imagine the former is most likely, although some people from the city think their numbers are much lessened upon their lines. They this day embarked their horses from Chester on board ships and brigs. From this it would seem as if they were going away; but in my opinion it is only a feint, and that they intend to cross over to Jersey and pay you a visit. Therefore keep a good look out below; if you do this, they cannot surprise you, because they must make a tedious debarkation of their horses. For all matters contained in yours of yesterday, I refer you to the Generals St. Clair, Knox, and Kalb, who went down to consult with you and the commodore. I expect a report from them to govern me in my operations towards assisting you. If you could get some countryman to go into Billingsport with a small supply of provisions, he might learn something of their intentions and numbers. I am, &c.

TO RICHARD HENRY LEE, IN CONGRESS.
Whitemarsh, 18 November, 1777.

Dear Sir, Your favor of the 7th instant should not have remained so long unanswered, but for the uncertainty of Colonel Pickering's acceptance of his new appointment. He has now determined to do this, which leads me to say, that I am really at a loss to recommend a proper person as a successor to the office of adjutant-general. The gentleman I named to you some time ago, you say will not answer. I knew but little of him myself, but I understood he was well acquainted with the duty, having served much to the satisfaction of General Mont VOL. V. N gomery (a good judge) in Canada, during his long and severe campaign in 1775.

That I might know the sense of the general officers upon this point of so much importance, that is, whether any of them were acquainted with, a person qualified for the discharge of the important duties of this office, I asked them collectively; but they either were not acquainted with a proper person, or did not incline to recommend any one. Colonel Lee, who was formerly recommended by Congress to fill this office, Colonel Wilkinson, Major Scull, and Colonel Innes were separately spoken of. The first is an active, spirited man, a good disciplinarian, and being, as he was, disappointed before by Colonel Pickering's unexpected acceptance of the office, may possibly look for it now. He writes a good hand, but how correctly, or with what ease, I cannot undertake to say, having had no opportunity of judging. The next genUeman, Wilkinson, I can say less of, because he has served for the most part in the northern department. General Gates I understand speaks highly of him. He is I believe a good grammatical scholar, but how diligent I know not. The next, Scull, is a young man, but an old officer, and very highly spoken of, for his knowl-

I have been duly honored with your favors of the 13th and 19th instant, with their enclosures. I am well assured Congress have not been inattentive to the necessities of the army; and that the deficiency in our supplies, particularly in the article of clothing, has arisen from the difficulty of importing, on account of the numerous fleet that lines our coast. However, I am persuaded that considerable relief might be drawn from the different States, were they to exert themselves properly. This I hope will be the case, as soon as they receive the pressing recommendations of Congress upon the subject.

It has been the unvaried custom of the enemy, from the commencement of the present contest, to try every artifice and device to delude the people. The message through John Brown was calculated for this end. I am surprised Mr. Willing should suffer himself to be imposed on by such flimsy measures. He knows that there is a plain, obvious way for General and Lord Howe to communicate any proposals they wish to make to Congress, without the intervention of a second and third hand. But this would not suit their views. I am sorry that Mr. Brown should be the bearer of the message; as, from the character I have had of him, he is a worthy, well-disposed man. It has been frequently mentioned, that he had interested himself much in behalf of our prisoners, and had afforded them every relief and comfort his circumstances would allow him to give. See Apmnux, No. Vn.

I have been endeavouring to effect an exchange of prisoners, upon principles of justice, and from motives of humanity; but at present I have no prospect of it. Yet General Howe has assured our officers it was his wish, and, if it could not be done, that he should readily agree to their release on parole. The enclosed copies of my letters and his answer will show Congress what has passed between us upon that subject; and, at the same time, that I had remonstrated against the severe and cruel treatment of the prisoners, and proposed the plan of sending in a suitable person to inquire into the facts, before the receipt of their resolution. Their sufferings, I am persuaded, have been great, and shocking to humanity. I have called upon General Howe for redress, and an explicit answer to my letter of the 14th. If I do not receive one by to-morrow night, with the most positive and satisfactory assurances that a proper conduct shall be observed towards them in future, we must retaliate, however much we wish to avoid severity, and measures that bear the smallest appearance of rigor or inhumanity.

Enclosed you will receive a list of sundry officers, who have been cashiered since the action of the 4th ultima I flatter myself, that these examples will involve many favorable and beneficial consequences. Besides these, there were many more brought to trial, who were acquitted; among them, General Maxwell and General Wayne, the former for charges against him while he commanded the light troops, the latter for charges against his conduct in the attack made on his division in the night of the 20th of September. The result of the court of inquiry against General Wayne not entirely exempting him from censure in his own opinion, he requested a court-martial; and, upon a full and minute investigation of the charges against him, he was honorably acquitted, and in terms of high respect.

I am sorry to inform Congress, that the enemy are now in possession of all the water defences. Fort Mifflin and that at Red Bank mutually depended oneach other for support; and the reduction of the former made the tenure of the latter extremely precarious, if not impracticable. After the loss of Fort Mifflin, it was found Red Bank could derive no advantages from the galleys and armed vessels; they could not maintain their station; and, in case of investiture, the garrison could have no supplies, no retreat, nor any hope of relief, but such as might arise from a superior force acting without on the rear of the enemy, and dislodging them. Under these circumstances, the garrison was obliged to evacuate it on the night of the 20th instant, on the approach of Lord Cornwallis, who had crossed the river from Chester with a detachment, supposed to be about two thousand men, and formed a junction with the troops lately arrived from New York, and those that had been landed before at Billingsport.

From General Varnum's account, I have reason to hope that we saved most of the stores, except a few heavy cannon; however, I cannot be particular in this instance. I am also to add, from the intelligence I have received, that most if not all the armed vessels have been burned by our own people, except the galleys, one brig, and two sloops, which are said to have run by the city. How far this might be founded in necessity, I am not able to determine; but I suppose it was done Under that idea, and an apprehension of their falling into the enemy's hands if they attempted to pass up the river.

Upon the first information I had of Lord Cornwallis's movement, I detached General Huntington's brigade to join General Varnum, and, as soon as possible, General Greene with his division; hoping that these, with Glover's brigade, which was on the march through Jersey, and which I directed to file off to the left for the same purpose, and with such militia as could be collected, would be able to defeat the enemy's design, and preserve the fort. But they were so rapid in their advances, that our troops could not form a junction and arrive in time to succour the garrison; which obliged them to withdraw. General Greene is still in Jersey; and, when Glover's brigade joins him, if an attack can be made on Lord Cornwallis with a prospect of success, I am persuaded it will be done. About a hundred and seventy of Morgan's corps are also gone to reinforce him. Generals Poor and Paterson, with their brigades, and Colonel Bailey with Learned's, are now in camp. The last arrived on Friday evening, the other two in the course of yesterday. I have not yet obtained returns of their strength; but, from the accounts of the officers, they will amount in the whole to twenty-three or twenty-four hundred rank and file. But I find many of them are very deficient in the articles of shoes, stockings, breeches, and blankets. Besides these, about three hundred and fifty men, detachments from Lee's, Jackson's, and Henley's regiments, have joined me. Yesterday evening the enemy burned several houses in the neighbourhood of Philadelphia, and they have committed the most wanton spoil in many others.

The remainder of Morgan's corps was rendered ilnfit to march by the want of shoes. There was much suffering in the army generally on this account. The following is an extract from the Orderly Book.

" The Commander-in-chief offers a reward of ten dollars to any person, who shall by nine o'clock on Monday morning produce the best substitute for shoes, made of raw hides. The commissary of hides is to furnish the hides, and the major-general of the day is to judge of the essays, and assign the reward to the best artist." — *Novcn&er 22tL*

A council of war was called, on the evening of the 24th of November, to consider the question of making an immediate attack on the enemy in Philadelphia. While Lord Cornwallis was absent in New Jersey with so large a body of troops, it was supposed by some that a fit opportunity presented itself for making a successful attack. General Washington bad reconnoitred the enemy's lines in person with this view. The subject was debated with earnestness, and, as there was a difference of opinion among the members of the council, they separated without coming to any decision. At the request of the Commander-in-chief, each officer sent in his written opinion the next morning, with his reason. During the night a messenger was likewise despatched to General Greene in Jersey, who communicated his views in writing. The result was, that eleven officers were opposed to the attack, and four in favor of it. Those in the affirmative were Stirling, Wayne, Scott, and Woodford; in the negative, Greene, Sullivan, Knox, Baron de Kalb, Smallwood, Maxwell, Poor, Paterson, Irvine, Duportail, and Armstrong.

I have the honor to be, &.c.

The plan suggested for the attack is thus described by Lord Stirling. " 1. That the enemy's lines on the north side of Philadelphia should be attacked at daylight by three columns properly flanked and supported. 2. That two thousand men should be drawn from General Greene and embarked in boats at Dunks's Ferry, proceed to Philadelphia, land at or near Spruce Street, push through the Common, and endeavour with a part to secure the bridge over the Schuylkill, and with the remainder to attack the enemy in the rear of their lines. 3. That five hundred of the Continental troops, with the militia under General Potter, should possess such of the hills on the other aide of the Schuylkill as command! and enfilade the enemy's lines; and while part of them carry on a brisk cannonade at that place, the rest proceed to the bridge over the Schuylkill, and wait an opportunity of attacking the works there in front, when the party from Spruce Street make an attack in the rear."

Such was the outline of the plan of attack, but it was by no mean satisfactory to the majority of the officers. The enemy's lines on the north ride of the city, from river to river, were sustained by a chain of fourteen redoubts, strengthened by *abatis* in some parts and by circular works in others. Each of the enemy's flanks was moreover protected TO THE PRESIDENT OF CONGRESS.

Head-Quarters, 26 November, 1777.

Sir, I wish the measures Congress have adopted may effectually suppress the disturbances in the western department. Should they prove successful, and the savages and wicked, deluded inhabitants receive a severe check, it is probable they will not be induced again to take part against us, or at least for some considerable time. Colonel Crawford set out yesterday evening, and will be with Congress, I expect, in the course of two or three days to take their commands. I was much obliged by the foreign intelligence you were pleased to transmit to me; it is agreeable and interesting; and I heartily wish there may be an early declaration of hostilities between France and Britain. From these advices, things seem to be getting into

a proper train for it; and it is not easily to be conceived, that it can be much longer delayed. However, our expectations have not been answered in this instance, and they may yet be held in suspense. The political reasons, that lead to delay on the part of France, I do not perfectly understand. As to Britain, her honor is lost in the contest with us, and the most indignant insults will scarcely be able to draw her attention from her present pursuits. The account of Mr. Lee having effected the purposes of his embassy at the court of Berlin is of great importance, if it be true. In such by a river, and the rear by the union of two rivers. To attack an army under such circumstances, without the greatest hazard of a failure, would require a large superiority of force, and the best disciplined troops; but in the present case, the enemy's force was almost equal in numbers to that under Washington, and in point of discipline and experience far superior. These considerations, with others of a similar tendency, were deemed sufficient to discourage an attack.

Vol. v. 22 o case, administration, however desirous they may be, will probably be disappointed in their schemes of further mercenary aids against us.

I must take the liberty to request the decision of Congress on the case of the nine first raised Virginia regiments, as early as circumstances will permit. If the plan proposed for reenlisting them is judged expedient, one capital inducement to that end, suggested by the officers, will cease if it is longer delayed. It is a matter of considerable importance, and of which I wjsh to be satisfied as soon as possible. I should also be happy in their determination respecting the Marquis de Lafayette. He is more and more solicitous to be in actual service, and is pressing in his applications for a command. I ventured before to submit my sentiments upon the measure, and I still fear a refusal will not only induce him to return in disgust, but may involve some unfavorable consequences. There are now some vacant divisions in the army, to one of which he may be appointed, if it should be the pleasure of Congress. I am convinced he possesses a large share of that military ardor, which generally characterizes the nobility of his country. He went to Jersey with General Greene, and I find he has not been inactive there. This you will perceive by the following extract from a letter just received from General Greene.

" The Marquis, with about four hundred militia and the rifle corps, attacked the enemy's picket last evening, killed about twenty, wounded many more, and took about twenty prisoners. The Marquis is charmed with the spirited behaviour of the militia and rifle corps; they drove the enemy about half a mile, and kept the ground until dark. The enemy's picket consisted of about three hundred, and were reinforced during the skirmish. The Marquis is determined to be in the way of danger." Mr. Arthur Lee's embassy to the court of Berlin did not turn out to be so successful as was anticipated. He received fair words and civil treatment, but little else. See his letters on the subject, in the *Diplomatic Correspondence of the American Revolution,* Vol. II. pp. 63, 68, 70, 76, 87, 103, 1U7.

By a letter from General Howe to General Burgoyne, which passed through my hands, he hinted that liberty might probably be granted for the prisoners to embark at Rhode Island, or some part of the Sound. This indulgence appearing to me inadmissible, I immediately wrote to General Heath to prevent him from giving the least countenance to the measure, in case it should be requested; and also to the Council of Massachusetts, and General Gates, lest he should extend his applications to them. The reasons, I am persuaded, will at once occur to Congress for my conduct in this instance, as well as for General Howe's; and I have been induced to mention it here, on a supposition that General Burgoyne may address them on the subject. If the embarkation is confined to Boston, it is likely that it will not take place before some time in the spring, or at least till towards the end of February; whereas, if it were allowed

at either of the other places, it might be made this month or the beginning of next, and the troops arrive in Britain by the month of January; a circumstance of great importance to us, as, the moment they get there, the most scrupulous and virtuous observance of the convention will justify the ministry in placing them in garrison, and sending others out to reinforce General Howe, or upon any other expedition, that they may think proper to undertake against us. Besides, compelling their transports to perform a long coasting voyage, at a tempestuous season, may bring on the loss of many, and be the means of deferring the embarkation for a long time.

The Marquis de Lafayette was not yet entirely recovered from his wound, and had only joined the army just in time to engage in this expedition aa a volunteer. At his request, General Greene gave him permission to reconnoitre Lord Comwallis, and make an attack if circumstances would warrant it. Comwallis was then in the act of sending his troops across the river at Gloucester. In reconnoitring, Lafayette advanced so near the enemy, that he was discovered on a sandy point near the mouth of a creek, which empties itself into the Delaware at Gloucester. A small detachment of dragoons was sent off to intercept him, which he saw across the creek. His guide was frightened, but soon became sufficiently collected to direct him into a back path, which took him out of the reach of the dragoons, before, they could advance to the bridge. He was obliged, also, to pass within musket-shot of an out-post; but he escaped uninjured, and joined his detachment. The following is his own account of the skirmish, as contained in a letter to General Washington.

" After having spent the most part of the day in making myself well acquainted with the certainty of the enemy's motions, I came pretty late into the Gloucester road between the two creeks. I had ten light-horse, almost one hundred and fifty riflemen, and two pickets of militia. Colonel Armand, Colonel Laumoy, and the Chevaliers Duplessis and Gimat were the French-

men with me. A scout of my men under Duplessis went to ascertain how near to Gloucester were the enemy's first pickets, and they found at the distance of two miles and a half from that place a strong post of three hundred and fifty Hessians, with field-pieces, and they engaged immediately. As my litt'.e reconnoitring party were all in fine spirits, I supported them. We pushed the Hessians more than half a mile from the place where their main body had been, and we made them run very fast. British reinforcements came twice to them, but, very far from recovering their ground, they always retreated. The darkness of the night prevented us from pursuing our advantage. After rt-ning on the ground we had gained, I ordered them to return very slowly to Haddonfield." —*MS. Letter, November 'Jtilh.*

The Marquis had one man only lulled, and six wounded. " I take the greatest pleasure," he added, " in letting you know that the cooduct of our soldiers was above all praise. I never saw men so merry, so spirited, and so desirous to go on to the enemy, whatever force they might have, as that small party in this little fight."

On the same day, that Congress received the above letter from General Washington, they voted that it would be highly agreeable to Congress for him to appoint the Marquis de Lafayette to the command of a division in the Continental army.—*Journal, December* 1st Three days afterwards it was proclaimed in public orders, that be was to take command of the division recently under General Stephen, who had bees dismissed from the army. That the Marquis had already made a favorable impression in the country, may be inferred from a letter written by Patrick Henry to Washington, in which he says; " I take the liberty of enclosing to you two letters from France to the Marquis de Lafayette. One of them is from his lady, I believe. I beg to be presented to hint in the most acceptable manner. I greatly revere his person and amiable character. " — *December* 6m.

November 27th. — Enclosed you will receive a copy of General Howe's letter in answer to mine of the 14th and 23d, which only came to hand last night, and at an instant when I was giving the commissary of prisoners instructions forthwith to confine a number of the officers in our hands, and to put the privates under very different restrictions from those they have been used to. I am m hopes the treatment of ours will be much better in future. Mr. Boudinot will immediately take measures for releasing the officers on parole, that we may relieve an equal number of ours. I should have been happy to effect a general exchange, or a partial one; but General Howe will not upon any terms but those he has ever insisted on. The enemy have got up several of their ships to the city. It is likely they have found a passage through the cbevaux-de-frise, or they may have removed them. I have the honor, &c In writing to his brother, November 26th, General Washington said; " Had the reinforcement from the northward arrived but ten days sooner, it would, I think, have put it in my power to save Fort Mifflin, which defended the chevaux-de-frise; and consequently have rendered Philadelphia a very ineligible situation for them this winter. They have also received a reinforcement from New York, but not quite so large, I believe, as ours. With truth I may add, that, till within these few days, I have never (notwithstanding the numbers given me by the world, and which it was not my interest to contradict) had so many men in the field, under my immediate command, as General Howe has had under his, although we have fought him twice, and prevented him hitherto from obtaining other advantages, than that of possessing himself of the city; which, but for the eclat it is attended with, brings no solid advantage to their arms. The militia, which have been called upon in aid of our troops (Continental I mean), have come out in such a manner, that, be o» TO MAJOR-GENERAL GREENE.

Head-Quarters, 28 November, 1777.

Dear Sir, Captain Duplessis has just delivered to me yours of this morning from Burlington. Every account from Philadelphia confirms the report, that the enemy mean to make a speedy move. I shall not be disappointed if they come out this night or very early in the morning. You will therefore push forward the rear brigades with all possible expedition, and, the moment that the troops and baggage have all passed, let the boats be instantly sent up the river to Coryell's Ferry; for one part of my information is, that the enemy are preparing to send boats up the Delaware, and it cannot be for any other purpose, than to destroy the remainder of our watercraft. I shall be glad that you would come on immediately upon the receipt of this, and send word back to the brigadiers to hasten their march. I am, &c fore you could get a second class of them, the first were always gone; by which means, although the sound of them was great, you never could increase your real numbers and strength." General Greene remained a week only in Jersey. His troops were already recrossing the Delaware at Burlington, on their way to the main army, when the above letter was written. As Fort Mercer had been evacuated, and all the posts on the river given up, and as Lord Cornwallis with his detachment had crossed over to Philadelphia, there was no longer any object to be gained by a large force in Jersey. General Washington's intelligence, as to the designs of the enemy, was well founded. In a despatch to the minister, dated November 27th, Sir William Howe said; " A forward movement against the enemy will immediately take place, and I hope will be attended with the success, that is due to the spirit and activity of his Majesty's troops." — *Parliamentary Register,* Vol. XI. p. 440.

General Dickinson made a descent upon Staten Island, November 27th, with about fourteen hundred men. He landed before day at Halstead's Point in three divisions, which marched into the Island seven miles and met at the appointed place of rendezvous. It was then ascertained, that the main body of the enemy, under Generals Skinner and Campbell, had escaped. Intelligence of the intended incursion had been received by General Skinner at three o'clock in the morning, which had given him time to draw off his troops. General Dickinson returned without effecting his object, but he received the approbation of the Commanderin-chief for his enterprise, and the judicious manner in which his plan had been laid. In the skirmishes on the Island, five or six of the enemy were killed and twenty-four taken prisoners. His own loss was three men taken and two wounded.— *General Dickinson's* MS. *Letter, Jfovem*6er28tt. See Appendix, No. VII.

TO SIR WILLIAM HOWE.

Head-Quarters, 28 November, 1777.

Sir,

In answer to your letter, which came to hand on Wednesday evening, I have to inform you, that I accede to the proposition contained therein, and have directed measures to be immediately taken for releasing all your officers upon the condition you mention. At the same time, I wish that a more extensive relief had been agreeable to you. I have sent Mr. Boudinot to examine into the state and wants of the prisoners, who are in Philadelphia, and request that he may obtain your permission for the same. He will also have an opportunity of agreeing with your commissary, upon the form and terms of parole for the officers to be mutually released, which I presume may not be improper, in order to prevent any misunderstanding on that head. Passports shall be granted for the commissaries or quartermasters you may appoint to carry supplies to the prisoners in our hands, when you choose to apply for them. Two only will be necessary; one for the person assigned to go to the eastward, the other for the officer having supplies for the prisoners in Pennsylvania, Maryland, and Virginia. Mr. Boudinot will also inform your commissary of the proportion of prisoners in each quarter.

When Major Stockton was first captured, I believe that he, and one or two officers taken with him, suffered the treatment which you mention. This was without my privity or consent. As soon as I was apprized of it, relief was ordered. But surely this event, which happened so long ago, will not authorize the charges in your letter of the 6th.

In a word, I shall be happy, as I ever have been, to render the situation of all prisoners in my hands as comfortable as I can; and nothing will induce me to depart from this rule, but a contrary line of conduct to those in your possession. Captivity of itself is sufficiently grievous, and it is cruel to add to its distresses.

I am, &.c.

TO MAJOR-GENERAL PUTNAM.

Head-Quarters, 2 December, 1777.

Dear Sir, The importance of the North River in the present contest, and the necessity of defending it, are subjects which have been so frequently and so fully discussed, and are so well understood, that it is unnecessary to enlarge upon them. These facts at once appear, when it is considered that it runs through a whole State; that it is the only passage by which the enemy from New York, or any part of our coast, can ever hope to cooperate with an army from Canada; that the possession of it is indispensably essential to preserve the communication between the eastern, middle, and southern States; and, further, that upon its security, in a great measure, depend our chief supplies of flour for the subsistence of such forces, as we may have occasion for, in the course of the war, either in the eastern or northern departments, or in the country lying high up on the west side of it. These facts are familiar to all; they are familiar to you. I therefore request you, in the most urgent terms, to turn your most serious and active attention to this infinitely important object. Seize the present opportunity, and employ your whole force and all the means in your power for erecting and completing, as far as it shall be possible, such works and obstructions as may be necessary to defend and secure the river against any future attempts of the enemy. You will consult Governor Clinton, General Parsons, and the French engineer, Colonel Radiere, upon the occasion. By gaining the passage, you know the enemy have already laid waste and destroyed all the houses, mills, and towns accessible to them. Unless proper measures are taken

to prevent them, they will renew their ravages in the spring, or as soon as the season will admit, and perhaps Albany, the only town in the State of any importance remaining in our hands, may undergo a like fate, and a general havoc and devastation take place.

To prevent these evils, therefore, I shall expect that you will exert every nerve, and employ your whole force in future, while and whenever it is practicable, in constructing and forwarding the proper works and means of defence. The troops must not be kept out on command, and acting in detachments to cover the country below, which is a consideration infinitely less important and interesting. I am, dear Sir, &,c General Washington wrote at the same time to Governor Clinton, with a good deal of solicitude, on this subject. " General Gates was directed by Congress," he remarked, " to turn his views to this matter; but, from some proceedings, that have just come to hand, he may be employed in the Board of War, if it should be his choice. Should this be the case, nothing would be more pleasing to me, and I am convinced nothing would more advance the interest of the States, than for you to take tho

Vol. r. 23 TO MAJOR-GENERAL GATES.

Head-Quarters, 2 December, 1777.

Sir,

I was yesterday favored with yours of the 23d of November, and am glad to find that you were upon your guard against any attempt of General Burgoyne to endeavour to change the place of embarkation. No transports have yet sailed from the Delaware, for the purpose of carrying the troops to Europe, nor do I hear that any have gone from New York. I can only attribute this delay to want of provision for the voyage. Bread we know is exceedingly scarce among them.

By a resolve of Congress of the 5th of November, you are directed, with a certain part of the northern army and the assistance of the militia of New York and the eastern States, to attempt the recovery of the posts upon the North River from the enemy, and to put them,

if recovered, in the best posture of defence. The enchief direction and superintendence of this business; and I shall be happy if the affairs of government will permit you. If they will, yon may rest assured, that no aid in my power to afford you shall be withheld, and there are no impediments on the score of delicacy or superior command, that shall not be removed." To this complimentary and Battering proposal, Governor Clinton replied; — " The legislature of this State New York is to meet on the 5th of next month. The variety of important business to be prepared for their consideration, and other affairs of government, will employ so great a part of my time, that 1 should not be able to give that attention to the works for the security of the river, which their importance, and the short time in which they ought to be completed, require. But you may rest assured, Sir, that every leisure hour shall be faithfully devoted to them, and my advice and assistance shall not on any consideration be withheld from the person, who shall be intrusted with the chief direction." — *MS. Letter, Drcrm*ler 2CMA. The same letter contains several important hints respecting the construction of new works on the river, and he especially recommends, that a "strong fortress should be erected at West Point, opposite to Fort Constitution." This was probably the first suggestion, from any official source, which led to the fortifying of that post.

emy having themselves evacuated Forts Montgomery and Clinton, while the resolve was in agitation, but of which the Congress could not at that time be informed, the first part falls of course; but the last deserves our most serious attention, as upon the possession of the North River depends the security of all the upper part of the government of New York, and the communication between the eastern, middle, and southern States. It is also the quarter, in which the enemy will probably attempt a diversion in the spring; as, from the small force they have remaining in Canada, there is not a possibility of their doing any thing on that side, till very late in the campaign, if at all. My not having heard from you, as to what steps you have taken towards carrying into execution the resolve for repairing the old works, or building new ones, or when you might be expected down into that part of the country, has made me hitherto delay recalling General Putnam from the command. But I beg leave to urge to you the necessity of your presence in that quarter, as speedily as possible; for I fear few or no measures have yet been taken towards putting matters in a proper train for carrying on these important works. General George Clinton will necessarily be employed in the affairs of his government; but I have written to him, and I am certain he will call for and contribute all the aid, that the State of New York can possibly afford. You are vested by the resolve of Congress with authority to demand a proportionable share of assistance from the eastern States.

General Howe has withdrawn himself close within his lines, which extend from the Upper Ferry upon the Schuylkill to Kensington upon the Delaware; they consist of a chain of strong redoubts connected by *abatis*. We have reconnoitred them well, but find it impossible to attack them while defended by a force fully equal to our own in Continental troops. The reinforcement from New York unluckily arriving before ours from the northward, it was out of my power to afford adequate relief to Fort Mifflin, which fell after a most gallant defence of seven weeks. The works upon the Jersey shore, which were of no great consequence after the reduction of Fort Mifflin, were evacuated, as it would have been impossible to support the garrison there. We have not yet determined upon a position for the army during the winter. That situation will undoubtedly be most eligible, which will afford best cover to the troops, and will at the same time cut off the enemy from resources of provision, which they may probably stand i n need of, when the navigation of the Delaware is obstructed by the ice. I am, Sir, &c.

TO THE PRESIDENT OF CONGRESS.

Head-Quarters, Whitemarsh, 10 December, 1777.

Sir, I have the honor to inform you, that in the course of last week, from a variety of intelligence, I had reason to expect that General Howe was preparing to give us a general action. Accordingly, on Thursday night he moved from the city with all his force, except a very inconsiderable part left in his lines and redoubts, and appeared the next morning on Chestnut Hill, in front of, and about three miles distant from, our right wing. As soon as their position was discovered, the Pennsylvania militia were ordered from our right, to skirmish with their light advanced parties; and I am sorry to mention, that Brigadier-General Irvine, who led them on, had the misfortune to be wounded and to be made prisoner. Nothing more occurred on that day.

On Friday night the enemy changed their ground, and moved to our left, within a mile of our line, where they remained quiet and advantageously posted the whole of the next day. On Sunday they inclined still further to our left; and, from every appearance, there was reason to apprehend they were determined on an action. In this movement, their advanced and flanking parties were warmly attacked by Colonel Morgan and his corps, and also by the Maryland militia under Colonel Gist. Their loss I cannot ascertain; but I am informed it was considerable, having regard to the number of the corps who engaged them. About sunset, after various marches and countermarches, they halted; and I still supposed, from their disposition and preceding manoeuvres, that they would attack us in the night or early the next morning; but in this I was mistaken. On Monday afternoon they began to move again, and, instead of advancing, filed off from their right; and the first certain account that I could obtain of their intentions was, that they were in full march towards Philadelphia by two or three routes. I immediately detached light parties after them to fall upon their rear; but they were not able to come up with them.

The enemy's loss, as I have observed, I cannot ascertain. One account from the city is, that five hundred wounded had been sent in; another is, that eighty-two wagons had gone in with men in this situation. These, I fear, are both exaggerated, and not to be depended upon. We lost twenty-seven men in Morgan's corps, killed and wounded, besides Major Morris, a brave and gallant officer, who is among the latter. Of the Maryland militia there were also sixteen or seventeen VOL. V. P wounded. I have not received further returns yet. I sincerely wish that they had made an attack; as the issue, in all probability, from the disposition of our troops, and the strong situation of our camp, would have been fortunate and happy. At the same time I must add, that reason, prudence, and every principle of policy, forbade us from quitting our post to attack them. Nothing but success would have justified the measure; and this could not be expected from their position.

The constant attention and watching I was obliged to give the enemy's movements would not allow me to write before; and this I believe was the less material, as I have reason to think your committee, who were in camp most of the time, and who are now here, transmitted an account of such occurrences as they deemed important in any degree. The first cause, too, Sir, and my engagements with the committee previous to the coming out of the enemy, will, I trust, sufficiently apologize for my not acknowledging before the honor of your favors of the 13th ultimo and the 1st instant, which came to hand in due order and time.

I have the honor to be, &c.

TO GOVERNOR LIVINGSTON.

Head-Quarters, Whitemarah, II December, 1777.

Sir, General Howe, after making great preparations, and threatening to drive us beyond the mountains, came out with his whole force last Thursday evening, and, after manoeuvring round us till the Monday following, decamped very hastily, and marched back to Philadelphia.

In my opinion, trying the officers taken by General Dickinson on Staten Island, for high treason, may prove to be a dangerous expedient. It is true, they left the State after such an offence was declared to be treason; but, as they had not taken the oaths, nor had entered into our service, it will be said they had a right to choose their side. Again, by the same rule that we try them, may not the enemy try any natural born subject of Great Britain, taken in arms in our service? We have a great number of them; and I therefore think, that we had better submit to the necessity of treating a few individuals, who may really deserve a severer fate, as prisoners of war, than run the risk of giving an opening for retaliation upon the Europeans in our service.

I am pleased to hear, that your Assembly are in so good a disposition to regulate the price of necessaries for the army. I could wish that they would not forget to regulate the prices of country produce, which the commissaries tell me has risen to so exorbitant a rate, that there is no purchasing a single article from the farmers. I am, &c.

The officers here mentioned were natives of New Jersey, who entered into the service of the enemy. As this was treason by the law of New Jersey, they were imprisoned, and the Governor considered it his duty to try them in the courts of justice. He conformed to General Washington's advice, however, and put them on the footing of prisoners of war.

The British General Campbell, then on Staten Island, had claimed these officers from Governor Livingston, and also another person, who bad been captured with them. The officers, three in number, were given up, but, in regard to the other person, Governor Livingston wrote; "He is no officer, and had committed a number of robberies in this State before he joined the enemy; and I can hardly think that General Campbell will be of the opinion, that, in consideration of law, a man can expiate the guilt of a prior robbery by a subsequent treason." TO THE PRESIDENT OF CONGRESS.

Head-Quarters, near the Gulf, 14 December, 1777.

Sir, On Thursday evening I had the honor to receive your favor of the 8th instant. From several letters, which have lately passed between General Howe and myself, I am fully convinced, that any propositions by me to release the Baron St. Ouary from captivity, either by an exchange or on parole, would be unavailing. He has explicitly stated his sentiments, and has declared himself to be utterly against a partial exchange. The situation of the Baron, through the interest and acquaintance of the Marquis de Lafayette with an officer in the guards, is much more comfortable than that of any of our officers, who are prisoners, he being on parole in the city, whilst they are all confined in the State-House. I do not know that it is the practice in Europe not to consider volunteers as prisoners. I am inclined to believe that it is not, and that they are generally held as such, unless the contrary is particularly stipulated by cartel. However this may be, they have been held in the present contest on both sides on the footing of other prisoners, and exchanged as such. Besides this, I fear that a proposition calculated for the peculiar benefit of the Baron, would be ill received by our unhappy officers, who have been much longer in confinement, whose sufferings are far greater than his, and who claim a right to exchange in due course.

In their resolve, respecting the Baron St. Ouary, Congress designated him as " a gallant gentleman from France, engaged as a volunteer in the service of the United States, and lately by the fortune of war made prisoner by the British." They instructed General Washington to apply for his release, on the ground that volunteers were not to be regarded as prisoners of war; but, if General Howe should not accede to this doctrine, then an enlargement by exchange or on parole wa» to bo solicited for the Boron St. Ouary. — *Journals, December 3d.*

The inquiries, directed in the resolutions contained in your letter of the 30th ultimo, respecting the loss of the forts in the Highlands and of Fort Mifflin, I shall order to be made, as soon as circumstances will admit. These, however, it is probable, will not be effected in a short time, from the situation of our affairs and inevitable necessity. On Thursday morning we marched from our old encampment, and intended to pass the Schuylkill at Matson's Ford, where a bridge had been laid across the river. When the first division and a part of the second had passed, they found a body of the enemy, consisting, from the best accounts we have been able to obtain, of four thousand men, under Lord Cornwallis, possessing themselves of the heights on both sides of the road leading from the river and the defile called the Gulf, which I presume are well known to some part of your honorable body. This unexpected event obliged such of our troops, as had crossed, to repass, and prevented our getting over till the succeeding night. This manoeuvre on the part of the enemy was not in consequence of any information they had of our movement, but was designed to secure the pass whilst they were foraging in the neighbouring country. They were met in their advance by General Potter, with part of the Pennsylvania militia, who behaved with bravery and gave them every possible opposition, till he was obliged to retreat from their superior numbers. Had we been an hour sooner, or had the least information of the measure, I am persuaded we should have given his Lordship a fortunate stroke, or obliged him to return without effecting his purpose, or drawn out all General Howe's force to support him. Our first intelligence was, that it was all out. Lord Cornwallis collected a good deal of forage, and returned to the city the night we passed the river. No

Vol. v. 24 P discrimination marked his proceedings. AD property, whether of friends or foes, that came in their way, was seized and carried oft'.

Enclosed is a copy of a letter from General Burgoyne, by which you will perceive he requests leave to embark his troops at Rhode Island, or at some place on the Sound; and, in case this cannot be granted, that he may be allowed, with his suite, to go there and return from thence to England. His first proposition, as I have observed upon a former occasion, is certainly inadmissible, and for reasons obvious to himself. As to the second, which respects the departure of himself and suite, Congress will be pleased to determine upon it and favor me with their sentiments by the first opportunity, that I may know what answer to give him. I learn from Mr. Griffin, who has just come from Boston, that this gentleman either holds, or professes to hold, very different ideas of our power from what he formerly entertained; that, without reserve, he has said it would be next to impossible for Britain to succeed in her views, and that he should with freedom declare his sentiments accordingly on his arrival in England; and that he seemed to think the recognition of our independence by the King and Parliament an eligible measure, under a treaty of commerce upon a large and extensive scale. How far these professions are founded in sincerity, it is not easy to determine; but if they are, what a mighty change! While I am on the subject of Mr. Burgoyne and his army, I would submit it to Congress, whether it will not be right and reasonable, that all expenses, incurred on their account for provisions, should be paid and satisfied previously to their embarkation and departure; I mean by an actual deposit of the money. Unless this is done, there will be little reason to suppose, that it will ever be paid. They have failed (that is, the nation) in other instances, as I have been told, after liquidating their accounts and giving the fullest certificates, and we cannot expect they will keep better faith with us than with others. The payment too, I should apprehend, ought to be in com, as it will enable us to administer some relief to our unfortunate officers and men who are in captivity.

" *In Congress, December 17th;* Resolved, that General Washington be directed to inform General Burgoyne, that Congress will not receive nor consider any proposition for indulgence or altering the terms of the convention of Saratoga, unless immediately directed to thoir own body." Congress had already voted, that a proposal for shipping the troops from any other place, than that stipulated in the convention of Saratoga, should be rejected. —*December 1st December 15th.* — Congress seem to have taken for granted a fact, that is really not so. All the forage for the army has been constantly drawn from Bucks and Philadelphia counties, and those parts most contiguous to the city; insomuch that it was nearly exhausted, and entirely so in the country below our camp. From these, too, were obtained all the supplies of flour, that circumstances would admit of. The millers in most instances were unwilling to grind, either from their disaffection or from motives of fear. This made the supplies less than they otherwise might have been, and the quantity, which was drawn from thence was little, besides what the guards, placed at the mills, compelled them to manufacture. As to stock, I do not know that much was had from thence, nor do I know that any considerable supply could have been had.

I confess I have felt myself greatly embarrassed with respect to a vigorous exercise of military power. An ill-placed humanity, perhaps, and a reluctance to give distress, may have restrained me too far; but these were not all. I have been well aware of the prevalent jealousy of military power, and that this has been considered as an evil, much to be apprehended, even by the best and most sensible among us. Under this idea, I have been cautious, and wished to avoid as much as possible any act that might increase it. However, Congress may be assured, that no exertions of mine, as far as circumstances will admit, shaH be wanting to provide our own troops with supplies on the one hand, and to prevent the enemy from getting them on the other. At the same time they must be apprized, that many obstacles have arisen to render the former more precarious and difficult than they usually were, from a change in the commissary's department, at a very critical and interesting period. I should be happy, if the civil authority in the several States, through the recommendations of Congress, or their own mere will, seeing the necessity of supporting the army, would always adopt the most spirited measures, suited to the end. The people at large are governed much by custom. To acts of legislation or civil authority they have ever been taught to yield a willing obedience, without reasoning about their propriety; on those of military power, whether immediate or derived originally from another source, they have ever looked with a jealous and suspicious eye. I have the honor to be, &c TO SIR WILLIAM HOWE.

Head-Quarters, 14 December, 1777.

Sir, The difficulty of supplying the troops of General Burgoyne's army with wood and provisions, from the country in the neighbourhood of Boston, induces me to request, that you would grant passports for vessels to be employed to bring them from places oa the coast. I cannot ascertain the number of vessels, that may be necessary for this business, or the names of the persons, who may be intrusted with the command of them. The passports, therefore, should be blank. In such case, they can be occasionally filled up; and, to prevent any doubts of their being improperly used, they may be countersigned by General Burgoyne. This I shall direct. The letters from General Burgoyne, which accompany this, I transmit to you by his request. I am, Sir, &,c TO MAJOR-GENERAL HEATH.

Head-Quarters, Gulf Mill, 17 December, 1777.

Dear Sir, I immediately forwarded the packets and letters from General Burgoyne and his officers to General Howe. As to General Burgoyne's request to me, to permit him to depart before his army, I did not think myself authorized to grant it, before I consulted Congress, to whom I transmitted a copy of his letter. I shall give him an answer as soon as I know their determination. I think it would have been highly improper to allow him the liberty of visiting your seaport towns. A man of his sagacity and penetration would make many observations, that might prove detrimental to us in future. Whenever you have occasion for directions in any matters respecting General Burgoyne and his troops, it will be best for you to write fully to Congress upon the subject, as they alone must determine in all cases which refer to them. I am, dear Sir, &.c. General Howe declined giving the passports here requested, assigning as a reason, that he thought it impossible to prevent their being improperly used, and that he hoped the troops would be permitted to embark at Rhode Island, which would render the supplies unnecessary. Bee his letter in the Appendix, No. VII. TO LIEUTENANT-GEXERAL BURGOYNE.

Head-Quarters, 17 December, 1777.

Sis,

I was, a few days ago, honored with yours of the 25th of November. The packets for Sir William Howe, and the letters for gentlemen in his army, were immediately forwarded to Philadelphia. As I did not conceive myself at liberty to answer either of your requests, without first consulting Congress, I have transmitted a copy of your letter to them, and have desired their determination as speedily as possible. As soon as I know the result, I shall take the earliest opportunity of acquainting you with it. I have the honor to be, &c TO GEORGE READ, PRESIDENT OF DELAWARE.

Head-Quarters, Gulf Mill, 19 December, 1777.

Sir, I have received information, which I have great reason to beb'eve is true, that the enemy mean to establish a post at Wilmington, for the purpose of countenancing the disaffected in the Delaware State, drawing supplies from that country and the lower parts of Chester county, and securing a post upon the Delaware River during the winter. As the advantages resulting to the enemy from such a position are most obvious, I have determined, and shall accordingly this day send off General Smallwood with a respectable Continental force, to take post at Wilmington before them. If General Howe thinks the place of that importance to him, which I conceive it to be, he will probably attempt to dispossess us of it; and as the force, which I can at present spare, is not adequate to making it perfectly secure, I expect that you will call out as many militia as you possibly can, to rendezvous without loss of time at

Wilmington, and put themselves 'under the command of General Smallwood. I shall hope that the people will turn out cheerfully, when they consider that they are called upon to remain within and defend their own State.

See this letter in the Appenoiz, No. VHL In a letter, which I had the honor of receiving from you some little time past, you express a wish, that some mode may be fallen upon, to procure the exchange of Governor MKinly. As this gentleman will be considered in the civil line, I have not any prisoner of war proper to be proposed for him. The application would go more properly to Congress, who have a number of State prisoners under their direction, for some of whom, Sir William Howe would, probably, exchange the Governor. I have the honor to be, &c.

TO MAJOR-GENERAL SMALLWOOD. Gulf Mill, 19 December, 1777.

Dear Sir, With the division lately commanded by General Sullivan, you are to march immediately for Wilmington, and take post there. You are not to delay a moment in putting the place in the best posture of defence, to do which, and for the security of it afterwards, I have written in urgent terms to the President of the Delaware State to give every aid he possibly can of militia. I have also directed an engineer to attend you for the purpose of constructing and superintending the works, and you will fix with the quartermaster on the number of tools necessary for the business; but do not let any neglect or deficiency on his part impede your operations, as you are hereby vested with full power to seize and take (passing receipts) such articles as are wanted. The commissary and forage-master will receive directions respecting your supplies in their way; but I earnestly request, that you will see that these supplies are drawn from the country between you and Philadelphia, as it will be depriving the enemy of all chance of getting them, and in this point of view it becomes an object to us of importance.

I earnestly exhort you to keep both officers and men to their duty, and to avoid furloughs except in cases of ab-

solute necessity. You will also use your utmost endeavours to collect all the stragglers from both brigades; and you are also to use your best endeavours to get the men clothed in the most comfortable manner you can. You will be particular in your observation of every thing passing on the river, and will communicate every matter of importance to, dear Sir, your most obedient servant. TO THE PRESIDENT OF CONGRESS.

Head-Quarters, Valley Forge, 22 December, 1777.

Sir,

On Saturday evening I had the honor to receive your favor of the 17th instant, with its enclosures. The next day I wrote to General Burgoyne upon the subject of his application, and transmitted to him a copy of the resolution of Congress founded thereon. That the matter might not be delayed, I despatched my letter by the express, who brought yours, he having informed me, that you expected he would be sent with it.

It is with infinite pain and concern, that I transmit to Congress the enclosed copies of sundry letters respecting the state of the commissary's department. In these, matters are not exaggerated. I do not know from what cause this alarming deficiency, or rather total failure of supplies, arises; but, unless more vigorous exertions and better regulations take place in that line immediately, this army must dissolve. I have done all in my power, by remonstrating, by writing, by ordering the commissaries on this head, from time to time; but without any good effect, or obtaining more than a present scanty relief. Owing to this, the march of the army has been delayed, upon more than one interesting occasion, in the course of the present campaign; and had a body of the enemy crossed the Schuylkill this morning, as I had reason to expect, from the intelligence I received at four o'clock last night, the divisions which I ordered to be in readiness to march and meet them could not have moved. It is unnecessary for me *to* add more upon the subject. I refer Congress to the copies, by one of which they will perceive, how very unfavorable also our prospect is of having any considerable supplies of salt provisions for the ensuing year.

Extracts from two letters, received on the 22d of December, will be enough to show the grounds upon which this statement is made. " I received an order," writes General Huntington, " to hold my brigade in readiness to march. Fighting will be by far preferable to starving. My brigade are out of provisions, nor can the commissary obtain any meat. I am exceedingly unhappy in being the bearer of complaints to Head-Quarters. I have used every argument my imagination can invent to make the soldiers easy, but I despair of being able to do it much longer." The next is from General Varnum. " According to the stying of Solomon, hunger will break through a stone-wall. It is therefore a very pleasing circumstance to the division under my command, that there is a probability of their marching. Three days successively we have been destitute of bread. Two days wo have been entirely without meat. The men must be supplied, or they cannot be commanded. The complaints are too urgent to pass unnoticed. It is with pain, that I mention this distress. I know it will make your Excellency unhappy; VOL. V. 25 Q

I would also take the liberty of reminding Congress of the necessity of filling, as soon as possible, the offices of quartermaster and adjutant general. These posts are of infinite importance, and without appointments to them it will be impossible to conduct the affairs of the army. The first office is now suffering much for want of a head to direct the great business of it; and the latter will be in the same predicament, in the course of a few days, by the departure of Colonel Pickering, who, since his appointment to the Board of War, has been waiting only for a successor.

Three o'clock, P. M. — Just as I was about to conclude my letter, your favor of the 20th came to hand. It would give me infinite pleasure to afford protection to every individual, and to every spot of ground, in the whole of the United States. Nothing is more my wish; but this is not possible with our present force. In all wars, from the nature of things, individuals and particular places must be exposed. It has ever been and ever will be the case, and we have only to pity and to regret the misfortune of those, who from their situation are subject to ravage and depredation. These facts are obvious to all; and if that system of conduct is pursued by an army, which is most likely to give the most extensive security, it is all that can be done or expected from it. but, if you expect the exertion of virtuous principles, while your troops are deprived of the necessaries of life, your final disppointment will be great in proportion to the patience, which now astonishes every man of human feeling." In a letter to Congress, dated October 8th, General Mifflin had tendered the resignation of his commissions of major-general and quartermaster-general, on the ground of ill health. His commission of quartermaster was accepted on the 7th of November, but the rank and commission of major-general, without the pay annexed to the office, was continued to him; and at the same time he was chosen a member of the new Board of War, which was constituted of persons not in Congress. This Board, by its first organization, was to consist of three members. The persons chosen were General Mifflin, Colonel Pickering, and Colonel Harrison. Before it went into operation, the Board was enlarged to five members, and, Harrison having declined the appointment, General Gates, Joseph Trumbull, and Richard Peters were chosen in addition to Mifflin and Pickering. Gates was made president of the Board, and recalled from his command in the northern department to fill that station. The salary of each member was two thousand dollars a year. The Board were intrusted with extensive powers, but they were obliged to ait in the place where Congress was held. All their proceedings were to be inspected by Congress or a committee once a month, and free access to the records was to be allowed at all times to any member of Congress.— *Journals, October 17th; November 7th, 07th.*

I assure you, Sir, no circumstance in the course of the present contest, or in my whole life, has employed more of my reflection or consideration, than in what manner to effect this, and to dispose of the army during the winter. Viewing the subject in any point of light, there was a choice of difficulties. If keeping the field was thought of, — the naked condition of the troops and the feelings of humanity opposed the measure; if returning to the towns in the interior parts of the State, which consistently with the preservation of the troops, from their necessitous circumstances, might have been justifiable, — the measure was found inexpedient, because it would have exposed and left uncovered a large extent of country; if cantoning the troops in several places, divided and distant from each other, — then there was a probability of their being cut off, and but little prospect of their giving security to any part. Under these embarrassments, I determined to take post near this place, as the best calculated in my judgment to secure the army, to protect our stores, and cover the country; and for this purpose we are beginning to hut, and shall endeavour to accomplish it as expeditiously as possible.

I have also, from a desire of preventing the enemy from an intercourse with the Delaware State, and from making incursions there, detached General Small wood with the Maryland forces to take post at Wilmington, which I had strong reason to believe the enemy intended. This however I cannot but consider as hazardous, and shall be happy if it does not turn out so. I have it also in contemplation to throw a bridge over the Schuylkill near this place, as soon as it is practicable; by means of which I hope we shall be able in a great measure, with the aid of the militia, to check the excursions of the enemy's parties on the other side.

As to Jersey, I am sensible of her sufferings and exertions in the present contest, and there is no State to which I would more willingly extend protection; but, as I have observed, it is not in my power to give it, in that degree, which seems to be wished and expected. I cannot divide the army (not superior, when collected, from sickness and other causes equally painful, to the enemy's force,) into detachments, contrary to every military principle, and to our own experience of the dangers that would attend it. If this is done, I cannot be answerable for the consequences. My feelings lead strongly to universal relief, but I have not the power to afford it; nevertheless, it has been and is still my intention, as soon as I have formed and secured this camp, to detach a small force to aid and countenance their militia. This is all, it appears to me, that can be done; and I hope the apprehensions in that quarter for the greater part will prove rather imaginary than well grounded, though I confess there are strong reasons to conclude, that the enemy will not be remiss in their acts of violence and injury there or any where else.

I have the honor to be, &c For particulars respecting the cantonment of the troops at Valley Forge, see Appendix, No. IX.

TO THE PRESIDENT OF CONGRESS.

Valley Forge, 23 December, 1777.

Sir,

Full as I was in my representation of the matters in the commissary's department yesterday, fresh and more powerful reasons oblige me to add, that I am now convinced beyond a doubt, that, unless some great and capital change suddenly takes place in that line, this army must inevitably be reduced to one or other of these three things; starve, dissolve, or disperse in order to obtain subsistence in the best manner they can. Rest assured, Sir, this is not an exaggerated picture, and that I have abundant reason to suppose what I say.

Yesterday afternoon, receiving information that the enemy in force had left the city, and were advancing towards Derby with the apparent design to forage, and draw subsistence from that part of the country, I ordered the troops to be in readiness, that I might give every opposition in my power; when behold, to my great mortification, I was not only informed, but convinced, that the men were unable to stir on account of provision, and that a dangerous mutiny, begun the night before, and which with difficulty was suppressed by the spirited exertions of some officers, was still much to be apprehended for want of this article. This brought forth the only commissary in the purchasing line in this camp; and, with him, this melancholy and alarming truth, that he had not a single hoof of any kind to slaughter, and not more than twenty-five barrels of flour! From hence form an opinion of our situation when I add, that he could not tell when to expect any.

All I could do, under these circumstances, was to send out a few light parties to watch and harass the enemy, whilst other parties were instantly detached different ways to collect, if possible, as much provision as would satisfy the present pressing wants of the soldiery. But will this answer? No, Sir; three or four days of bad weather would prove our destruction. What then is to become of the army this winter? And if we are so often without provisions now, what is to become of us in the spring, when our force will be collected, with the aid perhaps of militia to take advantage of an early campaign, before the enemy can be reinforced? These are considerations of great magnitude, meriting the closest attention; and they will, when my own reputation is so intimately connected with the event and to be affected by it, justify my saying, that the present commissaries are by no means equal to the execution of the office, or that the disaffection of the people is past all belief. The misfortune, however, does in my opinion proceed from both causes; and, though I have been tender heretofore of giving any opinion, or lodging complaints, as the change in that department took place contrary to my judgment, and the consequences thereof were predicted; yet, finding that the inactivity of the army, whether for want of provisions, clothes, or other essentials, is charged to my account, not only by the common vulgar but by those in power, it is time to speak plain in exculpation of myself. With truth, then, I can declare, that no man in my opinion ever had his measures more impeded than I have, by every department of the army.

Since the month of July we have had no assistance from the quartermaster-general, and to want of assistance from this department the commissary-general charges great part of his deficiency. To this I am to add, that, notwithstanding it is a standing order, and often repeated, that the troops shall always have two days' provisions by them, that they might be ready at any sudden call; yet an opportunity has scarcely ever offered, of taking an advantage of the enemy, that has not been either totally obstructed, or greatly impeded, on this account. And this, the great and crying evil, is not all. The soap, vinegar, and other articles allowed by Congress, we see none of, nor have we seen them, I believe, since the battle of Brandywine. The first, indeed, we have now little occasion for; few men having more than one shirt, many only the moiety of one, and some none at all. In addition to which, as a proof of the little benefit received from a clothiergeneral, and as a further proof of the inability of an army, under the circumstances of this, to perform the common duties of soldiers, (besides a number of men confined to hospitals for want of shoes, and others in farmers' houses on the same account,) we have, by a field-return this day made, no less than two thousand eight hundred and ninety-eight men now in camp unfit for duty, because they are barefoot and otherwise naked. By the same return it appears, that our whole strength in Continental troops, including the eastern brigades, which have joined us since the surrender of General Burgoyne, exclusive of the Maryland troops sent to Wilmington, amounts to no more than eight thousand two hundred in camp fit for duty; notwithstanding which, and that since the 4th instant, our numbers fit for duty, from the hardships and exposures they have undergone, particularly on account of blankets (numbers having been obliged, and still are, to sit up all night by fires, instead of taking comfortable rest in a natural and common way), have decreased near two thousand men.

We find gentlemen, without knowing

whether the army was really going into winter-quarters or not (for I am sure no resolution of mine would warrant the Remonstrance), reprobating the measure as much as if they thought the soldiers were made of stocks or stones, and equally insensible of frost and snow; and moreover, as if they conceived it easily practicable for an inferior army, under the disadvantages I have described ours to be, which are by no means exaggerated, to confine a superior one, in all respects well-appointed and provided for a winter's campaign, within the city of Philadelphia, and.to cover from depredation and waste the States of Pennsylvania and Jersey. But what makes this matter still more extraordinary in my eye is, that these very gentlemen,—who were well apprized of the nakedness of the troops from ocular demonstration, who thought their own soldiers worse clad than others, and who advised me near a month ago to postpone the execution of a plan I was about to adopt, in consequence of a resolve of Congress for seizing clothes, under strong assurances that an ample supply would be collected in ten days agreeably to a decree of the State (not one article of which, by the by, is yet come to hand), — should think a winter's campaign, and the covering of these States from the invasion of an enemy, so easy and practicable a business. I can assure those gentlemen, that it is a much easier and less distressing thing to draw remonstrances in a comfortable room by a good fireside, than to occupy a cold, bleak hill, and sleep under frost and snow, without clothes or blankets. However, although they seem to have little feeling for the naked and distressed soldiers, I feel superabundantly for them, and, from my soul, I pity those miseries, which it is neither in my power to relieve or prevent.

Alluding to the Memorial, or Remonstrance, of the legislature of Pennsylvania, respecting his going into winter-quarters.

It is for these reasons, therefore, that I have dwelt upon the subject; and it adds not a little to my other difficulties and distress to find, that much more is expected of me than is possible to be performed, and that upon the ground of safety and policy I am obliged to conceal the true state of the army from public view, and thereby expose myself to detraction and calumny. The honorable committee of Congress went from camp fully possessed of my sentiments respecting the establishment of this army, the necessity of auditors of accounts, the appointment of officers, and new arrangements. I have no need, therefore, to be prolix upon these subjects, but I refer to the committee. I shall add a word or two to show, first, the necessity of some better provision for binding the officers by the tie of interest to the service, as no day nor scarce an hour passes without the offer of a resigned commission; (otherwise I much doubt the practicability of holding the army together much longer, and in this I shall probably be thought the more sincere, when I freely declare, that I do not myself expect to derive the smallest benefit from any establishment that Congress may adopt, otherwise than as a member of the community at large in the good, which I am persuaded will result from the measure, by making better officers and better troops;) and, secondly, to point out the necessity of making the appointments and arrangements without loss of time. We have not more than three months, in which to prepare a great deal of business. If we let these slip or waste, we shall be laboring under the same difficulties all next campaign, as we have been this, to rectify mistakes and bring things to order.

Military arrangement, and movements in consequence, like the mechanism of a clock, will be imperfect and disordered by the want of a part. In a very

Vol. v. 26 sensible degree have I experienced this, in the course of the last summer, several brigades having no brigadiers appointed to them till late, and some not at all; by which means it follows, that an additional weight is thrown upon the shoulders of the Commander-in-chief, to withdraw his attention from the great line of his duty. The gentlemen of the committee, when they were at camp, talked of an expedient for adjusting these matters, which I highly approved and wish to see adopted; namely, that two or three members of the Board of War, or a committee of Congress, should repair immediately to camp, where the best aid can be had, and with the commanding officer, or a committee of his appointment, prepare and digest the most perfect plan, that can be devised, for correcting all abuses and making new arrangements; considering what is to be done with the weak and debilitated regiments, if the States to which they belong will not draft men to fill them, for as to enlisting soldiers it seems to me to be totally out of the question; together with many other things, that would occur in the course of such a conference; and, after digesting matters in the best manner they can, to submit the whole to the ultimate determination of Congress.

If this measure is approved, I would earnestly advise the immediate execution of it, and that the commissary general of purchases, whom I rarely see, may be directed to form magazines without a moment's delay in the neighbourhood of this camp, in order to secure provision for us in case of bad weather. The quartermaster-general ought also to be busy in his department In short, there is as much to be done in preparing for a campaign, as in the active part of it. Every thing depends upon the preparation that is made in the several departments, and the success or misfortunes of the next campaign will more than probably originate with our activity or supineness during this winter.

I have the honor to be, &c.

TO MAJOR-GENERAL CONWAY.

Head-Quarters, 30 December, 1777.

Sir,

I am favored with your letter of yesterday, in which you propose, in order to lose no time, to begin with the instruction of the troops. You will observe, by the resolution of Congress relative to your appointment, that the Board of War is to furnish a set of instructions, according to which the troops are to be manoeuvred. As you have made no mention of having received them, I suppose they are not come to you; when they do, I shall issue any orders which may be judged necessary to have them carried into immediate execution.

Conway had just been appointed by Congress inspector-general to the army, and promoted to the rank of major-general. He wrote to General Washington, respecting the mode of discharging his new duties, and added in regard to his late appointments; — "I accepted the office of inspector-general with the view of being instrumental to the welfare of the cause, and to the glory of the Commander-in-chief, in making his troops fit to execute his orders. The rank of major-general, which was given me, is absolutely requisite for this office, in order to be vested with proper authority to superintend the instruction and the internal administration. There is no inspector in the European armies under a major-general. However, Sir, if my appointment is productive of any inconvenience, or anywise disagreeable to your Excellency, as I neither applied nor solicited for this place, I am very ready to return to France, where I have pressing business; and this I will do with the more satisfaction, as I expect even there to be useful to the cause."—*MS. Letter, December 29tt*. It is remarkable that he should assert, as he does here, that he never applied for the appointment of major-general, when there are letters of an anterior date from him to Congress, in which he not only applies, but insists, with a forwardness almost amounting to impudence, that the rank ought to be bestowed on him, and uses a series of arguments to sustain his application.

Your appointment of inspector-general to the army, I believe, has not given the least uneasiness to any officer in it. By consulting your own feelings upon the appointment of the Baron de Kalb, you may judge what must be the sensation of those brigadiers, who by your promotion are superseded. I am told they are determined to remonstrate against it. For my own part I have nothing to do in the appointment of general officers, and

shall always afford every countenance and due respect to those appointed by Congress, taking it for granted, that, prior to any resolve of that nature, they take a dispassionate view of the merits of the officer to be promoted, and consider every consequence that can result from such a procedure; nor have I any other wish on that head, but that good, attentive officers may be chosen, and no extraordinary promotion take place, but where the merit of the officer is so generally acknowledged, as to obviate every reasonable cause for dissatisfaction thereat, f I am, Sir, &c.

When the Baron de Kalb received an appointment in the army, Conway sent a remonstrance to Congress, which begins as follows; — " It is with infinite concern, that I find myself slighted and forgot, when you have offered rank to persons, who cost you a great deal of money, and have never rendered you the least service. Baron de Kalb, to whom you have offered the rank of major-general, is my inferior in France." And then he proceeds to utter his complaints and objections, and to demand for himself the rank of major-general. f Conway's reply to this last clause of the letter is sufficiently indie live of his duplicity and vanity. — "What you are pleased to call aa extraordinary promotion," he says, " is a very plain one. There is nothing extraordinary in it, only that such a place was not thought of sooner The general and universal merit, which you wish every promoted officer might be endowed with, is a rare gift We see but few of merit so generally acknowledged. We know but the great Frederic in Europe, and the great Washington on this continent. I certainly never was so rash as to pretend to such a prodigious height. Neither do I pretend to any superiority in personal qualities over my brother brigadiers, for whom I have much regard. But you, Sir, and the great Frederic, know perfectly well, that this trade is not learnt in a few months. I have served steadily thirty years; that is, before some of my comrade brigadiers were born. Therefore I do not think that it will be found marvellous and incredible, if I command here a number of

men, which falls much short of what I have commanded there many years in an old army. TO GOVERNOR COOKE.
Valley Forge, 31 December, 1777.

Sir,

By Lieutenant-Colonel Barton, I was honored with your favor of the 5th ultimo, with its enclosures. The spirit and disposition of this gentleman for enterprise, and of the officers concerned with him, in capturing General Prescott, give them a high claim to the thanks and esteem of their country. Congress, persuaded of this, promoted Mr. Barton on the 24th instant to the rank and pay of a colonel in the service of the States, and recommended him to me for employment. To their and your recommendations I would willingly pay the utmost attention. But at present it is impossible for me to introduce Colonel Barton into the army, without injuring others and creating disgust, there being now a full and indeed over proportion of officers, of which he is convinced.

Under these circumstances I would take the liberty to mention, that, if your State should raise and continue troops for their own defence, his past merit and that of the other officers afford favorable grounds to hope, if they should be in command, that their services would be attended with no small benefits. I am, &c.

However, Sir, by the complexion of your letter, and by the two receptions you have honored mo with since my arrival, I perceive that I have not the happiness of being agreeable to your Excellency, and that I can expect no support in fulfilling the laborious duty of an inspectorgeneral. I do not mean to give you or any officer in the army the least uneasiness. Therefore I am very ready to return to France, and to thn army where I hope I shall meet with no frowns. I beg leave to wish your Excellency a happy new year and a glorious campaign."—*MS. Letter, December 31st.* VOL. V. R TO GOVERNOR LIVINGSTON.

Head-Quarters, Valley Forge, 31 December, 1777.

Sir,

It being of great importance to prevent the enemy from supplies of forage and provisions, I must take the liberty of requesting the interposition of your interest and authority for this purpose, and that the most speedy and suitable measures may be adopted and pursued, either by your direction, or that of the legislature or council, for the removal of all that lies in the vicinity of the Jersey shore, opposite to Philadelphia, or that may be within the reach of the enemy's foraging parties, excepting such as may be really essential for the inhabitants' use. They should be removed so far back from the water, that they will not be in danger of falling into the enemy's hands. I am not without power and directions from Congress to act myself in such instances. But I would wish the business to be done by civil authority, as their acts will create less jealousy and disgust, and be viewed in a much more unexceptionable light.

In a few days all our light-horse, excepting a few that will remain to do duty, will be sent to Trenton, to winter and recruit, it being a place under all circumstances the best adapted to that end. Besides recruiting, they will serve to protect the country from incursions by small parties of the enemy, and will give security to our stores and magazines. In addition to these, when we have secured and fortified our camp, if circumstances will possibly admit, I will send a few more troops. But I cannot promise that they will be many, the army being now much reduced, by the expiration of the service of several regiments, and from other causes equally distressing.

I sincerely feel for the unhappy condition of our poor fellows in the hospitals, and wish my powers to relieve them were equal to my inclination. It is but too melancholy a truth, that our hospital stores are exceedingly scanty and deficient in every instance, and I fear there is no prospect of their shortly being better. Our difficulties and distresses are certainly great, and such as wound the feelings of humanity. Our sick naked, and well naked, our unfortunate men in captivity naked! You were certainly right in representing the state of the sick, that they may be made more happy if possible. I have ordered a field-officer to be always in future at the hospitals, and hope that he will contribute all in his power to accommodate them, and prevent some of the inconveniences, which you mention, and which are of great moment. As to the directors, if they do not afford every aid in their power, their conduct is highly culpable, and deserves the severest reprehension. I assure you, Sir, I shall ever consider myself much obliged by your information of any grievances or abuses respecting the army, and shall never suppose that you step out of your proper line in giving it. We are all equally engaged in the present important struggle, and in the cause of humanity, and are equally concerned in pro moting them. I have the honor to be, &c.

TO THE PRESIDENT OF CONGRESS. Valley Forge, 2 January, 1778.

Sir,

I take the liberty of transmitting to you the enclosed copies of a letter from me to General Conway, since his return from York to camp, and of two letters from him to me, which you will be pleased to lay before Congress. I shall not in this letter animadvert upon them; but after making a single observation, submit the whole to Congress.

If General Conway means, by cool receptions, mentioned in the last paragraph of his letter of the 31st ultimo, that I did not receive him in the language of a warm and cordial friend, I readily confess the charge. I did not, nor shall I ever, till I am capable of the arts of dissimulation. These I despise, and my feelings will not permit me to make professions of friendship to the man I deem my enemy, and whose system of conduct forbids it. At the same time, truth authorizes me to say, that he was received and treated with proper respect to his official character, and that he has had no cause to justify the assertion, that he could not expect any support for fulfilling the duties of his appointment.

I have the honor to be, &,c

P. S. The enclosed extract from the proceedings of a council of general officers will show, that the office of inspector-general was a matter not of such modern date, as General Conway mentions it to be, and that it was one of the regulations in view for the reform of the army. The foreign officers, who had commissions and no commands, and who were of ability, were intended to be recommended to execute it; particularly the Baron d'Arendt, with whom the idea originated, and whose capacity seemed to be well admitted.

TO THE PRESIDENT OF CONGRESS. Valley Forge, 5 January, 1778.

Sir, I yesterday evening had the honor of your favor of the 1st instant, with its several enclosures. The letter you allude to, from the Committee of Congress and Board of War, came to hand on Saturday morning; but it does not mention the regulations adopted for removing the difficulties and failures in the commissary line. I trust they will be vigorous, or the army cannot exist. It will never answer to procure supplies of clothing or provision by coercive measures. The Bmall seizures made of the former a few days ago, in consequence of the most pressing and absolute necessity, when that, or to dissolve, was the alternative, excited the greatest alarm and uneasiness even among our best and warmest friends. Such procedures may give a momentary relief; but, if repeated, will prove of the most pernicious consequence. Besides spreading disaffection, jealousy, and fear among the people, they never fail, even in the most veteran troops under the most rigid and exact discipline, to raise in the soldiery a disposition to licentiousness, to plunder and robbery, difficult to suppress afterwards, and which has proved not only ruinous to the inhabitants, but, in many instances, to armies themselves. I regret the occasion that compelled us to the measure the other day; and shall consider it among the greatest of our misfortunes, if we should be under the necessity of practising it again.

I had received from the Board of War a copy of the resolutions of the 29 th ultimo, and published such parts in orders as were directed. I shall endeavour, as far as possible, to carry the intention of

Congress into execution, respecting the extra pay, and to prevent any from receiving it, who do not come under their description. The three packets with commissions came safe to hand. I have the honor to be, &c.

As soon as it was determined, that the army would go into winterquarters at Valley Forge, Congress directed General Washington to inform the officers and soldiers, that, in consequence of " their soldierly VOL. V. 27 R TO COLONEL SAMUEL B. WEBB.

Valley Forge, 8 January, 1778.

Sir,

I was this evening favored with your letter of the 29 th ultimo. I had heard before of your unfortunate expedition and captivity, and not without concern. It would give me pleasure to render you any services in my power; but it is impossible for me to comply with your request, without violating the principles of justice, and incurring a charge of partiality. You are sensible, that we have several officers now in-captivity with the enemy, of your rank and of Lieutenant-Colonel Campbell's rank, who have been in this unhappy situation much longer than you; some taken when General Thompson was defeated at the Three Rivers, early in 1776; others at Long Island in August following; others at Fort Washington; and a further number at the battle of Germantown. These gentlemen would surely exclaim loudly against my conduct, and with reason, were any distinctions to be made by concurrence or authority to their prejudice. So far as exchanges have depended on me, or as they rest with me, they have been and ever will be conducted on one principle, namely, to release those first, who were first captured, as far as circumstances of rank will apply. There is no other rule by which equal and impartial justice can be done.

I know there have been some exchanges contrary to this rule, but they were not made with my privity, consent, or approbation. In a word, you may rest assured, whenever circumstances will put it in my power to effect your exchange, and that of all the officers and privates, under the restrictions I have mentioned, there shall not be a moment's delay on my part; but on other terms, or in a different order, you will find on reflection I can never do it. Suppose yourself for an instant an officer taken at any of the above periods, you would consider it an injury, a wrong, an act of high injustice done you, if one captured on the 10th of December last, of your rank, was exchanged before you. Perhaps on your return, you may have interest enough with your acquaintances to obtain your release on parole, but you cannot do this on a principle of having an officer sent in on the like indulgence; the objections to an enlargement on parole out of due course in such case being the same, as to an exchange. I am, dear Sir, your most obedient servant.

patience, fidelity, and zeal in the cause of their country," one month's pay extraordinary would be given to each. — *Journals, December 30th.* After the troops had marched from Fishkill to join General Washington, according to his directions, General Putnam moved down, with a part of the forces that remained, on the east side of the Hudson. When General Dickinson made his descent upon Staten Island, Putnam ordered Parsons's and Warner's brigades to march towards Kingsbridge, with the view of making a diversion in that quarter. Putnam reconnoitred in person within three miles of Kingsbridge. But, there being no opportunity for acting with effect at that point, he diverged to New Rochelle, where he made a disposition to cross over to Long Island, and attack the forts at Huntington and Satauket. The enemy probably got intelligence of this design, for the forts were evacuated before the preparations were fully completed.

General Putnam remained near the Sound till the middle of December, when, in consequence of orders from the Commander-in-chief, he returned with his troops to the Highlands. But in the mean time an enterprise, in part unsuccessful, had been entrusted to the separate command of General Parsons and Colonel Webb. The object was a descent upon Long Island, with the intention to destroy the timber and boards prepared at the east end of the Island for barracks in New York; to destroy the shipping then at that place, from Newport, for wood; to attack a regiment stationed about eight miles eastward of Jamaica; and to remove or destroy whatever public stores should be found on the Island.

By the plan of operations Colonel Meigs was to land at Hempstead harbour, and attack the regiment near Jamaica; Colonel Webb was to land near Huntington to sustain Meigs, and afford such aid to the eastern division as should be wanted; and General Parsons was to command this division. Meigs was to cross from the Saw-pits; but, when the time arrived, the winds and waves were Bo boisterous, that he could not proceed. The other two divisions sailed from Norwalk on the evening of the 9th of December with fair prospects; but unfortunately Colonel Webb the next morning fell in with the British sloop of war, Falcon, and was forced on shore with his party so far from the beach, that they were all taken prisoners. When the boat was put out, the surf ran so high, that it immediately filled and sunk, and there were no means of escape. Parsons landed safely, took and destroyed a sloop loaded with timber, and also a great quantity of boards and wood. Captain Hart, of this party, with about forty men, attacked several boats near the shore, killed eight and wounded eleven, among whom was the captain of a sloop of war. General Parsons returned with all his men, and twenty of the enemy prisoners. The persons taken with Colonel Webb were four officers and twenty privates of his Continental regiment, and forty militia. — *MS. Letters of Putnam, Parsons, and Webb, December 16th,* 29tt.

TO THE PRESIDENT OF CONGRESS.

Valley Forge, 9 January, 1778.

Sir,

The power Congress have been pleased to vest me with, for appointing aids-de-camp, I shall use with economy, and I will not appoint more at any time than shall be necessary and essential to advance the public interest. Any future appointments, that may be material, will be made out of the line of the army, if circumstances will allow it. In general this has been the case. The proceedings of Congress for the detention of General Burgoyne and his army, or rather suspending their embarkation, till the convention of Saratoga is explicitly ratified and notified by the court of Britain, shall remain secret here till they are duly announced by Congress. This procedure, when known to the General, will chagrin him much; for I learn by a letter from General Heath, that the refusal to let his troops embark at Rhode Island, or in the Sound, had given him some uneasiness. I have nothing of importance to communicate; and have only to add, that I have the honor to be, with great respect, &c.

Hitherto the Commander-in-chief had been allowed three aids-decamp. He was now authorized to appoint as many as he should think proper. In cases where much service was required, it bad been hk custom to appoint extra aids, but no more than three could be entitled to pay and rank.

In compliance with the strong representations of the Commander-inchief, the Congress were at this time deliberating on the means of correcting abuses in the army, particularly in the departments for supplying provision and clothing. From the imperfect organization of these departments, or from bod management in administering them, great sufferings had been experienced by the soldiers during the preceding campaign. On the 10th of January, it was decided by Congress, that a committee should be sent to the camp, empowered to consult with General Washington, and, in conjunction with him, to mature a new system of arrangements for the administration of the army. The committee were invested with ample powers for effecting all the desirable objects of reform; or rather for digesting and reporting a plan of the same to Congress. The persons chosen were Dana, Reed, and Folsom in Congress; and Gates, Mifflin, and Pickering from the Board of War. When it was found, that these latter gentlemen were fully occupied by their official duties, they were excused, and two members of Congress, Charles Carroll and Gouverneur Morris, in addition to the above three, were chosen in their place. The committee therefore consisted of five members of Congress, who repaired immediately to Valley Forge. General Washington communicated to them a memoir, extending to fifty folio pages, exhibiting in detail the existing state of the army, the deficiencies and disorders, with their causes, and suggesting snch changes and improvements as he thought essential. This formed the basis of the plan adopted by the committee, who, after remaining in camp nearly three months, returned to Congress. The report, containing the result of their proceedings and the new scheme of the army, was approved.— *Journals, January 10th, 12th, 20th.* TO BARON STETXBEN.

Head-Quarters, Valley Forge, 9 January, 1778.

Sir,

I yesterday received the honor of yours from Portsmouth, enclosing the copy of a letter from Messrs. Franklin and Deane, the original of which I shall be glad to receive from your own hands, as soon as convenient for you to undertake the journey. As it will lie solely with Congress to make a suitable provision for you in the American army, you will be under the necessity of prolonging your journey, in order to lay before them at Yorktown the honorable testimonials, which you bear of your former services. I return you my thanks for the polite manner in which you express your desire of serving under me, and have the honor to be, Sir, your most obedient servant.

TO THE PRESIDENT OF CONGRESS.

Head-Quarters, 13 January, 1778.

Sir,

This will be delivered to you by the Chevalier de Mauduit Duplessis, who was among the first French officers, that joined the army of the United States. The gallant conduct of this young gentleman at Brandywine and Germantown, and his distinguished services at Fort Mercer, where he united the offices of engineer and commandant of artillery, entitle him to the particular notice of Congress. He made several judicious alterations in the works at Red Bank, showed great good conduct during the action in which the Hessians were repulsed, and was spoken of, in consequence, in terms of the highest applause, by the commanding officer of the post. After the evacuation was determined upon, he became the means of saving some valuable artillery and stores, and cheerfully undertook, as volunteer, the hazardous operation of blowing up the magazine, without the apparatus usually provided upon such occasions. I must further add in Monsieur Duplessis's favor, that he possesses a degree of modesty not always found in men, who have performed brilliant actions. It is with pleasure, therefore, that I recommend it to Congress to grant him a brevet of lieutenantcolonel; a reward due to his merit, and which will not have the inconvenience of occasioning any dissatisfaction in the corps to which he belongs.

See copies of the testimonials, and other particulars respecting *hr* Baron Steuben, in the Appendix, No. X.

As some particular circumstances have prevented Monsieur Duplessis from waiting upon Congress sooner, I hope there will be no difficulty in antedating the brevet, so that the recompense may more immediately follow the services, which he has done. At the same time, that there may not be any uneasiness on the part of Monsieur Fleury, whom Congress have been pleased to reward in the same way, and as their times of service are nearly equal in France, I would propose that Monsieur Duplessis's brevet should bear the same date, namely, the 26th of November. I have the honor, &,c TO MAJOR-GENERAL ARNOLD, f

Head-Quarters, Valley Forge, 20 January, 1778.

Dear Sir, Enclosed you will receive a commission, by which you will find, that you are restored to the rank you claim in the line of the army. This I transmit by direction of Congress, and in pursuance of their resolution of the

29th of November. The situation of my papers and the want of blank commissions prevented my doing it before. May I venture to ask whether you are upon your legs again, and, if you are not, may I flatter myself that you will be soon? There is none, who wishes more sincerely for this event, than I do, or who will receive the information with more pleasure. I shall expect a favorable account upon the subject; and as soon as your situation will permit, I request that you will repair to this army, it being my earnest wish to have your services the ensuing campaign. In hopes of this, I have set you down in an arrangement now under consideration, and for a command, which I trust will be agreeable to yourself, and of great advantage to the public.

CoDgress complied in every particular with the request contained in this letter. — *Journals, January 17th.* f General Arnold and General Lincoln were at this time in Albany, not having yet sufficiently recovered from their wounds to be removed from that place.

I have nothing of importance to inform you of in the military line, that is new or interesting. The enemy still remain in possession of Philadelphia, and have secured themselves by a strong chain of redoubts, with intrenchments of communication from the Schuylkill to the Delaware. We, on our part, have taken a post on the west side of the former about twenty miles from the city, and with much pains and industry have got the troops tolerably well covered in huts. We have to regret that we are not in more comfortable quarters, but these could not be found, unless we had retired to the towns in the more interior part of the State; the consequence of which would have been distress to the virtuous citizens of Philadelphia, who had fled thither for protection, and the exposure of a considerable tract of fertile country to ravage and rum.

I am, dear Sir, with great esteem and regard, &c TO MAJOR-GENERAL LINCOLN.

Head-Quarters, Valley Forge, 20 January, 1778.

My Dear Sir,

By the enclosed copies of two resolutions of Congress, you will perceive that they have restored General Arnold to the rank he claims in the line of general officers, and have directed me to grant him a commission for that purpose. This I have done, and he will receive it by the conveyance by which this goes.

From your peculiar situation, and being one of the officers within the operation of the resolves, I have been induced to communicate the matter to you. I am too sensible, my dear Sir, of your disposition to justice and generosity, of your wishes to see every man in the possession of his rightful claim, not to be convinced, that you will cheerfully acquiesce in a measure calculated for that end. In this instance General Arnold is restored to a violated right, and the restitution I hope will be considered by every gentleman concerned, as I am sure it will by you, as an act of necessary justice.

May I hope that you are recovered from your wound, and if you are not, that you will be soon? There is none, who wishes more sincerely for this event, than I do, or who will receive the information with more pleasure. I request that you will write to me upon the subject, and let your account be favorable and pleasing. As soon as your situation will permit, I shall be happy to see you, it being my earnest wish to have your services the ensuing campaign. In hope of this, I have set you down in an arrangement now under consideration. I am, Sir, &c.

TO SIR WILLIAM HOWE.

Head-Quarters, 20 January, 1778.

Sir,

Tour letter of the 8th instant, enclosing Lieutenant Eyre's representation, was duly received. I am not at liberty to contradict the facts, which he has related; but I am inclined to think, from his own statement, that his conduct has not been so discreet, as it should have been; and that, if he experienced a severer treatment, than had been usually imposed upon officers, prisoners with us, h proceeded in some measure at least from that cause. But were not this the case, if the insults and incivilities,

which Mr. Eyre complains of having suffered, were ever so unprovoked by him, though I wish not to justify them, yet I cannot forbear observing, that they are not to be wondered at, since the accounts generally received of the treatment of our officers in your hands are replete with instances of the most flagrant indignities, and even cruelties.

Americans have the feelings of sympathy, as well as other men. A series of injuries may exhaust their patience, and it is natural, that the sufferings of their friends in captivity should at length irritate them into resentment, and to acts of retaliation. If you suppose Mr. Eyre's representation to be just, and that he escaped from a rigorous confinement, under no obligation of parole, I cannot conceive upon what principle you still consider him my prisoner. But, if you are of a different opinion, I shall expect some gentleman of ours in your possession, who was taken in a similar character, in return for him. He was reported to me, at the time of his capture, as a volunteer, in which light I still view him. The officer you mention did not attend the flag of truce with my knowledge or consent. His conduct was reprehensible, and I hope an instance of this sort will not happen again.

Mr. James Bayard was taken prisoner near the Swedes' Ford, the day your army crossed the Schuylkill. He had just returned from college, and had no rank in or connexion with the army. He is not to be considered as a prisoner of war, but as a citizen, and as such his friends will propose an exchange for him.

I am, Sir, &c.

TO GOVERNOR LIVINGSTON.

Valley Forge, 20 January, 177&

Sir,

I last night received a letter from Colonel' Dayton, informing me, that John and Baker Hendricks and John Meeker had been apprehended upon a supposition of their carrying on an illegal correspondence with the enemy, as they had been several times upon Staten Island, and that they were to be tried for their lives in consequence.

In justice to these men, I am bound to take this earliest opportunity of informing you, that they were employed by Colonel Dayton last summer to procure intelligence of the movements of the enemy, while upon Staten Island, for which purpose I granted them passports, allowing them to carry small quantities of provisions, and to bring back a few goods, the better to cover their real designs. Colonel Dayton informs me, that they executed their trust faithfully. This I very well remember, that what intelligence he communiated to me, and which, he says, came principally through them, was generally confirmed by the event. Upon these considerations, I hope you will put a stop to the prosecution, unless other matters appear against them. You must be well convinced, that it is indispensably necessary to make use of such means to procure intelligence. The persons employed must bear the suspicion of being thought inimical; and it is not in their power to assert their innocence, because that would get abroad and destroy the confidence which the enemy puts in them. I have the honor to be, &c.

TO CAPTAIN HENRY LEE.

Valley Forge, 21 January, 1778.

My Dear Lee, Although I have given you my thanks in the general orders of this day, for the rate instance of your gallant behaviour, I cannot resist the inclination I feel to repeat them again in this manner. I needed no fresh proofs of your merit, to bear you in remembrance. I waited only for the proper time and season to show it; those, I hope, are not far off. I shall also think of and woi reward the merit of Lindsay, when an opening presents, as far as I can consistently; and I shall not forget the corporal, whom you have recommended to my notice. Offer my sincere thanks to the whole of your gallant party, and assure them, that no one felt pleasure more sensibly, or rejoiced more sincerely for your and their escape, than your affectionate, &c

" /Vow *Captain Lee's Letters*. —" I am to inform your Excellency of an action, which happened this morning, between a party of the enemy's dragoons and my troop of horse. They were near two hundred in number, and by a very circuitous route endeavoured to surprise me in quarters. About daybreak they appeared. We were immediately alarmed, and manned the doors and windows. The contest was very warm; the British dragoons trusting to their vast superiority in number, attempted to force their way into the house. In this they were baffled by the TO MAJOR-GENERAL HEATH.

Head-Quarters, Valley Forge, 22 January, 1778.

Dear Sir,

You will, I suppose, before this time have received orders from Congress, respecting the delaying of the embarkation of General Burgoyne and his army till the convention is ratified in Great Britain. By this step General Burgoyne will, it is more than probable, look upon himself as released from all former ties, and consequently at liberty to make use of any means to effect an escape. I would therefore have you increase the vigilance, and, if necessary, the strength of your guards. All magazines of arms should be removed from Boston and the neighbourhood; for if any attempt is made, it must be by first seizing upon arms to force their way.

I cannot think with you, that the operations of the next campaign will be against New England, unless the enemy are much more strongly reinforced, than I think they have any chance of being. They know the unanimity and spirit of the people too well to attempt it by detachment; and should they send a considerable body from Philadelphia, they must either remain besieged in the town, which would be ignominious, or risk a defeat should they come into the field with inconsiderable numbers. The troops, who went back from Philadelphia to New York, were I believe only intended for the security of that city. The garrison was so small, after the reinforcements had been sent to General Howe, that the inhabitants complained much of their being abandoned, and the troops were returned to quiet them. This being merely matter of opinion, it should not relax your endeavours to perfect the necessary defences of the harbour, and to fix upon signals which may at all times alarm the country upon any sudden invasion. I am, &c.

bravery of my men. After having left two killed and four wounded, they desisted and sheered off. We are trying to intercept them. Colonel Stevens has pushed a party of infantry to reach their rear. So well directed was the opposition, that we drove them from the stables and saved every horse. We have got the arms, some cloaks, &c. of their wounded. The only damage I at present know of, is a slight wound received by Lieutenant Lindsay. I am apprehensive about the patroles. The enterprise was certainly daring, though the issue of it very ignominious. I had not a soldier for each window." — *January 20th.*

Again; " We have at length ascertained the real loss of this day. Four privates, belonging to the patrole at the square, were taken, I am told they made a brave resistance. The quartermaster-sergeant, who imprudently ran from our quarters prior to the commencement of the skirmish, was also taken. The loss sustained stands thus; one sergeant and four privates taken; one lieutenant and two privates wounded. By what I can learn from the people of Derby, the enemy's loss is as follows; three privates dead; one commissioned officer, one sergeant, and three privates wounded."

TO COLONEL WALTER STEWART.

Head-Quarters, 22 January, 1778.

Dear Sir, I have been favored with yours of the 1sth. I should have answered it by the return of your officer, but he omitted to call upon me. I spoke to Mr. Blaine, commissary of purchases, respecting the insufficiency of his deputies. He promised to go over himself or send a proper person to assist you and to keep them to their duty. I am amazed at the report you make of the quantity of provision that goes daily into Philadelphia from the county of Bucks. I must beg you to look into the matter, and endeavour to find out whether it proceeds from the remissness of our guards, or whether any of our officers connive at it. This latter has been hinted to me.

I am told that General Lacey, who succeeds General Potter, is an active officer, and well acquainted with all the roads of that country. If any particular mode of cutting off this pernicious intercourse strikes you, be pleased to communicate it to him. The property taken, with the horses and carriages that transport it, should be seized without distinction; and if any of the persons are proper objects to make examples of, it must be done. They have had sufficient warnings, and cannot therefore plead ignorance in excuse of their crime.

I am, dear Sir, &.c TO MAJOR-GENERAL PUTNAM.

Valley Forge, 25 January, 1778.

Dear Sir, I begin to be very apprehensive that the season will entirely pass away, before any thing material will be done for the defence of Hudson's River. You are well acquainted with the great necessity there is for having the works there finished, as soon as possible; and I most earnestly desire, that the strictest attention may A brig had been taken in the Delaware by a party of troops belonging to the detachment under General Smallwood at Wilmington. The following request, sent by General Washington to General Smallwood, is characteristic of his liberality and enlargement of mind.

" A few days ago I received a very polite letter from Doctor Boyes, surgeon of the fifteenth regiment, British, requesting me to return him, some valuable medical manuscripts, taken in the brig Symmetry. He says they are packed in a neat kind of portable library, and consist of Doctor Cullen's Lectures on the Practice of Medicine, thirty-nine or forty volumes; Cullen's Lectures on the Institutions of Medicine, eighteen volumes; Anatomical Lectures, eight volumes; and Doctor Black on Chemistry, nine volumes; the whole in octavo. If they can be found, I beg that they may be sent up to me, that I may return them to the Doctor. I have no other view in doing this, than that of showing our enemies that we do not war against the sciences." be paid to every matter, which may contribute to finishing and putting them in a respectable state before the spring.

I wish you had not waited for returns of the militia to furnish me with a state of the troops in that quarter; and, if you do not get them in before you receive this, you will please to let me have an accurate return of the Continental troops alone, it being absolutely necessary that I should know the strength of your command as soon as possible. I congratulate you on the success of your two little parties against the enemy, which I dare say will prevent their making so extensive excursions for some time at least. One circumstance however I cannot avoid taking notice of, that our officers, who have been but a very short time in the enemy's hands, reap the advantages of any captures which happen to be made by us. This must not be practised in future, as it is the height of injustice, and will, if continued, draw upon us the censures of the officers, who have been for a long dme suffering all the rigors of a severe capdvity. The proper mode of proceeding is, to de liver them into the hands of the commissary of pris oners, who must be best acquainted with the propriety of complying with the claims of our officers in their hands. I shall represent your situation, in the money way, to the paymaster-general, and order such measures to be taken as may relieve you. I am, Sir, &,c.

The forts and other works in the Highlands were entirely demolished by the British, and it now became a question of some importance, whether they should be restored in their former positions, or new places should be selected for that purpose. About the beginning of January the grounds were examined by General Putnam, Governor Clinton, General James Clinton, and several other gentlemen, among whom was Radiere, the French engineer; and they were all, except Radiere, united in the opinion, that West Point was the most eligible place to be fortified. Radiere opposed this decision with considerable vehemence, and drew up a memorial designed to show, that the site of Fort Clinton poseemed advantages much superior to West Point. As the engineer was a man of science, and had the confidence of Congress and the Commander-inchief, it was deemed expedient by General Putnam to consult the Council and Assembly of New York, before he came to a final determination. A committee was appointed by those bodies, who spent three days reconnoitring the borders of the river in the Highlands, and they were unanimous in favor of West Point, agreeing herein with every other person authorized to act in the affair, except the engineer. It was accordingly decided, on the 13th of January, that the fortifications should be erected at West Point. — *Putnarig* MS. *LetUr,* January 130. — *Ra_ ditrr'i Memorial.*

General Putnam wrote, on the 13th of February, in reply to the above letter from the Commander-in-chief; —

" At my request the legislature of this State have appointed a committee, to affix the places and manner of securing the river, and to afford some assistance in expediting the work. The state of affairs now at this, post, you will please to observe, is as follows. The chain and accessary anchors are contracted for, to be completed by the first of April; and, from the intelligence I have received, there is reason to believe they will be finished by that time. Parts of the boom intended to have been wed at Fort Montgomery, sufficient for this place, are remaining. Some of the iron is exceedingly bad; this I hope to have replaced with good iron soon. The chevaux-de-frise will be completed by the time the river will admit of sinking them. The batteries near the water, and the fort to cover them, are laid out. The latter is within the walls six hundred yards around, twenty-one feet base, fourteen feet high, the *talus* two inches to the foot. This I fear is too large to be completed by the time expected. Governor Clinton and the committee have agreed to this plan, and nothing on my part shall be wanting to complete it in the best and most expeditious manner. Barracks and huts for about three hundred men are completed, and barracks for about the same number are nearly covered. A road to the river has been made with great difficulty.

" Meigs's regiment, except those under inoculation with the smallpox, is at the White Plains; and, until barracks can be fitted for their reception, I have thought best to continue them there, to cover the country from the incursions of the enemy. Dubois's regiment is unfit to be ordered on duty, there being not one blanket in the regiment. Very few have either a shoe or a shirt, and most of them have neither stockings, breeches, nor overalls. Several companies of enlisted artificers are in the same situation, and unable to work in,the field. Several hundred men are rendered useless, merely for want of necessary apparel, as no clothing is permitted to be stopped at this post. General Parsons has returned to camp some time since, and takes upon himself the command to-morrow, when I shall set out for Connecticut."

Vol. v. 29 TO THE BOARD OF WAR.
Valley Forge, 26 January, 1778.
Gentlemen,

This evening I have received a letter from Lieutenant-Colonel Smith at Lancaster, advising me of the confinement of the British officers, who were going with the clothing and medicine for the prisoners in our hands. This measure I consider rather unfortunate, as they came out by my permission, and in consequence of a stipulation between myself and General Howe. The officers are a Hessian and British regimental quartermaster, and a doctor and two mates. They had passports signed by one of my aids, who met them at our most advanced post, and were attended by a captain and lieutenant of our army.

Mr. Boudinot, I am persuaded, was mistaken in his representation respecting General Howe's forbidding any more provisions being sent in by water, as the only information he had was derived from a postscript in a letter from him to me, namely, " A sloop with flour has been received yesterday evening, for the use of the prisoners here; but I am to desire, that no more flags of truce may be sent by water, either up or down the river, without leave being previously obtained." As to clothing, I have no doubt but General Howe has denied us the liberty of purchasing. This is now a subject of difference between us, and the design of our insisting, that he shall

victual his troops in our hands by a certain day, is to oblige him to consent to that measure. But it should not, in my opinion, prevent him from sending clothes to the prisoners, especially as he had obtained my consent for the same, so long ago as the last day of November, in consideration of his assurances to permit a commissary of ours to go into Philadelphia, with necessaries for our people in his hands. Matters being thus circumstanced, and the conclusion of your letter to Colonel Smith directing the officers to be secured till further orders, either from the Board of War or from me, I have written to him to release and permit them to pursue their route. I have the honor, &c TO MAJOR-GENERAL GATES.

Valley Forge, 27 January, 1778.

Sir, Your two letters of the 24th instant came to hand. Before the receipt of the first, I had written to you upon the subject contained in it, in consequence of your letter to the commanding officer at Lancaster, which had been transmitted to me. As that will inform you fully respecting the British officers and clothing, I will not trouble you with a repetition of the matter. I must observe, however, that the number of officers and men, who came out, does not appear to me so very extraordinary, considering the various duties they have to perform, and the amount of wagons and necessaries they have in charge. The officers are under parole, and the party unarmed, nor will the state of this army admit large escorts to be detached; and if it were much more respectable, I should apprehend two officers sufficient to attend the flag. I should have been happy, if the officers and clothing had not been seized, as it destroys that confidence, which should ever be had in passports, and involves consequences of a delicate nature. In answer to the last clause of your letter, respecting the detention of the clothing, I refer you to my letter See a farther explanation of thia affair in Marshall's *Life of Washington*, Vol. III. p. 430.
of yesterday, by which you will perceive, that there is a particular agreement between General Howe and my-

self, under the sanction of which they came out

I am much obliged by your polite request of my opinion and advice on the expedition to Canada and other occasions. In the present instance, as I neither know the extent of the objects in view, nor the means to be employed to effect them, it is not in my power to pass any judgment upon the subject. I can only sincerely wish, that success may attend it, both as it may advance the pubUc good, and on account of the personal honor of the Marquis de Lafayette, for whom I have a very particular esteem and regard. Your letter was delivered to him in a little time after it came to my hands, and he proposes to set out for Yorktown to-morrow.

Agreeably to your request I shall order Hazen's regiment to march from Wilmington to this place, from whence it will immediately proceed towards Albany. As some particular purpose seems to be intended by desiring this regiment, I am induced to part with it, notwithstanding our force will ill bear the smallest diminution. I am, Sir, your most obedient servant.

TO MAJOR-GENERAL CHARLES LEE.
Valley Forge, 27 January, 1778.

Dear Sir, I last night received your favor of the 30th ultimo.t It gave me great pleasure to hear that you were released from your confined situation, and permitted so many indulgences. You may rest assured, that I feel myself very much interested in your welfare, and that every exertion has been used on my part to effect your exchange. This I have not been able to accomplish. However, from the letters, which have lately passed between Sir William Howe and myself upon the subject of prisoners, I am authorized to expect, that you will return in a few days to your friends on parole, as Major-General Prescott will be sent in on the same terms for that purpose. Indeed, till I saw Major Williams last night, I supposed that he had arrived either at New York or Rhode Island, having directed his releasement as soon as I was at liberty to do it. I will take the earliest opportunity to recommend to your friends, Mr. Nourse and

Mr. White, the care of your farm.

See Afpucdix, No. XI. t In that letter General Lee wrote;—"I have the strongest reason to flatter myself, that you will interest yourself in whatever concerns my comfort and welfare. I think it my duty to inform you, that my condition is much bettered. It is now five days that I am on my parole. I have the full liberty of the city and its limits; have horses at my command furnished by Sir Henry Clinton and General Robertson; am lodged with two of the oldest and warmest friends I have in the world, Colonel Butler and Major Disney of the forty-third regiment; with the former I was bred up from the age of nine years at school; the latter is a *commUito* from the time I entered the service in the forty-fourth. In short, my situation is rendered as easy, comfortable, and pleasant as possible, for a man who is in any sort a prisoner. I have nothing left to wish for, but that some circumstance may arise, which may make it convenient for both parties, that a general exchange may take place, and I among the rest reap the advantage. Give my love to all my friends, particularly to Greene, Mifflin, Reed, and Morgan, and be persuaded that I am most sincerely and devotedly yours." — *December* 30M.

Your request to Major Morris, in favor of Mrs. Battier, reached me only last night. I wish I had been informed of it sooner. I have enclosed a passport for her to Major Morris, and I doubt not but he will do every thing in his power to accommodate a lady, from whose husband you have received so many civilities. I am, dear Sir, with great esteem and regard, &c.

VOL. V. T TO SIR WILLAM HOWE.

Head-Quarters, 90 January, 1778.

Sir,

I have duly received your letter of the 19th ultimo. It is unnecessary to enter minutely into its contents, since the enclosed resolutions of Congress will show you, that the matter is now put upon a footing different from that mentioned by Mr. Boudinot; which, at the same time, you will be pleased to consider as final and decisive, and to reg-

ulate your measures accordingly. I should be glad, as soon as possible, to be favored with your determination in consequence, especially on those parts numbered in the margin of the resolves; to which I must expect a speedy and explicit answer.

There is one passage of your letter, which I cannot forbear taking particular notice of. No expression of personal politeness to me can be acceptable, accompanied by reflections on the representatives of a free people, under whose authority I have the honor to act. The delicacy I have observed, in refraining from every thing offensive in this way, entitled me to expect a similar treatment from you. I have not indulged myself in invective against the present rulers of Great Britain, in the course of our correspondence, nor will I even now avail myself of so fruitful a theme.

The quartermasters, permitted to go with the clothing, appeared to me sufficient for the purpose; for, though the prisoners are in different places, yet they lie chiefly on a direct communication. If upon any future occasion you should conceive a greater number requisite, you will inform me of it previously to their coming, and I shall be ready to comply, as far as I think myself justified. Whether your sending out more than one British quartermaster was an encroachment upon the spirit of the agreement between us, shall not now be matter of discussion. But can it be said there is any thing in it, that can reconcile the coming out of Captain MCleod *1* I have the honor to be, &c TO GOVERNOR LIVINGSTON.

Head-Quarters, 2 February, 1778.

Sir,

The recent detection of the wicked design you mention, gives me sensible pleasure; and I earnestly hope, that you may be alike successful in discovering and disappointing every attempt, which may be projected against you, either by your open or concealed enemies. It is a severe tax, however, which all those must pay, who are called to eminent stations of trust, not only to be held up as conspicuous marks to the enmity of the public adversaries to their country, but

to the malice of secret traitors, and the *envious intrigues* of false friends and factions.

I am obliged to you for the interest you take in the affair of the two Hendricks and Meeker; and I have no doubt that the measures adopted are, considering all things, best. You are pleased to intimate, that you would take pleasure in recommending, at the approaching session of your Assembly, any hints from me respecting the army, by which your State can advance the general interest. I should be happy in offering any such in my power; but, as there is now in camp a committee of Congress to confer with me at large on the measures proper to be adopted in every respect for the benefit of the army, whatever shall be thought necessary to this end will, of course, be communicated to you by Congress. I am, &c.

TO ELIAS BOUDINOT.

VaDey Forge, 3 February, 1778.

Dear Sir, A letter from Congress will accompany this, containing two resolutions relative to prisoners. You will perceive by them, that Congress go upon the presumption of our furnishing our prisoners in the enemy's hands wholly and entirely with provisions. Their fixing no rule for liquidating and accounting for the rations heretofore supplied by the enemy is a proof, that they do not intend them to continue, but expect our prisoners will hereafter be altogether victualled by ourselves. This is a matter, to which it will be necessary to attend carefully, both that a competent supply may be immediately ready for the purpose, and that there may be no deficiency in future; otherwise the consequences may be dreadful, for the past conduct of the enemy gives too much reason to apprehend, that they would not be very apt to relieve wants, to which we had undertaken wholly to administer. I am, Sir, &c.

TO BRIGADIER-GENERAL WAYNE.

Valley Forge, 9 February, 1778.

Sir,

The good people of the State of Pennsylvania, living in the vicinity of Philadelphia and near the Delaware River, having suffered much by the enemy's carrying off their property, without allowing them any compensation, thereby distressing the inhabitants, supplying their own army, and enabling them to protract the cruel and unjust war that they are now waging against these States; and whereas, by recent intelligence, I have reason to expect that they intend making another grand forage into this country; it is of the utmost conquence, that the horses, cattle, sheep, and provender, within fifteen miles west from the river Delaware, between the Schuylkill and the Brandywine, be immediately removed to prevent the enemy from receiving any benefit therefrom, as well as to supply the present exigencies of the American army.

I do therefore authorize, empower, and command you forthwith to take, carry off, and secure, all such horses as are suitable for cavalry or for draft, and all cattle and sheep fit for slaughter, together with every kind of forage, for the use of this army, that may be found in the possession of any of the inhabitants within the aforesaid limits, causing certificates to be given to each person for the number, value, and quantity of the horses, sheep, cattle, and provender so taken. Notice will be given to the holders of such certificates by the commissary and quartermaster-general when and where they may apply for payment, that they may not be disappointed in calling for their money.

All officers, civil and military, commissioners, and quartermasters, are hereby ordered to obey, aid, and assist you in this necessary business. All the provender on the islands between Philadelphia and Chester, which may be difficult of access, or too hazardous to attempt carrying off, you will immediately cause to be destroyed, giving directions to the officer or officers to whom this duty is assigned, to take an account of the quantity, together with the owners' names, as far as the nature of the service will admit. I am, Sir, &,c After executing these orders, Wayne passed over for a similar purpose into Jersey, where he was joined by Pulaski with a party of horse. Pulaski was stationed for the winter at Trenton. The

British followed Wayne into Jersey, crossing the river in two divisions, one landing at VOL. V. 30 T TO SIR WILLIAM HOWE.

Head-Quarters, 10 February, 1778.
Sir,
I received yesterday the favor of your letter of the 5th instant. In answer to whatever it contains concerning General Burgoyne's army, and the measures adopted relative to it, I have only to inform you, that this is a matter in which I have never had the least direction. It lies wholly with Congress; and the proposals you make on this head must be submitted to them. I have accordingly transmitted a copy of your letter, and shall be ready to forward to you any resolution they may take in consequence.

I shall omit animadverting on your observations with regard to the allowance and treatment to prisoners in your hands. It is a subject, which has been fully discussed in the progress of our correspondence; and the necessity of a further investigation is superseded, by your meeting me on the ground I have so long wished. The powers under which I act are entirely derived from Congress, and must of course be subject to such modifications, as they may think proper according to

Billingsport, and the other at Gloucester, amounting in all to more than three thousand men, with eight field-pieces. They attempted to surround Wayne in the night at Haddonfield, being in force vastly superior; but he received timely intelligence of their design, and retreated in the evening a few hours previously to the arrival of the enemy. After making a rapid incursion into the country, and collecting forage and cattle, the British returned to Philadelphia; but they were harassed by Wayne and Pulaski while debarking at the ferry, and a smart skirmish ensued. Pulaski exposed himself with his usual bravery. His horse was wounded. On the 14th of March, Wayne recrossed the river with his detachment at Burlington, and proceeded to destroy the forage accessible to the enemy in Philadelphia county and a part of Bucks, and to drive off the horses and cattle. He thus made

a circuit quite round the city.— *Wayne's MS. Lettert, March 5th, 14th.* See this letter in the Appensix, No. *XIL* circumstances to prescribe. But, holding myself fully authorized, by their instructions and intentions, to avail myself of the reasonable terms, which you are at this time willing to adopt for the mutual relief of prisoners, I shall explicitly close with your propositions to the following effect; — " That an exchange of all prisoners now in our possession, officer for officer, soldier for soldier, and citizen for citizen, so far as number and rank will apply," be carried into execution, as expeditiously as the nature of the case will admit, and without regard to any controverted point, which might prove an impediment to so desirable an end. And here, as I may not clearly understand your meaning, when you say, — "In the mean time I shall wait the arrival of the British officers, whom you have released upon their paroles, and shall without delay send an equal number to you in return," — I take occasion to request, that you will be pleased to favor me with an explanation; whether you intend to consider such officers, on both sides, as still continuing under the obligation of a parole, or as absolutely exchanged in pursuance of the general cartel. I see no reason why an effectual exchange should not at once operate with respect to them.

I also agree, that two commissioners from me shall meet a like number from you, on the 10th day of March in Germantown, at the King of Prussia Tavern, at eleven o'clock in the forenoon, to adjust upon equitable terms the difference you mention, and such other matters as they may be severally empowered to determine.

With respect to a general settlement of accounts, as it comprehends points with which I have no authority to interfere, it is not in my power to concur in the measure you suggest for that purpose. I am under the necessity of referring it to the decision of Congress. Considering a general exchange as being finally agreed on between us, I shall without delay order the prisoners in our hands to places in the vicinity of your different posts, which their respective situations may render most convenient; and shall give you notice as they arrive, that you may return a number equal to those sent in from time to time. I am, with due respect, Sir, &,c TO MAJOR-GENERAL GATES.

Head-Quarters, 14 February, 1778.

Sir,

I am favored with yours of the 9th instant, enclosing the proceedings of a general court-martial held by your order. It is a defect in our martial law, from which we often find great inconvenience, that the power of appointing general courts-martial is too limited. I do not find it can be legally exercised by any officer, except the Commander-in-chief, or the commanding general in any particular State. This circumstance would make it improper for me to ratify the sentence against Murray, did the nature of his crime require it; and, if it was thought inexpedient to let him pass unpunished, I should be under the necessity of ordering another court for his trial. But as there are some mitigating considerations, which you mention, it may perhaps be as well to remit the present sentence, without proceeding any further in the affair. I leave it to your judgment, either with my approbation to do this, or to make use of the enclosed order, to bring the offender to a second trial.

Had the constitution of the court been entirely regular, I do not conceive I could with propriety alter the capita punishment into a corporal one. The right of mitigating only extends, in my opinion, to lessening the degree of punishment, in the same species prescribed; and does not imply any authority to change the nature or quality of it altogether. I am, Sir, &c.

TO RICHARD HENRY LEE.

Valley Forge, 15 February, 1778.

Dear Sir, Your letter of the 2d ultimo, from Chantilly, enclosing Lieutenant-Colonel Frazer's orders for the management of the grenadiers and light-infantry in an action, and upon a march, came to my hands in the course of last month, and merits my thanks, as it may be of use to such corps, one of which,

consisting of lightInfantry, we are now forming. The enemy are governed by no principles that ought to actuate honest men; no wonder then, that forgery should be amongst their other crimes. I have seen a letter published in a handbill at New York, and extracts from it republished in a Philadelphia paper, said to be from me to Mrs. Washington, not one word of which did I ever write. Those contained in the pamphlet you speak of are, I presume, equally genuine, and perhaps written by the same author. I should be glad, however, to see and examine the texture of them, if a favorable opportunity to send them should present.

Alluding to a number of spurious letters, circulated in the name of General Washington, which it seems he had not yet seen. Mr. Lee had aaid, in the letter to which the above was an answer; — " The arts of the enemies of America are endless, but all wicked as they are various. Among other tricks, they have forged a pamphlet of letters, entitled ' Letters from General Washington to Several of his Friends, in 1776.' The design of the forger is evident, and no doubt it gained him a good beefsteak from his masters. I would send you this pamphlet, if it were not too bulky for the post, as it might serve to amuse your leisure hours during the inaction of winter."

Lord Cornwallis has certainly embarked for England, but with what view is not so easy to determine. He was eye-witness a few days before his departure to a scene, not a little disgraceful to the pride of British valor, in their manoeuvre to Chesnut Hill, and precipitate return, after boasting their intentions of driving us beyond the mountains.

I am very glad to find, that the Assembly of Virginia have taken matters up so spiritedly; but wish, instead of attempting to raise so many volunteers, they had resolved at all adventures to complete their regiments by drafting. If all the States would do this, and fall upon ways and means to supply their troops with comfortable clothing upon moderate terms, and Congress would make the commissions of officers of

some value to them, every thing would probably go well, making at the same time some reform in the different departments of the army; nothing standing in greater need of it, than the quartermasters and commissaries, as no army ever suffered more by their neglect; the consequences of this neglect are much to be dreaded. I am, dear Sir, your most obedient servant.

TO GOVERNOR GEORGE CLINTON.

Valley Forge, 16 February, 177S.

Dear Sir, It is with great reluctance I trouble you on a subject, which does not properly fall within your province; but it is a subject that occasions me more distress, than I have felt since the commencement of the war; and which loudly demands the most zealous exertions of every person of weight and authority, who is interested in the success of our affairs; I mean the present dreadful situation of the army for want of provisions, and the miserable prospects before us with respect to futurity. It is more alarming, than you will probably conceive; for, to form a just idea of it, it were necessary to be on the spot. For some days past, there has been little less than a famine in camp. A part of the army has been a week without any kind of flesh, and the rest three or four days. Naked and starving as they are, we cannot enough admire the incomparable patience and fidelity of the soldiery, that they have not been ere this excited by their suffering to a general mutiny and dispersion. Strong symptoms, however, of discontent have appeared in particular instances; and nothing but the most active efforts everywhere can long avert so shocking a catastrophe.

Our present sufferings are not all. There is no foundation laid for any adequate relief hereafter. All the magazines provided in the States of New Jersey, Pennsylvania, Delaware, and Maryland, and all the immediate additional supplies they seem capable of affording, will not be sufficient to support the army more than a month longer, if so long. Very little has been done at the eastward, and as little to the southward; and whatever we have a right to expect from those quarters must necessarily be very remote, and is, indeed, more precarious than could be wished. When the before-mentioned supplies are exhausted, what a terrible crisis must ensue, unless all the energy of the continent shall be exerted to provide a timely remedy!

Impressed with this idea, I am, on my part, putting every engine at work, that I can possibly think of, to prevent the fatal consequences, which we have so great reason to apprehend. I am calling upon all those, whose stations and influence enable them to contribute their aid upon so important an occasion; and, from your well known zeaL I expect every thing within the compass of your power, and that the abilities and resources of the State over which you preside will admit. I am sensible of the disadvantages it labors under, from having been so long the scene of war, and that it must be exceedingly drained by the great demands to which it has been subjected. But, though you may not be able to contribute materially to our relief, you can perhaps do something towards it; and any assistance, however trifling in itself, will be of great moment at so critical a juncture, and will conduce to the keeping of the army together, till the commissary's department can be put upon a better looting, and effectual measures concerted to secure a competent and permanent supply. What methods you can take, you will be the best judge of; but, if you can devise any means to procure a quantity of cattle, or other kind of flesh, for the use of this army, to be at camp in the course of a month, you will render a most essential service to the common cause. I have the honor to be, &,c The following extract from a letter written in camp by General Varnum, as brigadier of the day, to General Greene, not only presents a vivid picture of the distresses of the army, but shows the difficulties with which the Commander-in-chief had to contend, as well in witnessing the scenes of suffering among the soldiers, as in controlling the discontent and opposing opinions of his officers.

" The situation of the camp is such," says General Varnum, "that in all human probability the army must soon dissolve. Many of the troops are destitute of meat, and are several days in arrear. The horses are dying for want of forage. The country in the vicinity of the camp is exhausted. There cannot be a moral certainty of bettering our circumstances, while we continue here. What consequences have we rationally to expect? Our desertions are astonishingly great; the love of freedom, which once animated the breasts of those born in the country, is controlled by hunger, the keenest of necessities. If we consider the relation in which we stand to the troops, we cannot reconcile their sufferings to the sentiments of honest men. No political consideration can justify the measure. There is no local object of so much moment, as to cooceal the obligations which bind us to them. Should a blind attachment to a preconcerted plan fatally disaffect, and in the end force the army to mutiny, then will the same country, which now applauds our hermitage Valley Forge, curse our insensibility.

AN ADDRESS TO THE INHABITANTS OP NEW JERSEY, PENNSYLVANIA, DELAWARE, MARYLAND, AND VIRGINIA. Valley Forge, 18 February, 1778.

Friends, Countrymen, and Fellow Citizens,

After three campaigns, during which the brave subjects of these States have contended, not unsuccessfully, with one of the most powerful kingdoms upon earth, we now find ourselves at least upon a level with our opponents; and there is the best reason to believe, that efforts adequate to the abilities of this country would enable us speedily to conclude the war, and to secure the invaluable blessings of peace, liberty, and safety. With this view, it is in contemplation, at the opening of the next campaign, to assemble a force sufficient, not barely to cover the country from a repetition of those depredations which it has already suffered, but also to operate offensively, and to strike some decisive blow.

In the prosecution of this object, it is to be feared that so large an army may suffer for want of provisions. The distance between this and the eastern States, whence considerable supplies of flesh have been hitherto drawn, will necessarily render those supplies extremely precarious. And unless the virtuous yeomanry of New Jersey, Pennsylvania, Delaware, Maryland, and Virginia, will exert themselves to prepare cattle for the use of the army, during the months of May, June, and July next, great difficulties may arise in the course of the campaign. It is therefore recommended to the inhabitants of those States, to put up and feed immediately as many of their stock cattle as they can spare, so that they may be driven to this army within that period. A bountiful price will be given, and the proprietors may assure themselves, that they will render a most essential service to the illustrious cause of their country, and contribute in a great degree to shorten this bloody contest. But should there be any so insensible to the common interest, as not to exert themselves upon these generous principles, the private interest of those, whose situation makes them liable to become immediate subjects to the enemy's incursions, should prompt them at least to a measure, which is calculated to save their property from plunder, their families from insult, and their own persons from abuse, hopeless confinement, or perhaps a violent death.

" I have from the beginning viewed this situation with horror! It is unparalleled in the history of mankind to establish winter-quarters in a country wasted and without a single magazine. We now only feel some of the effects, which reason from the beginning taught us to expect aa inevitable. My freedom upon this occasion may be offensive; if so, I should be unhappy, but duty obliges me to speak without reserve. My own conscience will approve the deed, when some may perhaps look back with regret to the time, when the evil in extreme might have been prevented. There is no alternative, but immediately to remove the army to places where they can be supplied, unless effectual remedies can be applied on the spot, which I believe every gentleman of the army thinks impracticable." — MS. Letter, February 12tt.

VOL. V. 31 TJ TO GOVERNOR LIVINGSTON.

Valley Forge, 22 February, 177a

Sir,

I cannot but be sensible of the fresh proofs given of that zeal, which yourself in particular, and the State of New Jersey in general, have so uniformly manifested in the common cause, and of the polite regard you have in repeated instances shown to my applications. I lament the additional load of business heaped upon you from the sources you mention, and earnestly hope that painful experience will teach us so to correct our former mistakes and reform past abuses, as to lighten the burden of those, whose whole time and attention are devoted to the execution of their duty and the service of the public. I feel with you the absolute necessity of calling forth the united efforts of these States, to relieve our wants, and prevent in future a renewal of our distresses; and the impossibility of answering these purposes by partial exertions. Nothing on my part has been or will be omitted, that may in the least tend to put our affairs upon this only footing, on which they can have any stability or success. I shall be obliged to your Excellency to send immediately to camp the troop of horse you can spare. I have the honor to be, &,c.

TO THE PRESIDENT OF CONGRESS.

Head-Quarters, Valley Forge, 27 February, 1778.

Sir, In compliance with the resolution of Congress of the 5th instant, transmitted in your letter of the 7th, I was about to take measures for appointing a court-martial and bringing on the trials which they direct. But, on recurring to the papers you were pleased to send me, I do not find that the committee have made any particular charges against the officers, who are to be the subjects of trial. It was probably the intention of Congress, that these charges should be laid by me. But, as I might err in doing it, and not fully correspond with their views in the matter, especially as it would require, considerable time and thought to make myself suffi ciently acquainted with it from the papers collect-

ed, I should think it would be most advisable for Congress to state explicitly the charges they wish to have exhibited against the officers respectively; and then the business may be proceeded on with propriety.

Besides the above reasons, which operate generally against my exhibiting the charges, in the particular instance of General Schuyler it is impossible for me to do it, as I do not know what instructions he had received from Congress from time to time as to the objects of his command, nor precisely what these were. These appear to me necessary to be known, and essential to carry on a prosecution against him. When Congress shall have arranged these points, and are pleased to honor me with them, I will pursue the speediest measures to bring on the trials. The sooner this can be done, the better, as some of the parties are extremely anxious, and strongly importune it.

Baron Steuben has arrived at camp. He appears to be much of a gentleman, and, as far as I have had an opportunity of judging, a man of military knowledge, and acquainted with the world.

The enclosed extract of a letter from General Putnam will show how great the distresses are in that quarter for want of money. He has described their necessities so fully, that it is unnecessary for me to add upon the subject. I shall only observe, that his account is more than justified by many other letters, and that I am persuaded the earliest possible supply will be forwarded, and that the very important and interesting works carrying on there may not be the least retarded.

I am under some embarrassments respecting the thirteenth Virginia regiment. It was raised on the west side of the Allegany and towards Pittsburg, with assurances from the officers, it is said, that the men should not be drawn from that quarter. This circumstance, added to the disturbances by the Indians, and the exposed situation of their families, has been the cause of great desertions, and is at present the source of much uneasiness, and the more so, as part of the regiment was never marched

from thence. I think the whole should be united either here or there, and wish Congress to direct me upon the subject. At the same time that their case, if truly represented, seems to be hard, and to merit the indulgence they claim, I would observe, that the twelfth regiment from the western parts of the same State, and the eighth and twelfth Pennsylvania regiments from the frontier counties of this, have similar pretensions, and might become uneasy, and apply for a like indulgence.

Agreeably to the directions of Congress, I shall send a major-general to Rhode Island, though the number of officers here of this rank, from one cause and another, is greatly reduced, and more so than it ought to be in point of policy. Our loss of matrosses the last campaign, in killed and wounded, was considerable; and it has not been a little increased this winter by desertions from Colonel Procter's corps. From these circumstances, we are very weak in this line; and I request that Congress will be pleased to order Colonel Harrison's regiment of artillery to march from Virginia as early as the roads will admit, and join this army.

I have the honor to be, &c General Varnum suggested that a battalion of negroes might be raised in Rhode Island. The idea was communicated to Governor Cooke, who laid the subject before the Assembly. He reported the following result to General Washington. " Liberty is given to every effective slave to enter into the service during the war; and upon his passing muster he is absolutely made free, and entitled to all the wages, bounties, and encouragements given by Congress to any soldier enlisting into their aorvice. The masters are allowed at the rate of one hundred and twenty pounds for the most valuable slave, and in proportion for those of less value. The number of slaves in the State is not great, but it is generally thought that three hundred and upwards will be enlisted." — MS. Letter, February 2W.

TO BRYAN FAIRFAX.

Valley Forge, 1 March, 177a

Dear Sir, Your favor of the 8th of December came safe to my hands, after a considerable delay on its passage. The sentiments you have expressed of me in ihis letter are highly flattering, and merit my warmest acknowledgments, as I have too good an opinion of your sincerity and candor to believe that you are capable of unmeaning professions, and of speaking a language foreign to your heart. The friendship, which I ever professed and felt for you, met with no diminution from the difference in our political sentiments. I know the rectitude of my own intentions, and, believing in the sincerity of yours, lamented, though I did not condemn, your renunciation of the creed I had adopted. Nor do I think any person or power ought to do it, whilst your conduct is not opposed to the general interest of the people, and the measures they are pursuing; the latter, that is, our actions, depending upon ourselves, may be controlled, while the powers of thinking, originating in higher causes, cannot always be moulded to our wishes.

An early and intimate friendship subsisted between Washington and Bryan Fairfax, which does not appear to have been at any period of their lives interrupted, although they differed widely in their political sentiments. This was illustrated in a striking manner by the letters, that passed between them in the year 1774. (See VoL II. p. 388.) Mr. Fairfax considered the pretensions of Parliament unjustifiable, and believed there were many grievances, which ought to be redressed; bnt could not reconcile to himself the idea of taking up arms against the King. Differing thus from the majority of his countrymen and from his friends, he thought it his duty to go to England and remain there during the contest. With this aim he repaired to New York, having obtained a passport from the Commander-in-chief But when be axrived there, he was diverted from his purpose by having certain oaths prescribed to him, which his conscience would not allow him to take, being afraid they might prevent him from ever again seeing his wife and children. This hesitancy excited a prejudice against him, which he thought un-

reasonable, and he obtained permission from the British commander to return to his family. On his journey he again visited Genera

The determinations of Providence are always wise, often inscrutable; and, though its decrees appear to bear hard upon us at times, they are nevertheless meant for gracious purposes. In this light I cannot help viewing your late disappointment; for if you had been permitted to go to England, unrestrained even by the rigid oaths, which are administered on those occasions, your feelings as a husband and parent must have been considerably wounded in the prospect of a long, perhaps lasting, separation from your nearest relatives. What then must they have been, if the obligation of an oath had left you without a will / Your hope of being instrumental in restoring peace would prove as unsubstantial, as mist before the noon-day's sun, and would as soon be dispelled; for, believe me, Sir, Great Britain understood herself perfectly well in this dispute, but did not comprehend America. She meant, as Lord Camden, in his late speech in Parliament, clearly and explicitly declared, to drive America into rebellion, that

Washington, and was received by him with so much kindness, and such marked civilities, that he wrote him a letter of acknowledgments and thanks soon after he reached Virginia, to which the above is a reply. Ic that letter he said; —

" There are times when favors conferred make a greater impression than at others, for, though I have received many, I hope I have not been unmindful of them; yet that, at a time your popularity was at the highest and mine at the lowest, and when it is so common for men's resentments to run high against those, who differ from them in opinion, you should act with your wonted kindness towards me, has affected me more than any favor I have received; and could not be believed by some in New York, it being above the run of common minds." her own purposes might be more fully answered by it; but take this along with it, that this plan originated

in a firm belief, founded on misinformation, that no effectual opposition would or could be made. They little dreamt of what has happened, and are disappointed in their views.

Does not every act of Administration, from the Tea Act to the present session of Parliament, declare this in plain and self-evident characters? Had the commissioners any powers to treat with America 1 If they meant peace, would Lord Howe have been detained in England five months after passing the act? Would the powers of these commissioners have been confined to mere acts of grace, upon condition of absolute submission 1 No! surely, no! They meant to drive us into what they termed rebellion, that they might be furnished with a pretext to disarm, and then strip us of the rights and privileges of Englishmen and citizens.

The allusion here is to Lord Camden's remarks, in the debate respecting the reply to the King's Speech at the opening of Parliament, November 18th, 1777. The debate turned on American affairs, the causes of the dispute, and the mode in which the war had been conducted. Lord Camden, referring to some of the preliminary steps in the contest, said, " The people of America showed great dissatisfaction, but that did not fully answer the intentions of government. It was not dissatisfaction, but rebellion, that was sought; dissatisfaction might furnish a pretence for adding to the intolerable oppressions, that those people had for a series of years groaned under; but nothing short of something in the shape of rebellion, or nearly approaching to it, could create a decent apology for slaughter, conquest, and unconditional submission." Again, in regard to the address declaring Massachusetts Bay to be in rebellion, Lord Camden continued; " But all this did not do; the New Englanders were resolved not to verify the address; they were determined not be rebels; but only to prepare, should the worst happen, to be in a situation to defend themselves. Something more was still wanting, and that was obtained. Our troops were ordered to act effectively; aad self-defence was styled actual and declared rebellion." — Anson's *Parliamentary Register,* VoL X. pp. 30, 31.

If they were actuated by the principles of justice, why did they refuse indignantly to accede to the terms, which were humbly supplicated before hostilities commenced, and this country was deluged in blood; and now make their principal officers, and even the commissioners themselves, say that these terms are just and reasonable; nay, that more will be granted, than we have yet asked, if we will relinquish our claim to independency? What name does such conduct as this deserve? And what punishment is there in store for the men, who have distressed millions, involved thousands in ruin, and plunged numberless families in inextricable woe? Could that, which is just and reasonable now, have been unjust four years ago? If not, upon what principles, I say, does Administration act *1* They must either be wantonly wicked and cruel, or (which is only another mode of describing the same thing) under false colors are now endeavouring to deceive the great body of the people, by industriously propagating a belief, that Great Britain is willing to offer any terms, and that we will accept of none; thereby hoping to poison and disaffect the minds of those, who wish for peace, and to create feuds and dissensions among ourselves. In a word, having less dependence now in their arms than their arts, they are practising such low and dirty tricks, that men of sentiment and honor must blush at their fall. Among other manoeuvres in this way, they are forging letters, and publishing them as intercepted ones of mine, to prove that I am an enemy to the present measures, and have been led into them step by step, still hoping that Congress would recede from their claims. I am, dear Sir, your most obedient and affectionate, &c TO BRIGADIER-GENERAL WAYNE.

Valley Forge, 3 March, 1778.

Dear Sir, Yours of the 26th from Mount Holly came to hand last evening. I am pleased to hear, that you had so good intelligence of the designs and motions of the enemy, that you were

enabled to withdraw your detachment from Haddonfield before they invested it. Considering the disproportion of your strength to that of the enemy, all that can be expected of you is to wait upon and circumscribe them as much as possible. You will not fail to make use of your utmost exertions to destroy all the forage within their reach, because I imagine they are more in want of that than of any thing else. I have written to General Pulaski, to give you all the assistance that he can with the small body of cavalry that he has at Trenton. I can give you no other directions, than to throw as many obstacles as you can in the way of the enemy, to prevent them from executing their plan to any great extent; and I know of no way more effectual than driving off all the cattle and horses, that you possibly can, and destroying the forage that you think they would carry off.

I am, dear Sir, yours, &c.

TO COUNT PULASKI.

Head-Quarters, 3 March, 1778.

Sir,

I have received your favor of the 28th ultimo, informing me that you were proceeding with a part of Bland's regiment to join General Wayne. You will have received my instructions relative to the service, which you are to render. Your intention to resign is founded on reasons, which I presume make you think the measure necessary. I can only say, therefore, that it will always give me pleasure to bear testimony to the zeal and bravery, which you have displayed on every occasion. Proper measures are taking for completing the cavalry, and I have no doubt of its being on a respectable footing by the opening of the campaign. I am, Sir, &c.

TO THOMAS WHARTON, PRESIDENT OF PENN-

SYLVANIA.

Valley Forge, 7 March, 1778.

Sir,

There is nothing I have more at heart, than to discharge the great duties incumbent on me with the strictest attention to the ease and convenience of the people. Every instance, therefore, of hardship or oppression, exercised by the

officers of any department under my immediate control, gives me the most sensible concern, and should be immediately punished, if complaints were properly made and supported. That there has been some foundation for such complaints, and that they have affected the service, I cannot doubt, from the great delay and backwardness of the people in forwarding supplies and affording the means of transportation. Until the late wagon law of this State was passed, there being no means of procuring the service of the inhabitants but by military compulsion, quartermasters and commissaries, from the necessity of the case, seem to have been justified in impressing, though in many instances, perhaps, it has been done with circumstances of terror and hardship, which they ought to have avoided. But, when the legislature had by law made an arrangement, and put this important service under the care of their own officers, it was my full determination, by every means in my power, to support the law which had been passed, and avail myself of the resources of the State in the mode pointed out, under a full confidence, that the wisdom and forecast, which had marked out such a plan, would be accompanied with proportionate zeal and efficacy to carry it into execution.

Perhaps, Sir, I am not sufficiently informed, to judge properly where the present defect lies, and therefore I avoid imputing blame to any; but I would wish you, and the gentlemen in authority with you, to be assured, that nothing would give me more satisfaction, than to see the powers of the government so effectual for the supply and accommodation of the army, as to take away not only the necessity but even pretence of using any other than the ordinary civil authority. Give me leave further to remark, that the army seems to have a peculiar claim to the exertions of the gentlemen of this State, to make its present situation as convenient as possible; as it was greatly owing to their apprehensions and anxieties, expressed in a memorial to Congress, that the present position was taken, where with unparalleled patience they have gone through a severe and inclement winter, unprovided with any of those conveniences and comforts, which are usually the soldier's lot after the duties of the field are over.

The necessities of the service, Sir, are great; the duty required, I acknowledge, is burthensome and difficult at this inclement season; but it cannot be dispensed with. The army and the country have a mutual dependence upon each other; and it is of the last importance, that their several duties should be so regulated and enforced, as to produce, not only the greatest harmony and good understanding, but the truest happiness and comfort to each. Depending, therefore, upon a due and early attention to this important business, and promising myself no small relief from our present difficulties, I remain, Sir, with due respect and regard, yours, &c.

P. S. Since writing the foregoing, I have received a letter from Colonel Gibson at Lancaster, dated the 2d instant, an extract from which, with his order to the quartermaster and the answer, I enclose, to show how much we are distressed even in small matters; but our sufferings in camp, for want of forage and wagons, are beyond all description.

TO THE PRESIDENT OF CONGRESS.

Valley Forge, 7 March, 1778.

Sir, I take the liberty of transmitting to you copies of three letters from General Howe, of the 14th and 21st ultimo, and of the 2d instant, with their enclosures. The unhappy violation of the flag of truce has laid us under no small embarrassments, and has afforded the enemy good grounds for complaint and triumph at the same time. This however is the natural consequence, and must ever be the case, where different powers counteract each other in matters of the most delicate importance. There are some circumstances attending this affair, which it may possibly be in the power of Congress to throw light upon. If they can, I shall be obliged by their assistance.

VOL. V. V *March 5th.* — In consequence of the letters, which have lately passed between General Howe and my-

self, particularly those of the 5th and 10th ultimo, copies of which I had the honor to transmit to you in mine of the 8th, continued to the 14th, I was about to send commissioners to meet those appointed by General Howe for adjusting the disputed points between us, carrying into execution an exchange of prisoners, and improving the old cartel, as far as it might be practicable, for their better accommodation in future. This meeting was to be on the 10th instant; but, yesterday morning, Dunlap's paper of the 4th being put into my hands, I found that a resolution had been made on the 26th of February, calling for all accounts against prisoners in our hands, and declaring that no exchange should take place, till the balance due thereon to the United States is discharged. Some of the States are not required to exhibit their claims till the 1st of June. The time that would be taken to adjust them, and make a delivery of the prisoners, would more than exhaust all the ensuing summer.

This resolution I cannot consider as an intended infraction of my engagements with General Howe; yet its operation is diametrically opposite both to the spirit and letter of the propositions made on my part, and acceded to on his. I supposed myself fully authorized "by the instructions and intentions" of Congress to act as I did; and I now conceive, that the public as well as my own personal honor and faith are pledged for the performance.

By the direction of Congress, I in the first instance stipulated with General Howe an exchange of prisoners, " officer for officer, of equal rank, soldier for soldier, and citizen for citizen." This agreement they have ever approved, and repeatedly declared their willingness to carry into execution. Their resolution of the 24th of March last empowered me (on condition of General Lee being declared exchangeable) not only *"to proceed"* to the exchange of prisoners, according to the principles and regulations of the cartel before agreed on, but also to enter into such further principles and regulations as should appear to me most proper and advantageous. A subsequent

resolution of the 6th of June holds forth the same language, sanctions my conduct and reasonings in the negotiations about that time on the subject, and directs an adherence to them. No event has occurred since that period, by which I could conclude there was any alteration in the views of Congress; so far from it, that all my late letters breathing the same spirit with the former, and pointedly signifying my wish to bring about a general exchange, if not with an express, at least met with a tacit approbation. General Howe at length, by profession if not in reality, is willing to perform the agreement on the conditions required by me and confirmed by them.

It may be said, that, with whatever powers I was originally vested to negotiate an exchange, the resolution of the 19 th of December last was an abridgment of them, so far as to annex a new condition, the settlement and payment of accounts previous to its taking place. I had no conception of this being the case in the present instance, however the letter may warrant the construction. Besides the common principle of preventing the inconveniences, necessarily resulting from allowing the enemy to make their payments in paper currency, I had reason to imagine that General Burgoyne's army was more particularly the object of the concluding clause. This interpretation I the more readily adopted, for, exclusive of the affairs of that army, I verily believed, that, from the confused, defective state of our accounts relating to prisoners, there would be a considerable balance in favor of Mr. Howe. Nor was the situation of our accounts the only reason for this belief; the prisoners in our hands, especially those westward of the Delaware, as I am informed, have been in a great measure supported by their own labor, and at the expense of the enemy, who have had agents constantly among us. If this is the case, the reason of the resolve not applying, the effect ought not of course.

But perhaps it may be thought contrary to our interest to go into an exchange, as the enemy would derive more immediate advantage from it than we should. This I shall not deny; but it appeared to me, that, on principles of genuine, extensive policy, independent of the considerations of compassion and justice, we were under an obligation not to elude it. I have the best evidence, that an event of this kind is the general wish of the country. I know it to be the wish of the army; and no one can doubt, that it is the ardent wish of the unhappy sufferers themselves. We need only consult the tide of humanity, and the sympathies natural to those connected by the cement of blood, interest, and a common dread of evil, to be convinced, that the prevailing current of sentiment demands an exchange. If the country, the army, and even the prisoners themselves, had a precise idea of our circumstances, and could be fully sensible of the disadvantages, that might attend the giving our enemy a considerable reinforcement without having an equivalent, they might perhaps be willing to make a sacrifice of their feelings to motives of policy. But they have not this knowledge, and cannot be entrusted with it; and their reasonings, of necessity, will be governed by what they feel.

Were an opinion once to be established (and the enemy and their emissaries know very well how to inculcate it, if they are furnished with a plausible pretext), that we designedly avoided an exchange, it would be a cause of dissatisfaction and disgust to the country and to the army, of resentment and desperation to our captive officers and soldiers. To say nothing of the importance of not hazarding our national character but upon the most solid grounds, especially in our embryo state, from the influence it may have on our affairs abroad, it may not be a little dangerous to beget in the minds of our own countrymen a suspicion, that we do not pay the strictest observance to the maxims of honor and good faith.

It is prudent to use the greatest caution not to shock the notions of general justice and humanity, universal among mankind, as well in a public as a private view. In a business on the side of which the passions are so much concerned as in the present, men would be readily disposed to believe the worst, and cherish the most unfavorable conclusions. Were the letters, that have passed between General Howe and myself from first to last, and the proceedings of Congress on the same subject, to be published with proper comments, it is much to be feared, if the exchange should be deferred till the terms of the last resolve were fulfilled, that it would be difficult to prevent our being generally accused of a breach of good faith. Perhaps it might be said, that, while the enemy refused us justice, we fondly embraced the opportunity to be loud, persevering, incessant in our claims; but, the moment they were willing to render it, we receded from ourselves, and started new difficulties. This, I say, might be the reasoning of speculative minds; and they might consider all our professions as *mere* professions; or, at best, that

Vol. v. 33 v» interest and policy were to be the only arbiters of their validity.

Imputations of this nature would have a tendency to unnerve our operations, by diminishing that respect and confidence, which are essential to be placed in those, who are at the head of affairs either in the civil or military line. This, added to the prospect of hopeless captivity, would be a great discouragement to the service. The ill consequences of both would be immense, by increasing the causes of discontent in the army, which are already too numerous, and many of which are in a great measure unavoidable; by fortifying that unwillingness, which already appears too great, towards entering into the service, and of course impeding the progress both of drafting and recruiting; by dejecting the courage of the soldiery, from an apprehension of the horrors of captivity; and, finally, by reducing those, whose lot it is to drink the bitter cup, to a despair, which can only find relief by renouncing their attachments and engaging with their captors. These effects have already been experienced in part from the obstacles, that have lain in the way of exchanges; but if these obstacles were once to seem the result of system, they would become tenfold. Nothing has operated more disagreeably upon the minds of the militia, than the fear of captivity, on the footing on which it has hitherto stood. What would be their reasonings, if it should be thought to stand upon a worse *1*

If a present temporary interest is to be a ruling principle, it is easy to prove, that an exchange can never take place. The constitution of our army in respect to the term of service for which our men engage, and the dependence we are obliged to place on the militia, must for ever operate against us in exchanges, and forbid an equality of advantages. Should it be said, that there are times when it might be more peculiarly unequal and injurious, and that the present is such, on account of the weak condition of our army, I answer, that the delay necessarily involved in the previous negotiation on the subject, in delivering the prisoners from time to time in small numbers, and receiving others in their stead, and the mode of delivery at different places, will nearly bring the matter to the point we could wish, and give us leisure to reinforce this army, if it is to be done at alL so as to obviate in a great measure the ill consequences apprehended.

But if the argument of interest on a partial scale be pursued as far as it will go, not only the general consideration thrown out above, but special ones apposite to every situation will present themselves, that we ought not to exchange. *Now* we ought not, because our army is weak! When the season is more advanced, and it is time for the campaign to open, we ought not, because our army may be strong, and it will be our business to avail ourselves of our own strength, and the enemy's weakness, to strike some decisive blow! If they, by the protection of their shipping and impregnable works, should be able to baffle our attempts till the period of reinforcements from Europe arrive, it will surely then not be our interest to add numbers and strength to an enemy already sufficiently numerous and strong! Thus, by a parity of reasoning, the golden era will never come, which is to relieve the miseries of captivity. Our service must become odious; those who are out of it will endeavour to keep so; and those who are in it will wish to get out of it; every prisoner the enemy makes will be his soldier, rather than submit to a rigorous and despairing confinement.

If we do not seize the present propitious moment, when the necessities of the enemy press them to reasonable terms, to form and establish a liberal cartel, it is not impossible, in the vicissitudes and reverses of war, that a time may come when we should wish we had embraced it, and interest may strongly impel the enemy to decline it, except on the most unequal conditions. True policy, as well as good faith, in my opinion, binds us to improve the occasion. There are however some ambiguities in General Howe's conduct, which require explanation, and ought to put us upon our guard. I determined to make the affair of citizens (namely, to procure an exemption from captivity for them if possible, or, if not, since it cannot now be demanded as a matter of right, to fix their exchangeability upon the easiest and most unequivocal foundation,) an indispensable preliminary to any further procedure; and at the same time to secure the exchange of General Lee, and all other officers, who have been the particular objects of exception.

The interview intended between General Howe's commissioners and those on our part on the 10th instant is now postponed. I cannot doubt that Congress, in preservation of the public faith and my personal honor, will remove all impediments, that now oppose themselves to my engagements, and that they will authorize me, through commissioners appointed for the purpose, to negotiate a more extensive and competent cartel, upon such principles as may appear advantageous and founded in necessity, any resolutions heretofore to the contrary notwithstanding; and I must request, that they will favor me with their answer by the earliest opportunity.

The work, from its nature, will be difficult. Two parties are concerned, whose interests are more than opposite in a common view. We shall endeavour to act for the best, and to promote the public service as far as possible, though we may not be able to answer the expectations of all. But it should be remembered, that, although General Howe's want of men affords a prospect of favorable terms, yet he will not be disposed to sacrifice to it all considerations of general advantage in a contract of such a nature; and it is not even to be hoped, that it can take place except on principles of mutual benefit. I persuade myself, that the freedom I have taken in delivering my sentiments so fully upon this occasion will readily be excused, as it proceeds from a desire to place the motives of my conduct in a just point of view, and from an opinion of duty, that led me to a free discussion of a subject, which, considered in all its lights, will appear to comprehend consequences of the first delicacy and magnitude.

I have the honor to be, &c TO BRIGADIER-GENERAL PARSONS, AT WEST POINT.

Valley Forge, 8 March, 1778.

-dear Sir, Below you will receive a copy of my last dated the 5th, to which I will add a thought, which has occurred since the writing of it; and which, if the scheme is practicable at all, may add not a little to the success; namely, to let the officers and soldiers employed in the enterprise be dressed in red, and much in the taste of the British soldiery. Webb's regiment will afford these dresses; and it might not be amiss to know certainly the number of some regiment, that is quartered in the city. Under some circumstances, this knowledge may avail them, especially if the number on their own buttons should correspond thereto. I am, &c. After taking this letter into consideration, Congress voted to suspend the operation of their former resolves in the present instance, and authorized General Washington to proceed to an exchange of the prisoners then in the power of the enemy, without waiting for a previous settlement of accounts; but, in arranging any future cartels of exchange, he was required to act in conformity to the resolves, which ordered a liquidation of accounts for the support of prisoners, before they could be exchanged. — *Journals, March 18th.* COPT Or THE LETTER REFERRED TO ABOVE.

S Much, 1778. Dear Sir,

I learn from undoubted authority, that General Clinton quarters in Captain Kennedy's house in the city of New York, which you know is near Fort George, and, by reason of the late fire, stands in a manner alone. What guards may be at or near his quarters, I cannot with precision say; and therefore shall not add any thing on.this score, lest it should prove a misinformation. But I think it one of the most practicable, and surely it will be among the most desirable and honorable things imaginable to take him prisoner.

This house lying close by the water, and a retired way through a back yard or garden leading into it, what, but want of secrecy, if you have eight or ten whaleboats, can prevent the execution in the hands of an enterprising party? The embarkation might even be (and this I should think best) at King's Ferry, on the first of the ebb, and early in the evening. Six or eight hours, with change of hands, would row the boats under the west shore and very secretly to the city, and the flood-tide will hoist them back again; or a party of horse might meet them at Fort Lee. No ship of war is in the North River; at least there was none ten days ago; nor within four hundred yards of the Point; all being in the East River. I shall add no more. This is dropped as a hint to be improved upon, or rejected, as circumstances point out and justify.

I am, &c TO SIR WILLIAM HOWE.

Head-Quarters, 9 March, 1778.

Sir,

I have your letters of the 14th and 21st of February, and the 2d of March, of all which due notice shall be taken. Particular circumstances make it inconvenient for my commissioners to meet yours at the time appointed. I must, therefore, beg to have the meeting deferred till the 31st of March.

Mr. Boudinot, who has lately returned to camp from New York, informs me, that notwithstanding MajorGeneral Prescott has been several weeks in the city, in pursuance of our agreement for the liberation of officers on parole, General Lee is not permitted to come out; and that orders had been received from you to send him round to Philadelphia by water, that you might take his parole in person. There can be no reason to prevent his parole being taken where he is; and I must consider his being required to expose himself to the inconveniences of a sea-voyage at this season as altogether unnecessary. I had a right to expect, that he would have been released as soon as General Prescott went in; and must request, that you will accordingly give immediate orders for it. If you will be pleased to transmit your directions through me, for that purpose, I will carefully forward them. This would obviate the uncertainty and possible delay of a conveyance by water. I am, with due respect, Sir, &a

This delay was caused by the ill-timed resolve of Congress, which gave rise to General Washington's letter of the 8th. He hoped, that, by postponing the time, Congress would reconsider their proceedings, and enable him to comply with his promise, and this hope was realized. Yet the circumstance was very unfortunate, as it naturally created suspicions in the mind of General Howe, and produced an unfavorable impression. He wrote, March 24th, to Lord George Germain as follows. " The time appointed for the meeting of the commissioners being postponed by General Washington to the 31st of this month, without assigning any satisfactory reason, leads me to believe that neither he, nor those under whose authority he acts, are sincere in their professions to carry an exchange into execution at this time.

" TO THE MARQUIS DE LAFAYETTE

Head-Quarters, 10 March, 1778.

My Dear Marquis, I have had the pleasure of receiving your two favors of the 19th and 23d of February, and hasten to dispel those fears, respecting your reputation, which are excited only by an uncommon degree of sensibility. You seem to apprehend that censure, proportioned to the disappointed expectations of the world, will fall on you, in consequence of the failure of the Canadian expedition. But, in the first place, it will be no disadvantage to you to have it

known in Europe, that you had received so manifest a proof of the good opinion and confidence of Congress, as an important detached command; and I am persuaded, that every one will applaud your prudence in renouncing a project, in pursuing which you would vainly have attempted physical impossibilities. Indeed, unless you can be chargeable with the invariable effects of natural causes, and be See extracts from the letters, to which this is a reply, in the APxkdix, No. XI. arraigned for not suspending the course of the seasons, to accommodate your march over the Lake, the most prone to slander can have nothing to found blame upon.

However sensibly your ardor for glory may make you feel this disappointment, you may be assured, that your character stands as fair as ever it did, and that no new enterprise is necessary to wipe off this imaginary stain. The expedition, which you hint at, I think unadvisable in our present circumstances. Any thing in the way of a formal attack, which would necessarily be announced to the enemy by preparatory measures, would not be likely to succeed. If a stroke is meditated in that quarter, it must be effected by troops stationed at a proper distance for availing themselves of the first favorable opportunity offered by the enemy, and success would principally depend upon the suddenness of the attempt. This, therefore, must rather be the effect of time and chance, than premeditation. You undoubtedly have determined judiciously in waiting the further orders of Congress. Whether they allow me the pleasure of seeing you shortly, or destine you to a longer absence, you may assure yourself of the sincere good wishes of, dear Sir, &c.

P. S. Your directing payment of such debts as appear to be most pressing is certainly right. There is not money enough to answer every demand; and I wish your supplies of clothing had been better. Your ordering a large supply of provisions into Fort Schuyler was a very judicious measure, and I thank you for it.

TO MAJOR-GENERAL SULLIVAN.

Head-Quarters, 10 March, 1778.

Sir,

In pursuance of a resolve of Congress, dated the 21st of February last, by which I am directed to order a major-general to take the command of the troops in the State of Rhode Island, in the place of MajorGeneral Spencer, who has resigned, I have appointed you to that duty, and you are to proceed with all convenient despatch to enter upon it.

Congress have not communicated any thing to me on the subject of instructions. If they have any new object, which will occasion an alteration in those given to your predecessor, it is probable that they will make you particularly acquainted with their views. I am, &lc TO LIEUTENANT-GENERAL BURGOTNE.

Head-Quarters, 11 Much, 177a

Sir, I was only two days since honored with your very obliging letter of the 11th of February. Your indulgent opinion of my character, and the polite terms in which you are pleased to express it, are peculiarly flattering; and I take pleasure in the opportunity you have afforded me, of assuring you, that, far from suffering the views of national opposition to be embittered and debased by personal animosity, I am ever ready to do justice to the merit of the man and soldier, and to esteem where esteem is due, however the idea of a public enemy may interpose. You will not think it the language of unmeaning ceremony, if I add, that sentiments of personal respect, in the present instance, are reciprocal.

Viewing you in the light of an officer, contending against what I conceive to be the rights of my country, the reverses of fortune you experienced in the field cannot be unacceptable to me; but, abstracted from considerations of national advantage, I can sincerely sympathize with your feelings as a soldier, the unavoidable difficulties of whose situation forbade his success; and as a man, whose lot combines the calamity of ill health, the anxieties of captivity, and the painful sensibility for a reputation exposed, where he most values it, to the assaults of malice and detraction.

As your aid-de-camp went directly to

Congress, the business of your letter to me had been decided before it came to hand. I am happy, that their cheerful acquiescence in your request prevented the necessity of my intervention; and wishing you a safe and agreeable passage, with a perfect restoration of your health, I have the honor to be, very respectfully, &,c TO GEORGE WILLIAM FAIRFAX, IN ENGLAND.

Head-Quarters, Pennsylvania, 11 March, 1778.

Dear Sir, Immediately on my appointment to the command of the American army, and arrival at Cambridge, near Boston, in the year 1775, I informed you of the impracticability of my longer continuing to perform the duties of a friend, by having an eye to the conduct of your collector and steward; as my absence from Virginia would not only withdraw every little attention I otherwise might have given to your business, but involve my own in the same neglected predicament. What use you may have made of the information, I know not, having heard nothing from you these four years, nor been in Virginia these last three. I have heard, and fear it is true, that your seat (Belvoir) is verging fast to destruction. In what condition, and under what management, your estate in Berkeley is, I know not; and equally ignorant am I respecting the conduct of Peyton, but earnestly advise you to empower some person to attend to these matters, or the consequence is obvious.

General Burgoyne wrote in reply j — "I beg you to accept my sincerest acknowledgments for your obliging letter. I find the character, which I before knew to be respectable, is also perfectly amiable; and I should have few greater private gratifications in seeing our melancholy contest at an end, than that of cultivating your friendship."— *April 4th.*

Lord Fairfax, as I have been told, after having been bowed down to the grave, and in a manner shaken hands with Death, is perfectly restored, and enjoys his usual good health, and as much vigor as falls to the lot of ninety. Miss Fairfax was upon the point of marriage in December last with a relation of mine, a Mr. Whiting; but her ill health delayed it at that time, and what has happened since I am not informed. Your nieces in Alexandria are both married; the elder to Mr. Herbert, the younger to Mr. Harry Whiting, son of Frank in Berkeley. Mrs. Cary, her son Colonel Cary, Mr. Nicholas, Mrs. Ambler, and their respective families were all well about two months ago. Miss Cary is married to Tom Nelson, second son to the Secretary.

Mrs. Washington, who is now in quarters with me, joins in most affectionate compliments to Mrs. Fairfax and yourself with, dear Sir, &c TO THE PRESIDENT OF CONGRESS.

Valley Forge, 12 March, 1778.

Sir,

I am happy to find, that my past conduct respecting citizens, in the correspondence between General Howe and myself, is approved by Congress. They may rest assured, that their rights are strongly impressed on my mind; and that, in all my transactions, every support in my power shall be given to them. I Know their importance; and, in my expected negotiations with General Howe, if possible, I will exempt citizens from captivity. However, I cannot hope to effect it, as I cannot demand it as a matter of right; since Congress themselves, in their original resolve directing a proposition to be made for the exchange of prisoners, mentioned that of citizens, which implied a right of capturing them.

They may also be assured, that General Lee will not be forgotten. He has all along been a principal object in dispute; and, so far from doing any thing injurious to him, his right to be exchanged, and his releasement, are intended to be placed upon the most explicit, unambiguous footing. Indeed, from the spirit of General Howe's letters collectively taken, since his agreement to enlarge the officers on parole in the first instance, and his extension of it in the last to an exchange, though they are not free from ambiguities, it may be inferred, that, on sending in Lieutenant-Colonel Campbell and the Hessian field-officers captured at Trenton, an exchange of all officers will immediately commence. It seems to be a point with him, that it shall begin with them, as they have been longest in captivity. I have taken the liberty to enclose to you copies of three letters, which have just passed between General Howe

W» and myself, more particularly concerning General Lee, in which I have pushed matters respecting him as far as I thought it prudent at this time. Every precaution will certainly be used to prevent the enemy from gaining any advantage in the exchange of prisoners.

With great deference I would take the liberty to observe, that Congress seem to have carried the preamble of their resolve of the 26th ultimo, prohibiting the enlisting of prisoners and deserters, too far; and, through accident, to have recited a fact, that has never happened (at least to my knowledge), and which is injurious to us, namely, that prisoners had been enlisted by us. If any have, it is what I never knew. However, be this as it may, if the resolution has not been published, I could wish the preamble to be altered, and only to recite, " *that experience, &c. in deserters*" only. The resolution itself may stand as it does, comprehending a prohibition against the enlistment of both.

My reason for troubling Congress upon this occasion is, that we have always complained against General Howe, and still do, for obliging or permitting the prisoners in his hands to enlist, as an unwarrantable procedure, and wholly repugnant to the spirit at least of the cartel. This preamble seems to admit the practice on our part, which would certainly justify it in him, and is such evidence as must silence us in future (should it stand), and afford him an opportunity for recrimination, though, as I have suggested, I believe no prisoners have been enlisted by us; I am sure none have through compulsion. I have the honor to be, &c.

The preamble and resolve had probably been published before the above letter waa received by Congress, since they both now stand in the Journals as they were originally passed. " Whereas experience has) proved, that no confidence can be placed in prisoners of war or deserters from the enemy, who enlist into the Continental army, bat many losses and great mischiefs have frequently happened by them; therefore, Resolved, that no prisoners of war or deserters from the enemy be enlisted, drafted, or returned, to serve in the Continental army." — *February QGth.* TO CAPTAIN JOHN BARRY.

Head-Quarters, 12 March, 1778.

Sir, I have received your favor of the 9th instant, and congratulate you on the success, which has crowned your gallantry and address in the late attack upon the enemy's ships. Although circumstances have prevented you from reaping the full benefit of your conquest, yet there is ample consolation in the degree of glory, which you have acquired. You will be pleased to accept of my thanks for the good things, which you were so polite as to send me, with my wishes, that a suitable recompense may always attend your bravery.

I am, Sir, &c Captain Barry, of the navy, had manned four row-boats at Burlington, and proceeded down the river in the night with muffled oars, and undiscovered by the enemy. He reached the vicinity of Port Penn unmolested, where he had the good fortune to capture two ships and a schooner, of which he gave the following account. "The two ships were transports from Rhode Island loaded with forage, one mounting six four-pounders, with fourteen hands each. The schooner was in the engineering department, mounting eight double-fortified four-pounders, and twelve four-pound howitzers, and manned with thirty-three men." These vessels were taken by capitulation. There were several ladies on board, who, by the articles of surrender, were to be sent immediately to Philadelphia with their baggage. The exploit was considered highly creditable to Captain Barry, on account of the enterprise and daring he displayed in going down the river, when it was full of the enemy's shipping and small craft. He adds, at the conclusion of his letter to General Washington; " I should have transmitted the particulars before, but a fleet of the enemy's small vessels appearing in sight obliged me to burn one of the ships, and I fear the other will share the same fate after discharging her; but I am determined to hold the schooner at all events." TO SIR WILLIAM HOWE.

Valley Forge, 12 March, 1778.

Sir,

Your letter of the 10th came to hand last night. The meeting of our commissioners cannot take place till the time appointed in my last.f

I am not able to conceive on what principle it should be imagined, that any distinction, injurious to Lieutenant-Colonel Campbell and the Hessian field-officers, still exists. That they have not yet been returned on parole is to be ascribed solely to the remoteness of their situation. Mr. Boudinot informs me, that he momentarily expects their arrival, in prosecution of our engagement. You are well aware, that the distinction originally made, with respect to them, was in consequence of your discrimination to the prejudice of General Lee. On your receding from that discrimination, and agreeing to a mutual releasement of officers on parole, the difficulty ceased, and General Prescott was sent into New York, in full expectation, that General Lee would come out in return. So far from adhering to any former exception, I had particularly directed my commissary of prisoners to release Lieutenant-Colonel Campbell, in lieu of Lieutenant-Colonel Ethan Allen.

See Appendix, No. XIII. f The time appointed was the 31st of March, or rather General Washington found it necessary to defer the meeting till that time, on account of a resolve of Congress, which made this postponement necessary. The commissioners were Colonel William Grayson, Lieutenant-Colonels Harrison and Hamilton, and Elias Boudinot. Their instructions were dated on the 28th of March, and they were empowered to confer with the British commissioners, " and determine and agree upon a treaty and convention for the exchange of prisoners of war, and for all matters whatsoever, which may be properly contained therein, on principles of justice, humanity, and mutual advantage, and agreeably to the customary roles and practice of war among civilized nations."

I wish, Sir, I was not obliged to say, that there are some ambiguities still characterizing the measures taken concerning General Lee, which justify alarming surmises, notwithstanding all that has passed to the contrary. I have now been as explicit as you can desire, on the subject of Colonel Campbell and the Hessian gentlemen; and I hope to find you as explicit on the subject of General Lee, by giving directions, without further delay, to liberate him in place of General Prescott. General Lee's request, mentioned by you, to be permitted to come by land to Philadelphia, can be no objection to this requisition. It was founded upon your order to send him round by water to that place; and, conceiving it would be insisted on, that he should pass to Philadelphia, he preferred the mode of going by land, as the least inconvenient alternative. But the measure appears to me wholly improper, and a departure from our late stipulation, calculated to impose unnecessary hardships on that unfortunate gentleman, and to produce needless procrastination, at least, in allowing him the common benefit of a general agreement.

With due respect, I am, &c.

TO PHILIP SCHUYLER, JAMES DUANE, AND VOLKERT P. DOUW, COMMISSIONERS OF INDIAN AFFAIRS.

Valley Forge, 13 March, 1778.

Gentlemen,

You will perceive, by the enclosed copy of a resolve of Congress, that I am empowered to employ a body of four hundred Indians, if they can be procured upon proper terms. Divesting them of the savage customs exercised in their wars against each other, I think they may be made of excellent use as scouts and light

Vol. v. 35 troops, mixed with our own parties. I propose to raise about one half the number among the southern, and the remainder among the northern Indians. I have sent Colonel Nathaniel Gist, who is well acquainted with the Cherokees and their allies, to bring as many as he can from thence; and I must depend upon you to employ suitable persons to procure the stipulated number, or as near as may be, from the northern tribes. The terms made with them should be such as you think we can comply with; and persons well acquainted with their language, manners, and customs, and who have gained an influence over them, should accompany them. The Oneidas have manifested the strongest attachment to us throughout this dispute, and therefore I suppose, if any can be procured, they will be most numerous. Their missionary, Mr. Kirkland, seemed to have an uncommon ascendency over that tribe, and I should therefore be glad to see him accompany them.

If the Indians can be procured, I would choose to have them here by the opening of the campaign; and therefore they should be engaged as soon as possible, as there is not more time between this and the middle of May, than will be necessary to settle the business with them, and to march from their country to the army. I am not without hopes, that this will reach you before the treaty, which is to be held, breaks up. If it should, you will have an opportunity of knowing their sentiments, of which I shall be glad to be informed as soon as possible.

I have the honor to be, gentlemen, &c The Acts, as to the original movements for employing Indiana is the war, have already been examined. (VoL III. p. 494.) A short time before Congress passed the resolve, conferring the authority described above, the subject had been vehemently discussed in the British Parliament, (February 6th,) on a motion of Mr. Burke to call for the papers. which had passed between the ministry and the generals commanding in America, relative to the military employment of Indians. The act was denounced as criminal, and the ministers were censured with much asperity by the prominent opposition members for abetting and approving it. Mr. Burke said; — "No proof whatever had been given of the Americans having attempted offensive alliances with any one tribe of savages;

whereas the imperfect papers now before that House demonstrated, that the King's ministers had negotiated and obtained such alliances from one end of the continent of America to the other; that the Americans had actually made a treaty on the footing of neutrality with the famous Five Nations, which the King's ministers had bribed them to violate, and to act offensively against the colonies; that no attempt had been made in a single instance on the part of the King's ministers to procure a neutrality; that if the fact had been, that the Americans had actually employed those savages, yet the difference of employing them against armed and trained soldiers, embodied and encamped, and employing them against the unarmed and defenceless men, women, and children of a country, dispersed in their houses, was manifest, and left those, who attempted so inhuman and unequal a retaliation, without excuse." TO THE REVEREND ISRAEL EVANS.

Valley Forge, 13 March, 1778.

Reverend Sir, Your favor of the 17th ultimo, enclosing the Discourse, which you delivered to General Poor's brigade on the 18th of December, the day set apart for a general thanksgiving, never came to my hands till yesterday. I have read this performance with equal attention and pleasure; and, at the same time that I admire and feel the force of the reasoning, which you have displayed through the whole, it is more especially incumbent upon me to thank you for the honorable but partial mention you have made of my character; and to assure you, that it will ever be the first wish of my heart to aid your pious endeavours to inculcate a due sense of the dependence we ought to place in that all-wise and powerful Being, on whom alone our success depends; and, moreover, to assure you, that, with respect and regard, I am, Reverend Sir, &c.

Lord George Germain spoke in reply, and justified the conduct of administration. " He said the matter lay within a very narrow compass; the Indians would not have remained idle spectators; the very arguments used by the honorable gentleman, who made the

motion, were so many proofs that they would not. Besides, the rebels, by their emissaries, had made frequent applications to the Indians to side with them, the Vir ginians particularly; and he said, that some Indians were employed at Boston in the rebel army. Now taking the disposition of the Indians, with the applications made to them by the colonies, it amounted to a clear, indisputable proposition, that either they would have served against us, or that we must have employed them." Lord North said, on the.same side, that, in respect to the employment of Indians, he looked upon it as bad, but unavoidable. " TO THE PRESIDENT OF CONGRESS.

Head-Quarters, 14 March, 1778.

Sir,

This will be presented to you by Count Pulaski, who, from a conviction that his remaining at the head of the cavalry was a constant subject of uneasiness to the principal officers of that corps, has been induced to resign his command. Waving a minute inquiry into the causes of dissatisfaction, which may be reduced perhaps to the disadvantages under which he labored, as a stranger not well acquainted with the language, genius, and manners of this country, it may be sufficient to observe, that the degree of harmony, which is inseparable from the well-being and consequent utility of a corps, has not subsisted in the cavalry since his appointment, and that the most effectual as well as the easiest remedy is that, which he has generously applied.

Governor Pownall, who had resided long in America, and understood the Indian character perfectly, was of the same opinion. He proposed a scheme of his own. " I know," said he, " and therefore speak directly, that the idea of an Indian neutrality is nonsense; delusive, dangerous nonsense. If both we and the Americans were agreed to observe a strict neutrality in not employing them, they would then plunder and scalp both parties indiscriminately on both sides. Although this is my opinion, founded on the knowledge and experience I have had in these matters, yet I am persuaded, that if we and the Americans would come to some stipulation, or convention, that we would mutually and in a spirit of good faith not suffer the Indians to intermeddle, but consider and act against them as enemies, whenever they did execute hostilities against any of the British nation, whether English or Americans, all this horrid business might be prevented, or at least in a great measure restrained." Governor Pownall enlarged upon his scheme, and even offered to proceed himself to Congress, if duly authorized, and use his endeavours with that body to carry it into effect. — Almon's *Pmiianentary Regitttr,* Vol VIII. pp. 349, 353, 357.

Mr. Evans was chaplain to Poor's New Hampshire brigade.

The Count, however, far from being disgusted with the service, is led by his thirst of glory, and zeal for the cause of liberty, to solicit farther employment, and waits upon Congress to make his proposals. They are briefly, that he be allowed to raise an independent corps, composed of sixty-eight horse and two hundred foot, the horse to be armed with lances, and the foot equipped in the manner of light-infantry. The former he thinks he can readily fill with natives of good character, and worthy of the trust reposed in them. With respect to the other, he is desirous of more latitude, so as to have liberty of engaging prisoners and deserters from the enemy.

The original plan for the lance-men was to draft them from the regiments of horse. But, as this method would produce a clashing of interests, and perhaps occasion new disturbances, the Count prefers having a corps totally unconnected with any other. My advice to him, therefore, is to enlist his number of cavalry with the Continental bounty; and, if it should be found consonant to the views of Congress to allow his raising the number proposed over and above the establishment for the horse, then he would have them on the footing of an independent corps; if not, he

Vol. v. x might at all events have them as drafts; and in this case there would be no ground for complaint. With regard to the infantry, which the Count esteems essential to the success of the

cavalry, I have informed him, that the enlisting of deserters and prisoners is prohibited by a late resolve of Congress. How far Congress might be inclined to make an exception, and license the engaging of prisoners in a particular detached corps, in which such characters may be admitted with less danger than promiscuously in the line, I cannot undertake to pronounce.

I have only to add, that the Count's valor and active zeal on all occasions have done him great honor; and, from a persuasion that, by being less exposed to the inconveniences which he has hitherto experienced, he will render great services with such a command as he asks for, I wish him to succeed in his application.

I have the honor to be, &c.

P. S. It is to be understood, that the Count expects to retain his rank as brigadier, and, I think, is entitled to it from his general character and particular disinterestedness on the present occasion.

The rank of brigadier-general was continued to Count Pulaski, and he was authorized to raise and command an independent corps, to consist of sixty-eight horse and two hundred foot. The latter were to be equipped in the manner of light-infantry, and the former to be armed with lances. The mode of raising and organizing the corps was left to the direction of General Washington. — *Journals, March 28th.* TO GOVERNOR LIVINGSTON.

Valley Forge, 14 March, 1778.

Sir,

I have the honor of yours of the 2d instant; and, I can assure you, I feel myself very sensibly affected by the strenuous manner in which you express the public regard of the State and your personal friendship towards me. I only desire to be the object of both, while in your good opinion and that of the public I continue to merit them.

We seem hitherto to have mistaken each other, in respect to the troop of light-horse. I did not mean to enlist them into the Continental service, but only to engage them for a few months, while the Continental horse were re-

cruiting, upon the same terms that I engaged the Morris County horse last winter. It will be expected, that they provide their own horses, arms, and accoutrements, and be paid accordingly. If Captain Arnold will come into the service upon the above terms, I will immediately take him into employ. It is impossible to devise any other mode of disposing of deserters, than to let them go at large among us, provided there is no particular cause of suspicion against them. To confine them would effectually put a stop to a drain, which weakens the enemy more, in the course of a year, than you would imagine. I am pleased with the favorable account you give of Count Pulaski's conduct while at Trenton. He is a gentleman of great activity and unquestionable bravery, and only wants a fuller knowledge of our language and customs to make him a valuable officer. I am, &c.

TO MAJOR-GENERAL MCDOUGALL.

Head-Quarters, Valley Forge, 16 March, 1778.

Dear Sir,

I was favored with yours of the 17th ultimo in due time, and should have proceeded immediately upon the business of the inquiry, had not General Putnam's private affairs required his absence for some little time. I have appointed Brigadier-General Huntington and Colonel Wigglesworth to assist you in this matter; and, enclosed, you will find instructions empowering you, in conjunction with them, to carry on the inquiry agreeably to the resolve of Congress. You will observe by the words of the resolve, that the inquiry is to be made into the loss of Forts Montgomery and Clinton, in the State of New York, and into the conduct of the principal officers commanding those forts.

Hence the officer commanding in chief in that department will be consequentially involved in the inquiry; because, if he has been deficient in affording the proper support to those posts, when called upon to do it, the commandant and principal officers will of course make it appear by the evidence produced in their own justification. I am not certain whether General Putnam has yet returned to Fishkill; and I have therefore by the enclosed, which you will please to forward to him by express, given him notice that the inquiry is to be held, and have desired him to repair immediately to that post. General Huntington and Colonel Wigglesworth will set out as soon as they can make preparations for the journey.

Upon your arrival at the Highlands, you are to take upon you the command of the different posts in that department, of which I have advised General Putnam. Your time will at first be principally taken up with the business, which you now have in hand; but I beg that your attention may be turned, as much as possible, to the completion of the works, or at least to putting them in such a state, that they may be able to resist a sudden attack of the enemy. Governor Clinton has written his opinion very fully to Congress upon the propriety of ordering all the troops, except the garrison of Fort Schuyler, down to the Highlands, as all prospects of carrying on the northern expedition seem to have vanished. I have backed his opinion forcibly with my own, and hope, if Congress see matters in the light we do, that those troops may be instantly brought down.

There has been a resolve of Congress vesting Governor Clinton with the direction of the works erecting for the defence of the river, and requiring the commanding officer at Peekskill to aid him in the execution of the same. Governor Clinton, I understand, from his civil avocations, does not incline to take the immediate direction of the business, and the late commanding officer in that quarter has doubted from that resolve, whether his command or superintendency extended to the forts. To remove difficulties of this kind, by which the public service must suffer, and as I consider it essential to the nature of the command, that one officer should have the general control and direction of all the posts in the Highlands and their dependencies, and be answerable for them, you are to consider yourself as possessed of this general control and direction, and to act accordingly. If the

Governor has leisure from his official duties to undertake the more immediate management of the works, it will afford you a very desirable assistance.

I have written to Congress to give you every power necessary to promote the objects of your command; *Vol. x.* 36 x and in the mean time you are to consider yourself authorized, as far as can depend upon me, to take every measure conducive to that end. I am sensible this command will not be in itself the most agreeable piece of service, and that you would prefer a post on the principal theatre of action; but the vast importance of it has determined me to confide it to you, and I am persuaded your object is to be useful to the public. If you get things in a proper train by the opening of the campaign, so that the prosecution may be assigned to other hands, I shall be extremely happy to avail myself of your services with the main army. I am, &,c There had been a series of misapprehensions on the subject of constructing military works in the Highlands, as well as a train of obstacles to their progress. On the 5th of November, Congress had appointed General Gates to command in the Highlands, or rather had connected that post with the northern department, and invested him with ample powers to carry on the works; but, as he was made President of the Board of War, he never entered upon these duties. Again, on the 18th of February, Governor Clinton was requested to take the superintendence of the works; but the multiplicity of his civil employment made it necessary for him to decline the undertaking. Meantime General Putnam went to Connecticut, and left the post in charge of General Parsons. Unfortunately this officer conceived the notion, that he had no control over the works in the Highlands; that the resolves of Congress in regard to Gates and Clinton were personal, and not designed to apply to any one else; and that, having no direct instructions, he could not rightfully assume any authority in the matter. By the judicious advice of Governor Clinton, however, he was prevailed upon to exercise a proper supervision, till General

McDougall arrived. When these doubts in regard to the extent of command are considered, and also the tardy movements of the engineer in executing a plan, which he did not approve, the extreme fatigue of the service in the midst of winter, the privations and sufferings of the men, and the want of teams and other necessary aids, it is not surprising, that very slow progress had been made. General McDougall took the command on the 28th of March. Two days previously Kosciuszko arrived, who had been appointed engineer in the place of Radiere. From that time the works were pressed forward with spirit. To the scientific skill and sedulous application of Kosciuszko, the public was mainly indebted for the construction of the military defences at West Point.

TO MAJOR-GENERAL PUTNAM.

Valley Forge, 16 March, 177a

Dear Sir,

The Congress having, by a resolve of the 28th of November last, directed that an inquiry be made into the loss of Forts Montgomery and Clinton, and into the conduct of the principal officers commanding those forts, I have appointed Major-General MDougall, Brigadier-General Huntington, and Colonel Wigglesworth, to carry the resolve into execution. It is more than probable, that the conduct of the officer commanding at the time in that department will be involved in the inquiry, and I therefore desire, that you will repair immediately to Fishkill upon the receipt of this, to meet General MDougall and the other gentlemen.

General MDougall is to take the command of the posts in the Highlands. My reason for making this change is owing to the prejudices of the people, which, whether well or ill grounded, must be indulged; and I should think myself wanting in justice to the public and candor towards you, were I to continue you in a command, after I have been almost in direct terms informed, that the people of the State of New York will not render the necessary support and assistance, while you remain at the head of that department. When the inquiry is finished, I desire that you will return to Connecticut and superintend the forwarding on the new levies with the greatest expedition.

I am, &c General Putnam's advanced age, his good nature, and easy temperament were among the chief causes of the ill success of his command on the North River. His proceedings were not marked with the promptBess, decision, and energy, nor even with the military address, which had characterized his early years. If all these had been combined and exercised, it is probable there would still have been dissatisfaction, after the enemy had forced their way up the river, and laid waste its border. Not only were complaints uttered by the popular voice, but the political leaders of the State expressed discontent. Robert R. Livingston, then Chancellor of New York, wrote to General Washington on the subject in a pointed manner.

TO THE PRESIDENT OF CONGRESS.
Head-Quarters, Valley Forge, 16 March, 1778.

Sir, I have the honor to transmit to you a letter from Governor Clinton, which he enclosed to me for my perusal and consideration. The inconvenience he mentions, as resulting from the resolve respecting the appointment of a commandant for Forts Montgomery and Clinton, requires to be obviated. I do not conceive it to have been the design of Congress to make the command of those forts altogether distinct and independent on the general command of the posts in that quarter; but only to designate the rank of the officer, who should have the immediate charge of them. There is such an intimate connexion between the forts and the other posts and passes in the Highlands and their vicinity, that it is necessary for one officer to have the superintendency and control of the whole, and to be answerable for all. If this were not to be the case, but the command were to be divided, there might be wanting that cooperation between the garrisons and the troops without, which might be essential to their preservation and to the common purposes of defence. The assigning of a fixed number of men to the garrisons would not remove this inconvenience; for the cooperation would still be necessary. But if it were otherwise, I should not think the measure advisable, because we do not know what number of men we may have in the field next campaign; and the number for the defence of the Highlands must be proportioned to the general strength, and the force of the garrisons to that number.

" Vour Excellency," said he, " is not ignorant of the extent of General Putnam's capacity and diligence; and how well soever these may qualify him for this most important command, the prejudices to which his imprudent lenity to the disaffected, and too great intercourse with the enemy, have given rise, have greatly injured his influence. How far the loss of Fort Montgomery and the subsequent ravages of the enemy are to be attributed to him, I will not venture to say; as thia will necessarily be determined by a court of inquiry, whose determinations I would not anticipate. Unfortunately for him, the current of popular opinion in this and the neighbouring States, and as far as I can learn in the troops under his command, runs strongly against him. For my own part, I respect his bravery and former services, and sincerely lament, that his patriotism will not suffer him to take that repose, to which his advanced age and past services justly entitle him."—MS. Letter, January lth.

It must be remembered, that at this station there were innumerable applications for passports to go into New York, under the pretence of urgent business, and various matters of a private concern; and it wu thought General Putnam's good nature was too pliant on these occasions, and that too many opportunities were afforded for an improper intercourse between the disaffected and the enemy. At any rate, the symptoms of uneasiness appeared from such high sources, and were so decidedly manifested, that General Washington deemed it necessary to take notice of them, and to change the command.

On these considerations, having ordered General M Dougall to repair to the Highlands to assume the chief command there, I have comprehended the forts among the other objects of his trust; in the discharge of which I am persuaded he will manifest adequate zeal and ability. But as the resolve in question affords room for doubt, it will be proper to have it explained, so as more explicitly to ascertain the intention of Congress. I am perfectly in sentiment with Governor Clinton, on the propriety of drawing the troops from the northward to reinforce and carry on the works in the Highlands. From every thing I can learn, there seems to be no prospect of prosecuting the intended expedition into Canada. If so, I apprehend it can answer no valuable end to keep a body of troops in and about Albany. In the present circumstances of Canada, little is to be dreaded thence; the enemy, in all probability, will be well satisfied to act on the defensive, without risking the consequences of an attempt against us. A proper garrison at Fort Schuyler, and a small party by way of guard at Albany, with the militia of the country that may be occasionally drawn together, will be a sufficient security against the inroads of the enemy from Canada, or the depredations of the neighbouring Indians, supposing there were any of the tribes, whose dispositions were still actively hostile notwithstanding our late northern successes, which is by no means a natural supposition. All the men, that are not wanted for these purposes, would be of the most important utility in the Highlands.

If the arms and stores at Albany should be thought an objection to the plan, I would beg leave to observe, that Albany appears to me a most improper place for stationary arsenals or magazines, and that those which are there at present should be removed without delay. Besides, as they would be in most danger from an incursion up the North River, the best way to counteract that danger is to strengthen the passes in the Highlands, and obstruct the navigation; in order to which the reinforcing of them with the troops from the northward would be no inconsiderable step.

I have the honor to be, &c In consequence of this letter the Congress decided, that all the troop in the State of New York, including the whole northern department, should be under one general. officer, and that he should be authorized to draw together at the Highlands such parts of them as he should deem expedient. To supply the place of those at Albany, the Governor of New York was requested to furnish such a number of militia, as would be sufficient to protect the arsenal and magazines at that place, till the progress of the obstructions at the Highlands should put them out of danger of any sudden attempt from the enemy. — *Journals, March* 31.

TO JAMES BOWDOIN, PRESIDENT OF THE COUNCIL OF MASSACHUSETTS.

Valley Forge, 17 March, 177&

Sir,

It gives me inexpressible concern to have repeated information from the best authority, that the committees of the different towns and districts in your State hire deserters from General Burgoyne's army, and employ them as substitutes, to excuse the personal service of the inhabitants. I need not enlarge upon the danger of substituting, as soldiers, men, who have given a glaring proof of a treacherous disposition, and who are bound to us by no motives of attachment, instead of citizens, in whom the ties of country, kindred, and sometimes property are so many securities for their fidelity. The evils with which this measure is pregnant are obvious, and of such a serious nature, as make it necessary, not only to stop the farther progress of it, but likewise to apply a retrospective remedy, and if possible to annul it, so far as it has been carried into effect. Unless this is done, although you may be amused for the present with the flattering idea of speedily completing your battalions, they will be found, at or before the opening of the campaign, reduced by the defection of every British soldier to their original weak condition; and the accumulated bounties of the continent and of the State will have been fruitlessly sacrificed.

Indeed, General Burgoyne could hardly, if he were consulted, suggest a more effectual plan for plundering us of so much money, reinforcing General Howe with so many men, and preventing us from recruiting a certain number of regiments; to say nothing of the additional losses, which may be dreaded, in desertions among the native soldiers, from the contagion of ill example and the arts of seduction, which it is more than probable will be put in practice. This r.atter demands your immediate attention, and I flatter myself, that on a due consideration of the mischiefs, which must inevitably flow from the pernicious practice remonstrated against, you will not delay the application of the most extensive and efficacious remedy. I have the honor to be, with the greatest respect, Sir, &c TO THE REVEREND TIMOTHY DWIGHT.f

Head-Quarters, Valley Forge, 18 March, 1778.

Sir, I yesterday received your favor of the 8th instant, accompanied by so warm a recommendation from General Parsons, that I cannot but form favorable presages of the merit of the work you propose to honor me with the dedication of. Nothing can give me more pleasure, than to patronize the essays of genius, and a laudable cultivation of the arts and sciences, which had begun to flourish in so eminent a degree, before the hand of oppression was stretched over our devoted country; and I shall esteem myself happy, if a poem, which has employed the labor of years, will derive any advantage, or bear more weight in the world, by making its appearance under a dedication to me. I am, &c In another letter, dated March 31st, General Washington wrote to Mr. Bowdoin as follows. The evil, which I apprehended from the enlistment of deserters, has already made its appearance. One of the colonels informs me, that every British deserter sent to his regiment, except one, has already gone off. One of these people a few nights ago took off a light-horse with his accoutrements from an advanced picket. I hope, upon this proof of the infidelity of the above-described class, that a total stop will be put to the hiring of them." f Mr. Dwight, afterwards President of Yale College, was at this time chaplain to General Parsons's brigade. " The application, which is the 'subject of this letter," said he, in writing to General Washington, " is, I believe, not common in these American regions, yet I hope it will not on that account be deemed impertinence or presumption. For several years I have been employed in writing a poem on the Conquest of Canaan by Joshua. This poem, upon the first knowledge of your Excellency's character,-1 determined, with leave, to inscribe to you. If it will not be too great a favor, it will certainly be remembered with gratitude."

Mr. Dwight's letter was enclosed in one from General Parson?, in which he says of the poet; " He is a person of extensive literature, an amiable private character, and has happily united that virtue and piety, which ought ever to form the character of a gentleman, with the liberal and generous sentiments and agreeable manners of a gentleman. Of the merit of the performance he mentions, I am not a competent judge. Many gentlemen of learning, and taste for poetical writings, who have examined it with care and attention, esteem this work in the class of the best writings of the kind. He will be particularly obliged by your Excellency's consent, that it should make its first appearance under your patronage." — *Wut Point, March 7th.* TO BRIGADIER-GENERAL JOHN CADWALADER.

Valley Forge, 20 March, 1778.

My Dear Sir, Your favor of the 12th instant came safe to my hands and gave me sincere pleasure; as it encouraged a hope, which I had before entertained, of seeing you in camp again. Most sincerely do I wish it was in my power to point out some post or place in the army, which would invite you and fix you in it. We want your aid exceedingly; and the public, perhaps at no time since the commencement of the war, would be more benefited by your advice and assistance, than at the present moment, and throughout the whole of this campaign, which must be important and critical. One thing is certain; a seat at my board, and a square on my floor, shall always be reserved for you. But this, though it would add to my pleasure, is not the height of my wishes. I want to see you in a more important station.

VOL. V. 37 T

By death and desertion we have lost a good many men since we came to this ground, and have encountered every species of hardship, that cold, wet, and hunger, and want of clothes, were capable of producing; notwithstanding, and contrary to my expectations, we have been able to keep the soldiers from mutiny or dispersion; although, in the single article of provisions, they have encountered enough to have occasioned one or the other of these in most other armies. They have two or three times been days together without provisions; and once, six days without any of the meat kind. Could the poor horses tell their tale, it would be in a strain still more lamentable, as numbers have actually died from pure want. But, as our prospects begin to brighten, my complaints shall cease.

It gives me much pleasure to hear, that the recruiting service in the counties near you is in so hopeful a way; but I despair of seeing our battalions completed by any other means than drafting. The importance of the place you speak of is obvious. It has engrossed much of my thoughts; but in our present situation and under our present prospects it is one of those things, that is more likely to become an object of our desire, than attainment.

I have every reason short of absolute proof to believe, that General Howe is meditating a stroke against this army. He has drawn, some say two thousand, and others twenty-five hundred, men from New York, who I believe are arrived at Philadelphia, as a number of transports have just past Wilmington in their way up the Delaware; and reports from Newport say, that the garrison there had orders to be in readiness to embark by the 20th instant. Their invalids had gone off for England, and the women and children for New York. I am, &.c TO THE MARQUIS DE LAFAYETTE.

Head-Quarters, 20 March, 1778.

Sir, In pursuance of a resolve of Congress of the 13th instant, a copy of which is enclosed, I am to desire, that you will without loss of time return to camp, to resume the command of a division of this army; and that you will communicate a similar order to MajorGeneral de Kalb. By the second resolve of the same date, you will see that I am empowered to order Hazen's or any other regiment from the northward to join this army. I intend no other change for the present, than to have Van Schaick's regiment marched to the Highlands to receive the orders of Major-General MDougall, and I desire, that you will give orders in consequence to the commanding officer of that regiment. I anticipate the pleasure of seeing you, and with sincere assurances of esteem and regard, remain, dear Sir, yours, &,c.f This conjecture, as to General Howe's designs, was doubtless without foundation. It does not appear from his letters, that he had formed any plans of attacking the American army at Valley Forge. As late as the 19th of April, he wrote to the minister; " The enemy's position continues to be at Valley Forge and Wilmington. Their force has been diminished during the course of the winter by desertion, and by detachments to the back settlements, where the Indians make constant inroads; but the want of green forage does not yet permit me to take the field, and their situation is too strong to hazard an attack with a prospect of success." — *Parliamentary Register,* Vol. XI. p. 465. f The Canada expedition having failed, from the want of proper means and suitable preparations for carrying it into effect, the Marquis de Lafayette and Baron de Kalb were directed by Congress to repair to the main army. — *Stcrct Journals,* VoL L p. 65. Conway was left with the command at Albany, but he remained only a abort time, when by order of Congress he joined the army under General McDougall in the Highlands. TO THE PRESIDENT OF CONGRESS. Head-Quarters, Valley Forge, 21 March, 177&

Sir,

In consequence of the resolves transmitted to me, I have despatched an express to the Marquis de Lafayette and Baron de Kalb, to recall them from the northward; and, instead of ordering down Hazen's regiment to rejoin this army, I have ordered Van Schaick's immediately to the Highlands, where the public works are in a manner at a stand for want of hands. Van Schaick's is a full and fresh regiment; Hazen's but weak in point of numbers, and must be considerably fatigued from their late long march.

Enclosed you have the copy of a letter, which 1 received a few days ago from Doctor Rush. As this letter contains charges of a very heinous nature against the director-general, Doctor Shippen, for mal-practices and neglect in his department, I could not but look upon it as meant for a public accusation, and have therefore thought it incumbent upon me to lay it before Congress. I have showed it to Doctor Shippen, that he may be prepared to vindicate his character, if called upon. He tells me, that Doctor Rush made charges of a private nature before a committee of Congress, appointed to hear them, which he could not support. If so, Congress will not have further occasion to trouble themselves in the matter.

I have the honor to be, &c.

They had marched from Wilmington in Delaware, during the eerer season of winter. TO SIR WILLIAM HOWE. Head-Quarters, 22 March, 1778.

Sir,

You are under a mistake as to the rank of Mr. Ethan Allen, which is only that of lieutenant-colonel; and as such he has been returned and considered by your commissary, Mr. Loring. The fact truly is, to the best of my information, that, at the time of his capture, he had an appointment as lieutenant-colonel from the State of New York, in a regiment commanded by Colonel Warner. Though he may have been called Colonel in some letters of mine, it was either through misconception at the time, or by a concise and familiar mode of expression, which frequently applies that term to a lieutenant-colonel. I shall, therefore, expect him in exchange for Mr. Campbell.

The conduct of Lieutenant-Colonel

Brooks, in detaining John Miller, requires neither palliation nor excuse. I justify and approve it. There is nothing so sacred in the character of the King's trumpeter, even when sanctified by a flag, as to alter the nature of things, or to consecrate infidelity and guilt. He was a deserter from the army under my command; and, whatever you have been pleaded to assert to the contrary, it is the practice of war and nations to seize and punish deserters wherever they may be found. His appearing in the character he did was an aggravation of his offence, inasmuch as it added insolence to perfidy. My scrupulous regard to the privileges of flags, and a desire to avoid every thing, that partiality itself might affect to consider as a violation of them, induced me to send orders for the release of the trumpeter, before the receipt of your letter; the improper and peremptory terms of which, had it not been too late, would have strongly operated to produce a less compromising conduct. I intended at the time to assure you, and I wish it to be remembered, that my indulgence in this instance is not to be drawn into precedent; and that, should any deserters from the American army hereafter have the daring folly to approach our lines in a similar manner, they will fall victims to their rashness and presumption.

This conjecture, as to Ethan Allen's rank, is not precisely accurate. He was not commissioned in the regiment of Green Mountain Boys, as it was called, which was raised by the authority of New York, in the summer of 1775, and commanded by Seth Warner, with the rank of *lieutenant-colonel.* The only commission, which Ethan Allen had received, was that conferred upon him by the committees of Bennington and the adjoining settlements before the war, when the people of the Green Mountains resolved to take up arms in defence of their rights against what they deemed the unjust encroachments of the New York government, in claiming and seizing their lands. He waa then made their military leader, with the rank *of colonel-commandant.* — SceSpARJts's *IAJe of Ethan Men,* in *The Library of*

American Biography, VoL L pp. 246, 291.

Before I conclude, I think it proper to inform you, that Colonel Grayson, Lieutenant-Colonels Harrison and Hamilton, and Elias Boudinot, commissary-general of prisoners, are the gentlemen appointed on my part to meet your commissioners. I am, Sir, &c.

TO THE PRESIDENT OF CONGRESS.
Valley Forge, 24 March, 1778L

Sir, What may be the designs of Congress, with respect to the establishment of the army, I know not; but I do most earnestly and devoutly recommend a ijpeedy adoption of them, and the appointment of officers, as our present situation at this advanced season b truly alarming, and to me highly distressing, as I am convinced that we shall be plunged into the campaign before our arrangements are made, and the army properly organized.

The numberless disadvantages, resulting from the late appointment of general officers last year, make me look forward with infinite anxiety this; for, after all the wisdom that Congress or their committee can use in the choice of officers, many will be disgusted; resignations of some and perhaps non-acceptance of others will follow. Before matters then can be brought to a proper tone, much time will be lost, and a great deal of trouble and vexation encountered; to overcome which, is not the work of a day; and, till they are overcome, confusion, disorder, and loss must prevail. In the mean while, order, regularity, and discipline, which require the vigilance of every officer to establish, and must flow from the general officers in every army, are neglected or not entered upon in time. Thus it happened last year; and brigades and divisions became vacant, to the great injury of the service.

As it is not improper for Congress to have some idea of the present temper of the army, it may not be amiss to remark in this place, that, since the month of August last, between two and three hundred officers have resigned their commissions, and many others were with difficulty dissuaded from it. In the Vir-

ginia line only, not less than six colonels, as good as any in the service, have left it lately; and more, I am told, are in the humor to do so.

Highly advantageous also would it be, if the recruits and drafts from North Carolina and Virginia were not suffered to halt on their way to camp, under pretence of getting equipped, but sent forward and incorporated into the different regiments of their respective States, as soon as it could be done. Out of the number of men said to be drafted in Virginia last fall, and others from North Carolina, very few have joined the army; but, owing to desertion and other causes, they have dwindled to nothing; and this will always be the case with new recruits, especially those who are unwillingly drawn forth, if much time is spent in getting them to their regiments under the care of proper officers. This shows the necessity (if the season and other powerful reasons did not loudly call for it) of hastening them to the army.

My solicitude for the preservation of the communication of the North River gives me very uneasy sensations on account of our posts there, and will excuse my again asking if the troops to the northward, except such as are necessary for the defence of Fort Schuyler, can be so advantageously employed as at the works on that river. A respectable force at those posts would awe New York, and divide General Howe's force or expose the city. To depend too much upon militia is, in my opinion, putting every thing to hazard. If I should appear uncommonly anxious, respecting the several matters contained in this letter, by repeating them, Congress will do me the justice, I hope, to believe, that I am actuated by no views but such as are prompted by circumstances and the advanced season.

I have the honor to be, &c.
TO MAJOR-GENERAL HEATH.
Valley Forge, 25 March, 1778.

Dear Sir,

I hope that no time will be lost in removing General Burgoyne's troops from Boston after the receipt of the resolution of Congress for that purpose. If they remain within reach of that part of the enemy's force, which are at Newport, I think it more than probable, that they will make an effort to rescue them.

You will exert yourself in forwarding on the recruits for such of the Massachusetts regiments as are with the army. They need not remain to be inoculated, as that can be done conveniently upon their arrival in camp, and the doctors say the men will be much healthier through the campaign, than if they had been inoculated at home and marched immediately upon their recovery. I am particularly pressing in this matter, because I have many reasons for thinking, that General Howe means to call in reinforcements and attack us before we receive ours. Four regiments are actually embarked at New York, and accounts from Rhode Island say they are about evacuating Newport.

Some little time past, I wrote to the President and Council of Massachusetts, informing them that several of the towns had hired British deserters, and sent them on by way of substitutes. Since writing that letter, eleven of these people have come from one district, and I doubt not many more will follow. I shall be obliged to send them back, or they will most certainly, as they ever have done, desert again to the enemy and carry off their arms. I desired the Council to put a stop to this practice, and I beg you will mention it to them, and point out the injury it does the service. By a late resolve of Congress, there is an absolute prohibition to the enlistment of deserters, it being better to be deficient in the quota, than to have such men.

I am, &c TO COLONEL ARMANI).
Valley Forge, 25 March, 177a
Sir,

I yesteiday received your letter from Yorktown. You must have misunderstood me, if you thought I gave you permission to raise a new and separate corps. I told you I had no power to grant such a request, but that, if you could obtain such a permission from Congress, or the committee of Congress in camp, I should have no objection to the measure and to your enlisting prisoners. I

am certain I never gave you any encouragement to enlist deserters, because I have ever found them of the greatest injury to the service, by debauching our own men, and I had therefore given positive orders to all recruiting officers not to enlist them upon any terms. The Congress have since made an express resolve against it, and also against enlisting prisoners.

As you say your two lieutenants were promised the rank of captains by the Marquis de Lafayette, I cannot do any thing in that matter until I have seen the Marquis, who is expected from Albany shortly. When the committee of Congress found that the corps formerly commanded by you was diminished below fifty men, they determined to reduce it and to throw the men into some regiment. I hope you will understand me clearly, when I again assure you, that I have no powers to authorize the raising of new corps; and, as you are upon the spot, you will have a good opportunity of making application to the Congress for such a command as you seem desirous of having.

I am, Sir, yours, &c t TO JOHN TERNANT.
Head-Quarters, 26 March, 1778.
Sir,

I was favored with your letter yesterday. As you seem to have taken it for granted, that your services are rejected, and intimate an inconsistency in my not discouraging from the beginning the application made in your behalf, it is incumbent upon me to assure you, that I have not given up the idea of your becoming one of the sub-inspectors, on the terms expressed in my last letter, and acceded to by you; and, consequently, that the want of consistency depends upon your interpretation of some parts of my conduct towards you.

I will not however conceal from you, that, foreseeing some difficulties in the way, I declined announcing your appointment precipitately and before the other sub-inspectors were chosen, that the whole might be declared at the same time. Having now in my own mind fixed upon these gentlemen, though all of them are not in camp, I have not the

smallest objection to your entering upon the duties of the office, as I am persuaded it will afford much relief to Baron Steuben and benefit the service. I am, Sir, &c.

TO MAJOR-GENERAL ARMSTRONG.
Valley Forge, 27 March, 1778.

Dear Sir, I fear your apprehensions as to the augmentation of the army, at least in good time, will appear to have been but too well founded. Some of the States have but lately drafted their men, others have proceeded but a very little way in recruiting, and some have not yet fixed upon the mode of completing their regiments. Even those men, that are already drafted or enlisted, are to be drawn together, most of them probably to be inoculated and all of them to be disciplined. By accounts from the eastward, the troops are about evacuating Rhode Island, and two regiments of Hessians and two of British are actually embarked at New York, whether with an intent to form some new expedition, or to reinforce General Howe at Philadelphia, cannot yet be determined, but I think the latter most probable. If General Howe draws his strength together before we have collected ours, nothing can hinder him from moving against us but ignorance of our numbers; and I do not think we have any right to count upon that, considering the knowledge he appears to have had the last campaign.

A French officer of engineers, who desired to enter the America army, and to whom General Washington offered the post of a Bubordinal inspector under Baron Steuben.

I shall say no more of the Canada expedition, than that it is at an end. I never was made acquainted with a single circumstance relating to it.

I am fully of opinion, that the enemy depend as much or more upon our own divisions, and the disaffection which they expect to create by sending their emissaries among the people, than they do on the force of their arms. The situation of matters in this State is melancholy and alarming. We have daily proof, that a majority of the people in this quarter are only restrained from supplying the enemy with horses and every kind of necessary, through fear of punishment; and, although I have made a number of severe examples, I cannot put a stop to the intercourse. It is plain from several late instances, that they have their emissaries in every part of the country. A lieutenant has been detected in Lancaster county purchasing horses, in conjunction with the inhabitants, one of whom and the lieutenant have been executed. Foui fine teams were taken a few days ago, going into Philadelphia from the neighbourhood of Yorktown, and 1 doubt not but there are many more such intentions yet undiscovered. I am convinced, that more mischief has been done by the British officers, who have been prisoners, than by any other set of people; during their captivity they have made connexions in the country, they have confirmed the disaffected, converted many ignorant people, and frightened the lukewarm and timid by their stories of the power of Britain. I hope a general exchange is not far off, by which means wc shall get rid of all that set of people; and I am convinced, that we had better, in future, send all officers in upon parole, than keep them among us.

If the state of General Potter's affairs will admit of returning to the army, I shall be exceedingly glad to see him, as his activity and vigilance have been much wanted in the course of the winter. The quota of militia, stipulated by the State, has never been above half kept up, and sometimes I believe there has not been a single man. General Lacey has not now above seventy. The country upon the east side of the Schuylkill has been by these means exceedingly exposed, as it has not been in my power to cover it with the effective Continental troops, who instead of relaxation have been upon fatigue the whole winter.

When the weather is such, that you think you can take the field without injury to your health, I shall be glad to see you with the army, as I am, with sincere regard, dear Sir, &c.
TO MAJOR-GENERAL MCDOUGALL.
Valley Forge, 31 Much, 1778.

Dear Sir,
That part of the troops at New York have left that place, admits of no doubt. The accounts of their number differ; some say four regiments, two British and two Hessian, some two thousand three hundred, and others two thousand five hundred men, all of whom, there is reason to believe, are arrived at Philadelphia, as a fleet consisting of near fifty transports, the same number that left New York, passed Wilmington about five days ago. By report, Rhode Island was to be evacuated, and the garrison brought to Philadelphia. This, if true, evidently proves, that General Howe intends an early campaign, to take advantage of our weak slate.

What is to be done? We must either oppose our whole force to his in this quarter, or take the advantage of him in some other; which leads me to ask your opinion of the practicability of an attempt upon New York, with Parsons's brigade, Nixon's, and the regiments of Van Schaick, Hazen, and James Livingston, aided by militia from the States of New York and Connecticut; such I mean as can speedily be drawn together. On this subject, and the advisableness of such an enterprise, I would have you consult Governor Clinton and General Parsons, and them only. In considering this matter, provisions will be found a capital object; not merely on account of the quantum necessary for the support of such a force, as may be thought adequate for your own operations, but in respect to this army, which must depend materially upon the eastern States for beef and pork, and must at all events be attended to as a primary object.

If, in viewing this matter in every light the importance of it deserves, you shall be of opinion, that it can be undertaken with a fair prospect of success, I shall not withdraw any part of the aforementioned troops to this army; if, on the other hand, too much danger and difficulty should appear, to warrant the attempt, I desire that Van Schaick's regiment, which has been ordered to Fishkill, may be directed to march without delay to join me. It is unnecessary, I am sure, for me to add, that the most

profound secrecy should attend your operations, if the scheme is adopted; and if not, hints of such a measure being in agitation should be dropped, in order to divide the attention of the enemy.

I am, with sincere esteem, dear Sir, &c TO THE PRESIDENT OF CONGRESS.
Head-Quarters, Valley Forge, 3 April, 1778.
Sir,
Captain Lee of the light dragoons, and the officers under his command, having uniformly distinguished themselves by a conduct of exemplary zeal, prudence, and bravery, I took occasion, on a late signal instance of it, to express the high sense I entertained of their merit, and to assure him, that it should not fail of being properly noticed. I was induced to give this assurance from a conviction, that it is the wish of Congress to give every encouragement to merit, and that they would cheerfully embrace so favorable an opportunity of maniTesting this disposition. I had it in contemplation at the time, in case no other method more eligible could be adopted, to make him an offer of a place in my family. I have consulted the committee of Congress upon the subject, and we were mutually of opinion, that giving Captain Lee the command of two troops of horse on the proposed establishment, with the rank of major, to act as an independent partisan corps, would be a mode of rewarding him very advantageous to the service. Captain Lee's genius particularly adapts him to a command of this nature; and it will be the most agreeable to him of any station in which he could be placed.
It was the opinion of General MDougall, in which Governor Clinton and General Parsons concurred, that the enterprise was not practicable. " The condition and strength of these posts," he replied, " utterly forbid it; especially when the consequence of a misfortune in the attempt is duly considered, as it may affect the supplies to your army, and the general influence such an event may have on the operations of the campaign." — *FuhkUl, Apnl 13th.*
I beg leave to recommend this measure to Congress, and shall be obliged by

their decision as speedily as may be convenient. The campaign is fast approaching, and there will probably be very little time to raise and prepare the corps for it. It is a part of the plan to give Mr. Lindsey the command of the second troop, and to make Mr. Peyton captain-lieutenant of the first. I am, with the highest esteem and respect, &c TO COLONEL JOSIAS C. HALL.

Head-Quarters, 3 April, 1779.

Sir, However painful it is to me to signify my public disapprobation of a sentence solemnly pronounced by a court-martial, it is a disagreeable sensation from which my duty forbids me to exempt myself in particular instances; such a one is that, which makes the subject of your favor of the 26th ultimo. A refusal to obey the commands of a superior officer, especially where the duty required was evidently calculated for the good of the service, cannot be justified, without involving consequences subversive of all military discipline. A precedent manifestly too dangerous would be established, of dispensing with orders, and subordination would be at an end, if men's ideas were not rectified in a case of this kind, and such notice taken, as has been on my part.

The above recommendation waa confirmed by Congress in all its particulars. In the preamble to the resolve, it is stated, that" Captain Henry Lee, of the Light Dragoons, by the whole tenor of his conduct during the last campaign, has proved himself a brave and prudent officer, rendered essential service to his country, and acquired to himself, and the corps he commanded, distinguished honor." — Journal, *April "IK.*

As far as the matter personally regards you, I feel additional concern; but I can by no means discover that necessity of retiring from the service in support of a mistaken opinion, which you remotely hint at. On the contrary, from the crisis at which our affairs have arrived, and the frequent defection of officers seduced by views of private interest and emolument to abandon the cause of their country, I think every man, who does not merely make profession of patriotism, is bound by indissoluble ties

to remain in the army. My advice, in which I flatter myself you will coincide, after a dispassionate review of this matter, is, therefore, that differences may be mutually forgotten, and that the whole may subside; to which your love of the service will I hope in no small degree contribute, and I am, &c Colonel Hall had written, — " Whatever your Excellency's determination may be, I shall submit to it without repining, because it will be dictated by candor, and calculated for the benefit of the service. If I should be under the necessity of retiring, though confined to a narrower sphere of action, still a deep sense of duty, and a warm attachment to the liberties of my country, shall be my leading principles, and no personal injury shall ever induce me to forget the great obligations due to society."

Vol. v. 39 % TO THE PRESIDENT OF CONGRESS.

Head-Quarters, Valley Forge, 4 April, 1778.

Sir,

I have now the honor to acknowledge your several letters of the 21st, 29th, and 30th ultimo, with their enclosures, which have been duly received. It gives me pain to observe they appear to contain several implications by which my sensibility is not a little wounded. I find myself extremely embarrassed by the steps I had taken towards an exchange of prisoners, and the formation of a general cartel making more ample provision for their future accommodation and relief. The views of Congress seem to be very different from what I supposed them, when I entered into my late engagements with General Howe. Their resolution of the 30th ultimo, pointedly requiring a strict adherence to all former ones upon the subject, will.in all probability render them impracticable. I considered some of thenresolutions as dictated on the principle of retaliation, and did not imagine the terms they contained would be insisted upon in negotiating an agreement calculated to remedy the evils which occasioned them. In most respects they might be substantially complied with; but there are some points to which an exact conformity

must of necessity destroy the idea of a cartel. One is the obliging of the enemy to pay gold and silver. on equal terms for Continental currency, estimating the articles supplied them at their actual prices with us, as seems to be the design of the resolve of the 19th of December; another is the subjecting of the inhabitants of these States, taken in arms against them, to trial and punishment, agreeably to the resolve of the 30th of the same month.

The following remarks contained in a letter, written by Colonel Hamilton to Governor Clinton, will show in what manner the proceeding of Congress, in regard to exchanges, were viewed by the writer. A lie was at that time one of General Washington's confidential aids, it may be presumed that he expresses without much qualification the private sentiments of his general.

" Lately," he observes, " a flag with provisions and clothing for the British prisoners, with General Washington's passport, was seized at Lancaster. The affair was attended with circumstances of violence. Still more lately, General Washington's engagement with General Howe, for an exchange of prisoners, has been violated. Congress have resolved, that no exchange shall take place till all accounts are settled and the balance due the United States paid. The beauty of it is, that, on a fair settlement, we shall without doubt be in Mr. Howe's debt; and in the mean time we detain his officers and soldiers, as a security for the payment. The operation of this resolve, though it docs not plainly appear upon the face of it, is to put off an exchange, perhaps for ever. At any rate, it cannot take place all next summer.

" It is thought to be bad policy to go into an exchange; but, admitting this to be true, it is much worse policy to commit such frequent breaches of faith, and ruin our national chamctcr. Whatever refined politicians may think, it is of great consequence to preserve a national character; and if it should once seem to be a system in any State to violate its faith, whenever it is the least inc tvenicnt to keep it, it will unquestionably have an ill effect upon foreign negotiations, and tend to bring Government at home into contempt, and of course to destroy its influence. The general notions of justice and humanity are implanted in almost every human breast, and ought not to be too freely shocked. In the present case, the passions of the country and army are on the side of an exchange; and a studied, attempt to avoid it will disgust both, and tend to make the service odious. It will injure drafting and recruiting, discourage the militia, and increase the discontents of the army. The prospect of hopeless captivity cannot but be very disagreeable to men constantly exposed to the chance of it. Those, whose lot it is to fall into it, will have little scruple to get rid of it by joining the enemy.

" It is said not to be our present interest to exchange, because we should endeavour, by and by, to take advantage of the enemy's weakness to strike some decisive blow. If we should fail in this, which I believe We shall, when they get reinforced, we shall not think it our interest to add to the strength of an enemy, already strong enough, and so on *ad infinitum*. The truth is, considered in the mere view of barter, it never can be our interest to exchange; the constitution of our army, from the short term of enlistment, and the dependence we are obliged to place in the militia, are strongly opposed to it; and, if the argument of present interest be adhered to, we never can exchange. I may venture to assert, there never can be a time more proper than the present, or rather a month or two hence; and, go about it as soon as we please, the previous negotiations necessary, and other circumstances, will of course procrastinate it for some time. And I would ask, whether in a republican State and a republican army, such a cruel policy as that of exposing those men, who are foremost in defence of their country, to the miseries of hopeless captivity, can succeed? " — *MS. Letter, March 12th.*

I am well aware that appearances ought to be upheld, and that we should avoid as much as possible recognising by any public act the depreciation of our currency; but I conceive this end would be answered, as far as might be necessary, by stipulating, that all money payments should be made in gold and silver, being the common medium of commerce among nations, at the rate of four shillings and six pence for a Spanish milled dollar; by fixing the price of rations on an equitable scale relatively to our respective circumstances; and by providing for the payment of what we may owe, by sending in provision and selling it at their market. The rates of money, and the prices of provisions and other commodities, differ everywhere; and, in treaties of a similar nature between any two States, it is requisite, for mutual convenience, to ascertain some common ratio, both for the value of money in payments, and for the rates of those articles on which they may arise.

It was determined on mature consideration not to conclude any thing expressly, that should contradict the resolution of the 30th of December; but at the same time, if it is designed to be the rule of practice, it is easy to perceive it would at once overturn any cartel that could be formed. General Howe would never consent to observe it on his part, if such a practice were to exist on ours. Though the law ought not to be contravened by an express article admitting the exchangeability of such persons, yet, if it is not suffered to sleep, it is in vain to expect the operation of it will be acquiesced in by the enemy.

The measures I have taken must evince, that it is my determination to pay the fullest attention to the interests of citizens, and to the rights of General Lee, in the treaty; and I think it but justice to the gentlemen appointed to negotiate it to declare, that I know them to be so fully impressed with the importance of both those objects, as to make them cheerfully observant of the injunctions of Congress, so far as not to conclude any agreement, of which the exchange of General Lee and the alternative respecting citizens are not essential parts. These points had been early determined on.

It is with no small concern, that I have been obliged to trouble Congress upon the subjects of this letter; and, should they appear to them in the same light they do to me, and should it be thought proper to remove the obstacles, which now oppose the 'business in hand, I must request they will be pleased to communicate their determination as expeditiously as possible, that the commissioners may govern themselves accordingly, and either proceed to forming a cartel, or put an end to the negotiation. Before the resolves of the 30th came to hand, they had met, and been in treaty two days, with a prospect of a favorable accommodation.

This point is so clear, that the ground taken by Congress, and adhered to with pertinacity, seems very extraordinary. By the resolution of the 30th of December, all loyalists, or Americans in the British service, who should be taken in arms, were to be sent to the respective States to which they belonged, and suffer the penalties inflicted by the laws of such States upon traitors. Such a resolution was an effectual bar to any agreement for a general exchange. The British commander was as much bound in honor and justice to protect these persons, as he was to protect the British officers or soldiers; and in some respects more so, inasmuch as they had made greater sacrifices in supporting the causo of the King.

I am happy to inform Congress, that General Lee will be out on parole tomorrow in place of General Prescott; and I have every reason to expect, if the negotiation can be continued upon admissible terms, that his exchange will immediately follow the releasement of Colonel Campbell and the Hessian field-officers. It is agreed, that Lieutenant-Colonel Allen shall be exchanged for Lieutenant-Colonel Campbell.

I have the honor to be, &c TO MAJOR-GENERAL MCDOUGALL.

Head-Quarters, Valley Forge, 8 April, 1778.

Dear Sir,

The fleet which arrived in the Delaware, as mentioned in mine of the 31st ultimo, came from New York, but they had very few troops on board; so that if those transports, which were at the Hook with the troops, have sailed, I know not certainly where they are gone. General Lee, who came out of Philadelphia a few days ago upon parole, says he thinks they were to go to Rhode Island to replace some troops, who were to be brought from thence to New York.

The practicability of the enterprise mentioned in mine of the 31st ultimo will depend entirely upon circumstances, and must be still, as it was then, left to your own good judgment, and that of the gentlemen with whom I desired you to consult. The sending of Van Schaick's regiment must also depend upon the intelligence you receive from New York. If you find that the enemy are not in a situation to make an attempt upon you, but still too strong for you to attempt any thing against them with a probability of success, I would have you in that case send the regiment forward as quick as possible.

See the answer to this letter in the Appendix, No. AiV

I am, dear Sir, with regard, yours, &c
TO THE PRESIDENT OF CONGRESS.

Valley Forge, 10 April, 1778.

Sir,

I have had the honor of receiving your favor of the 4th instant, enclosing a resolve of Congress of the same date, empowering me to call forth five thousand militia from the States of Maryland, Pennsylvania, and New Jersey. I thank Congress for the power; at the same time it is incumbent on me to assure them, that, granting the practicability of collecting such a number, it would prove a work of time, difficulty, and expense; to evince which, I need only recur to the experience of last campaign on similar occasions, and to remind you that it was not possible to obtain a thousand men, nor sometimes even one hundred, from this State, although the former number was required and promised, for the purpose of covering during the winter the country between the Schuylkill and the Delaware. General McDougall was now pursuing the construction of the works at West Point. He wrote that the fort was so nearly enclosed as to resist a sudden attack of the enemy. But the heights near it were such, that the fort would not

be tenable if the enemy should possess them. " For this reason," he added, " we are obliged to make some works on them. It will require five thousand men effectually to secure the grounds near the fort, which command it. And these objection exist against almost all the points on the river, proper for erecting works to annoy the shipping. Mr. Kosciuszko is esteemed by those, who have attended the works at West Point, to have more practice than Colonel Radiere, and his manner of treating the people is more acceptable than that of the latter; which induced General Parsons and Governor Clinton to desire the former may be continued at West Point. "—*April 13th.*

The great end of my letter to Congress, of the 24th ultimo, seems to have been mistaken. My views were not turned to reinforcements of militia. To know whether the old establishment of the army, or the new as agreed upon by the committee, is the choice of Congress, and in what manner the regiments of this State and the additional are to be reduced, and officers for the whole appointed, was my object. These are objects of the greatest moment, as they may, in their consequences, involve the fate of America; for I will undertake to say, that it is next to impossible, when the season is so far advanced, properly to accomplish those changes, appointments, and the dependent arrangements for the ensuing campaign. Should any convulsion happen, or movement take place, they will be altogether impracticable. Justice to my own character, as well as duty to the public, constrains me to repeat these things; their consequences are more easily conceived than described.

It may be said by some, Sir, that my wish to see the officers of this army upon a more respectable establishment is the cause of my solicitude, and carries me too far. To such I can declare, that my anxiety proceeds from the causes above mentioned. If my opinion is asked with respect to the necessity of making this provision for the officers, I am ready to declare, that I do most religiously believe the salvation of the

cause depends upon it, and, without it, your officers will moulder to nothing, or be composed of low and illiterate men, void of capacity for this or any other business. To prove this, I can with truth aver, that scarce a day passes without the offer of two or three commissions; and my advices from the eastward and southward are, that numbers who had gone home on furlough mean not to return, but are establishing themselves in more lucrative employments. Let Congress determine what will be the consequence of this spirit.

Personally, as an officer, I have no interest in their decision, because I have declared, and I now repeat it, that I never will receive the smallest benefit from the half-pay establishment; but, as a man who fights under the weight of a proscription, and as a citizen, who wishes to see the liberty of his country established upon a permanent foundation, and whose property depends upon the success of our arms, I am deeply interested. But, all this apart, and justice out of the question, upon the single ground of economy and public saving, I will maintain the utility of it; for I have not the least doubt, that, until officers consider their commissions in an honorable and interested point of view, and are afraid to endanger them by negligence and inattention, no order, regularity, or care, either of the men or public property, will prevail. To prove this, I need only refer to the general courts-martial, which are constantly sitting for the trial of them, and the number who have been cashiered within the last three months for misconduct of different kinds. At no period since the commencement of the war have I felt more painful sensations on account of delay, than at the present; and, urged by them, I have expressed myself without reserve.

By a letter just received from General Weedon, I am informed of his intention to resign, if General Woodford should be restored to his former rank, which he had not then heard. General Muhlenberg is now balancing on the same point. One, therefore, if not two brigadiers, will be wanted for that State. The disadvantages resulting from the frequent resignations in the Virginia line, the change of commanding officers to the regiments, and other causes equally distressing, have injured that corps beyond conception, and have been the means of reducing very respectable regiments in some instances to a mere handful of men; and this will ever be the case, till officers can be fixed by something equivalent to the sacrifice they make. To reason otherwise, and suppose that public virtue alone will enable men to forego the ease and comforts of life, to encounter the hardships and dangers of war for a bare subsistence, when their companions and friends are amassing large fortunes, is viewing human nature rather as it should be, than as it really is.

Vol. v. 40 A A

The clothier-general of the army, as well as the heads of every other department, should be in camp near the Commander-in-chief; otherwise it is impossible that the operations of war can be conducted with energy and precision. I wish most sincerely that this, as not the least essential part of the business settled with the committee, were decided, and a thorough investigation were had into the conduct of this department. I shall make no apology for the freedom of this letter. To inform Congress of such facts as materially affect the service, I conceive to be one great and essential part of my duty to them and myself. My agreement with the committee entitled me to expect upwards of forty thousand Continental troops, exclusive of artillery and horse, for the service of the ensuing campaign, including those to be employed in' the defence of the North River. Instead of these, what are my prospects'!

Major-General the Marquis de Lafayette is arrived at camp, and will resume the command of his division. The Baron de Kalb is expected in a few days.

I have the honor to be, &c TO COLONEL STEPHEN MOYLAN.

Valley Forge, 11 April, 177a

Dear Sir,

Your return of the cavalry is really vexatious; but what can be expected when officers prefer their own ease and emolument to the good of their country, or to the care and attention, which they are in duty bound to pay to the particular corps they command? In every service but ours, the winter is spent in endeavouring to make preparation for the ensuing campaign. I desire you will make strict inquiry into the conduct of every officer present, and find out whether those absent have gone upon furlough regularly obtained; and if it appears, that they have been negligent in point of duty or are absent without leave, arrest and have them brought to trial; for I am determined to make examples of those, to whom this shameful neglect of the cavalry has been owing. If there has been any deficiency on the part of the commissary of forage, let the commanding officer of Sheldon's make it appear in his own justification.

I am, &c.

To The Officer Commanding Sheldon's Light Dragoons.

Valley Forge, 14 April, 177a

Sir, I scarce know which is greatest, my astonishment or vexation, at hearing of the present low condition of your horse. To have them in good order against the period, which is now just at hand, you were exempted from the fatigues of a winter's campaign, and permitted to retire to the best quarters the country afforded for the express purpose of recruiting them. I deprived myself of the advantages of their services, which were essential both for the security of my camp, and stopping the intercourse with the city; but for what purpose did I do this? Why to furnish the officers and men, it seems, with opportunities of galloping about the country, and, by neglect of the horses, reducing them to a worse condition than those, which have been kept upon constant and severe duty the whole winter. How you can reconcile this conduct to your feelings as an officer, and answer it to your country, I know not.

I am, Sir, &c.

TO THE PRESIDENT OF CONGRESS.

Valley Forge, 18 April, 1778.

Sir, On Thursday evening I had the honor to receive your two letters of the 14th instant. I am much obliged by the fresh assurances, which Congress are pleased to make me of their confidence; and they may be satisfied that I wish nothing more ardently, than that a good and perfect agreement should subsist between us. The negotiation between the commissioners is ended without effecting a cartel; nor do I suppose, from the information I have received on the subject, that there is any good prospect that one will ever be formed, or at least for a great while, on a liberal and extensive plan. A report of the proceedings of the commissioners on our part, at their several meetings, I take the liberty to enclose. The old agreement, I presume, continues; and under it we must carry on exchanges.

Commissioners from General Washington and General Hove met at Germantown on the 31st of March, where they remained three days.

General Muhlenberg has communicated his determination to resign, but has promised not to leave his brigade till Congress shall appoint another general in bis room, provided it is done in any reasonable time. By postponing my call upon the militia, as mentioned in my last of the 10th, I did not mean to decline it altogether. I did not see the necessity of calling out five thousand for the sole purpose of defence; and, in the present situation of things, I cannot perceive my way sufficiently clear for offensive measures, as I do not know when to expect the recruits from the different States, nor what prospect the commissary has of provision; as we only get it yet from hand to mouth, assembling the militia, unless for the purpose of defence, should be the last thing done, as they soon become impatient, and are very expensive in the articles of stores, camp utensils, and provisions.

They met again April 6th, at Newtown, in Bucks county. A difficulty arose at the outset concerning the nature of the powers contained in General Howe's commission. It was given on no other authority than his own, whereas the commission from General Washington expressly specified, that it was " in virtue of full powers to him delegated." This defect was objected to by the American commissioners, and the subject was referred to General Howe, who declined altering the commission, declaring at the same time, " that he meant the treaty to be of a personal nature, founded on the mutual confidence and honor of the contracting generals, and had no intention, either of binding the nation, or extending the cartel beyond the limits and duration of his own command." As this was putting the matter on a totally different footing from that contemplated in General Washington's commission, by which Congress and the nation were bound, and as General Howe's commissioners refused to treat on any other terms, the meeting was dissolved, without any progress having been made in a cartel. It was intimated by the British commissioners, as a reason why General Howe declined to negotiate on a national ground, that it might imply an acknowledgment inconsistent with the claims of the English government. The papers, which passed between the commissioners of the two parties, were published by order of Congress. — See *Remembrancer,* Vol. VI. p. 315. The American commissioners were Colonels Grayson, Harrison, Hamilton, and Mr. Elias Boudinot. Their conduct was approved by Congress.

AA»

The enclosed draft of a bill was brought to headquarters yesterday afternoon, by a gentleman who informed me, that a large cargo of them had been just sent out of Philadelphia. Whether this insidious proceeding is genuine, and imported in the packet, which arrived a few days ago, or contrived in Philadelphia, is a point undetermined and immaterial; but it is certainly founded in principles of the most wicked, diabolical baseness, and meant to poison the minds of the people, and detach the wavering at least from our cause. I suppose it will obtain a place in the papers, and am not without anxiety that it will have a malignant influence. I would submit it, whether it will not be highly expedient for Congress to investigate it in all its parts, and to expose in the most striking man-

ner the injustice, delusion, and fraud it contains. I trust it will be attacked, in every shape, in every part of the continent.

I have the honor to be, &c The paper here referred to contained a draft of Lord North's *Conciliatory Bills,* as they were called. They had made their way with quick despatch to General Washington's camp. They arrived in New York on the 14th of April, and were published on the 15th by Governor Tryon, accompanied by a declaration certifying that they were genuine copies of the drafts sent to him by Lord George Germain. He added; " To prepare the way for the return of peace, the above bills were read in the House of Commons on the 19th day of February last, in pursuance of the unanimous resolve of the House on the 17th of the same month; and I have his Majesty's command to cause them to be printed and dispersed, that the people at large may be acquainted with their contents, and with the favorable disposition of Great Britain towards the American colonies." Lord North's speech, on presenting the bills to Parliament, was likewise published at the same time. None of these particulars had come to General Washington's knowledge, when he wrote the above letter. From the manner in which he speaks of the bills, aa well as from his next letter to Congress, it is evident that he considered them a forgery at the time he was writing. Nor was he singular in this opinion. Mr. Laurens, President of Congress, in a letter to Governor Clinton, said, "I differ from gentlemen, who suppose the performance originated under authority in England. It appears to me to be destitute of the most essential marks. I believe it to be of Philadelphia TO THE PRESIDENT OF CONGRESS.

Valley Forge, 20 April, 1778.

Sir, When I addressed you on the 18th, I was doubtful whether the draft of the bill then transmitted was not spurious and contrived in Philadelphia; but its authenticity, I am almost certain, is not to be questioned. The information from Philadelphia seems clear and conclusive, that it came over in the packet,

with Lord North's speech on the introduction of it into Parliament. I enclose a paper containing his speeeh, which just came to hand. This bill, I am persuaded, will pass into a law. Congress will perceive by the minister's speech, that it aims at objects of the greatest extent and importance, and will no doubt in one way or other involve the most interesting consequences to this country. I have the honor to be, &c TO MAJOR-GENERAL GREENE.

Head-Quarters, 20 April, 1778.

Sir,

There seem to be but three general plans of operation, which may be premeditated for the next campaign; one, the attempting to recover Philadelphia and destroy the enemy's army there; another, the endeavouring to transfer the war to the northward by an enterprise against New York; and a third, the remaining quiet in a secure, fortified camp, disciplining and arranging the army till the enemy begin their operations, and then to govern ourselves accordingly. Which of these three plans shall we adopt?

facture, probably under bints from the other side of the water." — *MS. Letter, April* 20ft. This letter was sent as a circular to all the general officers in camp. General Greene had been appointed quartermaster-general, on the 2d of March, but he retained his rank of major-general in the army.

If the first, what mode of execution shall we pursue, and what force will be requisite, estimating the present numbers of the enemy in Philadelphia to be ten thousand men, exclusive of marines and seamen, whose aid may be called in? Shall we endeavour to effect the purpose by storm, by regular approaches, or by blockade, and in what particular manner?

If the second, shall we attempt to take New York by a *coup de main* with a small force, or shall we collect. a large force, and make an attack in form? In either case, what force will be necessary, estimating the number of the enemy in and about New York at four thousand men, and what disposition shall we make so as to effect the enterprise, and at the same time toprotect the country here and secure our stores?

If the last, what post shall we take, so as to keep the army in a state of security, to afford cover to the country and to our magazines, and to be in a situation to counteract the future motions of the enemy?

The Commander-in-chief thinks it unnecessary to make any comments on these questions, as the general officers will no doubt fully weigh every circumstance proper to be considered, and, sensible of the importance of the objects, to which their attention is called, will make their opinions the result of mature deliberation.

I am, &c.

Each of the officers sent a written reply to the above queries. They differed widely in opinion. Wayne, Paterson, and Maxwell recommended an attack on Philadelphia. Knox, Poor, Varnum, and Muhlenberg were in favor of an attack on New York. Greene thought it best for the main body nf the army to remain at Valley Forge, but that an attack should be made on New York by a detachment of four thousand regulars, joined to the eastern militia; that General Washington should command this expedition in person, and leave General Lee to command in Pennsylvania. Lord Stirling was for operating against both New York and Philadelphia. Lafayette, Steuben, and Duportail had doubts as to the expediency of any attack upon the enemy, till the army should be strengthened and put in a better condition; and they were inclined to adopt the third plan suggested by the Commander-in-chief. TO JOHN BANISTER, DELEGATE IN CONGRESS.

Valley Forge, 21 April, 1778.

Dear Sir,

I thank you very much for your obliging tender of a friendly intercourse between us; and you may rest assured that I embrace it with cheerfulness, and shall write you freely, as often as leisure will permit, on such points as appear to me material and interesting. I am pleased to find, that you expect the proposed establishment of the army will succeed; though it is a painful consideration, that

matters of such pressing importance and obvious necessity meet with so much difficulty and delay. Be assured, the success of the measure is a matter of the most serious moment, and that it ought to be brought to a conclusion as speedily as possible. The spirit of resigning commissions has been long at an alarming height, and increases daily.

The Virginia line has sustained a violent shock in this instance. Not less than ninety have already resigned to me. The same conduct has prevailed among the officers from the other States, though not yet to so considerable a degree; and there are but too just grounds to fear, that it will shake the very existence of the army, unless a remedy is soon, very soon, applied. There is none, in my opinion, so effectual as the one pointed out. This, I trust, will satisfy the officers, and at the same time it will produce no present additional emission of money. They will not be per suaded to sacrifice all views of present interest, and en counter the numerous vicissitudes of war, in the defence of their country, unless she will be generous enough on her part to make a decent provision for their future support. I do not pronounce absolutely, that we shall have no army if the establishment fails, but the army which we may have will be without discipline, without energy, incapable of acting with vigor, and destitute of those cements necessary to promise success on the one hand, or to withstand the shocks of adversity on the other. It is indeed hard to say how extensive the evil may be, if the measure should be rejected, or much longer delayed. I find it a very arduous task to keep the officers in tolerable humor, and to protract such a combination for quitting the service, as might possibly undo us for ever.

That is, an establishment of half-pay for the officers after the termination of the war. A plan for this purpose had been agreed upon by the committee in camp, and was now under debate in Congress. It was thought extremely important by General Washington, as appears by some VOL. V. 41

The difference between our service and

that of the enemy is very striking. With us, from the peculiar, unhappy situation of things, the officer, a few instances excepted, must break in upon his private fortune for present support, without a prospect of future relief. With them, even companies are esteemed so honorable and so valuable, that they have sold of late from fifteen to twenty-two hundred pounds sterling; and I am credibly informed, that four thousand guineas have been given for a troop of dragoons. You will readily determine how this difference will operate; what effects it must produce. Men may speculate as they will; they may talk of patriotism; they may draw a few examples from ancient story, of great achievements performed by its influence; but whoever builds upon them, as a sufficient basis for conducting a long and bloody war, will find himself deceived in the end. /We must take the passions of men as nature has given them, and those principles as a guide, which are generally the rule of action. I do not mean to exclude altogether the idea of patriotism. I know it exists, and I know it has done much in the present contest. But I will venture to assert, that a great and lasting war can never be supported on this principle alone. It must be aided by a prospect of interest, or some reward. For a time it may, of itself, push men to action, to bear much, to encounter difficulties; but it will not endure unassisted by interest. of his preceding letters, and he used his utmost endeavours to promote it; but there was a division in Congress. Some of the members were wholly opposed to it, particularly a majority of the members from the eastern States, as encouraging too far the idea of a standing army; others were of opinion, that Congress had no power to act in the matter, without special instructions from the States; and others were for limiting the time. This variety of opinion caused embarrassment m Congress, and delay in adopting the report of the committee for the new arrangements of the army. For other particulars respecting the subject of half-pay, see Sfamcs's *Life of Gouvernevr Morrit,* VoL I. p. 152.

The necessity of putting the army upon a respectable footing, both as to numbers and constitution, is now become more essential than ever. The enemy are beginning to play a game more dangerous, than their efforts by arms (though these will not be remitted in the smallest degree), which threatens a fatal blow to the independence of America, and of course to her liberties. They are endeavouring to ensnare the people by specious allurements of peace. It is not improbable they have had such abundant cause to be tired of the war, that they may be sincere in the terms they offer, which, though far short of our pretensions, will be extremely flattering to minds, that do not penetrate far into political consequences; but, whether they are sincere or not, they may be equally destructive; for, to discerning men nothing can be more evident, than that a peace on the principles of dependence, however limited, after what has happened, would be to the last degree dishonorable and ruinous. It is however much to be apprehended, that the idea of such an event will have a very powerful effect upon the country, and if not combated with the greatest address will serve, at least, to produce supineness and disunion. Men are naturally fond of peace, and there are symptoms which may authorize an opinion, that the people of America are pretty generally weary of the present war. It is doubtful, whether many of our friends might not incline to an accommodation on the grounds held out, or which may be, rather than persevere in a contest for independence. If this is the case, it must surely be the truest policy to strengthen the army, and place it upon a substantial footing. This will conduce to inspire the country with confidence; enable those at the head of affairs to consult the public honor and interest, notwithstanding the defection of some and temporary inconsistency and irresolution of others, who may desire to compromise the dispute; and, if a treaty should.be deemed expedient, will put it in their power to insist upon better terms, than they could otherwise expect.

There was at this time in Parliament a small party in favor of granting independence to America, and of instructing the commissioners to make a treaty on that footing. Governor Pownall held out this idea, and enforced it with strong arguments, in the debate on the address to the King, in reply to his message accompanying the declaration of the French ambassador, which gave notice of the treaty between France and the United States. " This treaty," said Governor Pownall, " does not alter my idea of the probability of our having even yet peace with America, if we will but take the way that leads to it, and the only one that is open. Nothing but the perverseness of our own conduct can cross it. We know that the Americans are and must be independent; and yet we will not treat with them as such. If government itself retains the least idea of sovereignty, it has already gone too far for that; if it entertains the least hope of peace, it has not gone far enough; and every step we shall take to put the Americans back from independency, will convince them the more of the necessity of going forward." — *Parliamentary Debates, March 17th,* 1778.

Besides the most vigorous exertions at home to increase and establish a military force upon a good basis, it appears to me advisable, that we should immediately try the full extent of our interest abroad, and bring our European negotiations to an issue. I think France must have ratified our independence, and will declare war immediately, on finding that serious proposals of accommodation are made; but lest, from a mistaken policy or too exalted opinion of our power from the representations she has had, she should still remain indecisive, it were to be wished, that proper persons should be instantly despatched, or our envoys already there instructed to insist pointedly on her coming to a final determination, f It cannot be fairly supposed, that she will hesitate a moment to declare war, if she *is* given to understand, in a proper manner, that a reunion of the two countries may be the consequence of procrastination. A European war and a' European alliance would effectually answer our purposes. If the step I now mention should be eligible, despatches ought to be sent at once by different conveyances, for fear of accidents. I confess, it appears to me a measure of this kind could not but be productive of the most salutary consequences. If possible, I should also suppose it absolutely necessary to obtain good intelligence from England, pointing out the true springs of this manoeuvre of the ministry; the preparations of force they are making; the prospects there are of raising it; the amount, and when it may be expected.

This was true, although the fact was not yet known in America. The treaties of commerce and alliance between France and the United States were signed on the 6th of February. The first meeting between the French Minister and the American Commissioners, for the purpose of negotiating a treaty, was held at Versailles on the. 12th of December. It was stated, in an article of the treaty of alliance, to be its direct end, " to maintain effectually the liberty, sovereignty, and independence, absolute and unlimited, of the United States, as well in matters of government as commerce. " — See *Diplomatic Correspondence,* VoL L pp. 355, 364. f It seems there were some fears at this moment, as to the effect which might be produced on the American people, by the advances of the British ministry in Lord North's propositions. In a reply to General Washington's circular letter, asking the advice of the general officers respecting a plan of the campaign, the Marquis de Lafayette stated, aa reasons for vigorous measures, the expected reinforcements of the enemy, and the approaching arrival of three commissioners, " whom I fear," said he, " more than ten thousand men." — *MS. Letter, April 25th.*

General Washington himself, in a letter to his brother, written a few days after the above, speaks as follows, alluding to the British commissioners. " It will require," he observes, all the skill, wisdom, and policy of the first abilities of these States to manage the helm, and steer with VOL. V. B B

It really seems to me, from a comprehensive view of things, that a period is fast approaching, big with events of the most interesting importance; when the counsels we pursue, and the part we act, may lead decisively to liberty or to slavery. Under this idea, I cannot but regret that inactivity, that inattention, that want of something, which unhappily I have but too often experienced in our public affairs. I wish that our representation in Congress was full from every State, and that it was formed of the first abilities among us. Whether we continue to prosecute the war or proceed to negotiate, the wisdom of America in council cannot be too great. Our situation will be truly delicate. To enter into a negotiation too hastily, or to reject it altogether, may be attended with consequences equally fatal. The wishes of the people, seldom founded on deep disquisitions, or resulting from other reasonings than their present feelings, may not entirely accord with our true policy and interest. If they do not, to observe a proper line of conduct for promoting the one, and avoiding offence to the other, will be a work of great difficulty.

judgment to the haven of our wishes, through so many shelves and rocks as will be thrown in Out way. This, more than ever, is the time for Congress to be filled with the first characters from every Stale, instead of having a thin assembly, and many States totally unrepresented, as is the case at present. I have often regretted the pernicious, and what appears to me fatal policy of having our ablest men engaged in the formation of the more local governments, and filling offices in their respective States, leaving the great national concern (on which the superstructure of all and every of them absolutely depends, and without which none can exist,) to be managed by men of more contracted abilities. Indeed, those at a distance from the seat of war live in such perfect tranquillity, that they conceive the dispute to be in a manner at an end; and those near it are so disaffected, that they only serve as embarrassments. Between the two, therefore, time slips away without the necessary means for opening the campaign in season or with propriety."

Nothing short of independence, it ap-

pears to me, can possibly do. A peace on other terms would, if I may be allowed the expression, be a peace of war. The injuries we have received from the British nation were so unprovoked, and have been so great and so many, that they can never be forgotten. Besides the feuds, the jealousies, the animosities, that would ever attend a union with them; besides the importance, the advantages, which we should derive from an unrestricted commerce; our fidelity as a people, our gratitude, our character as men, are opposed to a coalition with them as subjects, but in case of the last extremity. Were we easily to accede to terms of dependence, no nation, upon future occasions, let the oppressions of Britain be ever so flagrant and unjust, would interpose for our relief; or, at most, they would do it with a cautious reluctance, and upon conditions most probably that would be hard, if not dishonorable to us. France, by her supplies, has saved us from the yoke thus far; and a wise and virtuous perseverance would, and I trust will. free us entirely.

I have sent to Congress Lord North's speech, and the two bills offered by him to Parliament. They are spreading fast through the country, and will soon become a subject of general notoriety. I therefore think they had best be published in our papers, and persons of leisure and ability set to work to counteract the impressions they may make on the minds of the people.

Before I conclude, there are one or two points more, upon which I will add an observation or two. The first is, the indecision of Congress and the delay used in coming to determinations on matters referred to them. This is productive of a variety of inconveniences; and an early decision, in many cases, though it should be against the measure submitted, would be attended with less pernicious effects. Some new plan might then be tried; but, while the matter is held in suspense, nothing can be attempted. The other point is, the *jealousy,* which Congress unhappily entertain of the army, and which, if reports are right, some members labor to establish. You may be assured, there is noth-

ing more injurious, or more unfounded. This jealousy stands upon the commonly received opinion, which under proper limitations is certainly true, that standing armies are dangerous to a State. The prejudices in other countries have only gone to them in time of *peace,* and these from their not having in general cases any of the ties, the concerns, or interests of citizens, or any other dependence, than what flowed from their military employ; in short, from their being mercenaries, hirelings. It is our policy to be prejudiced against them in time of *toar*; though they are citizens, having all the ties and interests of citizens, and in most cases property totally unconnected with the military line.

If we would pursue a right system of policy, in my opinion, there should be none of these distinctions. We should all, Congress and army, be considered as one people, embarked in one cause, in one interest; acting on the same principle, and to the same end. The distinction, the jealousies set up, or perhaps only incautiously let out, can answer not a single good purpose. They are impolitic in the extreme. Among individuals the most certain way to make a man your enemy is to tell him you esteem him such. So with public bodies; and the very jealousy, which the narrow politics of some may affect to entertain of the army, in order to a due subordination to the supreme civil authority, is a likely means to produce a contrary effect; to incline it to the pursuit of those measures, which they may wish it to avoid. It is unjust, because no order of men in the Thirteen States has paid a more sacred regard to the proceedings of Congress than the army; for without arrogance or the smallest deviation from truth it may be said, that no history now extant can furnish an instance of an army's suffering such uncommon hardships as ours has done, and bearing them with the same patience and fortitude. To see men, without clothes to cover their nakedness, without blankets to lie on, without shoes (for the want of which their marches might be traced by the blood from their feet), and almost as often without provisions as with them, marching through the frost and snow, and at Christmas taking up their winter-quarters within a day's march of the enemy, without a house or hut to cover them, till they could be built, and submitting without a murmur, is a proof of patience and obedience, which in my opinion can scarce be paralleled.

There may have been some remonstrances or applications to Congress, in the style of complaint, from the Vol. v. 42 BB» army, (and slaves indeed should we be, if this privilege were denied,) on account of their proceedings in particular instances; but these will not authorize nor even excuse a jealousy, that they are therefore aiming at unreasonable powers, or making strides dangerous or subversive of civil authority. Things should not be viewed in that light, more especially as Congress in some cases have relieved the injuries complained of, which had flowed from their own acts.

In respect to the volunteer plan, I scarce know what opinion to give at this time. The propriety of a requisition on this head will depend altogether on our operations. Such kind of troops should not be called for, but upon the spur of the occasion, and at the moment of executing an enterprise. They will not endure a long service; and, of all men in the military line, they are the most impatient of restraint and necessary government.

As the propositions and the speech of Lord North must have proceeded from despair of the nation's succeeding against us; or from a rupture in Europe, that has actually happened, or certainly will happen; or from some deep political manoeuvre; or from what I think still more likely, a combination of the whole, would it not be good policy, in this day of uncertainty and distress to the Tories, to avail ourselves of the This conjecture was well founded. There is no room to doubt, that, when the *Conciliatory Mils* were brought before Parliament by,Lord North, the ministry were convinced a negotiation was pending between the French court and the American commissioners. During the debate (February 17th), and in reply to

Lord North's speech, Mr. Fox affirmed,, upon information on which reliance might be placed, that a treaty had already been signed; and when the question was pressed by Mr. Grenvillc upon Lord North, he answered, "that be could not say from authority that the treaty alluded to was signed; that, indeed, it was possible, nay too probable, but not authenticated by the ambassador." — Almon's *Parliamentary Register,* VoL vTO. pp. 385, 389.

occasion, and for the several States to hold out pardon to all delinquents returning by a certain day? They are frightened, and this is the time to operate upon them. After a short consideration of the matter, it appears to me, that such a measure would detach the Tories from the enemy, and bring things to a much speedier conclusion, and of course be a means of saving much public treasure.

I trust you will excuse, not only the length of my letter, but the freedom with which I have delivered my sentiments. The subjects struck me as important and interesting, and I have only to wish, that they may appear to you in the same light.

I am, dear Sir, with great regard, &c.
TO GOVERNOR LIVINGSTON.
Head-Quarters, 23 April, 1778.

Dear Sir, Enclosed I transmit to you a Philadelphia paper, containing the drafts of two bills, introduced into Parliament by Lord North, and his speech upon the occasion. Their authenticity is not questioned in Philadelphia; and I have not the smallest doubt, but there will be some overtures made to us similar, or nearly so, to the propositions held forth in the drafts. You will see that their aim is, under offers of peace, to divide and disunite us; and, unless their views are early investigated and exposed in a striking manner and in various shapes by able pens, I fear they will be but too successful. and that they will give a very unhappy if not a ruinous cast to our affairs. It appears to me, that we have every possible motive to urge us to exertion. If they are still for war, of which there can be no doubt, since they are straining every sinew and nerve

to levy troops, it behoves us to be prepared. If for peace, our preparations are equally essential, as they will enable us to treat with honor and dignity. There are many important concessions in the speech, which I hope will be improved to our advantage. If your leisure will possibly permit, I should be happy that the whole should be discussed by your pen.

This measure was adopted by Congress, two days after the abov letter was written. — *Journal, April 23J.*

I am, dear Sir, with great esteem and regard, &c

P. S. After I had closed the foregoing letter, and when I was just about to despatch it by express, I received your favors of the 17th and 20th instant, with Governor Tryon's letters, both of the same import. I send you a copy. The enclosures alluded to are the drafts of the two bills. Can you conceive of any thmg equal to the shifts and stratagems of the British ministry? If we conduct our affairs with firmness and wisdom, we must do well. The "Resolution," so called in Towne's paper, must be an arrant forgery, as I never had the least intimation of it; and to suppose such a one could have passed, is to suppose almost the existence of an impossibility. The forgery is calculated for the most wicked purposes, to excite an opposition in the people to the measures for drafting, and to render them ineffectual. There is nothing the enemy will not attempt, to carry their ends.

A forged article, purporting to be two resolves of Congress, had been published by the British, with all the formalities of place, date, and the signatures of the president and secretary, the object of which wa to foment discontents in the American army and prevent enlistments. The article declared in substance, that, whereas the mode adopted by many of the States for filling up their quotas, by enlistment and drafts for six and nine months, was found to produce constant fluctuation ia the number of the army and want of discipline, it was resolved that all the troops then in the army, and such as must afterwards be enlisted or drafted, should be deemed troops of the United States during the war, and that General Washington and other commanding officers were required to apprehend and punish as deserters all, who should leave the army under pretence of their terms of service being expired. These spurious resolves were dated February 20th. They may be found in Hugh Gaine'a *Ncxc York Gazette,* of the 9th of March.

The only proceedings of Congress, for drafting, that I have seen, were passed on the 26th of February, and are a recommendation to the several States, "to fill up their respective regiments by drafts from the militia, to serve nine months after they appear at the places appointed for their rendezvous, dischargeable before the end of that period, in proportion as recruits, enlisted for 'three years or during the war, may join the regiments in which they are." What a contrast between these proceedings and the forgery! I shall transmit the paper to Congress immediately, that they may pursue proper steps for counteracting this wicked publication.

TO MAJOR-GENERAL MCDOtTGALL.

Valley Forge, 22 April, 1778.

Dear Sir, I am perfectly satisfied with your delay of the enterprise proposed by you, as I am certain it has been founded upon substantial reasons. Congress having, by their resolve of the 15th instant, directed General Gates to resume the command of the northern department, and to repair forthwith to Fishkill for that purpose, I imagine he will proceed immediately thither. Upon his arrival there, I must desire you to return to this army and take the command of your division. As Colonel Radiere and Colonel Kosciuszko will never agree, I think it will be best to order Radiere to return, especially as you say Kosciuszko is better adapted to the genius and temper of the people.

It is painful to reflect upon the number of valuable officers, who have been obliged to quit the service on account of the disproportion between their pay and every necessary of life. I do not yet know what Congress will determine, as to the new arrangement and provision for the army; but if the gentlemen mentioned by you are such as will be an acquisition to the service, I would wish you to endeavour to persuade them to remain until they see what Congress will do. If they cannot be prevailed upon to wait till that time, you will see that they are not indebted to their regiments or to the public, and give them discharges.

I am, &c.

TO MAJOR-GENERAL CHARLES LEE.

Valley Forge, 22 April, 177B.

Dear Sir, Mr. Boudinot, at Commissary Loring's request, met him at Germantown yesterday; from whence he is just returned, after having agreed on a final exchange of yourself and other officers, with that gentleman.

That delay may not produce danger, I shall send in a flag to-morrow for your parole; and, when obtained,

I shall most cordially and sincerely congratulate you on your restoration to your country and to the army.

I could not however refrain, till the happy event should take place, from rejoicing with you on the probability of it, nor from expressing my wish of seeing you in camp, as soon as you can possibly make it convenient to yourself, after you are perfectly at liberty to take an active part with us; of which I shall not delay giving you the earliest notice. I have received your favor of the 13th instant from Yorktown. The contents shall be the subject of conversation, when I have the pleasure of seeing you in circumstances to mount your hobbyhorse, which will not, I hope, on trial be found quite so limping a jade, as thj one on which you set out for York. I am, &c

On being re-appointed to this command, General Gates was invested with extensive powers for completing the works on the North River, and was " authorized to carry on operations against the enemy if any favorable opportunity should offer." For effecting these purposes, he could call for the artificers and militia of the State of New York and the eastern States. It was enjoined upon him, however, in his instruction, " not to undertake any expedition against New York, without previously consulting the Commander-in-chief." The instructions were drawn up by a committee of Congress, of which Gouvcrneur Morris was chairman; and caution seems to have been used to guard against a revival of the difficulties, which had recently threatened the peace of the army, if not the safety of the country.

General Lee had written; — "I have reason to hope, that Congress will unembarrass the negotiation of the commissioners, with respect to a general exchange of prisoners, of all matters which I myself think foreign to the purpose, and that I shall soon be at liberty to take an active part; but I could wish that they would bo a little more expeditious.

I perhaps ought to make an apology to you for a liberty I have taken;

but if it is regarded in a proper point of view, I am in hopes it can neither be considered a step of indelicacy towards you, nor by General

Howe as any violation of the parole I have given.

" You must know, that it has long been the object of my studies how to form an army in the most simple manner possible. I once wrote a treatise, though I did not publish it, for the use of the militia of England. By reading Machiavel's *Institution,* and Marshal Saxe, I

have taken it into my head, that I understand it better than almost any man living. In short, I am mounting on a hobby-horse of my own training, and it runs away with me. Indeed I am so infatuated with it,

that I cannot forbear boasting its excellences on all occasions to friends and enemies. You must excuse me, therefore, if I could not forbear recommending the beast to some members of Congress." — *MS. Letter,*

Afril 130.

TO THE PRESIDENT OF CONGRESS.

Valley Forge, 23 April, 1778.

Sir,

I take the liberty to transmit to you a letter, which I received yesterday from Governor Tryon, enclosing the drafts of the two bills I forwarded before, with his certificate of the manner in which they came to his hands, accompanied by his more extraordinary and imperti-nent request, that, through my means, the contents should be communicated to the officers and men of this army. This engine of the ministry, from Governor Livingston's account, is very industri-ously circulating copies of these drafts, in obedience to their and his royal mas-ter's mandates. The letter which I en-close, and a triplicate, came to hand at one time; some future conveyance, it is probable, will present to me the dupli-cate.

I would also take the liberty to en-close to you the "Evening Post," No. 475, which Governor Livingston was so obliging as to send to me yesterday. Were we not fully satisfied, from our experience, that there are no artifices, no measures too black or wicked for the enemy or their adherents to attempt, in order to promote their views, we might be astonished at the daring confidence, in defiance of the opinion of the world, manifested in a publication in this pa-per, purporting to be a resolution of Congress, of the 20th of February. This proceeding is infamous to the last de-gree, and calculated to produce the most baneful consequences by exciting an opposition in the people to our drafting system, and embarrassing at least the only probable mode now left us for rais-ing men. I think it of great importance, that the forgery should be announced in the most public manner, and am the more induced to this opinion from Governor Livingston's account of the disagreeable operation it has had, and is likely to produce, if not contradicted. If it is, and with a few strictures, I should hope that it will excite in the breasts of all our countrymen a just and generous contempt of the enemy for such a dirty, wicked proceeding.

I was last night honored with your favor of the 18th instant, with the pro-ceedings alluded to. A general plan of operations for the campaign is indis-pensably essential to be settled. I have thought much upon the subject; and some propositions respecting it were put into the hands of all the general of-ficers here on Tuesday evening for their consideration. I also intended to send

a messenger this day to meet General Gates, supposing him to be on his way to Hudson's River, and to request his call at this camp, that we might enter in-to a full and free discussion of the point. There is not a moment to be delayed in forming some general system, in my opinion; and I only wait the arrival of Generals Gates and Mifflin to summon a council for the purpose. I have the honor to be, &c.

P. S. It is confidently reported, and I have little doubt of the truth of it, that Sir William Howe is recalled, and that General Clinton is to succeed him in the command. I have also the pleasure to transmit a list of sundry officers ex-changed on the 21st instant.
Lord George Germain's letter to Gen-eral Howe, signifying bis Majesty's ac-quiescence in his request to be relieved from the command, was dated February 4th. He was directed at the same time to deliver np his orders and instructions to Sir Henry Clinton as his successor. The letter was received by Sir William Howe on the 9th of April. VOL. V. 43 C
C TO MAJOR-GENERAL GATES.
Head-Quarters, Valley Forge, 24 April, 1778.

Sir,

It being indispensably necessary, that some general plan of operation should be settled for the present campaign, and perceiving that Congress have been pleased to appoint you to command on the North River, I am to request, if you should not find it too inconvenient, that you will make a digression from your route thither, and favor me with a call at this camp, that we may enter upon a discussion of the point, and form some general system. The propriety of this measure, particularly at this advanced period, will be so obvious to you, that it is unnecessary to add upon the subject.

I am, Sir, your most obedient servant.
TO GOUVERNEUR MORRIS, IN CON-GRESS.
Valley Forge, 25 April, 1778.

Dear Sir, I received your obliging fa-vor of the 18th instant yesterday evening. I thank you much for the ex-planatory hints it contains, and could have wished it had come to hand a little

sooner. I have many things to say to you, but as the express, who will deliver you this, is going with 'despatches, which will not admit of delay, I shall content myself with taking notice of one matter, that appears to me to require im-mediate remedy.f A similar invitation was sent to General Mifflin. t *From Gowernew Morris's Letter.* — "We have determined to scad Gates to Hudson's River, where he is to command very largely. Bat

The resolution of Congress directs the council to be formed of major-gen-erals and the chief engineer, who, you say, is to be a member *officially.* By this the commanding officer of artillery is negatively excluded, who, by the prac-tice of armies, and from the very nature of his appointment, is more *officially* a member than the other. According to my ideas, both or neither ought to be there; or, if an official preference is due to one more than the other, it is to the commander in the artillery line. I do not know what motives induced the dis-crimination in this instance; but I should suppose it will at least be felt; and I will further add, though prejudices may be entertained by some against General Knox, there is no department in the army, that has been conducted with greater propriety, or to more advantage, than the one in which he presides, ow-ing principally if not wholly to his man-agement. Surely whatever plans may be come into, the artillery will have no small share in the execution.

You say, *All xcill yet be well.* I wish it heartily; but I am much mistaken, if there are not some secret and retrograde springs in motion to disprove it. I wish you could announce the provision for officers concluded. It seems to me the basis of all our operations. Rehe is to re-ceive instructions, which shall be prop-er. You are directed to call a council of *major-generah,* in which the chief engineer is *officially* to be a member, and to which, by a subsequent resolu-tion, Generals Gates and Mifflin were *ordered* to repair. As these gentlemen ought not to receive orders *immediately* from Congress, they are, as you will see, permitted to leave the Board of War upon *your* order. This *amendment* was therefore acquiesced in unanimously.

" Apropos, of your council of war. Should you determine on any thing, which, considering the course of human affairs, is, I confess, rather improbable, let Congress know nothing about it. A secret should never be trusted to many bosoms. I will forfeit any thing, except reputation, that it will not be well kept, even by those necessarily confided in. " — *April 18th.* See the whole letter in Sfarks's Life of *Gouverneur Morris,* Vol. L p. 164.

signation after resignation is taking place; not here only, but of officers acting east of Hudson's River. I am, with great esteem and regard, dear Sir, &,c TO THE PRESIDENT OF CONGRESS.
Valley Forge, 25 April, 177&

Sir, I beg leave to inform Congress, that the report of the commissioners coming, according to intelligence received yesterday by a person of Philadelphia, is confidently believed; and it is there thought, that they will very soon arrive, f I think it almost certain that the matter will not be delayed, as the conduct of ministry, in not sending them immediately after their former propositions, has been much reprobated, and as it may be of much importance to improve the first impressions of the people upon the occasion. Lord Amherst, Admiral Keppel, and General Murray, are said to be the persons appointed; and it is likely they are vested with both civil and military powers. The information was through the channel of a sensible, intelligent man, well known, and of esteemed credit. He is connected with the British army, having two or three brothers in it. I shall transmit the"earliest accounts I receive from time to time on this very interesting subject.
Mr. Morris wrote in reply; — " Knox will attend the Council. Conway has resigned, and his resignation has been accepted. The affairs of the army are necessarily delayed by the foreign affairs, which have broken in upon us. As to the half-pay, matters stand thus. The questions have been carried; but by an entry on the minutes there is an agreement,

that a final question shall be put, whether it be finally determined in Congress, or sent to the several States. When a motion is made for the purpose, the yeas will be Massachusetts, Rhode Island, Connecticut, Jersey, and South Carolina; the nays will be New York, Maryland, Virginia, and Georgia. Pennsylvania is in a mighty flimsy situation on that subject, having indeed a mighty flimsy representation. I wish Boudinot were here. Delaware is absent, who is with us; as k North Carolina, also absent. New Hampshire is absent, who is against us." — *MS. Letter, May 1st.*
When the question was put, two weeks afterwards, whether the subject of making allowance to the officers after the war should be referred to the several States, it was decided in the negative, by a vote which accorded exacUy with Mr. Morris's prediction.—*Journals, May 13iA.*
f Commissioners for effecting a reconciliation with the Americana, ar cording to the tenor of Lo-d North's bills for that purpose.

I have the honor to be, &c.f TO GOVERNOR LIVINGSTON.
Valley Forge, 36 April, 1778.
Sir,

Your reasoning, upon the subject of deserters attending flags, is certainly right, and not to be disputed. Their appearing in that character is an additional crime, and it is the practice of war, in such instances, founded This information, in regard to the names of the commissioners, proved to be erroneous.
f The expectations of the British ministry, in regard to what they called the Conciliatory Propositions, may be inferred from Lord George Germain's letter on the subject to Sir Henry Clinton, in which he says;
" If that be true, which has been repeatedly declared by the colonial assemblies, and is still asserted by many persons, who pretend to be well informed of the dispositions of the inhabitants, that the generality of the people desire nothing more, than a full security for the enjoyment of all their rights and liberties under the British constitution, there can be no room to doubt, that the

generous terms now held out to them will be gladly embraced, and that a negotiation will immediately take place upon the arrival of the new commission, and be so far advanced before the season will admit of military operations, as to supersede the necessity of another campaign. So speedy and happy a termination of the war could not fail to gratify the King, as the peace, prosperity, and happi ness of all his subjects have ever been his most ardent wish." — *MS. Letter, Whitehall, March 8th.*

Instructions were at the same time communicated, that, in case the attempt at a reconciliation did not succeed, the war was to be prosecuted with vigor, and a plan for the campaign was suggested. Five CC on the principles of common reason and the delicacy of truces, to execute them immediately. This is the custom in general cases. How far the circumstances, which attended the enlistment of Job Hetfield, require a discrimination in his favor, is a point perhaps of some difficulty. I find, by inquiry of General Maxwell, that he was enlisted and sworn; but yet that there was a sort of coercion, which might distinguish it from an act perfectly free and voluntary. Upon the whole, I think his detention and confinement justifiable, which I would prefer to capital punishment. At the same time, you will permit me to observe, that, from the expediency of flags, and the necessity of such an intercourse between warring powers, it is the constant usage for the party detaining, or executing, to inform the other side of the reasons.

I have taken the freedom to commit to your care a letter for Major-General Tryon, which you will be pleased to send by a flag to Staten Island, or to such other post as you may deem most proper. I transmit to you a copy of our correspondence, which on his part is pretty similar, it is probable, to his addresses to your officers. Determined that I should get some of his obliging letters, he made out a first, a second, and a third, all of the same tenor and date. I am persuaded you will be under some difficulty, which to admire most, his impertinence or his folly.

I am, dear Sir, &c.

days after the above letter was written, the French ambassador made known to the British cabinet, that a treaty had been signed between the French government and the commissioners from the United States. The instructions to Sir Henry Clinton were then essentially altered. These facts render it probable, that the British ministers had not positive knowledge of the signature of the treaty, before it was communicated by the French ambassador, although they undoubtedly had strong i for suspecting it. TO MAJOR-GENERAL WILLIAM TRYON.

Head-Quarters, Valley Forge, 26 April, 1778.

Sir,

Your letter of the 17th, and a triplicate of the same, were duly received. I had had the pleasure of seeing the drafts of the two bills, before those which were sent by you came to hand; and I can assure you they were suffered to have a free currency among the officers and men under my command, in whose fidelity to the United States I have the most perfect confidence. The enclosed Gazette, published the 24th at Yorktown, will show you, that it is the wish of Congress, that they should have an unrestrained circulation.

I take the liberty to transmit to you a few printed copies of a resolution of Congress of the 23d instant, and to request that you will be instrumental in communicating its contents, so far as it may be in your power, to the persons who are the objects of its operation. The benevolent purpose it is intended to answer will, I persuade myself, sufficiently recommend it to your candor. I am, Sir, &c.f The bills were published by order of Congress. They met with a different fate in Rhode Island, according to General Sullivan's account, who then commanded at Providence. " We have nothing new in this quarter," he says in writing to General Washington, " save that General Pigot politely requested me to disperse his hand-bills, which I refused. I delivered them over to the Assembly. I since hear, that while I was viewing the sea-coast below the enemy,

the populace rose and burnt them under the gallows." — *MS. Letter, May 1st.* f This was a fair retort upon Governor Tryon, who had sent to General Washington copies of the Conciliatory Bills, with a request that he would circulate them. The resolve, enclosed in the above letter, recommended to the legislatures of the several States, or to the executive authority of each State possessing the power, to issue proclamations offering pardon, under certain specified limitations and restrictions, " to such of their inhabitants or subjects as had levied war against any of the States, or adhered to, aided,-or abetted the enemy, and who should surrender themselves to any civil or military officer in any of the States, and return to the State to which they belonged before the 10th of June." This resolve was suggested by a hint in General Washington's letter of the 21st of April to Mr. Banister.

TO THE PRESIDENT OF CONGRESS.

Valley Forge, 27 April, 177&

Sir, I had the honor yesterday afternoon to receive your letter of the 24th, continued to the 25th, with its important enclosures. Congress will be pleased to accept my sincere thanks for the fresh instance of confidence manifested in their resolution of the 23d, and other proceedings; and they may rest assured, that whatever powers are entrusted to me shall be invariably directed to promote the interest of these States. If in any case there should be a misapplication or a failure in the execution, it will be the effect of mistake and not of design. I shall take measures for distributing the report of the committee on Lord North's bills, and the resolution of the 23d, inviting delinquents to return to their allegiance and to the protection of these States. This proceeding appears to me founded in great good policy; and I should hope, that it will be attended with many valuable consequences; but this can only be proved by the event.

The draft of the *Conciliatory Bills,* communicated to Congress in General Washington's letter of the 18th, was referred to a committee of three, consisting of Gouvcmeur Morris, Drayton, and Dana. The bills were regarded as gen-

uine by the committee, analyzed, examined in their various parts, and censured throughout as totally inadequate to the expectations of the Americans, and as affording no solid basis for a reconciliation. The report, expressing these sentiments, was discussed by Congress, and *unanimously* adopted. It contains the declaration, " that these United States cannot with propriety hold any conference or treaty with any commissioners on the part of Great Britain, unless they shall, as a preliminary thereto, either withdraw their fleets and armies, or else in positive and express terms acknowledge the independence of the said States." This was effectually closing the door against the commissioners long before their arrival. The report was drawn up by Gouverneur Morris. It is ingenious and able. — *Journals, April 22i.*

Though I wish most heartily for the aid of General Lee in council and upon every other occasion, yet, as the time of his return is uncertain, or at least it will be several days before it takes place, and as it seems to me, that there is not a moment to lose in forming some general system for our operations, I should think it inexpedient for General Gates to delay coming to camp till his arrival. After a plan is digested, there will be a great deal of time expended before things will be in a proper train for execution. The season is fast advancing, and the period, which may be most favorable for any designs we may form, will presently arrive. I have written to Major-General Tryon a few lines in answer to his letter, a copy of which is enclosed. I have the honor to be, &,c.

TO MAJOR-GENERAL PUTNAM.

Head-Quarters, Valley Forge, 29 April, 1778.

Dear Sir,

I am pleased to hear, that your prospect of procuring recruits and drafts for the army bore a more favorable appearance, than when you wrote before. I must beg you to forward on all those for the regiments at this camp as fast as possible. I expect in a few days a general plan of operations for the campaign will be settled; if one similar to that which you mention should be fixed upon, your assistance will still be wanting in Connecticut to arrange and forward the militia, which we shall have occasion to draw from that State, and therefore I wish you to continue there till you hear from me. I am, dear Sir, &c.

Vol. v. 44 TO MAJOR-GENERAL HEATH.

Valley Forge, 29 April, 1778.

Dear Sir,

I am glad to hear that General Burgoyne is gone, and I wish his departure had been much earlier. At the time of his capture, he certainly must have entertained very favorable impressions of our force, and perhaps in point of good policy he should have been allowed to depart, before they were in the smallest degree done away, and before he could have obtained any accurate ideas of our affairs. He must yet, in vindication of his conduct, speak largely of our powers.

It is astonishing that officers will, in direct violation of the resolution of Congress, of my recruiting instructions, and the most evident principles of policy, founded in experience, persevere in enlisting deserters from the British army. Supposing it might be done in any case, yet there is every possible objection to the measure in the instance of deserters from General Burgoyne's army. These troops did not originally come into our hands through choice; they were conquered, and brought into our possession by compulsion. Those apprehensions of punishment, in case of return, which may operate on the minds of *deserters,* they feel nothing of. So far from the most distant chance of punishment, they will be applauded by the commanders of the British army for their fidelity and attachment to their prince, and their enlisting with us will be considered as a high stroke of policy, and the only probable mode they could adopt to effect their escape. We are counting on men, who cannot be confided in, and who will embrace the earliest opportunity to leave us and strengthen the enemy, at the expense of arms, clothes, and bounty on our part.

But very few if any of those, who deserted from General Burgoyne, and who came on with the two detachments under Lieutenant-Colonel Smith, now remain with him; they are gone. In like manner, a detachment from Colonel Henley, which marched from Boston sixty strong, arrived here two or three days ago with thirteen men only; and, had it not been for a detachment of New Hampshire troops, it is highly probable, that not one of them would have been seen. Thirty of the sixty are now in Easton jail, having formed a plan at that place to go off in a body. The rest, except thirteen, had escaped before. If we would wish to reinforce the enemy with the whole of Mr. Burgoyne's army, we cannot pursue a mode, that will be more effectual or more certain, than to enlist it into our service; but it may be done with less injury by sending them the men, unarmed, without clothes, and without paying them an exorbitant bounty. If nothing else will restrain officers from pursuing such a pernicious, ruinous practice, they must be made to pay for all expenses and losses occasioned by it. Indeed there is nothing that can compensate for the injury.

I am, dear Sir, &,c.

TO THE PRESIDENT OF CONGRESS.

Head-Quarters, 30 AprU, 1778.

Sir, The extensive ill consequences, arising from a want of uniformity in discipline and manoeuvres throughout the army, have long occasioned me to wish for the establishment of a well organized inspectorship; and the concurrence of Congress in the same views has induced me to set on foot a temporary institution, which, from the success that has hitherto attended it, gives me the most flattering expectations, and will, I hope, obtain their approbation.

Baron Steuben's length of service in the first military school in Europe, and his former rank, pointed him out as a person peculiarly qualified to be at the head of this department. This appeared the least exceptionable way of introducing him into the army, and one that would give him the most ready opportunity of displaying his talents. I therefore proposed to him to undertake the office of inspector-general, which he agreed to with the greatest cheerfulness, and has performed the duties of it with a zeal and intelligence equal to our wishes. He has two ranks of inspectors under him; the lowest are officers charged with the inspection of brigades, with the title of brigade-inspectors; the others superintend several of these. They have written instructions relative to their several functions; and the manoeuvres, which they are to practise, are illustrated by a company, which the Baron has taken the pains to train himself.

The brigade-inspectors were chosen by the brigadier and commanding officers of regiments in each brigade. The inspectors are Lieutenant-Colonels Barber of Jersey, Brooks of Massachusetts, Davis of Virginia, and Monsieur Ternant, a French gentleman. The reason for employing him, apart from his intrinsic merit and abilities, was his possessing the French and English languages equally, which made him a necessary assistant to Baron Steuben. He is content to serve without rank, until, after an experiment of his abilities, Congress shall determine what he is entitled to.

Upon the arrival of Lieutenant-Colonel Fleury in camp, as he was unemployed, and had exercised the office of aid-major in France, the Baron proposed to have him employed as an inspector; in which I readily acquiesced, as Congress had given him the rank and pay of lieutenant-colonel. There may be other foreign officers in Continental pay, idle for want of being attached to some corps, of whose services we might avail ourselves in this way, which is the only method of disposing of them, unless they could be formed into a distinct corps. From the extraordinary fatigue and close attention of the officers employed in the inspectorship, I did not think it amiss to let them entertain hopes, that Congress would allow some addition to the pay, which they derive from their rank, and I take the liberty of recommending the measure. I would propose twenty dollars a month for the brigadeinspectors, and thirty for the inspectors, in addition to their pay in the line.

I should do injustice if I were to be longer silent with regard to the merits of Baron Steuben. His knowledge of his profession, added to the zeal which he has discovered since he began upon the functions of his office, leads me to consider him as an acquisition to the service, and to recommend him to the attention of Congress. His expectations with respect to rank extend to that of major-general. His finances, he ingenuously confesses, will not admit of his serving without the incidental emoluments; and Congress, I presume, from his character, and their own knowledge of him, will without difficulty gratify him in these particulars.

The Baron is sensible, that our situation requires a few variations in the duties of his office from the general practice in Europe, and particularly that they must necessarily be more comprehensive; in which, as well as in his instructions, he has skilfully yielded to circumstances. The success, which has hitherto attended VOL. V. DD the plan, enables me to request with confidence the ratification of Congress, and is I think a pledge of the establishment of a well combined general system, which insurmountable obstacles have hitherto opposed.

I have the honor to be, &c TO THE PRESIDENT OF CONGRESS.

Vtlley Forge, 30 April, 1778.

Dear Sir, I thank you much for your obliging favor of the 27th. I think with you, that a most important crisis is now at hand, and that there cannot be too much wisdom in all our counsels for conducting our affairs to a safe and happy issue. There should, in my opinion, be a full representation of the States in Congress, which I have often regretted has not been the case for a long time past. I also concur with you in sentiment, that gentlemen any where, whose abilities might be of essential service, in case of a treaty with the British commissioners, ought to be called forth for the purpose. It will be a work of infinite importance, and the result may lead to happiness or to misery, to freedom or to slavery. The enemy are determined to

try us by force and by fraud; and while they are exerting their utmost powers in the first instance, I do not doubt but they will employ men in the second, versed in the arts of dissimulation. It appears to me, that nothing short of independence can possibly do. The injuries we have received from Britain can never be forgotten, and a peace upon other terms would be the source of perpetual feuds and animosity. Besides, should Britain, from her love of tyranny and lawless domination, attempt again to bend our necks to the yoke of slavery, and there is no doubt but she would, for her pride and ambition are unconquerable, no nation would credit our professions, or grant us aid. At any rate, her favors would be obtained upon the most disadvantageous and dishonorable terms.

I sincerely wish the provision for officers, so long the subject of discussion, was established. It is certainly equitable, and in my opinion essential. Day after day and hour after hour produce resignations. If they Mere confined to bad officers, or to those of little or no character, they would be of no consequence. But it is painful to see men, who are of a different cast, who have rendered great services to their country, and who are still and may be most materially wanted, leaving the army, on account of the distresses of their families, and to repair their circumstances, which have been much injured by their zeal and the part they have taken in defence of our common rights. The provision, if adopted, would not produce present relief, nor a present expense; yet it would be a compensation in future for their misfortunes and their toils, and be some support to their injured constitutions.

If the measure is to be submitted to the legislatures of the several States for their concurrence, the delay, supposing it should be assented to, will I fear be attended with effects, that will only be regretted when too late. But the chance in such case will be rather against the adoption; for there are but few of the legislatures, which are impressed with the real state of. things, or which can without difficulty be fully informed of them; and while this matter is held in

suspense, every thing is at a stand, and the most fatal consequences may result from it. I do not to this hour know whether, putting half-pay out of the question, the old or new establishment is to take place; how to dispose of the officers in consequence; whether the instituting several other corps, as agreed to by the committee and referred by them to Congress, is adopted or not. In a word, I have no ground to form a single arrangement upon, nor do I know whether the augmentation of the cavalry is to take place or was rejected, in order that I may govern myself thereby. Equally unable am I to answer the incessant applications of the officers of the Pennsylvania and Additional Battalions, who, knowing the intended reduction of some of these corps, are held in suspense, uncertain what part to act. In short, our present situation is beyond description irksome and dangerous. But I will trouble you no further, than to assure you, that I am, dear Sir, &c.

TO THE PRESIDENT OF CONGRESS.

Valley Forge, 1 May, 1778.

Sir, In compliance with the request of Congress, I shall immediately call upon the officers in the army to take the oath of allegiance and abjuration. This I should have done as soon as the resolution passed, had it not been for the state of the army at that time, and that there were some strong reasons, which made it expedient to defer the matter. My opinion upon the subject.of a future provision for the officers has been so fully, and I trust so necessarily and equitably urged, that I shall not add further respecting it, except my sincere wishes that the establishment was determined on. Nothing in my idea can be more just; and I am certain there is nothing more essential. The present unsettled state of the army is hurtful in the extreme.

Since my letter of the 27th, I have received authentic information of the sailing of a very large number of transports from Philadelphia; two hundred, it is said. They went down the Delaware the beginning of the week, light and empty. I have not been able to learn any thing of their destination; nor can I form a conjecture upon the occasion, that is the least satisfactory.

With infinite pleasure I beg leave to congratulate Congress on the very important and interesting advices brought by the frigate *Sensible.* General MDougall and Mr. Deane were so obliging as to transmit to me the outlines of the good tidings. As soon as Congress may think it expedient, I shall be happy to have an opportunity of announcing to the army, with the usual ceremony, such parts of the intelligence as may be proper, and sanctioned by authority. I have mentioned the matter to such officers as I have seen; and I believe no event was ever received with a more heart-felt joy. I have the honor to be, &c.

TO MAJOR-GENERAL MCDOUGALL.

Head-Quarters, 1 May, 1778.

Dear Sir, I return you my thanks for your favor of the 27th ultimo, and heartily congratulate you on the important intelligence contained in it. As the matter is related, in general terms, France appears to have acted with politic generosity towards us, and to have timed her declaration in our favor most admirably for her own interests and the abasing of her ancient rival One immediate good consequence I flatter myself will attend this intelligence, which is, that the States will shake off their languor, and be stimulated to complete their battalions. I am, wkh great regard, dear Sir, &,c.

Simeon Deane, brother to Silas Deane one of the American Commissioners in Paris, was the bearer of the despatches containing the treaties between France and the United States. He came over in the French frigate *SaxsMe,* of thirty-six guns, which was sent by the King for the express purpose, and arrived at Falmouth (now Portland) in Casco Bay, on the 13th of April, after a passage of thirty-five days. He reached Yorktown on Saturday, the 2d of May. Congress had adjourned tin Monday, but the members were immediately summoned to assemble by the president, and the despatches were read. VOL. V. 45 D D TO THE PRESIDENT OF CONGRESS.

Head-Quarters, Valley Forge, 3 May,

177b.

Sir,

In a letter from General Schuyler, I received the proceedings of a Board of Commissioners for Indian affairs, held at Albany the 15th of last month. It appears by them and some other accounts I have seen, that there is but little prospect of succeeding in the plan for engaging a body of Indians from that quarter to serve with this army. The advantage which the enemy possess over us, in having the means of making presents much more liberally than we can, has made a strong impression upon their minds, and seems to be more than a counterbalance for any arguments we can offer to conciliate their attachment. They also appear to be apprehensive for their own safety, and rather to wish for aid and protection from us, than to be willing to leave their habitations and come to our assistance.

The measure proposed was by way of experiment, as one which might possibly be attended with valuable consequences, and, if it could have been effected without much difficulty, might have been worth a trial But, as the scheme does not well correspond with their present disposition, and may serve to increase our embarrassments in keeping them even in tolerably good humor, I am inclined to think it would be most advisable to relinquish the attempt. They may be told of what has happened in Europe, with proper embellishments, and that our affairs are now upon such a footing as to render their aid in the field unnecessary, and that all we require of them is their friendship and good wishes. This and promises of protection may have a very powerful and happy effect. It is of great importance to counteract the temptations held out by the enemy, and to secure the good will of the Indians, who appear at least to be in a state of hesitancy and indecision, if nothing worse. Congress I am persuaded will do every thing in their power to promote these desirable ends. I have the honor to be, &c.

TO THE PRESIDENT OF CONGRESS.

Head-Quarters, Valley Forge, 4 May, 177&

Sir, Last night at eleven o'clock I was honored with your despatches of the 3d. The contents afford me the most sensible pleasure. Mr. Simeon Deane had informed me by a line from Bethlehem, that he was the bearer of the articles of alliance between France and the States. I shall defer celebrating this happy event in a suitable manner, until I have liberty from Congress to announce it publicly. I will only say, that the army are anxious to manifest their joy upon the occasion. Enclosed you have a letter, which I received a few days ago from Lord Stirling, and which, at his request, I lay before Congress with its contents.

Ihmthe Orderly Book, May 6th. — "It having pleased the Almighty Ruler of the Universe to defend the cause of the United American States, and finally to raise us up a powerful friend among the princes of the earth, to establish our liberty and independency upon a lasting foundation; it becomes us to set apart a day for gratefully acknowledging the divine goodness, and celebrating the important event, which we owe to his divine interposition. The several brigades are to be assembled for this purpose at nine o'clock to-morrow morning, when their chaplains will communicate the intelligence contained in the Postscript of the Pennsylvania Gazette of the 2d instant, and offer up thanksgiving, and deliver a discourse suitable to the occasion. At half after ten o'clock a cannon will be fired, which is to be a signal for the men to be under arms; the brigade-inspectors will then inspect their dress and arms and form the battalions according to the instructions given them, and announce to the commanding officers of the brigade that the battalions are formed.

I am, with the greatest esteem and respect, &c.

TO MAJOR-GENERAL HEATH.

Valley Forge, 5 May, 1778.

Dear Sir, Notwithstanding the immense advantages, which we shall derive from the acknowledgment of our independence by, and our late alliance with, the court of France, yet much remains to be done to extricate ourselves entirely from our oppressors. Even taking it for granted, that the enemy, from the situation of European affairs, cannot be further reinforced, their remaining strength, if collected and properly directed, is formidable. The Congress, sensible of this, have wisely determined not to relax in their preparations for war, and have earnestly recommended it to every State to complete its quota of Continental troops, and to hold its militia ready for service.

" The commanders of brigades will then appoint the field-officers to the battalions, after which each battalion will be ordered to load and ground their arms. At half past eleven a second cannon will be fired as a signal for the march, upon which the several brigades will begin their march by wheeling to the right by platoons, and proceed by the nearest way to the left of their ground by the new position; this will be pointed out by the brigade-inspectors. A third signal will then be given, on which there will be a discharge of thirteen cannon; after which a running fire of the infantry will begin on the right of Woodford's, and continue throughout the front line; it will then be taken upon the left of the second line and continue to the right. Upon a signal given, the whole army will huzza, *Long live the King of* /Vance; the artillery then begins again and fires thirteen rounds; this will be succeeded by a second general discharge of the musketry in a running fin?, and huzza, *Long live the friendly European Powers.* The last discharge of thirteen pieces of artillery will be given, followed by a general running fire, and huzza, *The American State."*

The following is an extract from a letter, written by an officer who wae present. " Last Wednesday was aet apart as a day of general rejoicing, when we had a *feu de joie* conducted with the greatest order and rcgelaxity. The army made a most brilliant appearance; after which his Excellency dined in public, with all the officers of his army, attended with a band of music. I never was present where there was such unfeigned and perfect joy, as was discovered in every countenance. The entertainment

was concluded with a number of patriotic toasts, attended with huzzas. When the General took his leave, there was a universal clap, with loud huzzas, which continued till he had proceeded a quarter of a mile, during which time there were a thousand hats tossed in the sir. His Excellency turned round with his retinue, and huzzaed several times." — *Valley Forge, May 9th.*

I cannot account for a late manoeuvre of the enemy in any other manner, than by supposing they are about making some change in the disposition of their forces. They have lately sent near two hundred sail of light transports from Philadelphia. If they evacuate Rhode Island, and carry the troops from thence to New York, the brigades upon the North River should be reinforced by recruits as speedily as possible; and if the troops are brought from Rhode Island to Philadelphia, this army will in like manner stand in need of assistance. I therefore must again request you to forward the recruits, drafts, furloughed men, and those recovered from the hospitals, to the North River, with as much expedition as possible.

There were fears at this time, that the country, confiding in the aid and prowess of France, now pledged to sustain American independence, would remit the necessary exertions for carrying on the war. The favorable result of the contest was now considered as beyond a doubt. Even Washington said, in a letter to General Putnam, of the same date as the above, I hope that the fair and, I may say, *certain* prospect of success will not induce us to relax." Robert Morris also, in a letter to General Washington, thus wrote. " When I congratulate your Excellency on the great good news lately received from France, you will not expect me to express my feelings. Were I in your company, my countenance might show, but my pen cannot describe them. Most sincerely do I give you joy. Our independence is undoubtedly secured; our country must be free." — *May 9tt.*

I had a letter a few days ago from the Board of War, in which they desire to know whether you had ever been able to

do any thing more towards the exchange between Brigadier-General Thompson and BrigadierGeneral Hamilton. If you cannot succeed in that, they desire you to feel the pulse of the two other brigadiers, for either of whom we would willingly exchange General Thompson. The foreigners have thought themselves partially treated by General Howe, in regard to exchanges, and if you were to propose the matter to the foreign brigadiers, and either of them should incline to it, perhaps General Howe would accede, rather than give umbrage.

As the balance of officers is much against us in the case of prisoners, and may long remain so, unless we can effect exchanges between ours with the enemy and those of General Burgoyne's army, I must request that you will take occasion to inform the latter, that, on their application, or indeed without it, we shall readily consent on our part to their releasement for our officers of the same rank. If there should be any number, who wish this to take place, they had better write at the same time to General Howe, or the commanding officer at Philadelphia; and you will send me a list of their rank and names, that a like number, who have been longest in confinement, may be directed to return, if their request is complied with. I am, &c.

TO MAJOR-GENERAL McDOUOALL.

Valley Forge, 5 May, 1778.

Dear Sir,

I have written pressingly to General Heath and General Putnam to forward the recruits of Massachusetts and Connecticut to the North River, with all possible despatch. If they arrive there during the continuance of your command, you will be pleased, agreeably to former orders, to send on immediately those belonging to the regiments that are here.

I very much fear that we, taking it for granted, that we have nothing more to do, because France has acknowledged our independency and formed an alliance with us, shall relapse into a state of supineness and perfect security. I think it more than probable, from the situation of affairs in Europe, that the enemy will receive no considerable if any reinforcements. But suppose they should not, their remaining force, if well directed, is far from being contemptible. In the desperate state of British affairs, it is worth a desperate attempt to extricate themselves; and a blow at our main army, if successful, would have a wonderful effect upon the minds of a number of people, still wishing to embrace the present terms, or indeed any terms offered by Great Britain. It behoves us therefore to make ourselves as respectable as possible, that, if the enemy continue in their detached state, we may endeavour to destroy them by piecemeal; and that if, on the contrary, they collect themselves, they may not fall heavily upon us in some quarter. I cannot help thinking, from a late uncommon movement of their shipping, that they have something of this kind in view. Near two hundred sail of light transports have gone down the Delaware within a week past. New York is too valuable to be evacuated but upon the last extremity, and I therefore incline to think that the movement, if any, will be from Rhode Island. If the troops should be brought from thence to New York, we must provide for the posts upon the North River, in proportion to the addition to the strength of the enemy; if to Philadelphia, we must draw down our force accordingly. For these reasons it is my wish to see the eastern recruits brought on towards the North River as quickly as possible. If there should be no alteration in the position of the enemy, you will, as before mentioned, send on those intended for the regiments here without loss of time. If there should be a move, we must alter our plan, without loss of time. I am, &c

A council of war was held on the 8th of May, at which were present the Major-Generals Gates, Greene, Stirling, Mifflin, Lafayette, Kalh, Armstrong, and Steuben; and the Brigadiers Knox and Duportail. This council was convened by order of Congress.

The Commander-in-chief first laid before the council the state of the enemy's forces, which were estimated at somewhat more than sixteen thousand men rank and file fit for the field, be-

sides cavalry and artillery. Of these about ten thousand were in Philadelphia, four thousand in New York, and two thousand on Rhode Island.

The Continental force amounted to about fifteen thousand, besides horse and artillery. Of these eleven thousand eight hundred were at Valley Forge, comprehending the sick present, and those on command, who might be called into action on an emergency. The detachment at Wilmington consisted of fourteen hundred. On the North River were eighteen hundred. When all the reinforcements were brought in, that it was reasonable to anticipate, the whole army fit for action could not be expected to amount to more than twenty thousand men. With thia state of the two armies before them, the council were requested to decide what measures it was best to pursue.

After a full and unreserved discussion, it was the unanimous opinion of the council, that the line of conduct most consistent with sound policy, and best suited to promote the interests and safety of the United States, was to remain on the defensive and wait events, and not attempt any offensive operation against the enemy, till circumstances should afford a fairer opportunity of striking a successful blow. As the enemy were strongly fortified by nature, and by artificial works, in all their position, it would require a greatly superior force to attack them, with any hop of a favorable issue. It was agreed, that to take Philadelphia by storm was impracticable, and that thirty thousand men would be requisite for a blockade. The Continental force could not bo so much increased by the militia, even if that description of troops could be relied on for such an enterprise. In short, strong objections were believed to exist against all offensive movements. General Lee, who was not present at the council, signed his name to their written decision. Baron Steuben sat in the council, having been two days before appointed by Congress inspector-general, with the rank and pay of major-general.

TO MAJOR-GENERAL ARNOLD.
Valley Forge, 7 May, 1778.

Dear Sir,

A gentleman in France having very obligingly sent me three sets of epaulettes and sword-knots, two of which, professedly, to be disposed of to any friends I should choose, I take the liberty of presenting them to you and General Lincoln, as a testimony of my sincere regard and approbation of your conduct. I have been informed, by a brigade-major of General Huntington's, of your intention of repairing to camp shortly; but, notwithstanding my wish to see you, I must beg that you will run no hazard by coming out too soon.

I am sincerely and affectionately your obedient, &,c TO THE PRESIDENT OF CONGRESS.

Valley Forge, 12 May, 1778.

Sir,

After much consideration upon the subject, I have appointed General MIntosh to command at Fort Pitt, and in the western country, for which he will set out as soon as he can accommodate his affairs. I part with this gentleman with much reluctance, as I esteem him an officer of great worth and merit,, and as I know his services here are and will be materially wanted. His firm disposition and equal justice, his assiduity and good understanding, added to his being a stranger to all parties in that quarter, pointed him out as a proper person; and I trust extensive advantages will be derived from his command, which I could wish was more agreeable. He will wait on Congress for their instructions.

The above estimate of the British forces in America was probably short of the true number. See Appendix, No. XV. General Arnold's wound, received at Saratoga, was not yet healed VOL. V. 46 E E

The enclosed copy of a letter from General Dickinson to me will inform Congress of the fate of the Continental frigates in the Delaware; a fate (in the situation in which they were left) I had long predicted, and which I had taken much pains to avert, by using every argument in my power to have them sunk. In that case, their destruction would have been at least a work of time, difficulty, and expense, and might have been perhaps prevented. About one o'clock on Thursday I got notice of an intended move of the enemy by water; and, conjecturing the destination of it, I had a detachment under General Maxwell (whose tour of duty it was) ready to march towards the Delaware by four o'clock; but a heavy rain prevented their moving till next morning.

I have been happy in the exchange, and a visit from Lieutenant-Colonel Allen. His fortitude and firmness seem to have placed him out of the reach of misfortune. There is an original something in him, that commands admiration; and his long captivity and sufferings have only served to increase, if possible, his enthusiastic zeal. He appears very desirous of rendering his services to the States, and of being employed; and at the same time he does not discover any ambition for high rank. Congress will herewith receive a letter from him; and I doubt not they will make such provision for him, as they may think proper and suitable..

Colonel Allen waa exchanged for Colonel Campbell on the 5th of May, and immediately proceeded from Elizabethtown to Head-Qoartera. — See the Lipk or Ethak Alleu, in the *Library of American Bugrwpky,* VoL L p. 321.

I take pleasure in transmitting a Philadelphia paper of the 9th, which came to hand yesterday evening, containing a message from his Most Christian Majesty to the court of London, in consequence of the treaty between him and these States, and his Britannic Majesty's Address to the Lords and Commons. The message is conceived in terms of irony and derision, more degrading to the pride and dignity of Britain, than any thing she has ever experienced since she has been a nation. It is not an actual declaration of war, but it certainly must produce one.

I have the honor to be, &c TO GOVERNOR LIVINGSTON.

Valley Forge, 12 May, 1778.

Dear Sir, I was a few days ago honored with yours, informing me of the probable strength of militia, which might be collected in your State, if called upon. This was a piece of infor-

mation, which I wanted more for my guidance in future, than for any sudden plan. There are several matters, which render the drawing together of a large body of forces just at this time impracticable. The deranged state of the commissary and quartermaster-general's departments, with which you are well acquainted, are sufficient obstacles. Every thing is doing to put the quarter mastership upon a proper and respectable footing; and I hope that the new commissary-general, with the assistance of the States, will be able to make such arrangements, that we shall, some time hence, be able to victual a very considerable body of men, should any advantageous prospects, from drawing them together, present themselves. We know but little yet of the intentions of the enemy, or of their expectations in respect to reinforcements; and therefore cannot determine whether an offensive or defensive plan is to be adopted by us. I could therefore wish, that some plan might be digested for calling out a given number of militia, should there be occasion, armed and accoutred, and in every respect ready for the field upon the shortest notice. Perhaps something similar to the minute companies, which were instituted at the commencement of this war, might answer the purpose.

See the Message and Address in the *Annual Register, for the Year* 1778, pp. 290, 291. — Almon's *Remembrancer,* Vol. V. p. 119.

The late visit of the enemy to Bordentown has fully verified my predictions of what would be the fate of the frigates and other vessels there. So soon as the enemy had got full possession of the river, I urged the gentlemen of the Navy Board to scuttle and sink the frigates immediately. They objected to sinking them at that time, but said, that they would have them ballasted and ready to sink upon the approach of the enemy. I then wrote to them, that, as they might depend upon it the attack would be sudden, so they would find that those, entrusted with the execution of the business, would not be able to effect it, before the enemy had possession of the vessels. The event has proved it. Had

hulks of such bulk been sunk, it would have taken considerable time to weigh them. Upon the first intimation of the design, I detached General Maxwell, with a strong party, to endeavour to prevent it; but the mischief was done by the time he reached the Cross Roads, and the enemy had returned again. I am, &. c.

TO BRIGADIER-GENERAL NELSON.

Head-Quarters, Valley Forge, 15 May, 1778.

Dear Sir,

I thank you for your exertions to raise a body of cavalry for reinforcing and relieving those belonging to the army, which by the severe service of the last campaign are much reduced. As motives of generosity and duty bring your corps to the field, I flatter myself they will render essential services, and that their conduct will be such, as to merit the approbation of their country.

I congratulate you most sincerely on the part, which France has taken in our affairs. The public prints will inform you of the treaty with us, and of her message to the court of London in consequence. The latter was communicated through the Philadelphia press, and it must have been more galling and degrading to the pride and ambition of Britain, than any thing she has experienced since she was a nation. In a paper of the 13th from the same quarter, it is said, "The directors of the Bank had waited on Lord North, to know whether a war would happen as soon as expected, who answered it was inevitable; that all the governors had been ordered forthwith to repair to their respective stations in England, Ireland, and elsewhere." A further paragraph states, " that a messenger extraordinary had been despatched to Lord Grantham, Brigadier-general of the Virginia militia. EE ambassador at the court of Madrid, instructing him to demand categorically, whether that court meant to aid the French in their present unjustifiable conduct with respect to American disputes, or to preserve the strictest neutrality, with further directions, in case of an evasive answer, to leave the Spanish dominions immediately. It is added,

that the declaration of war was only suspended to know the event of the demand." Matters appear abroad to be in as favorable a train as we could wish, and if we are not free and happy, it will be owing to a want of virtue, prudence, and management among ourselves. I am, dear Sir, &c. TO THE MARQUIS DE LAFAYETTE.
Camp, 17 May, 1778.

Dear Sir,

I received yesterday your favor of the 15th instant, enclosing a paper subscribed by sundry officers of General Woodford's brigade, setting forth the reasons for not taking the oath of abjuration, allegiance, and office; and I thank you much for the cautious delicacy used in communicating the matter to me. As every oath should be a free act of the mind, founded on the conviction of its propriety, I would not wish, in any instance, that there should be the least degree of compulsion exercised; nor to interpose my opinion, in order to induce any to make it, of whom it is required. The gentlemen, therefore, who signed the paper, will use their own discretion in the matter, and swear or not swear, as their conscience and feelings dictate.

At the same time, I cannot but consider it as a circumstance of some singularity, that the scruples against the oath should be peculiar to the officers of one bri gade, and so very extensive. The oath in itself is not new. It is substantially the same with that required in all governments, and therefore does not imply any indignity; and it is perfectly consistent with the professions, actions, and implied engagements of every officer. The objection, founded on the supposed unsettled rank of the officers, is of no validity, rank being only mentioned as a further designation of the party swearing; nor can it be seriously thought, that the oath is either intended to prevent, or can prevent, their being promoted, or their resignation.

The fourth objection, stated by the gentlemen, serves as a *key* to their scruples; and I would willingly persuade myself, that their own reflections will point out to them the impropriety of the whole proceeding, and not suffer them

to be betrayed in future into a»similar conduct. I have a regard for them all, and cannot but regret, that they were ever engaged in the measure. I am certain they will regret it themselves. Sure I am, that they ought.. I am, my dear Marquis, your affectionate friend and servant.

General Woodford's brigade consisted of Virginia troops, and was in the division commanded by the Marquis de Lafayette. The oath required by Congress to be taken by every officer was as follows. — "I do acknowledge the United States of America to be free, independent, and sovereign States, and declare that the people thereof owe no allegiance or obedience to George the Third, King of Great Britain; and I renounce, refuse, and abjure any allegiance or obedience to him; and I do swear (or affirm) that I will, to the utmost of my power, support, maintain, and defend the said United States against the said King George the Third and his heirs and successors, and his or their abettors, assistants, and adherents, and will serve the said United States in the office, which I now hold, with fidelity, according to the best of my skill and understanding."—*Journals, February 3d.* Twenty-six officers of General Woodford's brigade signed and sent a memorial to the Marquis de Lafayette, stating their reasons against taking the oath in the words following.
" 1. The tenor of the oath they in some measure consider an indignity; they will not undertake to determine it unnecessary; an indignity, as it presupposes that some of them have acted contrary to their sentiments; it may be unnecessary, for those officers, who ventured their live and fortunes in support of American Independence, could have no other reason but the apparent one.
TO THE MARQUIS DE LAFAYETTE.
Instructions.

Sir, The detachment under your command, with which you will immediately march towards the enemy's lines, is designed to answer the following purposes; namely, to be a security to this camp and a cover to the country between the Delaware and the Schuylkill, to inter-

rupt the communication with Philadelphia, to obstruct the incursions of the enemy's parties, and to obtain intelligence of their motions and designs. This last is a matter of very interesting moment, and ought to claim your particular attention. You will endeavour to procure trusty and intelligent spies, who will advise you faithfully of whatever may be passing in the city, and you will without delay communicate to me every piece of material information you obtain.

" 2. As many officers at present are injured in their rank, and cannot possibly continue in the army exactly in their present situation, they apprehend it would be an impropriety in them to swear to continue in their present posts, as the rank of the juror is to be taken when the oath is administered.

" 3. Would not the oath debar an officer from the privilege of resigning, when circumstances might render it indispensably necessary that he should quit the army?

" 4. The taking of the oath, while the present establishment continues, most of the subscribers are of opinion, would lay them under a pointed restraint in endeavouring to procure a change, which the whole army have long, not only most ardently wished for, but conceived absolutely necessary for its preservation; a change, that would put them on an honorable and advantageous footing. "

At the request of the officers, these reasons were presented by the Marquis de Lafayette to the Commander-in-chief. It is presumed, that their scruples were satisfied by the above letter, and that they took the oath, since the objections were peculiar to themselves, and not advanced by any other part of the army.

A variety of concurring accounts make it probable, that the enemy are preparing to evacuate Philadelphia. This is a point, which it is of the utmost importance to ascertain; and, if possible, the place of their future destination. Should you be able to gain certain intelligence of the time of their intended embarkation, so that you may be able to take advantage of it, and fall upon the rear of the enemy in the act of withdrawing, it will be a very desirable event. But this will be a matter of no small difficulty, and will require the greatest caution and prudence in the execution. Any deception or precipitation may be attended with the most disastrous consequences.

You will remember, that your detachment is a very valuable one, and that any accident happening to it would be a very severe blow to this army. You will therefore use every possible precaution for its security, and to guard against a surprise. No attempt should be made, nor any thing risked, without the greatest prospect of success, and with every reasonable advantage on your side. I shall not point out any precise position to you; but shall leave it to your discretion to take such posts occasionally, as shall appear to you best adapted to the purposes of your detachment. In general, I would observe, that a stationary post is unadvisable, as it gives the enemy an opportunity of knowing your situation, and concerting plans successfully against you. In case of any offensive movement against this army, you will keep yourself in such a state as to have an easy communication with it, and at the same time harass the enemy's advance.

Our parties of horse and foot between the rivers are to be under your command, and to form part of

Vol. v. 47 your detachment. As great complaints have been made of the disorderly conduct of the parties, which have been sent towards the enemy's lines, it is expected that you will be very attentive in preventing abuses of the like nature, and will inquire how far complaints already made are founded in justice.

Given under my hand, at Head-Quarters, this 18th day of May, 1778.

TO GOUVERNEUR MORRIS, IN CONGRESS.

Valley Forge, 18 May, 177&

My Dear Sir, Your favor of the 15th instant gave me singular pleasure. I thank you for the agreeable intelligence it contains, which, though not equal to my wishes, exceeded my expectations; and is to be lamented only for the delay. The evils in consequence of this will soon, as I have often foretold, be manifested in the moving state of the army, if the departments of the quartermaster' and commissary will enable us to stir and keep pace with the enemy, who, from every account, are busy in preparing for their departure from Philadelphia; whether for the West Indies, a rendezvous at New York to prepare for their voyage, or for some other expedition, time only can discover. The sooner, however, the regimental regulations and other arrangements are set about, the sooner they will be finished; and for God's sake, my dear Morris, let me recommend it to you to urge the absolute necessity of this measure with all your might.

After long debates the question of half-pay was finally settled by a kind of compromise. It was decided, that all military officers, commissioned by Congress, who should continue in the service during the war, and not hold any office of profit in the States, should be entitled to receive annually after the conclusion of the war one half of their present pay, for the term of *seven years,* provided that no general officer of the artillery, cavalry, or infantry should receive more than the half-pay of a colonel, and that this gratuity should extend to no officer, who should not take an oath of allegiance to the United States, and actually reside within the same. The non-commissioned officers, instead of half-pay, were entitled to receive a specific reward of eighty dollars at the end of the war. To the resolution in this form there were but two dissenting Toices, Mr. Lovell of Massachusetts, and Mr. Wolcott of Connecticut. — *Journals, May 15th.* In the plan first reported by the committee to Congress, the half-pay was to continue for life, and to extend to the widows of officers, who should be slain. It was also to be transferable under the control of Congress, and the officers were to be again called into service when necessary.

As the council held at this camp was by order of Congress, and the members constituting it were pointed out by them, it was determined, out of respect to that body, to treat the new members with civility. Indeed, the wish of all here, that no private differences should interrupt that harmony, which is so necessary in public councils, had no small share in the amity that appeared. Contrary, I own, to my expectation, the same sentiments, respecting the measures to be pursued, pervaded the whole. Our resolutions of consequence were unanimous.

I was not a little surprised to find a certain gentleman, who, some time ago, when a cloud of darkness hung heavy over us, and our affairs looked gloomy, was desirous of resigning, to be now stepping forward in the line of the army. But if he can reconcile such conduct to his own feelings, as an officer and a man of honor, and Congress have no objection to his leaving his seat in another department, I have nothing personally to oppose to it. Yet I must think, that gentleman's stepping in and out, as the sun happens to beam forth or become obscure, is not *quite* the thing, nor *quite* just, with respect to those officers, who take the bitter with the sweet.

General Mifflin had resigned his commissions of major-general and quartermaster-general, on the 8th of October. His resignation of the latter office was accepted by Congress, when he was appointed to the Board of War; but the rank and commission of major-general were continuod to him, with the proviso, that no pay should be annexed to that office, till a further order of Congress. It seems his views were afterwards changed, and, on the 21st of May, Congress gave him leave to join the army under General Washington.

I am told that Conway, from whom I have received another impertinent letter, dated the 23d ultimo, *demanding* the command of a division of the Continental army, is, through the medium of his friends, soliciting his commission again. Can this be? And, if so, will it be granted?

I am, very sincerely and affectionately, &c.

Conway had sent a petulant letter to Congress, complaining of 01 treatment, and asking an acceptance of his resignation; and then be was vexed and mortified, that ho should be taken at his word. After the Canada expedition had been abandoned, he was ordered to join the army under General MDougall at Fishkill. He was again ordered back to Albany, whereupon he wrote the above-mentioned letter to the President of Congress, from which the following is an extract character istic of its author.

" If an attack is made in that quarter," said he, " the inhabitants will look up to me for assistance. I shall not have it in my power to make any opposition, and, though undeservedly, my character must suffer. Therefore, Sir, I expect you will make my resignation acceptable to Congress. I am determined not to expose myself to dishonor, to gratify the envy and malice of my enemies, whoever they may be. I have been boxed about in a most indecent manner. I declined no occasion of serving. I trust I am as able in leading a division as any officer of my rank in the American army. What is the meaning of removing mt from the scene of action on the opening of a campaign? I did not deserve this burlesque disgrace, and my honor will not permit me to bear it. If my services arc not thought necessary, why do yon not mention it to me fairly? It is not becoming to the dignity of Congress to give such usage to an officer of my age and rank." — *MS. Letter, FishkOl, JlpHL sOd.*

This tone of anger and insult was more than the beat friends of the writer could withstand or excuse. Apologies were attempted by some of the members, yet no opposition was made to accepting his resignation. But it appeared, that his design was misapprehended, although expressed in the strongest language. In reply to a letter from the President of Congress, communicating the resolution by which his resignation was accepted, he endeavoured to explain his meaning, and added; " I am willing to apologize for the orthographical and grammatical faults; I am an Irishman, and learnt my English in France, but I do not conceive that any of these letters could be construed into a request to resign. I had no thoughts of resigning, while there was a prospect of firing a single shot, and especially at the beginning of this campaign, which in my opinion will be a very hot one." — *Albany, May 18th.* TO THE PRESIDENT OF CONGRESS.

Valley Forge, 18 May, 1778.

Sir,

I shall announce the resolution of the 15th to the army, and would flatter myself it will quiet in a great measure the uneasinesses, which have been so extremely distressing, and prevent resignations, which had proceeded, and were likely to be at such a height, as to destroy our whole military system. It has experienced no inconsiderable shock, particularly in the line of some States, from the loss of several very valuable officers.

The letter and brevet for Colonel Allen I will transmit by the first opportunity. He left camp eight days ago. From a variety of concurring circumstances, and the uniform report of persons, who have left Philadelphia within four days past, it would appear that the enemy mean to evacuate the city. It is said they have already embarked a part of their heavy cannon and baggage, and that transports are fitted and fitting for their horse, and taking in hay. The accounts further add, that there has been a press for some nights in the city, and several men obtained in this way, and carried aboard ship; also that there had been an increased number of vendues. These circumstances all indicate an evacuation; but I have not been able to learn the objects of their future operations. I wrote to General Gates yesterday upon the subject, that he may be prepared in the best manner the situation of things will admit, in case they should be destined for the North River, and I'desired him to retain for the present all the eastern recruits intended for this army.

This letter produced no favorable impression in Congress. The author himself soon followed, and on the 7th of June wrote from Yorktown to bis friend Gates, who was then at Fishkill; — "I had never a sufficient dea of cabals until I reached this place. My reception, you may imagine, was not a warm one. I must except Mr. Samuel Adams, Colonel Richard Henry Lee, and a few others, who are attached to you, and who cannot oppose the torrent. Before my arrival, General Mifflin had joined General Washington's army, where he commands a division. One Mr. Carroll from Maryland, upon whose friendship I depended, is one of the hottest of the cabal. He told me a few days ago, almost literally, that any body, who displeased or did not admire the Commanderin-chief, ought not to be kept in the army." — See Sparrs' *Lift of Gouverneur Morris,* Vol. I. p. 109.

VOL. V. F F

The quartermaster-general and commissary of provisions are directed to use every possible exertion for putting the affairs of their departments in a train to facilitate a movement, in case it should be necessary. But such have been the derangements and disorders in them, that we must be greatly embarrassed for a considerable time yet.

A valuable detachment, under the command of the Marquis de Lafayette, marched this morning, which is intended to move between the Delaware and the Schuylkill, for restraining the enemy's parties and procuring intelligence, and to act as circumstances may require.

I cannot help feeling for the prisoners in possession of the enemy. If they evacuate Philadelphia, those unhappy men will be dragged away with them, and perhaps to a more miserable confinement. But, supposing their future treatment should not be worse, or even that it should be more comfortable than their past, the idea of being removed farther from their friends, and farther from relief, must distress them to the last degree. I have the honor to be, &c.

TO JEREMIAH POWELL, PRESIDENT OF THE COUNCIL OF MASSACHUSETTS.

Valley Forge, 19 May, 1778.

Sir,

Two days ago I had the honor to receive your favor of the 25th ultimo, with the resolutions alluded to. I sincerely wish that the drafts, determined to be furnished by the several States, were with the army. It has ever been our misfortune not to be in a condition to avail ourselves of circumstances, which otherwise might have been most favorable. However, I trust in the end all will be well. There is yet a call for our most strenuous and prudent exertions.

I am happy to see the precautions, which the Court have taken to prevent the enlisting of deserters, or prisoners of war. No practice has been more impolitic or injurious, in proportion to the extent. But few of the former have proved faithful; and I believe there is not a single instance, where the latter have not deserted, when they had an opportunity. The enlisting of prisoners, or soldiers in the circumstances of those of General Burgoyne's army, is far less justifiable, than enlisting deserters, inasmuch as they are not under the smallest anxiety or fear of any consequences, that would attend their return; but, on the contrary, they have every reason to conclude, that their desertion will be considered as a meritorious act, worthy of applause, and a strong manifestation of their attachment to the service of their prince. Measures more effectual, though far less expensive, could not be easily adopted by us, to reinforce the enemy with the whole of the army, included in the Convention of Saratoga, than permitting the troops to enlist among us. Of a detachment of sixty in this predicament, which marched to join Colonel Henley's regiment, only twelve or thirteen reached camp. Part of the remainder made their escape, and the residue formed a plan for the same purpose, mutinied, and are now in prison. I am determined, where any are recruited, to call the officers to an account, and to make them answer for the consequences resulting from their desertion, so far as possible.

The General Court, or Assembly, of Massachusetts.

From a variety of concurring circumstances, it would appear, that the enemy mean to evacuate Philadelphia, and are preparing to embark. I cannot learn with certainty the cause. However, it is prob-

able, if the event happen, that it will be in consequence of the changes which have taken place, and which are likely to take place, in Europe. The objects of their future operations are also unknown; but, from the intelligence received, New York is supposed to be the place of their first destination. It is said, that houses are preparing there for their reception, and particularly for many families of Philadelphia, who have been their fast adherents. Indeed, if there is a war between France and Britain, which seems to be inevitable, Philadelphia is an ineligible situation for the army under Sir William Howe, or perhaps Sir Henry Clinton. Before I conclude, I beg leave to return you my warmest thanks for your kind wishes, and to request that you will present my best respects to the Honorable Council.

I have the honor to be, &c TO THE PRESIDENT OF CONGRESS.

Head-Quarters, Valley Forge, 24 May, 1778.

Sir,

I have transmitted to General Howe a copy of the resolution respecting prisoners; and, supposing him willing to effect an exchange immediately, I have written to Mr. Boudinot and requested him, as he is in possession of all the papers concerning them, to come to camp without delay, and superintend the business on our part. The provost establishment is a necessary one, and the corps shall be formed, as soon as proper officers can be fixed on.

On the night of the, 19th the enemy moved out in force against the detachment under the Marquis de Lafayette, mentioned in my letter of the 18th, which made a timely and handsome retreat in great order over the Schuylkill at Matson's Ford. Our loss was nine men in the whole. The enemy's loss is supposed to be something more. Their march was circuitous and rapid, and I should imagine many of their men suffered from it. General Clinton, it is said, commanded in person.

The accounts from Philadelphia are still in favor of an evacuation. It is certain that a great deal of baggage is on shipboard, and that they still seem busy

in packing up. There are other reports which say, that it is only a detachment which is going, and that the West Indies are conjectured to be the place of their destination.

I beg leave to lay before Congress a memorial and remonstrance of the field-officers of North Carolina, founded on the suspension and dismission of Captain See Appendix, No. XVL

Vol. v. 48 *r T*

John Vance of the artillery, through the means of the House of Commons of that State. It is with reluctance, that I interfere with the decisions of any civil or legislative body; however, I cannot help thinking, that the proceedings respecting Captain Vance are of an extraordinary nature, and such as involve consequences, which may deeply affect and interest the rights of every officer, or at least all under the rank of brigadiers. I should suppose no individual State can or ought to deprive an officer of rank, derived from the States at large; and that it will not be improper for Congress to prohibit the exercise of such a power. I do not know what the merits or demerits of Captain Vance are, (the memorial speaks very favorably of him,) nor do I apprehend they can make a part of the question. The principle and practice are what I cannot reconcile to my ideas of propriety. Congress, I am persuaded, will give the memorial that attention, which the objects of it seem to deserve, and I have only to refer them to the Journals of the House, which contain the whole of the proceedings against Captain Vance, that have come to my knowledge.

I have the honor to be, &.c.
TO GENERAL HENRY LEE, VIRGINIA.
Valley Forge, 25 May, 1778

Dear Sir, If any thing of greater moment had occurred, than declaring that every word contained in the pamphlet, which you were obliging enough to send me, was spurious, I should not have suffered your favor of the 6th instant to remain so long unacknowledged. These letters are written with a great deal of art. The inter mixture of so many family circumstances (which, by the by, want foundation in truth) gives an air of plausibility, which renders the villany greater; as the whole is a contrivance to answer the most diabolical purposes. Who the author of them is, I know not. From information, or acquaintance, he must have had some knowledge of the component parts of my family; but he has most egregiously mistaken facts in several instances. The design of his labors is as clear as the sun in its meridian brightness.

The favorable issue of our negotiation with France is matter for heartfelt joy, big with important events, and it must, I should think, chalk out a plain and easy road to independence. From this I hope we shall not depart, from a mistaken opinion, that the great work is already finished; nor, to finish it, adopt measures of precipitation. Great Britain, since the declaration of the King of France through the Marquis de Noailles, has no choice but war. Under their present circumstances, how they will conduct it, is a matter not so easily understood, as all their ways have been ways of darkness. That they will be under a necessity of giving up the continent, or their islands, seems obvious to me, if the accounts we have received of the French force in the West Indies be true. Halifax and Canada will, I presume, be strengthened; and, if they can afford a garrison sufficient, they may attempt to hold New York, unless every idea of subjugating America is given up, in which case their whole resentment will be levelled at France.

I am not aware, that the author of these spurious letters was ever ascertained. The first in the series was printed in Rivington's *Royal Gazette,* on the 14th of February, 1778. Whether the pamphlet had been previously printed I am not able to determine. The following title was prefixed. " Letters from General Washington to several of his Friends, in the Year 1776; in which are set forth a fairer and fuller View of American Politics, than ever yet transpired, or the Public could be made acquainted with through any other Channel." The preface vouches for their genuineness, and states that they were copied from the first drafts, found in the possession of

General Washington's servant Billy, who had been left behind unwell at the evacuation of Fort Lee. They purport to have been written in New York, in the months of June and July, 1776, and are addressed to Mr. Lund Washington, Mr. Custis, and Mrs. Washington. The object of the fabricator was to disparage General Washington, and create distrust in the minds of his countrymen, by showing from his private sentiments unguardedly expressed to his friends, that he was acting a hypocritical part, being in reality opposed to the war. The disguise was too flimsy to conceal so nefarious a purpose, although pains were taken by the enemy to circulate the letters in newspapers and pamphlets.

The enemy are making every preparation, and seem to be upon the point of leaving Philadelphia. In my own judgment, and from many corresponding circumstances, I am convinced they are bound to New York; whether by land or water, whether as a place of rendezvous, or to operate on the North River, is not so clear. Our situation here, on account of the sick and stores, is embarrassing, as I dare not detach largely to harass the enemy, in case of a land movement through the Jerseys, before they have actually crossed the Delaware; and then it will be too late, as their distance to South Amboy will be much less than ours, and nothing to obstruct them. To this may be added the advantage of a day's march, which they must gain of us. Were it not for the number of our sick (upwards of three thousand in camp), and the securing of our stores, which are covered by our present position and strength, I could take such a post in Jersey, as would make their passage through that State very difficult and dangerous to them. But the impracticability of doing this, without exposing this camp to insult and injury is well known to them; and some part of their conduct justifies a report, that, at all events, they will aim a blow at this army before they go off.

I observe what you say respecting the recruits, or rather drafts, from Virginia. I was never called upon by the State for officers, or directed by Congress to send

any to aid in the business; but, thinking such a measure might be necessary, I ordered the officers of the disbanded regiments, and such as had gone to Virginia on furlough, to call upon and receive the governor's orders, with respect to the marching of them to camp. That something has been wrong in conducting the drafts, and assembling the men, admits of no doubt; for, out of the fifteen hundred ordered last fall, and the two thousand this spring, we have received only twelve hundred and forty-two, which is such a deficiency, that I have made a representation thereof to the State. I am, &c.

TO MAJOR-GENERAL GATES.

Valley Forge, 25 May, 1778.

Sir, I was yesterday favored with yours of the 21st instant. The enemy have been constantly busy since my last in embarking their cannon and stores. I do not yet find, that any troops have gone on board. They give out, that they mean to attack this army before they go off, but I rather think, if they move at all by land, it will be across Jersey. In this uncertainty, I cannot alter my position, until they change theirs. I hold the army ready to move at the shortest notice towards the North River, should circumstances require it. In the mean time, I would have you make yourself as respectable as possible, by stopping all the recruits, and calling in as many militia as you can feed. I cannot account for the evacuation of Kingsbridge and Fort Washington, if they mean to keep the city, especially the latter, which is the key to the Island.

I would have you by all means exchange the British convalescents, and direct our deputy-commissary of prisoners to receive those in return for them, who have been longest in captivity. You will undoubtedly take the proper precautions when the prisoners pass our posts upon the river. You may depend upon having constant intelligence of the motions of the enemy in this quarter from me, and I shall depend upon the same from you. I am, &c.

TO BRIGADIER-GENERAL MCINTOSH.

Camp, Valley Forge, 36 May, 177&

Sir,

The Congress having been pleased to direct me to appoint an officer to command at Fort Pitt, and on the western frontiers, in the room of Brigadier-General Hand, I am induced, but not without reluctance, from the sense I entertain of your merit, to nominate you, as an officer well qualified from a variety of considerations to answer the objects they have in view. I do not know particularly what the objects are, which Congress have in contemplation in this command; and I therefore request that you will, as soon as you conveniently can, repair to Yorktown and receive their instructions respecting them. I have only to add, that I shall be happy to hear from you as often as opportunity will permit, and my warmest wishes, that your services may be honorable to yourself and approved by your country. I am, Sir, with great esteem and regard, your most obedient servant.

TO THE PRESIDENT OF CONGRESS.

Valley Forge, 29 May, 1778.

Dear Sir,

Your polite favor of the 5th instant, I duly received, and thank you much for the information contained in it. At the same time, I earnestly request that you will indulge me with an excuse for not answering it before. A constant crowd of business, and the intervention of a variety of circumstances, have been the cause, and not an inattention to the rules of civility or to those of friendship.

Your letter gave me the first intimation of the disagreement between our commissioners. The event is disagreeable and painful; and, unless they can bring themselves to harmonize, their proceedings will not probably consult the public interest, so well as they otherwise might. It is certain, they will not have that degree of respect, either at home or abroad. Their embassy is a most interesting one, and may involve consequences which will lead, in no small degree, to the happiness or misery of their country. I hope reflection and a due consideration will set them right.

The act of the 22d of April will certainly require the commissioners,! if they come at all, to be vested with much more ample powers than Lord North's

bills professed, or their mission will be ridiculously mortifying. Indeed men, who would come out under the powers expressed in the bills, after all that has passed, deserve to be mortified in the extreme. I am happy the report and consequent resolution were previous to the treaty and alliance with France being known. The Parliament have been so much parties to this war, and to all the proceedings respecting it, that it would seem the Crown itself has no authority, either to continue or to end it, or to do any thing else, without their express concurrence.

The history of the doings of the American commissioners in Paris, and of their disagreements, may be found in the first volume of the *Diplomatic Correspondence of the American Revolution.* t The British commissioners expected from England.

I sincerely wish the military arrangement to be completed. The delay is attended with great inconvenience and injury. While it remains open, our whole system cannot but be imperfect. I know that Congress have a variety of important matters to call their attenion; but, I assure you, there are few if any that are more interesting than this. The question of half-pay being decided, I shall not trouble you with a further discussion of the subject. It must be granted, however, that, in the situation of our affairs, the measure or something substantially the same had become necessary. Nor can I, after balancing in my mind and giving the subject the fairest consideration I am capable of, esteem it unjust. I assure you, Sir, however we may have differed in sentiment on this point, I am fully convinced that the rtrictest candor forms a part of your character, and request you to believe, that I am, with great attachment and esteem, &.c President Laurens was strongly opposed to the scheme of half-pay for life. In this respect he was somewhat singular, as nearly all the southern delegates were its advocates. His reasons were contained is the letter, to which the above was an answer.

" I view the scheme," says he, " as altogether unjust and unconstitutional in

its nature, and full of dangerous consequences. It is an unhappy dilemma to which we seem to be reduced; provide for your officers in terras dictated to you, or lose all the valuable soldiers among them; establish a pension for officers, make them a separate body to be provided for by the honest yeomanry and others of their fellow-citixena, many thousands of whom have equal claims, upon every ground of loss of estate and health, or lose your army and your cause. That such provision will be against the grain of the people has been unwarily testified by its advocates, whom I have heard converse upon the subject.

P. S. I most sincerely wish, that Congress would lay the charge, and order the trial of the major-generals in disgrace. St. Clair is exceedingly uneasy and distressed at the delay; and with pain I add, that the proceeding, or more properly not proceeding, in this matter, is looked upon as cruel and oppressive.

TO MAJOR-GENERAL GATES.

Valley Forge, 29 May, 1778.

Sir,

If the States will not or cannot send their quota of troops into the field, it is no fault of mine. I have been urgent in my requisitions on that head; and whatever consequences may arise from the deficiency, they will not, I trust, be chargeable on me. I cannot detach

Indeed they have furnished strong ground for opposition against an immediate compliance with the demand. If we cannot make justice one of the pillars, necessity may be submitted to at present; but republicans will at a proper time withdraw a grant, which shall appear to have been extorted. Were I in private conversation with an officer on this point, I should not despair of fairly balancing every grievance he might suppose to be peculiar to the army, by instances of losses and inconveniences in my own property and person; and I count myself very happy compared with thousands, who have as faithfully adhered to our original compact.

" Would to God, gentlemen had followed the noble, patriotic example of their Commander-in-chief. How superior are many of the gentlemen now in my contemplation (for I know many with whom I do not converse) to the acceptance of half-pay, contributed to by widows and orphans of soldiers, who had bled and died by their sides, shackled with a condition of being excluded from the privilege of serving in offices in common with their fellow-citizens, bated in every House of Assembly as the drones and incumbrances of society, pointed at by boys and girls, —' There goes a man, who robs me every year of part of my pittance.' I think, Sir, I do not overstrain. This will be the language of republicans. How pungent, when applied to gentlemen, who shall have stepped from the army into a good remaining estate! How much deeper to some, who, in idleness and by peculation, have amassed estates in the war! I am most heartily disposed to distinguish the gallant officer and VOL. V. 49 G G the reinforcement you request. The enemy are yet in possession of Philadelphia in full force, and we hav« near four thousand men in this camp sick of the smallpox and other disorders. I have sent the whole of the Jersey troops to that State, to harass the enemy in their march, in case they proceed to New York by land; and General Maxwell, who commands them, is ordered, as soon as they shall have passed through, or the moment he is informed that they are embarked, to repair with all possible expedition to Newburg, and take your directions. The whole of the army, besides, is under marching orders, and, as soon as Philadelphia is evacuated, will move as fast as circumstances will admit towards the North River. I have writte» to Colonel Sheldon, and directed him to proceed immediately with his regiment to Fishkill.

I am, Sir, your most obedient servant TO OOVERWOR CLINTON.

Valley Forge, 29 May, 1778.

Dear Sir,

Some days ago I received your favor of the 8th instant, and am much obliged by the measures you hare taken to recover the box. I am happy to find, by a letter from General Schuyler, that the Indian nations, which had discovered an unfriendly disposition, seem to be well affected, and to afford grounds to hope for a friendly alliance between us. If this can be effected, or if we can only keep them from falling upon our frontiers, it would be a fortunate circumstance; as we may not only then employ nearly the whole of the Continental force, wherever Sir Henry Clinton's movements require it, but also derive greater aid from the militia in cases of exigency. Our treaty and alliance with France, when well understood by them, I am persuaded will have a favorable influence on their conduct. That the enemy mean to evacuate Philadelphia is almost reduced to a certainty. It is as much so, as an event can be, that is contingent. Their baggage and stores are nearly if not all embarked; and, from our intelligence, there is reason to conclude, that many days will not elapse before they abandon it. All accounts concur, that New York will be the place of their first destination. Whether they will move by sea Or land cannot be ascertained; but the weight of circumstances is in favor of the latter. *I* have sent a brigade to Jersey, which, with the militia I expect will collect under General Dickinson, I hope will give them some small annoyance; more cannot be done. If the States had furnished their quota of men, or any thing like it, and the great departments of quartermaster and commissary had not been in a state of almost inextricable confusion, a more favorable opportunity could not have presented itself for giving the troops in Philadelphia a decisive stroke. After the enemy have passed through Jersey, if that should be their route, or embarked, the brigade, which is there, is ordered to proceed with all possible expedition to Newburg; and the main body if not the whole of this army will move immediately after the same way. This I mention for *your oxen* information. I thank you much for your exertions to complete your battalions. Colonel Malcom's regiment will proceed with the rest of the army, and will then have an opportunity of recruiting.

soldier by the most liberal marks of esteem, and desirous of proper provision for all, who shall stand in need. I would not except even some of the brave, whose expenses have been princely in extravagance, while they complained of insufficiency of pay"

The opinions and arguments of President Laurens, in opposition to the scheme of half-pay, are expressed much more at large in a letter, from him to Governor Livingston, who declared himself a disciple of the same school. " In my private judgment," said the Governor, " I should be totally against the plan of allowing the officer half-pay after the war; it is a very pernicious precedent in republican States; will load us with an immense debt, and render the pensioners themselves) ia a great measure useless to their country."—Sedgwick's.Lf/c e/ *V'Uliam Livingston,* pp. 272, 281 In the battle of Princeton a small box was taken from the enemy, which was supposed to contain hard money. It was put into an ammunition cart, and disappeared. Suspicions had recently rested upon a subordinate officer in the army, who was at this time in the State of New York. Governor Clinton's aid in detecting the theft, and recovering the box, had been solicited.

I am, dear Sir, &c TO LANDON CARTER.

Valley Forge, 30 Mty, 177a

My Dear Sir,

I thank you much for your kind and affectionate remembrance and mention of me, and for that solicitude for my welfare, which breathes through the whole of your letters. Were I not warm in my acknowledgments for your distinguished regard, I should feel that sense of ingratitude, which I hope will never constitute a part of my character, nor find a place in my bosom. My friends therefore may believe me sincere in my professions of attachment to them, whilst Providence has a just claim to my humble and grateful thanks, for its protection and direction of me, through the many difficult and intricate scenes, which this contest has produced; and for its constant interposition in our behalf, when the clouds were heaviest and seemed ready to burst upon us.

To paint the distresses and perilous

situation of this army in the course of last winter, for want of clothes, provisions, and almost every other necessary, essential to the well-being, I may say existence, of an army, would require more time and an abler pen than mine; nor, since our prospects have so miraculously brightened, shall I attempt it, or even bear it in remembrance, further than as a memento of what is due to the great Author of all the care and good, that have been extended in relieving us in difficulties and distress.

The accounts which you had received of the accession of Canada to the Union were premature. If is a measure much to be wished, and I believe would not be displeasing to the body of the people; but, while Carleton remains among them, with three or four thousand regular troops, they dare not avow their sentiments, if they really are favorable, without a strong support. Your ideas of its importance to our political union coincide exactly with mine. If that country is not with us, from its proximity to the eastern States, its intercourse and connexion with the numerous tribes of western Indians, its communion with them by water and other local advantages, it will be at least a troublesome if not a dangerous neighbour to us; and ought, at all events, to be in the same interest and politics, as the other States.

If all the counties in Virginia had followed the example of yours, it would have been a fortunate circumstance for this army; but instead of fifteen hundred men, under the first draft, and two thousand from the second, we have by an accurate return made to me four days ago received only twelve hundred and fortytwo in the whole. Hence, unless you conceive our country possessed of less virtue, or less knowledge in the principles of government than other States, you may account for the multitude of men, which undoubtedly you have heard our army consisted of, and consequently for many things, which, without such a key, would seem mysterious.

That is, Virginia, it having been customary before the revolution for people to speak of the colony in which they were born, as their cotcruVy. GO

With great truth I think I can assure you, that the information you received from a gentleman at Sabine Hall, respecting the disposition in the northern officers to see me superseded in my command by General Gates is without the least foundation. I have very sufficient reasons to think, that no officers in the army are more attached to me, than those from the northward, and of those, none more so than the gentlemen, who were under the immediate command of Gates last campaign. That there was a scheme of this sort, in fact, last fall, admits of no doubt; but it originated in another quarter; with three men, who wanted to aggrandize themselves. Finding no support, but, on the contrary, that their conduct and views, when seen into, were likely to undergo severe reprehension, they slunk back, disavowed the measure, and professed themselves my warmest admirers. Thus stands the matter at present Whether any members of Congress were privy to tbJ6 scheme, and inclined to aid and abet it, I shall not take upon me to say; but I am well informed, that no whisper of the kind was ever heard in Congress.

The drafts of bills as mentioned by you, and which have since passed into accounts of British legislation, are so strongly marked with folly and villany, that one can scarcely tell which predominates, or how to be surprised at any act of a British minister. This last trite performance of Master North's is neither more nor less than an insult to common sense, and shows to what extremity of folly wicked men in a bad cause are sometimes driven; for this " rude Boreas," who

" Conway, Gates, and Mifflin.

was to bring America to his feet, knew at the time of drafting these bills, or had good reason to believe, that a treaty had actually been signed between the court of France and the United States. By what rule of common sense, then, he could expect that such an undisguised artifice would go down in America I cannot conceive. But, thanks to Heaven, the tables are turned; and we, I hope, shall have our independence secured, in

its fullest extent, without cringing to this Son of Thunder, who I am persuaded will find abundant work for his troops elsewhere; on which happy prospect I sincerely congratulate you and every friend to American liberty.

I am sorry it is not in my power to furnish you with the letter required, which, with many others, was written to show, that I was an enemy to independence, and with a view to create distrust and jealousy. I never had but one of them, and that I sent to Mrs. Washington, to let her see what obliging folks there are in the world. As a sample of it, I enclose to you another letter, written for me to Mr. Custis, of the same tenor, which I happen to have by me. It is no easy matter to decide, whether the villany or artifice of these letters is greatest. They were written by a person, who had some knowledge or information of the component parts of my family, and yet they are so deficient in circumstances and facts, as to run into egregious misrepresentations of both.

I have spun out a long letter, and send it to you in a very slovenly manner; but, not having time to give it with more fairness, and flattering myself into a belief, that you had rather receive it in this dress than not at all. I shall make no other apology for the interlineations and scratches you will find in it, than you will please to allow to my hurried situation. I am, dear Sir, &lc. TO MAJOR-GENERAL LEE.

Head-Quarters, 30 May, 1778.

Sir,

Poor's, Vanium's, and Huntington's brigades are to march in one division under your command to the North River. The quartermaster-general will give you the route, encampment, and halting-days, to which you will conform as strictly as possible, to prevent interfering with other troops, and that I may know precisely your situation every day. Leave as few sick and lame on the road as possible. Such as are absolutely incapable of marching with you are to be committed to the care of proper officers, with directions to follow as fast as their condition will allow.

Be strict in your discipline, suffer no

rambling, keep the men in their ranks and the officers with their divisions, avoid pressing horses as much as possible, and punish severely every officer or soldier, who shall presume to press without proper authority. Prohibit the burning of fences. In a word, you are to protect the persons and property of the inhabitants from every kind of insult and abuse.

Begin your march at four o'clock in the morning at the latest, that it may be over before the heat of the day, and that the soldiers may have time to cook, refresh, and prepare for the ensuing day. I am, &c.

P. S. *June 18th.* — The foregoing instructions may serve you for general directions, but circumstances have varied since they were written. You are to halt on the first strong ground after passing the Delaware at Coryell's Ferry, till further orders, unless you should receive authentic intelligence, that the enemy have proceeded by a direct route to South Amboy, or still lower. In this case you will continue your march to the North River, agreeably to former orders, and by the route already given you. If my memory does not deceive me, there is an advantageous spot of ground at the ferry to the right of the road leading from the water.

TO THE PRESIDENT OF CONGRESS.

Head-Quarters, Valley Forge, 31 May, 1778.

Sir, ' I shall inform Major Lee of the new arrangement of his corps, and will appoint the officers required. Major Beatty is not in camp. The letter addressed to him shall be forwarded by the first opportunity to Princeton, where I presume he will be found, f That for Captain Smith is already despatched to him. J

The enemy are yet in Philadelphia, though the whole chain of information for several days past afforded grounds to believe, that they would have evacuated it before now. I should suppose they are nearly prepared to do it, though the removal of the stores and baggage of so large an army requires considerable time.

June 1st. — I should be glad to know, in case Philadelphia is evacuated, whether any and what line of conduct is to be pursued respecting the goods that may be left. Such articles, as come under the denomination of public stores, will of course be taken by the proper officers for the use of the States. The point on which I wish direction is, with respect to goods and merchandise, private property. I do not know whether any considerable quantity may be left; but it has been suggested, that, from an expectation of the sort, there are some bringing into light their gold and silver for the purpose of buying up. If there should be clothing suitable for the army, perhaps there might be.nothing unjust in the public taking the preference, and Congress appointing one or two intelligent, active persons of address, acquainted with the city and with those who have the goods, with proper powers to purchase them. Major Lee's partisan corps of light dragoons was enlarged to three companies instead of two, and the appointment of the additional officers was referred to General Washington. t Major John Beatty was elected commissary-general of prisoners, in the place of Elias Boudinot, who had resigned, having been appointed a delegate in Congress from New Jersey. t Captain Robert Smith was chosen secretary to the Board of War, in the place of Colonel Wilkinson resigned. Captain Smith did not accept the appointment, and the office was filled by Joseph Nourse. VOL. V. 50

Whatever measure may be thought expedient, it will be necessary to adopt it as early as possible, as the evacuation will probably take. place in a short time. Mr. Robert Morris, I should imagine, if the purchasing scheme is determined on, will be able to point out proper persons. Some gentlemen have mentioned Messrs. Samuel Howell and Thomas Franklin as well qualified, both on account of their integrity and attachment to our cause, and from their knowledge of the city and residence in it ever since the enemy had the possession. I have the honor to be, &c.

TO SIR HENRY CLINTON.

Head-Quarters, 31 May, 1778.

Sir, I had the honor last night to receive your favor of the 30th instant. I am sorry that I cannot see the necessity of the interview you propose. If you, or Lord Howe, have any despatches for Congress, and think fit to transmit them to my care, they shall be forwarded by the earliest opportunity. If you have any for me of a military nature, for none other can come properly under my consideration, I wish them to be communicated in writing, and in the usual way. This will prevent any trouble on the part of Colonel Paterson, and must answer, I should suppose, all the purposes you may have in view. I have the honor to be, Sir, &c.

TO MAJOR-GENERAL DICKINSON.

Head-Quarters, Valley Forge, 5 Jane, 1778.

Dear Sir,

Your favor of yesterday came safe to hand. What the real designs of the enemy are, remains yet to be discovered. Appearances and a thousand circumstances induce a belief, that they intend to pass through the Jerseys to New York. Your last intelligence however is a let to this opinion, inasmuch as it contradicts a former report of their assembling a number of boats in Prince's Bay. That they will either march to Amboy, and from thence pass to Staten Island, or embark below the chevaux-de-frise scarcely admits of a doubt; and the first being much the most probable, I would recommend it to you to be in the most perfect readiness for their reception, as you may rely upon it, that their march will be rapid whenever it is begun, t Sir Henry Clinton took command of the British army in Philadelphia, on the 11th of May, in the place of Sir William Howe, who shortly afterwards returned to England. — See Appendix, No. XVII. t The enemy had resolved to evacuate Philadelphia as early as the 23d of May, and perhaps before. On that day General Clinton wrote to Lord George Germain, that he had determined to leave Philadelphia and proceed to New York with the whole army, as soon as it could bo done. The first intention was to go by water, but twelve days aibtr the date of the letter mentioned above he wrote again as follows; — " I found it impracticable to embark the forces in order to proceed to New York by water, as there are not transports enough to receive the whole at once, and therefore a great part of the cavalry, all our provision train, and the persons whose attachment to the government has rendered them objects of vengeance to the enemy, must have been left behind. I am to add to this, that, if we should afterwards have been detained by contrary winds, General Washington might have seized the opportunity of making a decisive push at New York, all accounts from thence seeming to indicate an intent of that sort. These reasons have induced me to resolve on marching through Jersey."— *MS. LeUert, May 23d, June Slk.*

I take the liberty of giving it to you as my opinion, also, that the way to annoy, distress, and really injure the enemy on their march (after obstructing the roads as much as possible) with militia, is to suffer them to act in very light bodies. Were it not for the horse, I should think the parties could not be too small, as every man in this case acts as it were for himself, and would, I conceive, make sure of his man between Cooper's Ferry, and South Amboy, as the enemy's guards in front, flank, and rear, must be exposed, and may be greatly injured by the concealed and well directed fire of men in ambush. This kind of annoyance ought to be incessant day and night, and would I think be very effectual. I shall add no more, than that I am, with very sincere regard, dear Sir, &,c.

General Clinton likewise added, that a large part of the baggage and stores of the army, and valuable merchandise necessary for the troops, were already embarked on board transports; and, also, that the refugee were provided for in those vessels.

Orders for evacuating Philadelphia had been sent by the ministry, dated March 21st, immediately after the French government had publicly declared, that a treaty had been made with the United States. Gordon says *(History,* Vol. III. p. 130.), that the order for evacuation was brought out by the commissioners, and that it was a secret erea to

them. But the fact is, it was contained in the instructions to Sir Henry Clinton, as the successor of Sir William Howe, and was leceivad by him several days before the arrival of the commissioners.

TO SIR HENRY CLINTON.

Head-Quarters, 9 June, 1778.

Sir, At nine o'clock this evening, I had the honor to receive your Excellency's letter of this date. I do not conceive myself at liberty to grant the passport you request for Doctor Ferguson, without being previously instructed by Congress on the subject. I shall despatch a copy of your letter to them; and will take the earliest opportunity of communicating their determination. I have the honor to be, Sir, &c The King's ship of war, Trident, of sixty-four guns, having on board the commissioners for carrying into effect Lord North's bills, arrived in the Delaware River on the 4th of June. The commissioners were the Earl of Carlisle, George Johnstone, and William Eden. To these were joined Lord Howe and Sir William Howe, but they did not act, the former being chiefly with the fleet, and the latter having returned to England. General Clinton took the place of General Howe in the commission. Dr. Adam Ferguson, Professor of Moral Philosophy in the University of Edinburgh, was the secretary.

After the arrival of the commissioners in Philadelphia, General Clinton wrote to Washington requesting a passport for Dr. Ferguson to proceed to Congress with despatches. This request was declined, and the letter containing it was forwarded to Congress. Not waiting for the result, the commissioners forwarded their papers to Congress, which were received on the 13th of June, at the moment they were debating on a proper reply to General Clinton's request for a passport. Among other papers in the packet was an *Address* to the Congresa, which the President was desired to read immediately. He proceeded in reading it, till he came to a part containing strong expressions of disrespect to the King of France, when he was interrupted, and the House directed him to seal up the papers, and adjourned. The sub-

ject was again resumed, and on the 17th a reply was ordered to be returned to the commissioners, signed by the President, the substance of which was in accordance with the former proceedings in regard to Lord North's bills. No encouragement was held out, that a conciliation could possibly be effected on the proffered terms. After expressing a readiness to make peace whenever the King of Great Britain should manifest a sincero disposition for that purpose, the President of Congress added, —" The only solid proof of this disposition will be, an explicit acknowledgment of the Independence of these States, or the withdrawing of his fleets and armies." To neither VOL. V. H H TO JOHN AUGUSTINE WASHINGTON.

Camp, near Valley Forge, 10 June, 1778.

Dear Brother, We have been kept in anxious expectation of the enemy's evacuating Philadelphia for upwards of fourteen days; and I was at a loss, as they had embarked all their baggage and stores on board transports, and had passed all those transports, a few only excepted, below the chevaux-de-frise, to account for their delay; when, behold, on Friday last the additional commissioners, to wit, Lord Carlisle, Governor Johnstone, and Mr. William Eden, arrived at the city. Whether this has heretofore been the cause of the delay, I shall not undertake to say, but more than probably it will detain them for some days to come. They give out, as i ' — I understand, that we may make our own terms, provided we will return to our dependence on Great Britain. But if this be their expectation, and they have no other powers than the Acts give them, which we have seen, there will be no great trouble in managing a negotiation, nor will there be much time spent in the business, I apprehend. They talk as usual of a great reinforcement, but whether the situation of affairs between them and France will admit of this, is not quite so clear. My wishes lead me, together with other circumstances, to believe that they will find sufficient employment, for their reinforcements at least, in other quarters. Time, however, will discover and reveal things more fully to us.

of these conditions was it in the power of the commissioners to accede; and much less was it the intention of Parliament to grant either of them. There was no rational hope, therefore, of any success to the negotiation, or even of a formal beginning. — *MS. Letter from President Laurens to General Washington, June 14A.— Journals, VHh, Ylth.*

Adolphus, in his *History of England,* (Vol. III. 4th ed. p. 89,) says, " Application was made to General Washington for a passport for Dr. Ferguson, to convey overtures to Congress, but this favor was harshly refused, and the letters of the commissioners forwarded by common military posts." And then he speaks of the " wanton insolence of this proceeding." Such coarseness of language and illiberality of sentiment would seem unworthy of notice, if they were not from a respectable source. In truth the passport was not refused, but General Washington thought it not consistent with his duty to grant it, without the previous approbation of Congress. Before an answer could possibly be received, the commissioners sent out their despatches through the usual channel of a flag. The above letter to Sir Henry Clinton is a sufficient comment on the charge of insolence. It is needless to say, that this writer is astonished at the blindness and obstinacy of the Americans, in not acceding to the terms of the commissioners, which, in his opinion, " pra£fered more real freedom, than, under all circumstances, could be expected to flow from an acquiescence in their unsupported independence." Party prejudice and national antipathy are but indifferent qualifications for a historian.

Out of your first and second drafts, by which we ought to have had upwards of thirty-five hundred men for the regiments from your State, we have received only twelve hundred and forty-two in all. I need only mention this fact, in proof of what other States do; of our prospects also; and as a criterion by which you may form some estimate of our real numbers when you hear them, as I doubt not you often do, spoken of m

magnified terms. From report, however, I should do injustice to the States of Maryland and New Jersey, were I not to add, that they are likely to get their regiments nearly completed. The extreme fatigue and hardships, which the soldiers underwent in the course of the winter, added to the want of clothes and provisions, have rendered tham very sickly, especially in the brigade you have mentioned (of North Carolina). Many deaths have happened in consequence, and yet the army is in exceedingly good spirits.

You have doubtless seen a publication of the treaty with France, and the message of the King of France by his ambassador to the court of London, with the King's speech to Parliament and their addresses upon the occasion. If one were to judge of the temper of these courts from the above documents, war I should think must have commenced long before this time; and yet the commissioners say, that it had not taken place on the 28th of April, and that the differences between the two courts were likely to be accommodated. But I believe not a word of it.

I am sorry to hear of Billy Washington's ill health, but hope he is recovering. Mrs. Washington left this place the day before yesterday for Mount Vernon. My love to my sister and the family is most sincerely offered, and I am, with the truest regard and affection, yours, &c.

TO THE PRESIDENT OF CONGRESS. 11 June, 1778.

Dear Sir, I thank you for your favor of the 8th, which was duly received. I must take the freedom to hint to you, that if in the packets transmitted by this conveyance there are any letters for persons, with whom you are not acquainted, or in whose firmness and attachment you have not an entire confidence, it may not be improper to open them. This, I am persuaded, would be the case. However, I am the more induced to mention it, as the obvious, nay almost sole design of sevejal letters, which have come to my hands, is to give the commissioners the most favorable characters for candor and integrity, and to

establish a belief, that they have the most competent and extensive powers. The letters coming sealed was sufficient to awaken my suspicions, and I shall not transmit a single one of this complexion. I am convinced that you and I move on the same principle, and therefore I am certain that I hazard nothing in taking this liberty. I am, dear Sir, with great friendship and esteem, &c TO WILLIAM EDEN, COMMISSIONER FROM THE COURT OF GREAT BRITAIN TO AMERICA.

Head-Quarters, IS June, 1778.

Sir, On Wednesday evening I had the honor to receive your polite favor of the 9th instant. If an occasion shall present itself of an interview with Dr. Ferguson, you may rely, Sir, I shall esteem myself happy in showing him the civilities due to his literary and social character. I thank you much for your care of the letters addressed to myself. The one from your brother, Sir Robert, gave me particular satisfaction, as it not only excited a pleasing remembrance of our past intimacy and friendship, during his residence in this country, but also served to show, that they had not been impaired by an opposition of political sentiments. And you will permit me to add, that if the situation of national affairs would admit, I should be no less desirous of cultivating your acquaintance, than you would be of mine.

It will be observed that this letter, although addressed to tho President of Congress, was strictly of a private nature, and not intended to be communicated to the House. There are several of this kind, particularly during the presidency of Mr. Laurens, which will be readily discovered by their contents. The above letter was accompanied with the despatches from the commissioners, and many private letters from England to members of Congress and others. In his reply, President Laurens wrote; — " Yesterday there was an extraordinary motion on our floor for calling upon members to lay before Congress such letters as tbey had received from the commissioners and other persons, meaning persons in Great Britain, on political subjects. I could not forbear offering some objections; it appeared to be a dangerous attempt to stretch the power of Congress. My letters had been read by many members, and were at the service of every gentleman, who should request a perusal, but I could never consent to have my property taken from me by an order from my fellow-citizens destitute of authority for the purpose. This circumstance, and some remarks which followed, have induced me to put Governor Johnstone's letter and my intended answer into Mr. Drayton's hands, who is collecting materials for displaying the governor's good designs. " — f.S. *Letter, June 18th.* VOL. V. 51 HH»

With respect to the other letters, I shall transmit them to the persons to whom they are directed, as opportunities may offer. I have the honor to be, with great personal respect, Sir, &c.

TO GOVERNOR JOHNSTONE, COMMISSIONER FROM THE COURT OF GREAT BRITAIN TO AMERICA, t

Head-Quarters, 12 Jane, 1778.

Sir, I have had the honor to receive your very obliging letter qf the 10 th instant. The sentiments you are pleased to entertain of me cannot but be extremely flattering, separated as we are by the circumstances of our political stations, and they have a just claim to my warmest acknowledgments. If in the course of events an opportunity should be afforded me, you may be assured I shall take pleasure in showing Dr. Ferguson every civility it may be in my power to render.

Sir Robert Eden had been for several years governor of Maryland, f George Johnstone was a Scotchman by birth, and was in the first part of his life attached to the naval service, in which he rose to the rank of post-captain. In 1763 he was appointed Governor of West Florida, and he seems to have formed acquaintance in other parts of America. After his return to England he became a member of Parliament, and was commonly called Governor Johnstone.

I shall ever be happy to relieve the anxiety of parted friends; and where letters are calculated either to this end, or to effect matters of mere private concern, they will have the earliest conveyance. I have the honor to be, with much personal esteem and regard, &c.

TO MAJOR-GENERAL GATES.

Head-Quartern, Valley Forge, 12 June, 1778.

Sir,

I have your favor of the 8th instant, with its several enclosures. Whether the intention of the enemy is to make the present campaign offensive or defensive, time alone must discover; but if the former, I cannot think they mean to operate against the eastern States in any other manner, than by laying waste their coast and destroying their seaport towns. They will never venture into a country full of people, whom they have always found ready to give them the most spirited opposition. Should the North River be their object, I can, as I have mentioned in my former letters, march such a part of this army thither by the time they can reach it, that they will not be able to effect any thing by a *coup de main.*

The arrival of the commissioners from Great Britain, upon the 7th instant, seems to have suspended the total evacuation of Philadelphia. The transports, except a few store-ships and victuallers, have fallen down the river, and many of the troops are in Jersey, where they have thrown over a number of their horses and wagons. They seem to be waiting until the commissioners shall have announced themselves to Congress, and found whether a negotiation, under their present powers, can be brought about. They asked liberty, upon the 9th, to send their secretary, Dr. Ferguson, to Yorktown; but, not knowing whether this would be agreeable to Congress, I refused the request until I should know their sentiments. I am, &c.

General Gates had expressed an opinion, that during the ensuing campaign the enemy would operate up the North River and against the eastern States. TO MAJOR-GENERAL CHARLES LEE.

Head-Quarters, 15 June, 1778.

Dear Sir,

I have received your letter of this date, and thank you, as I shall any officer, over whom I have the honor to be placed, for his opinion and advice in matters of importance; especially when they proceed from the fountain of candor, and not from a captious spirit, or an itch for criticism.

No man can be more sensible of the defects of our present arrangement, than I am; no man more sensible of the advantage of having the commander and commanded of every corps well known to each other, and the army properly organized. Heaven and my own letters to Congress can witness, on the one hand, how ardently I have labored to effect these points during the past winter and spring; the army, on the other, bears witness to the effect. Suspended between the old and new establishments, I could govern myself by neither with propriety; and the hourly expectation of a committee, for the purposes of reducing some regiments and changing the establishment of all, rendered a mere temporary alteration unnecessary, which from its uncertainty and shortness could effect no valuable end. That I had a *power* to shift regiments and alter brigades every day, if I chose to do it, I never entertained a doubt; but the *efficacy* of the measure I have very much questioned, as frequent changes, without apparent causes, are rather ascribed to caprice and whim, than to stability and judgment.

The mode of shifting the major-generals from the command of a division, in the present tranquil state of affairs, to a more important one in action and other capital movements of the whole army, is not less disagreeable to my ideas, than repugnant to yours, but is the result of necessity. For, having recommended to Congress the appointment of lieutenant-generals for the discharge of the latter duties, and they having neither approved nor disapproved the measure, I am hung in suspense; and being unwilling, on the one hand, to give up the benefits resulting from the command of lieutenant-generals in the cases abovementioned, or to deprive the divisions of their major-generals for ordinary duty on the other, I have been led to adopt a kind of medium course, which, though not perfect in itself, is in my judgment the best that circumstances will admit of, till Congress shall have decided upon the proposition before them. Your remark upon the disadvantages of an officer's being suddenly removed from the command of a division to a wing, though not without foundation, as I have before acknowledged, does not apply so forcibly in the present case, as you seem to think. There is no major-general in this army, that is not pretty well known, and who may not, if he chooses, soon become acquainted with such officers as may be serviceable to him. Their commands being announced in general orders, and the army prepared for their reception, a major-general may go with the same ease to the command of a wing consisting of five brigades, as to a division composed of two, and will be received with as little confusion, since the brigades remain perfect and no changes have happened in them.

Mr. Boudinot's conjecture of the enemy's intention, although it does not coincide with mine, is nevertheless worthy of attention; and the evils of the measure have been guarded against, as far as it has been in my power, by removing the stores and provisions as fast as possible from the Head of Elk and the Susquehanna, and by exploring the country, surveying the roads, and marking the defiles and strong grounds; an engineer and three surveyors having been employed in this work nearly a month, though their report is not yet come in. Boats are also prepared on the Susquehanna for the transportation of our troops, in case we should find it necessary to move that way. But nevertheless it gives me real pleasure to find you have turned your thoughts that way, and are revolving the questions contained in your letter; and here let me again assure you, that I shall be always happy in a free communication of your sentiments upon any important subject relative to the service, and only beg that they may come directly to myself. The custom, which many officers have, of speaking freely of things and reprobating measures, which upon investigation may be found to be unavoidable, is never productive of good, but often of very mischievous consequences.

General Mifflin had just obtained leave to be absent from the army, and proceed to CongTess, in consequence of a resolve passed on the 11th of June, directing General Washington to order an inquiry to be made into his conduct, and that of the officers under him, while be was quartermaster-general. Dr. Gordon states this to have been the effect of " some secret manoeuvres " of certain officers in the army, who were extremely dissatisfied, that General Mifflin should come forward at the opening of the campaign to share in its honors, after having escaped the distresses they had suffered in winter-quarters; especially as he had once tendered a resignation of his commission, and expressed a wish to retire from the service.

I am, &,c TO JOSEPH REED, DELEGATE IN CONGRESS FROM PENNSYLVANIA.

Valley Forge, 15 June, 1778.

Dear Sir,

I thank you much for your friendly favor of this date, and your polite attention in submitting the draft of your letter to Governor Johnstone to my perusal. I return it again; but, before you transcribe a fair copy, I would wish to see you upon the subject of it. Perhaps there are some parts of it which might receive a small alteration. In the present situation of things, all correspondence of this nature must and will be weighed and scanned with a scrupulous exactness; and even compliment, if carried far, may not pass entirely uncensured. So adroitly had the British made their preparations for a removal from Philadelphia, that it was even at this late hour doubtful what course they intended to pursue. From many concurring circumstances, which he watched narrowly, General Washington was at length convinced, that they intended to march through Jersey. But the views of others were quite different; and only three days before the enemy actually crossed the river, and took up their line of march, General Lee wrote to the Commander-in-chief as follows.

" My opinion is, that, if they are in a capacity to act offensively, they will either immediately from Philadelphia, or, by a feint in descending the river as far as Newcastle, and then, turning to the right, march directly and rapidly towards Lancaster, by which means they will draw us out of our present position, and oblige us to fight on terms perhaps very disadvantageous; or that they will leave Lancaster and this army wide on the right, endeavour to take post on the lower parts of the Susquehanna, and, by securing a communication with their ships sent round into the bay for this purpose, be furnished with the means of encouraging and feeding the Indian war, broke out on the western frontier. This last plan I mention as a possibility, but as less probable than the former.

" If they are not in a capacity to act offensively, but are still determined to keep footing on the continent, there arc strong reasons to think, that they will not shut themselves up in towns, but take possession of some tract of country, which will afford them elbow-room and sustenance, and which is so situated as to be the most effectually protected by their command of the waters; and I have particular reasons to think, that they have cast their eyes for this purpose on the lower counties of Delaware, and some of the Maryland counties on the Eastern Shore. If they are resolved on this plan, it certainly will be very difficult to prevent them, or remove them afterwards, as their shipping will give them such mighty advantages. Whether they do or do not adopt any one of these plans, there can no inconvenience arise from considering the subject, nor from devising means of defeating their purposes, on the supposition that they will.

There is another consideration, which weighs with me. Congress at this instant, perhaps, are deliberating on an answer to the address, which they have received from the commissioners. Should your letter, therefore, considered as coming from a member, contain sentiments repugnant to theirs, an unfavorable use, more than probably, will be made of it.

I am, dear Sir, your affectionate, &c
TO THE PRESIDENT OF CONGRESS.

Head-Quarters, 18 Jane, 1778.

Sir,

Baron Steuben will have the honor to

deliver you this. I do not know particularly the extent of his business at York; but, from what he has communicated, it is in part to get the duties and powers of his appointment minutely defined and settled. I enclose a copy of orders on the 15th instant, which were issued to quiet the minds of the general officers, and to remove a spirit of jealousy, which but too apparently was rising among them. These contain my ideas of the principal duties of the inspector's office, and, I have reason to think, are generally agreeable to the army. While I am on this subject, I must do justice to the Baron's intelligence, zeal, and indefatigable industry, from which we have experienced very happy effects. I have the honor to be, &c.

" In short, I think it would be proper to put these queries to ourserrea. Should they march directly towards Lancaster and the Susquehanna, or indirectly from Newcastle, what are we to do? Should they, though it is less probable, leave this army, and even Lancaster wide on the right, and endeavour to establish themselves on the lower parts of the Susquehanna, what are we to do? And, should they act only on the defensive, and attempt to secure to themselves some such tract of country as I have mentioned, what measures are we to pursue? These are matter I really think worthy of consideration." — *MS. Letter, June ISA.* General Reed'was probably at this time in camp, as one of taw committee from Congress for arranging the army. TO THE PRESIDENT OF CONGRESS. Head-Quarters, half after eleven, A. M, 18 June, 1778.

Sir,

I have the pleasure to inform Congress, that I was this minute advised by Mr. Roberts that the enemy evacuated the city early this morning. He was down at the Middle Ferry on this side, where he received the intelligence from a number of citizens, who were on the opposite shore. They told him that about three thousand of the troops had embarked on board transports. The destruction of the bridge prevented him from crossing. I expect every moment official accounts on the subject.

I have put six brigades in motion; and the rest of the army are preparing to follow with all possible despatch. We shall proceed towards Jersey, and govern ourselves according to circumstances. As yet I am not fully ascertained of the enemy's destination; nor is there wanting a variety of opinions, as to the route

Vol. v. 52 Ii they will pursue, whether it will be by land or sea, admitting it to be to New York. Some think it probable, in such case, that the part of their army, which crossed the Delaware, will march down the Jersey shore some distance, and then embark. There is other intelligence corroborating Mr. Roberts's, but none official is yet come. I have the honor to be, &c

P. S. A letter from Captain MLane, dated in Philadelphia, this minute came to hand, confirming the evacuation. A Council of War was held on the 17th of June, in which the following questions were proposed by the Commander-in-chief, and discussed.

" Whether any enterprise ought to be undertaken against the enemy in their present circumstances? Whether the army should remain in the position it now holds, till the final evacuation of the city, or more immediately towards the Delaware? Whether any detachment of it shall be sent to reinforce the brigade in the Jerseys, or advanced towards the enemy to act as occasion shall require, and endeavour to take advantage of their retreat? If the enemy march through Jersey, will it be prudent to attack them on the way, or more eligible to proceed to the North River in the most direct and convenient manner, to secure the important communication between the eastern and southern States? In case such measures should be adopted, as will enable this army to overtake the enemy in their march, will it be prudent, with the aid which may reasonably be expected from the Jersey militia, to make aa attack upon them, and ought it to be a partial or a general one? "

There being a great variety of opinions among the officers, General Washington requested each one to communicate his views in writing; which was accordingly done the next day; but not till the decided movements of the enemy had made it demonstrable, that they were advancing through Jersey. The main point to be considered, therefore, was the expediency of attacking them on their march. Nearly all the officers were opposed to an attack, on account of the inequality of force, bat others thought it should depend on circumstances. This was probably the impression of General Washington, when he put the army in i to cross the Delaware.

TO BRIGADIER-GENERAL WAYNE.

Instructions.

Sir,

You are to proceed with the first and second Pennsylvania regiments, and the brigade late Conway's, by the direct route to Coryell's Ferry, leaving a proper interval between your division and General Lee's, so as to prevent their interfering with each other. The instructions given to General Lee, are to halt on the first strong ground after passing the Delaware at the said ferry, until further orders; unless he should receive authentic intelligence, that the enemy have proceeded by the direct road to South Amboy, or still lower; in this case he is to continue his march to the North River. Given at Head-Quarters, this 18th day of June, 1778.

TO THE PRESIDENT OF CONGRESS.

Head-Quarters, six o'clock, P. M, 18 June, 1778.

Sir,

Since I had the honor of addressing you this forenoon, I have received your letter of the 17th, with its several enclosures. I am happy in the approbation of Congress respecting my conduct to Dr. Ferguson. I could not find, after the maturest consideration on the subject, that his passage through the country could be in any wise material, or answer any other purpose than to spread disaffection.

I shall take every measure in my power to prevent an intercourse between the army and the enemy, and also between the inhabitants and the latter. You may rest assured, that whatever letters come from their lines shall be, as they ever have been, minutely inspected; and whenever they import any thing of an insidious cast, they shall be suppressed. In this I trust I shall not offend against any rule of right, nor the strictest propriety. The letter for the commissioners I shall transmit by the earliest opportunity; however, their departure from Philadelphia will prevent their getting it as soon as they otherwise would have done. I cannot say that I regret the delay; for there is no knowing to what acts of depredation and ruin their disappointed ambition might have led. And permit me to add, that I think there was no other criterion for Congress to go by, than the one they have adopted. The proceedings of the 22d of April, it is probable, have reached Britain by this time, and will show that the present powers of the commissioners, or at least those we are obliged to suppose them to possess, are wholly incompetent to any valuable end.

I have appointed General Arnold to command in Philadelphia, as the state of his wound will not permit his services in a more active line. Colonel Jackson, with a detachment of troops, is to attend him; and I flatter myself that order will be preserved, and the several purposes answered, expressed by Congress in their resolution of the 4th instant. The General set out this evening, and I shall move with the main body of the army at five in the morning to-morrow.

I have the honor to be, &c The object of this resolve was to protect the inhabitant of Phua. dolphin from suffering any insult or injury to their property or person after the evacuation. It was required, that no transfers, removal, or ales of goods or merchandise in the possession of the inhabitants should be allowed, till it should be ascertained by a joint committee, appointed by Congress and the government of Pennsylvania, whether any of I belonged to the King of Great Britain or his subjects.

P. S. By this conveyance you will be pleased to receive the proceedings of the court of inquiry, respecting the losses of the forts in the Highlands.

TO MAJOR-GENERAL ARNOLD.
Instructions.

Sir,

You are immediately to proceed to Philadelphia and take the command of the troops there. The principal objects of your command you will find specified in the enclosed resolve of Congress of the 4th instant, which you will carefully execute. You will take every prudent step in your power to preserve tranquillity and order in the city, and give security to individuals of every class and description, restraining as far as possible, till the restoration of civil government, every species of persecution, insult, or abuse, either from the soldiery to the inhabitants, or among each other. I leave it to your own discretion to adopt such measures as shall appear to you most effectual, and at the same time least offensive, for answering the views of Congress, to prevent the removal, transfer, or sale of any goods, wares, or merchandise, in possession of the inhabitants of the city, till the property of them can be ascertained in the mode directed.

The quartermaster-general will send one of his assistants into the city, who will take your directions and give you all the aid in his power. He is to search out any public stores belonging to the enemy, and convert them to the use of the army. Given under my hand, at Head-Quarters, this 19th day of June, 1778.

TO MAJOR-GENERAL GATES.
Four o'clock, 20 June, 1778.

Sir, I think it necessary to inform you by the return oi the express, who brought your packet for Congress, that I am now with the main body of the army within ten miles of Coryell's Ferry. General Lee is advanced with six brigades, and will cross to-night or to-morrow morning. By the last intelligence the enemy were near Mount Holly, and moving very slowly; but, as there are so many roads open to them, their route could not be ascertained. I shall enter the Jerseys to-morrow, and give you the earliest notice of their movements and whatever may affect you. As the supplies of forage and provision in your quarter will be objects of the utmost importance, they will there-

fore claim your attention. I am, Sir, &c.

TO MAJOR-GENERAL ARNOLD.
Ten Miles from Coryell's, 21 June, 1778.

Dear Sir, This will be delivered to you by Major Wemp, who has the conduct and care of some warriors from the Seneca nations, who are also accompanied by a few of our Oneida and Tuscarora friends. The enclosed extract of a letter from our Indian commissioners at Albany will inform you of the Senecas' business in this quarter. I cannot give them the smallest account of Astyarix, of whom they are in pursuit, nor did I ever hear of his captivity, till I was advised of it a few days ago by General Schuyler. They have been treated with civility; but at the same time I told them of their hostilities, and that as soon as the British army were gone, if they did not immediately cease from them, I would turn our whole force against them and the other Indian nations, who have taken a like bloody part against us, and cut them to pieces. They have also had a view of the main body of the army, and been told of our great resources of men and number of troops elsewhere. I hope this circumstance, with the evacuation of Philadelphia and their own evidence of it, added to our civilities and some presents, will have a happy effect upon the temper and disposition of their nation when they return. I wish you to order them such trinkets, and the like, as you may judge necessary, keeping up however a distinction between them and the Oneidas and Tuscaroras, who are our friends. I would have the favors and presents to these greatly to exceed.

Major Wemp has despatches from the Sachems for all the warriors, and the men who were here before, to return home immediately. Such as remained, I believe are with Monsieur Tousard. I shall be glad that you will have them collected, and all *presented,* after which they may return to their nation, in obedience to their Sachems' orders, if they incline. I have given the Senecas a letter to Congress respecting Astyarix's releasement, if he can be found.

I received your favor yesterday. If

Morgan's corps could have been on the rear of the enemy, they might have harassed them, but not without considerable risk. They are now advancing, as the whole army is, to the Delaware. We have been much impeded by rain. The troops with General Lee crossed the river last night. I am, in haste, dear Sir, &c.

TO THE PRESIDENT OF CONGRESS.

Head-Quarters, near Coryell's, 23 June, 1778.

Sir, I have the honor to inform you that I am now in Jersey, and that the troops are passing the river at Coryell's, and are mostly over. The latest intelligence I have had respecting the enemy was yesterday from General Dickinson. He says they were in the morning at Morestown and Mount Holly; but that he had not been able to learn what route they would pursue from thence; nor was it easy to determine, as, from their situation, they might either proceed to South Amboy, or by way of Brunswic. We have been a good deal impeded in our march by rainy weather. As soon as we have cleaned the arms, and can get matters in train, we propose moving towards Princeton, in order to avail ourselves of any favorable occasions, that may present themselves, of attacking or annoying the enemy. I have the honor to be, &c.

TO MAJOR-GENERAL DICKINSON.

Head-Quarters, Hopewell, 34 June, 1778.

Sir, As the several detachments of Continental troops, employed in harassing the enemy on their march, will have the greatest need of intelligent guides, not only for their own safety, but to enable them to direct their offensive operations with greater precision, it will be necessary that among the militia, which you shall think proper to annex to each party, there be persons perfectly acquainted with the roads and communications, which it is most interesting to the different commanding officers to know. The disposition for these detachments is as follows. Morgan's corps is to gain the enemy's right flank; Maxwell's brigade to hang on their left; Brigadier-General Scott is now marching with a very respectable detachment destined to gall the enemy's left flank and rear. Two or three hundred Continentals, and such volunteers as General Cadwalader has been able to collect, have crossed the Delaware, and are now marching to the enemy's rear. Colonel White's detachment of horse is to join General Scott. Enclosed is a letter for Colonel Morgan, which you will forward. I am, &,c.

TO THE MARQUIS DE LAFAYETTE.

Instructions.

Sir,

You are immediately to proceed with the detachment commanded by General Poor, and form a junction as expeditiously as possible with that under the command of General Scott. You are to use the most effectual means for gaining the enemy's left flank and rear, and giving them every degree of annoyance. All Continental parties, that are already on the lines, will be under your command, and you will take such measures, in concert with General Dickinson, as will cause the enemy the greatest impediment and loss in their march. For these purposes you will attack them as occasion may require by detachment, and, if a proper opening should be given, by operating against them with the whole force of your command. You will naturally take such precautions, as will secure you against surprise, and maintain your communication with this army. Given at Kingston, this 25th day of June, 1778.

Vol. v. 53 TO MAJOR-GENERAL LEE.

Cranberry, 26 June, 1778.

Dear Sir,

Your uneasiness on account of the command of yesterday's detachment fills me with concern, as it is not in my power fully to remove it without wounding the feelings of the Marquis de Lafayette. I have thought of an expedient, which, though not quite equal to the views of either of you, may in some measure answer both; and that is, to make another detachment from this army for the purpose of aiding and supporting the several detachments now under the command of the Marquis, and giving you the command of the whole, under certain restrictions; which the circumstances arising from your own conduct yesterday render almost unavoidable.

The expedient I would propose, is, for you to march towards the Marquis with Scott's and Varnum's brigades. Give him notice, that you are advancing to support him, and that you are to have the command of the whole advanced body; but, as he may have formed some enterprise with the advice of the officers commanding the several corps under his command, which will not admit of delay or alteration, you will give him every assistance and countenance in your power. This, as I observed before, is not quite the thing; but may possibly answer, in some degree, the views of both. That it may do so, and the public service receive benefit from the measure, is the sincere wish of, dear Sir, your most obedient servant.

In the council of war General Lee had been strongly opposed to attacking the enemy, and, when this measure was resolved upon, be gave up the command of the advanced divisions to Lafayette; bat be afterwards altered his mind, and requested to be restored to the command. TO THE MARQUIS DE LAFAYETTE. Cranberry, 26 June, 1775.

My Dear Marquis, General Lee's uneasiness on account of yesterday's transaction rather.increasing than abating, and your politeness in wishing to ease him of it, have induced me to detach him from this army with a part of it, to reinforce or at least cover the several detachments at present under your command. At the same time that I felt for General Lee's distress of mind, I have had an eye to your wishes, and the delicacy of your situation; and have therefore obtained a promise from him, that, when he gives you notice of his approach and command, he will request you to prosecute any plan you may have already concerted for the purpose of attacking or otherwise annoying the enemy. This is the only expedient I could think of to answer the views of both. General Lee seems satisfied with the measure, and I wish it may prove agreeable to you, as I am, with the warmest wishes for your honor and glory, and with the sincerest esteem and affection, yours, &c.

TO THE PRESIDENT OF CONGRESS.

Engliahtown, half after eleven, A. M, 28 June, 1778.

Sir, I was duly honored with your favor of the 20th instant, with the report to which it referred, and trust my situation will apologize for my not answering it before. I am now here with the main body of the army, and pressing hard to come up with the enemy. They encamped yesterday at Monmouth Court-House, having almost the whole of their front, particularly their left wing, secured by a marsh and thick wood, and their rear by a difficult defile, from whence they moved very early this morning. Our advance, from the rainy weather, and the intense heat when it was fair, (though these may have been equally disadvantageous to them,) has been greatly delayed. Several of our men have fallen sick from these causes; and a few unfortunately have fainted, and died in a little time after.

We have a select and strong detachment more forward, under the command of Major-General Lee, with orders to attack their rear if possible. Whether the detachment will be able to come up with it, is a matter of question, especially before they get into strong grounds. Besides this, Morgan, with his corps, and some bodies of militia, are on their flanks. I cannot determine yet at what place they intend to embark. Some think they will push for Sandy Hook, whilst others suppose they mean to go to Shoal Harbour. The latter opinion seems to be founded in the greater probability, as, from intelligence, several vessels and craft are lying off that place. We have made a few prisoners; and they have lost a good many men by desertion. I cannot ascertain their number, as they came in to our advanced parties, and pushed immediately into the country. I think five or six hundred is the least number in the whole, that have come in. They are chiefly foreigners.

I have the honor to be, &.c When Sir Henry Clinton left Philadelphia, it was his purpose, if circumstances would admit, to march directly to Brunswic and

embark his troops on the Rariton River. Till he arrived at Cross wicks and Allentown, his march was in that direction, although equally in a line to Sandy Hook. At this point it was necessary for him to determine which route to pursue, and he chose the latter, as he was informed that General Washington had crossed the Delaware with his whole army, and was stationed on the line to Brunswic.

TO THE PRESIDENT OF CONGRESS.

Fields, near Monmouth Court-House, 29 June, 1778.

Sir, I have the honor to inform you, that, about seven o'clock yesterday morning, both armies advanced on each other. About twelve, they met on the grounds near Monmouth Court-House, when an action commenced. We forced the enemy from the field, and encamped on the ground. They took a strong post in our front, secured on both flanks by morasses and thick woods, where they remained till about twelve at night, and then retreated. I cannot at this time go into a detail of matters. When opportunity will permit, I shall take the liberty of transmitting to Congress a more particular account of the proceedings of the day.

I have the honor to be, &c.

TO MAJOR-GENERAL ARNOLD.

Englishtown, 30 June, 1778.

Dear Sir, As we are again in possession of Philadelphia, and it may possibly happen, that, in the course of the war, the enemy may form some design against it, either in reality or appearance, I have sent General Duportail to examine what defence may be essential for its security, and to make his report to me, as soon as the nature of the business will admit. In order to facilitate this, I am to request, that you will give him every aid i n your power, which he may consider material for informing his judgment and making a well digested plan. For the particulars on this head I refer you to General DuportaiPs instructions.

VOL. V. J J

Colonel Jackson's regiment having joined the army, and being thus far advanced from the station to which it was

lately assigned, it will proceed with me to the Hudson River. Colonel Hartley's was to have marched from Yorktown about the time we left Valley Forge, which you will order to supply the place of the former, unless Congress shall have directed another disposition of it, which they wish to remain. In your next, let me know the state of your wound.

I am, dear Sir, with great regard and esteem, &c.

TO THE PRESIDENT OF CONGRESS.

Englishtown, 1 July, 1778.

Sir,

I embrace this first moment of leisure to give Congress a more full and particular account of the movements of the army under my command since its passing the Delaware, than the situation of our affairs would heretofore permit. I had the honor to advise them, that, on the appearances of the enemy's intention to march through Jersey becoming serious, I had detached General Maxwell's brigade, in conjunction with the militia of that State, to interrupt and impede their progress by every obstruction in their power, so as to give time to the army under my command to come up with them, and take advantage of any favorable circumstances that might present themselves. The army having proceeded to Coryell's Ferry, and crossed the Delaware at that place, I immediately detached Colonel Morgan with a select corps of six hundred men to reinforce General Maxwell, and marched with the main body towards Princeton.

The slow advance of the enemy had greatly the air of design, and led me, with others, to suspect that General Clinton, desirous of a general action, was endeavouring to draw us down into the lower country, in order, by a rapid movement, to gain our right, and take possession of the strong grounds above us. This consideration, and to give the troops time to repose and refresh themselves from the fatigues they had experienced from rainy and excessively hot weather, determined me to halt at Hopewell township about five miles from Princeton, where we remained till the morning of the 25th. On the preceding day I made a second detachment of fifteen hundred chosen troops under Brigadier-General Scott, to reinforce those already in the vicinity of the enemy, the more effectually to annoy and delay their march. The next day the army moved to Kingston; and, having received intelligence that the enemy were prosecuting their route towards Monmouth Court-House, I despatched a thousand select men under Brigadier-General Wayne, and sent the Marquis de Lafayette to take the command of the whole advanced corps, including Maxwell's brigade and Morgan's light-infantry, with orders to take the first fair opportunity of attacking the enemy's rear.

In the evening of the same day the whole army marched from Kingston, where our baggage was left, with intention to preserve a proper distance for supporting the advanced corps, and arrived at Cranberry early the next morning. The intense heat of the weather, and a heavy storm unluckily coming on, made it impossible to resume our march that day without great inconvenience and injury to the troops. Our advanced corps, being differently circumstanced, moved from the position it had held the night before, and took post in the evening on the Monmouth road about five miles from the enemy's rear, in expectation of attacking them next morning on their march. The main body having remained at Cranberry, the advanced corps was found to be too remote, and too far upon the right, to be supported in case of an attack either upon or from the enemy; which induced me to send orders to the Marquis to file off by his left towards Englishtown, which he accordingly executed early in the morning of the 27th.

The enemy, in marching from Allentown, had changed their disposition, and placed their best troops in the rear, consisting of all the grenadiers, light-infantry, and chasseurs of the line. This alteration made it necessary to increase the number of our advanced corps; in consequence of which I detached Major-General Lee with two brigades to join the Marquis at Englishtown, on whom of course the command of the

whole devolved, amounting to about five thousand men. The main body marched the same day, and encamped within three miles of that place. Morgan's corps was left hovering on the enemy's right flank; and the Jersey militia, amounting at this time to about seven or eight hundred men, under General Dickinson, on their left.

The enemy were now encamped in a strong position, with their right extending about a mile and a half beyond the Court-House to the parting of the roads leading to Shrewsbury and Middletown, and their left along the road from Allentown to Monmouth, about three miles on this side of the Court-House. Their right flank lay on the skirt of a small wood, while their left was secured by a very thick one, a morass running towards their rear, and their whole front covered by a wood, and, for a considerable extent towards the left, with a morass. In this situation they halted till the morning of the 28th. Matters being thus situated, and having had the best information, that, if the enemy were once arrived at the Heights of Middletown, ten or twelve miles from where they were, it would be impossible to attempt any thing against them with a prospect of success, I determined to attack their rear the moment they should get in motion from their present ground. I communicated my intention to General Lee, and ordered him to make his disposition for the attack, and to keep his troops constantly lying upon their arms, to be in readiness at the shortest notice. This was done with respect to the troops under my immediate command.

About five in the morning General Dickinson sent an express, informing that the front of the enemy had begun their march. I instantly put the army in motion, and sent orders by one of my aids to General Lee to move on and attack them, unless there should be very powerful reasons to the contrary, acquainting him at the same time, that I was marching to support him, and, for doing it with the greater expedition and convenience, should make the men disencumber themselves of their packs and blankets. After marching about five

miles, to my great surprise and mortification, I met the whole advanced corps retreating, and, as I was told, by General Lee's orders, without having made any opposition, except one fire, given by a party under the command of Colonel Butler, on their being charged by the enemy's cavalry, who were repulsed. I proceeded immediately to the rear of the corps, which I found closely pressed by the enemy, and gave directions for forming part of the retreating troops, who, by the brave and spirited conduct of the officers, aided by some pieces of well-served artillery, checked the enemy's advance, and gave time to make a disposition of the left wing and second line of the army upon an eminence, and in a wood a little in the rear, covered

Vol. v. 54 Jj» by a morass in front. On this were placed some batteries of cannon by Lord Stirling, who commanded the left wing, which played upon the enemy with great effect, and, seconded by parties of infantry detached to oppose them, effectually put a stop to their advance.

General Lee being detached with the advanced corps, the command of the right wing, for the occasion, was given to General Greene. For the expedition of the march, and to counteract any attempt to turn our right, I had ordered him to file off by the new church, two miles from Englishtown, and fall into the Monmouth road, a small distance in the rear of the CourtHouse, while the rest of the column moved directly on towards the Court-House. On intelligence of the retreat, he marched up and took a very advantageous position on the right. The enemy by this time, finding themselves warmly opposed in front, made an attempt to turn our left flank; but they were bravely repulsed and driven back by detached parties of infantry. They also made a movement to our right with as little success, General Greene having advanced a body of troops with artillery to a commanding piece of ground; which not only disappointed their design of turning our right, but severely enfiladed those in front of the left wing. In addition to this, General Wayne advanced with a body of troops, and kept up so severe and well-directed a fire, that the enemy were soon compelled to retire behind the defile where the first stand in the beginning of the action had been made.

In this situation the enemy had both their flanks secured by thick woods and morasses, while their front could only be approached through a narrow pass. I resolved nevertheless to attack them; and for that purpose ordered General Poor, with his own and the Carolina brigade, to move round upon their right, and General Woodford upon their left, and the artillery to gall them in front. But the impediments in their way prevented their getting within reach before it was dark. They remained upon the ground they had been directed to occupy during the night, with the intention to begin the attack early the next morning; and the army continued lying upon their arms in the field of action, to be in readiness to support them. In the mean time the enemy were employed in removing their wounded, and about twelve o'clock at night marched away in such silence, that, though General Poor lay extremely near them, they effected their retreat without his knowledge. They carried off all their wounded, except four officers and about forty privates, whose wounds were too dangerous to permit their removal.

The extreme heat of the weather, the fatigue of the men from their march through a deep sandy country almost entirely destitute of water, and the distance the enemy had gained by marching in the night, made a pursuit impracticable and fruitless. It would have answered no valuable purpose, and would have been fatal to numbers of our men, several of whom died the preceding day with heat.

Were I to conclude my account of this day's transactions, without expressing my obligations to the officers of the army in general, I should do injustice to their merit, and violence to my own feelings. They seemed to vie with each other in manifesting their zeal and bravery. The catalogue of those, who distinguished themselves, is too long to admit of particularizing individuals. I cannot, however, forbear mentioning Brigadier-General Wayne, whose good conduct and bravery through the whole action deserves particular commendation. The behaviour of the troops in general, after they recovered from the first surprise occasioned by the retreat of the advanced corps, was such as could not be surpassed. All the artillery, both officers and men, that were engaged, distinguished themselves in a remarkable manner.

Enclosed, Congress will be pleased to receive a return of our killed, wounded, and missing. Among the first were Lieutenant-Colonel Bunner of Pennsylvania, and Major Dickinson of Virginia, both officers of distinguished merit, and much to be regretted. The enemy's slain, left on the field, and buried by us, according to the return of the persons assigned to that duty, were four officers and two hundred and forty-five privates. In the former number was the honorable Colonel Monckton. Exclusive of these, they buried some themselves, as there were several new graves near the field of battle. How many men they may have had wounded cannot be determined; but, from the usual proportion, the number must have been considerable. There were a few prisoners taken.

The peculiar situation of General Lee at this time requires that I should say nothing of his conduct. He is now in arrest. The charges against him, with such sentence as the court-martial may decree in his case, shall be transmitted for the approbation or disapprobation of Congress, as soon as it shall be passed.

Being fully convinced by the gentlemen of this country, that the enemy cannot be hurt or injured in their embarkation at Sandy Hook, the place to which they are going, and unwilling to get too far removed from the North River, I put the troops in motion early this morning, and shall proceed that way, leaving the Jersey brigade, Morgan's corps, and other light parties (the militia being all dismissed) to hover about them, to countenance desertion, and to prevent depredations as far as possible. After they embark, the former will take post in the neighbourhood of Elizabeth town, the latter rejoin the corps from which they were detached.

I have the honor to be, &c TO MAJOR-GENERAL GATES.

Brunswic, 3 July, 1778.

Sir,

I have the pleasure of informing you, that the loss of the enemy in the action of the 28th was more considerable than we at first apprehended. By the return of the officers, who had charge of the burying parties, it appears that they left two hundred and forty-five non-commissioned officers and privates dead on the field, and four officers, one of whom was the honorable Colonel Monckton of the grenadiers. Our loss was seven officers and fifty-two rank and file killed, and seventeen officers and one hundred and twenty rank and file wounded. Among the former were Lieutenant-Colonel Bunner of Pennsylvania and Major Dickinson of Virginia, who were the only officers of rank. There were several fresh graves and burying-places found near the field, in which the enemy put their dead before they quitted it. These were exclusive of the two hundred and forty-five before mentioned. We have made upwards of one hundred prisoners, including forty privates and four officers left wounded at Monmouth Court-House. The number of their wounded we can only guess at, as they were employed in carrying them off during the action and till midnight, when they stole off as silent as the grave. Finding that the enemy had during the action pushed their baggage to Middletown, and that they, by marching off in the night after the engagement, would gain that place before there was any possibility of overtaking their rear, I determined to give over the pursuit. From the information of General Forman, and many gentlemen well acquainted with the country, I found it would be impossible to annoy them in their embarkation, as the neck of land, upon which they now are, is defended by a narrow passage, which being possessed by a few men would effectually oppose our whole force. Besides this consideration, I thought it highly expedient to turn towards the North River. I marched from Englishtown on the 30th of last month, and arrived here yesterday with the whole army, except Maxwell's brigade and Morgan's corps, who are left upon the rear of the enemy to prevent their making depredations, and to encourage desertions, which still prevail to a considerable degree.

For other particulars respecting the battle of Monmouth, see Apperort, No. XVIII.

The march from Englishtown was inconceivably distressing to the troops and horses. The distance is about twenty miles through a deep sand without a drop of water, except at South River, which is half way. This, added to the intense heat, killed a few and disabled many of our men, and killed a number of our horses. To recruit the former upon the airy, open grounds near this place, and to give the quartermaster-general an opportunity of providing the latter, will occasion a short halt, but you may depend that we will be with you as soon as possible. My present intention is to cross By an official return from General Arnold, dated the 4th of July, the number of deserters, who had then arrived in Philadelphia during the march of the enemy through Jersey, was five hundred and seventy-six. Of these one hundred and thirty-six were British, and four hundred and forty German troops. On the 8th of July the number had increased to above six hundred. the North River at King's Ferry; but, should you be of opinion, that it will be in the power of the enemy to hinder our passage, be pleased to inform me, as it would be losing much time to be obliged to turn up from thence, and march through the Clove. The route by King's Ferry is so much the shortest and best, that if the passage could be kept open by throwing up works and mounting some cannon upon them, I think it would be worth while to have it done. But this I leave to your determination. I am, &c.

TO JOHN AUGUSTINE WASHINGTON.
Brunswic, 4 July, 1778.

Dear Brother,

Before this will have reached you, the account of the battle of Monmouth will probably get to Virginia; which, from an unfortunate and bad beginning, turned out a glorious and happy day. The enemy evacuated Philadelphia on the 18th instant. At ten o'clock that day I got intelligence of it, and by two o'clock, or soon after, had six brigades on their march for the Jerseys, and followed with the whole army next morning. On the 21st we completed our passage over the Delaware at Coryell's Ferry, about thirty-three miles above Philadelphia, and distant from Valley Forge about forty miles. From this ferry we moved down towards the enemy, and on the 27th got within six miles of them.

General Lee, having the command of the van of the army, consisting of full five thousand chosen men, was ordered to begin the attack next morning, so soon as the enemy began their march; to be supported by me; but, strange to tell! when he came up with the enemy, a retreat commenced; whether by his order, or from other causes, is now the subject of inquiry, and consequently improper to be descanted upon, as he is in arrest, and a court-martial is sitting for his trial. A retreat, however, was the fact, be the causes what they may; and the disorder arising from it would have proved fatal to the army, had not that bountiful Providence, which has never failed us in the hour of distress, enabled me to form a regiment or two (of those that were retreating) in the face of the enemy and under their fire; by which means a stand was made long enough (the place through which the enemy were pursuing being narrow) to form the troops, that were advancing, upon an advantageous piece of ground in the rear. Here our affairs took a favorable turn, and, from being pursued, we drove the enemy back over the ground they had followed, and recovered the field of battle, and possessed ourselves of their dead. But as they retreated behind a morass very difficult to pass, and had both flanks secured with thick woods, it was found impracticable with our men, fainting with fatigue, heat, and want of water, to do any thing more that night. In the morning we expected to renew the action; when, behold, the enemy had stolen off silently in the night, after having sent away their wounded. Getting a night's march of us, and having but ten miles to a strong post, it was judged expedient not to follow them any further, but to move towards the North River, lest they should have any design upon our posts there.

I observe what you say respecting voluntary enlistments, or rather your scheme for raising two thousand volunteers; and I candidly own to you, that I have no opinion of it. These measures only tend to burthen the public with a number of officers, without adding one jot to our strength, but greatly to confusion and disorder. If the several States would but fall upon some vigorous measures to fill-up their respective regiments, nothing more need be asked of them. But while these are neglected, or in other words ineffectually and feebly attended to, and these succedaneums tried, we can never have an army to be depended upon.

The enemy's whole force marched through the Jerseys, excepting the regiment of Anspach, which, it is said, they were afraid to trust, and therefore sent them round to New York by water with the commissioners. I do not learn that they have received much of a reinforcement as yet; nor do I think they have a prospect of any worth speaking of, as I believe they stand very critically with respect to France. As the post waits, I shall only add my love to my sister and the family, and strong assurances of being, with the sincerest regard and love, your most affectionate brother.

TO MAJOR-GENERAL ARNOLD.
Brunswic, 6 July, 1778.

Dear Sir,

I received your favor of the 30th ultimo, and thank you much for your kind and affectionate congratulations. As you will have seen before this the account of the action transmitted to Congress, I shall only add, that since that was given, more of the enemy have been found dead in the woods near the field of action, and on their route; and that desertion yet prevails to a considerable degree. I have also been favored with Major Franks's letter of the 4th, and was sorry to find you had been afflicted with a violent oppression in the stomach. I hope you are released from it, and I shall also be happy to hear, that your leg is in a very fair way of recovering.

Vol. v. 55 K K

Sir Henry Clinton has really suffered much in the line of desertion. I am persuaded his army, from this cause, and the action, has experienced a diminution of two thousand men at least, since it left Philadelphia. Our left wing moved yesterday morning, and our right this, on the route to the North River. I am, &c.

TO MAJOR-GENERAL LORD STIRLING AND THE MEMBERS OF THE GENERAL COURT-MARTIAL FOR THE TRIAL OF MAJOR-GENERAL LEE. 7 July, 177a

Gentlemen, On further consideration of the adjournment of the court-martial to Morristown, it appears to me, that the matter is liable to many great and almost insuperable objections. Should the court remain there, it would be necessary for more officers to be drawn directly from the army, than could be prudently spared; and the frequent occasions there will be of calling on the same witnesses on several, and often on the same points in question, would cause such a detention of them as might be very injurious. From these considerations I am induced to change the place of the court's sitting, and to request that they will adjourn from Morristown to Faramus Church, which will be immediately in the route of the army. The court will be pleased to notify General Lee and the witnesses of the removal, in such a way as they shall deem most proper. I am, &c This estimate includes the *tcounded,* as appears by an extract from another letter, in which he says; — "Without exaggeration their trip through the Jerseys, in killed, wounded, prisoners, and deserters, baa cost them at least two thousand men, and of their best troops." As more than six hundred deserters went back to Philadelphia, and many joined the American army on the march, and others escaped into the country, the whole number of deserters may perhaps be fairly estimated at eight

hundred. To these add three hundred killed, and one hundred prisoners, and the absolute loss will be twelve hundred; leaving eight hundred of the estimated two thousand for the wounded, which is a proportion of less than three to one between the wounded and the killed.

TO THE PRESIDENT OF CONGRESS.
Camp, near Brunswic, 7 July, 1778.

Sir,

I have the honor to inform you, that, on Sunday morning, the left wing of the army moved towards the North River; the right followed yesterday; and the second line, which forms the rear division, is also now in motion. I shall advance as fast as I can consistently with the circumstances of the weather and the health of the troops. The enemy, from the advices of our parties of observation, were nearly if not all embarked yesterday. They have continued to desert upon all occasions.

I should be extremely happy if the committee appointed to arrange the army would repair to it as soon as possible. Congress can form no adequate idea of the discontents prevailing on account of the unsettled state of rank, and the uncertainty in which officers are, as to their future situation. The variety of hands in which the power of granting commissions and filling up vacancies is lodged, and other circumstances, have occasioned frequent instances of younger officers commanding their seniors, from the former having received their commissions, and the latter not; and these not only in the line of the army at large, but in their own brigades, and even in their own regiments. This, it will be readily conceived, is necessarily productive of much confusion, altercation, and complaint, and requires the speediest remedy.

Lord Stirling was president of the court-martial for the trial of General Lee. The court met at Brunswic on the 4th of July, and continued sitting nearly every day till the 12th of August, when it was closed. It moved with the army, and convened successively at Brunswic, Paramus, Peekskill, and Northcastlo.

By accounts from Monmouth, more

of the enemy's dead have been found. It is said the number buried by us and the inhabitants exceeds three hundred.

I have the honor to be, &c TO THE PRESIDENT OF CONGRESS.
11 July, 177a

Dear Sir,

I this morning had the pleasure of receiving your polite and friendly letter of the 7th. My warmest acknowledgments are due for the indulgent terms in which you express your sense of my conduct, in our late rencounter with the British army. Not to be pleased with the approbation and esteem of any of the virtuous and discerning part of my countrymen would indicate a want of sensibility; but I assure you, my dear Sir, there is no man on whose good opinion and friendship I set a higher value than on yours; and every fresh instance I receive of them cannot fail of affording me the most sincere and genuine satisfaction. At the same time, it is both a pleasing and a humiliating consideration to me, that the partiality of my friends greatly overrates the importance of my services. With every sentiment of respect and esteem, I am, dear Sir, &c.

Congress had adjourned to Philadelphia. President Laurens wrote from that place; — "I arrived here on Thursday last, but hitherto have not collected a sufficient number of States to form a Congress; consequently I have received no commands. Your Excellency will therefore be pleased to accept this as the address of an individual, intended to assure you, Sir, of my hearty congratulations with my countrymen, on the success of the American arms under your immediate command at the battle of Monmouth, and more particularly of my own happiness in the additional glory achieved by you in retrieving the honor of these States in the moment of an alarming dilemma. It is not my design to attempt encomiums. I am as unequal to the task as the act is unnecessary. Love and respect for your Excellency are impressed on the heart of every grateful American, and your name will be revered by posterity. Our acknowledgments are especially due to Heaven for the preservation of your person, necessarily exposed for the solvation of America to the most imminent danger on the late occasion." — *MS. Letter, July 70k,* TO MAJOR-GENERAL ARNOLD.

Head-Quarters, Paramus, 11 July, 1778.

Dear Sir,

The left wing of the army is advanced four miles lrom this place, and nineteen miles from King's Ferry; the other two divisions are moving after it, with proper intervals. The enemy, since quitting the Jerseys, have encamped in three divisions on Staten Island, New York Island, and Long Island. It does not appear to be their design, or even practicable for them immediately, to commence any offensive operations. This consideration, added to the intense heat of the weather, determines me to move very leisurely, and spare the troops as much as possible. My hurry was so great, when I last wrote, that I omitted returning you my thanks for your obliging care in forwarding a letter to Mrs. Washington. You will be so good as to accept them now, and excuse the delinquency.

The intelligence of the French fleet's sailing from KK

Toulon gives some weight to the accounts, which have been received by a flag-boat from New York, of the arrival of a French fleet off Chesapeake Bay, and induces me to congratulate you on it as a matter worthy of credit. A vigorous press is said to have taken place in the harbour of New York, for the purpose of manning their large ships, which are ordered to be ready for sea. I am, with great regard, dear Sir, &.c.

TO THE PRESIDENT OF CONGRESS.

Camp, at Paramus, 12 July, 1778.

Sir, The vote of approbation and thanks, which Congress have been pleased to honor me with, gives me the highest satisfaction, and at the same time demands a return of my sincerest acknowledgments. The other resolution I communicated with great pleasure to the army at large in yesterday's orders. The left wing of the army, which advanced yesterday four miles beyond this, moved this morning on the route towards King's Ferry. The right and second line, which make the last divi-

sion, are now here, where they will halt for a day or two, or perhaps longer, if no circumstances of a pressing nature cast up, in order to refresh themselves from the great fatigues they have suffered from the intense heat of the weather.

' Resolved, unanimously, that the thanks of Congress be gives to General Washington for the activity with which he marched from the camp at Valley Forge-in pursuit of the enemy; for his distinguished exertions in forming the lino of battle; and for his great good conduct in leading on the attack and gaining the important victory of Monmouth over the British grand army, under the command of General Sir Henry Clinton, in their march from Philadelphia to New York." —. JbtyTtt.

We have had it reported for two or three days through several channels from New York, that there is a French fleet on the coast; and it is added, that the enemy have been manning with the utmost despatch several of their ships of war which were there, and have pushed them out to sea. How far these facts are true, I cannot determine; but I should think it of infinite importance to ascertain the first, if possible, by sending out swift-sailing cruisers. The most interesting advantages might follow the information. I will try, by every practicable means that I can devise, to obtain an accurate account of the enemy's fleet at New York. I have the honor to be, &,c.

TO WILLIAM HENRY DRAYTON, DELEGATE IN

CONGRESS.

Head-Quarters, Paramus 12 July, 1778.

Dear Sir, Permit me to assure you, that the cordial terms of your obliging favor of the 5 th afforded me the most sensible pleasure. It naturally is my ardent wish, that my well-meant endeavours for the prosperity of my country may meet the approbation of my countrymen; and I cannot but be peculiarly flattered by every instance of esteem from the discerning part of them. The want of a longer personal acquaintance rather increases than lessens my obligation for your politeness on the present occasion, which certainly could need no

apology on that or on any other account. I need not say, that I shall be happy in every occasion of cultivating a continuance of your friendship and convincing you that I am, with great regard, dear Sir, &.c.

William Henry Drayton, of South Carolina, was one of the earliest and most active defenders of the liberties of his country in the first stages of the revolutionary movements. His writings contributed equally to enlighten the public mind, and enforce the claims of justice. A charge to the Grand Jury of Charleston, delivered by him as Chief Justice of South Carolina, on the 23d of April, 1776, is one of the most important historical documents of that period, whether considered in regard to the facts it contains, or the force of its arguments. He was an efficient member of Congress, and was conspicuous for the part he took in counteracting the objects of the British commissioners, by several spirited and well written essays in the newspapers. He died in Philadelphia, September 3d, 1779, at the age of thirty-six. See John Drayton's *Memoirs of the American Revolution,* Vol. I. p. xxvi; Vol. II. p. 259. TO GOVERNOR TRUMBULL.

Paramus, 14 July, 1778.

Sir, I last night received a letter from Congress, informing me of the arrival of a French fleet on our coast, extracts from which I have the honor to enclose. In addition to that information, I have to-day received intelligence tolerably authentic of its arrival oft' the Hook. Every thing we can do to aid and cooperate with this fleet is of the greatest importance. Accounts from New York speak of a Cork fleet, which is momently expected there; for the safety of which the enemy are extremely alarmed. It is probable, that this fleet, to avoid the French fleet, will be directed to take its course through the Sound. If this should be the case, it might answer the most valuable purposes, were the eastern States to collect beforehand all the frigates and armed vessels, which they can get together for the purpose, at some convenient place for interrupting their passage that way. If the whole or any considerable part of the Cork fleet could be taken, or destroyed, it would be a fatal blow to the British army, which it is supposed at this time has but a very small stock of provisions on hand. Should the project I have now suggested appear to you eligible, I beg the favor of you to transmit copies of it, and of the enclosed extracts, to the neighbouring States, and to endeavour to engage their concurrence. From the nature of the river, even small armed boats may be useful, as the frigates cannot protect the transports. I have the honor to be, with the greatest respect and esteem, &c.

This fleet sailed from Toulon on the 12th of April, but did not reach the mouth of the Delaware till the 8th of July. It had on board M. Gerard, the French Minister Plenipotentiary to the United States. After ascertaining, that the British had evacuated Philadelphia, and that th« shipping had left the Delaware, Count d'Estning despatched a Teasel up the river with the minister on board, and proceeded with the fleet to Sandy Hook, where he arrived on the 11th of July. APPENDIX. APPENDIX. No. I. pp. 11, 59.

MARQUIS DE LAFAYETTE.

Lafayette was but eighteen years old when he first conceived the project of joining the Americans, and risking his fortune and reputation in their cause. In the summer of 1776 he was stationed on military duty at Metz, being then an officer in the French army. It happened at this time, that the Duke of Gloucester, brother to the King of England, was at Metz, and a dinner was given to him by the commandant of that place. Several of the principal officers were invited, and among others Lafayette. Despatches had just been received by the Duke from England, and he made their contents the topic of conversation. They related to American affairs, the recent declaration of independence, the resistance of the colonists, and the strong measures adopted by the ministry to crush the rebellion.

The details were new to Lafayette. He listened with eagerness to the conversation, and prolonged it by asking

questions of the Duke. His curiosity was deeply excited by what he heard, and the idea of a people fighting for liberty had a strong influence upon his imagination. The cause seemed to him just and noble, from the tepresentations of the Duke himself; and before he left the table the thought came into his head, that he would go to America, and offer his services to a people, who were struggling for freedom and independence. From that hour he could think of nothing but this chivalrous enterprise. He resolved to return to Paris and make further inquiries.

When he arrived in that city, he confided his scheme to two young friends, Count Segur and Viscount de Noailles, and proposed that they should join him. They entered with enthusiasm into his views; but, as they were dependent on their families, it was necessary to consult their parents, who reprobated the plan and refused their consent. The young men faithfully kept Lafayette's secret. His VOL. V. LL situation was more fortunate, as his property was at his own disposal, ' and he possessed an annual revenue of nearly two hundred thousand lines.

He next explained his intention to the Count de Broglie, who told him that his project was so chimerical and fraught with so many hazards, without a prospect of the least advantage, that he could not for a moment regard it with favor, nor encourage him with any advice, which should prevent him from abandoning it immediately. When Lafayette found him thus determined, he requested that at least he would not betray him, for he was resolved to go to America. The Count de Broglie assured him, that his confidence was not misplaced; but, said he, " I have seen your uncle die in the wars of Italy, I witnessed your father's death at the battle of Minden, and I will not be accessory to the ruin of the only remaining branch of the family." He then used all his powers of argument and persuasion to divert Lafayette from his purpose, but in vain. Finding his determination unalterable, the Count de Broglie said, as he could render him no aid, he would intro-

duce him to the Baron de Kalb, who he knew was seeking an opportunity to go to America, and whose experience and counsels might be valuable.

Through this channel Lafayette procured an interview with Silas Deane, who explained to him the state of things in America, and gave him encouragement. Deane was formal, spoke little French, and the conversation was not very copious. As he had not yet been acknowledged in any public character, and was surrounded by the British ambassador's spies, it was thought advisable, that, to avoid suspicion, no more interviews should take place. The affair was afterwards managed by the intervention of Mr. Cannichael. An agreement was at length concluded, by the terms of which the Marquis de Lafayette was to join the American service, and to receive from Congress the appointment of major-general. A vessel was about to be despatched with arms and other military supplies for the American army, in which it was proposed he should take passaire.

At this juncture came the news of the evacuation of New York, the loss of Fort Washington, the retreat across Jersey, and the numerous disasters attending the campaign. The friends of America were in despair. The plan of sending a vessel with munitions of war was abandoned. Lafayette was advised to give up the scheme, and not to make so hopeless a sacrifice in an adventure, that at best must end in utter disappointment. These representations and prospects, so far from disheartening him, rather increased his ardor in the pursuit of his object. " My zeal and love of liberty," said be, " have perhaps been hitherto the prevailing motives; but now I see a chance for usefulness, which I had not anticipated. I have money; I will purchase a ship, which shall convey to America myself, my companions, and the freight for Congress." By this time Franklin and Arthur Lee had joined Deane as commissioners. To a proposal so disinterested and generous they could not object; they could only admire the spirit which dictated it; and he hastened immediately to put it in execution.

He entrusted his secret to Dubois-Martin, secretary to the Count de Broglie, whom he despatched to Bordeaux, with instructions to purchase a vessel. This was done; but the vessel wanted repairs, and other preparations were necessary. To prevent discovery during the delay in getting things ready, he took the opportunity to fulfil a previous engagement, which was now claimed by the Prince de Poix, to visit England in company with him. The two friends arrived in London, where they received many marks of civility and attention from the King and persons of rank. It was the policy of the ministers at this time to make it appear, that a good understanding existed between the English and French courts, and the visit of these young noblemen was a circumstance favorable to that end. They stayed about three weeks in London, when Lafayette received intelligence that his vessel was ready at' Bordeaux, and he returned to France; but not without some displeasure on the part of the Marquis de Noailles, the French ambassador in London, who thought his departure too abrupt and unceremonious. The British King and ministry always supposed, that the Marquis de Noailles was acquainted with Lafayette's design to go to America during this visit. But this was a mistake. Lafayette has ofien been heard to say, that neither the Marquis de Noailles nor any other individual in London had knowledge of his purpose. British writers have also charged him with having gone there to obtain information, which should be useful to the Americans. This suspicion is equally without foundation. So far from taking advantage of his situation for such a purpose, his delicacy restrained him from making such a use of his opportunities, as would, under other circumstances, have been particularly agreeable to him. It was on this ground alone, that he declined accepting a proposal to visit the naval armament at Portsmouth, which was then fitting out for America.

He did not enter Paris on his return, but went to Passy, where he remained concealed, and saw only Segur and a very few other friends. After three days he set off for Bordeaux; but on arriving there he found that his vessel was not entirely ready. He soon discovered, also, that his precautions had not been effectual, that his departure was known at Versailles, and that an arrest by order of the King would immediately follow him. He adopted the only mode of escape, that of setting sail without delay. He proceeded to Passage, the nearest port in Spain, where he proposed to wait for his ship's papers. He had hardly reached that harbour, when two officers arrived by land from Bordeaux, with a *Icttrc de cachet* from the King prohibiting his departure. At the same time came letters from the ministers and his family, insisting on his return. Lord Stormont's spies had detected his movements, and that ambassador had communicated the intelligence to Lafayette's fatherin-law. The *kttrc de cachet* commanded him to repair to Marseilles, and there wait for further orders. The letters from the ministers were severe, charging him with violating his oath of allegiance to the King, and of rashly committing an act, which might involve the government with other powers. His family censured him in a tone of pointed reprimand, assuring him that his conduct, if persisted, '"» would ruin both them and himself. It must be observed, however, that his wife did not join in this outcry; she approved of his enterprise from the beginning, and threw no obstacles in his way. The family were preparing for a tour in Italy, and the design was, that he should meet them at Marseilles, go with them on this tour, and thus be diverted from his American project.

From Passage he was obliged to return with the officers to Bordeaux, where he reported himself to the commandant. He wrote to the ministers and his friends, replying to their charges, and vindicating himself in the best manner he could. He reminded them, that an officer in the King's Irish regiment had been permitted to go over and join the British forces, and added that be saw no reason why the same privilege should not be allowed to other officers in regard to the Americans, who were an independent people, and contending for just principles. Indeed, this had already been done in the case of Duportail, and three other engineers belonging to the King's army, who had obtained special permission to enter the American service. These reasons and precedents he thought would justify him in asking the same permission. To his family he wrote, that his resolution was fixed, and he hoped they would aid his views. As to his oath of allegiance, he observed to some of his correspondents, that when the ministers should be faithful to their pledges to the people, they might with a better grace talk about a violation of an oath to the government. This hint got to the ears of the ministers and gave offence.

In short, he had little hope of succeeding in his petition; and he accordingly wrote to M. Cogny, a particular friend very intimate at court, requesting him to watch carefully what passed, and, should he be convinced a prohibition would be issued against his American plan, to let him know it with all possible despatch. He sent a trusty courier to Versailles, who speedily came back with a letter from Cogny informing him, that there was much excitement against him at court, that the British ambassador had made strong representations, and that there was not the remotest prospect of his receiving a favorable reply.

Lafayette lost no time in taking the course, on which he had already resolved. He intimated to the commandant, that he would proceed to Marseilles, and commenced the journey. An officer by the name of Mauroy, who wished to visit America, was his companion. They entered the carriage together; but, as soon as they left the environs of Bordeaux, Lafayette disguised himself in the dress of a courier, mounted a horse, and rode forward to procure relays at the post-houses. They soon diverged from the road to Marseilles, and took the direction to Bayonne. In that city they were obliged to stop for two or three hours. While Mauroy executed some important commission of business, Lafayette lay on the straw in the stable. Fresh horses were procured, and they continued their route, Lafayette still preserving the costume and character of a courier. At the little village of St. Jean de Luz, while calling for horses, he was detected by the daughter of the man who kept the post-house. She had seen him a few days before on his way from Passage to Bordeaux. He made a signal to the girl to keep silence, which she understood; and when Lafayette's pursuers came up, and inquired if such a person had passed, she was faithful to the signal, replying that a carriage had gone along, but it contained no such person as they described. This answer occasioned much uncertainty as to the object of their pursuit, and it is believed to have been the cause of his not being overtaken by them before he reached his vessel at Passage. A favorable wind wafted him quickly to sea. Baron de Kalb, and eleven other officers of different ranks seeking service in America, constituted his retinue.

His time was employed on the voyage, as far as a severe attack of seasickness would permit, in studying the English language, and reading books on military tactics. The ship's papers were VOL. V. 57 LL.

taken out for the French Islands in the West Indies, and the Captain sailed in that direction. While on the voyage Lafayette told him, that it was his intention to run directly for the coast of America. This was promptly declined by the Captain, on the ground that the papers protected the ship only to the French Islands; and should they be taken by the English in attempting to go into an American port, they would all inevitably be sent prisoners to Halifax, and detained in captivity no one could tell how long. This was a dilemma, which Lafayette had not anticipated, and he finally told the Captain that the vessel was his property, that every person on board ran an equal risk, that he was determined at all hazards to sail by the shortest course to the American coast, and that, if he refused to put the vessel upon that track, he would deprive him of the command and give it to the

nest officer. The Captain acceded, but with a reluctance, which made Lafayette suspect there were other motives besides personal apprehension; and he found, on inquiry, that the Captain had goods in the ship to the amount of eight thousand dollars. When this was known, he offered a pledge of security, that in case they should be captured, and the cargo lost, he would pay this amount to the Captain, although the goods had been put on board without his authority. He also feared, what proved to be true, that orders would be seat to the West Indies to arrest him.

At some distance from the coast a privateer was descried making towards them. It was supposed to be English, and hasty preparations were made for defence; but it turned out to be American, and no molestation was offered. Land was soon discovered, and they approached the shore near Georgetown in South Carolina, having fortunately escaped two British cruisers. The same strong north easterly wind, which brought the French vessel to the coast, had driven the cruisers to the south, and thus left an open passage far that vessel, which otherwise would probably have been captured.

It was dark before they came so near the shore as to be able to land. Lafayette and some of the officers entered the ship's boat, which was rowed to the beach. Here they debarked, and a distant light served to guide them. When they arrived near the boose whence the light proceeded, the dogs growled and barked, and the people within supposed them to be a party of marauders from the enemy's vessels. Before gaining admittance, it was demanded of them who they were and what they wanted. Baron de Kalb was their interpreter, he having before been in America, and acquired some facility in speaking the English language. At length suspicions were removed, and the strangers were received with a cordial welcome and a generous hospitality. Lafayette retired to rest, rejoiced that he had at last attained the haven of his wishes, and was safely landed in America beyond the reach of his pursuers. The morning was beauti-

ful. The novelty of every thing around him, the room, the bed with mosquito-curtains, the black servants who came to ascertain his wants, the beauty and strange appearance of the country as he saw it from his window, clothed in luxuriant verdure, all conspired to produce a magical effect, and to impress him with indescribable sensations. He found himself in the house of Major Huger, a gentleman not more remarkable for his hospitality, than for his worth and highly respectable character. Major Huger provided horses to convey him and his companions to Charleston. The vessel likewise went into Charleston harbour. A letter written by Lafayette to his wife will explain his situation and feelings at this time.

" Charleiton, 19 June, 1777.

" My last letter to you, my dear love, has informed you, that I arrived safely in this country, after having suffered a little from sea-sickness during the first weeks of the voyage; that I was then, the morning after I landed, at the house of a very kind officer; that I had been nearly two months on the passage, and that I wished to set off immediately. It spoke of every thing most interesting to my heart; of my sorrow at parting from you, and of our dear children; and it said, besides, that I was in excellent health. I give you this abstract of it, because the English may possibly amuse themselves by seizing it on its way. I have such confidence in my lucky star, however, that I hope it will reach you. This same star has befriended me, to the astonishment of every body here. Trust to it yourself, and be assured that it ought to calm all your fears. I landed after having sailed several days along a coast, which swarmed with hostile vessels. When I arrived, every body said that my vessel must inevitably be taken, since two British frigates blockaded the harbour. I even went so far as to send orders to the captain, both by land and sea, to put the men on shore and set fire to the ship, if not yet too late. By a most wonderful good fortune, a gale obliged the frigates to stand out to sea for a short time. My vessel came in at noon-day, without meeting friend or foe.

" At Charleston I have met General Howe, an American officei now in the service. The Governor of the State is expected this evening from the country. All with whom I wished to become acquainted here, have shown me the greatest politeness and attention. I feel entirely satisfied with my reception, although I have not thought it best to go into any detail respecting my arrangements and plans. I wish first to see Congress. I hope to set out for Philadelphia in two days. Our route is more than two hundred and fifty leagues by land. We shall divide ourselves into small parties. I have already purchased horses and light carriages for the journey. Some French and American vessels are here, and are to sail together to-morrow morning, taking advantage of a moment when the frigates are out of sight. They are armed, and have promised me to defend themselves stoutly against the small privateers, which they will certainly meet. I shall distribute my letters among the different ships.

" I will now tell you about the country and its inhabitants. They are as agreeable as my enthusiasm had painted them. Simplicity of manners, kindness, love of country and of liberty, and a delightful equality every where prevail. The wealthiest man and the poorest are on a level; and, although there are some large fortunes, I challenge any one to discover the slightest difference between the manners of these two classes respectively towards each other. I first saw the country life at the house of Major Huger. I am now in the city, where every thing is very much after the English fashion, except that there is more simplicity, equality, cordiality, and courtesy here than in England. The city of Charleston is one of the handsomest and best built, and its inhabitants among the most agreeable, that I have ever seen. The American women are very pretty, simple in their manners, and exhibit a neatness, which is every where cultivated even more studiously than in England. What most charms me is, that all the citizens are brethren. In America, there are no poor, nor even what we call peasantry. Each individual has his own

honest property, and the same rights as the most wealthy landed proprietor. The inns are very different from those of Europe; the host and hostess sit at table with yon, and do the honors of a comfortable meal; and, on going away, you pay your bill without higgling. When one does not wish to go to an inn, there are country-houses where the title of a good American is a sufficient passport to all those civilities paid in Europe to one's friend.

" As to my own reception, it has been most agreeable in every quarter; and to have come with me secures the most flattering welcome. I have just passed five hours at a grand dinner, gives in honor of me by an individual of this city. Generals Howe and Moultrie, and several officers of my suite, were present. We drank healths and tried to talk English. I begin to speak it a little. To-morrow I shall go with these gentlemen to call on the Governor of the State, and make arrangements for my departure. The next day the commanding officers here will show me the city and its environs, and then I shall set out for the army.

" Considering the pleasant life I lead in this country, my sympathy with the people, which makes me feel as much at ease in their society as if I had known them for twenty years, the similarity between their mode of thinking and my own, and my love of liberty and of glory, one might suppose that I am very happy. But you are not with me; my friends are not with me; and there is no happiness for me far from you and them. I ask you, if you still love me; but I put the same question much oftener to myself, and my heart always responds, Yes. I am impatient beyond measure to hear from you. I hope to find letters at Philadelphia. My only fear is, that the privateer, which is to bring them, may be captured on her passage. Although I suppose I have drawn upon me the special displeasure of the English, by taking the liberty to depart in spite of them, and by landing in their very face, yet I confess they will not be in arrears with me, should they capture this vessel, my cherished hope, on which I so fondly

depend for letters from you. Write frequent and long letters. You do not know the full extent of the joy with which I shall receive them. Embrace Henrietta tenderly. May I say embrace tenderly our *children?* The father of these poor children is a rover, but a good and honest man at heart; a good father, who loves his family dearly, and a good husband, who loves his wife with all his heart.

" Remember me to your friends and my own, to the dear society, once the society of the court, but which by the lapse of time has become the society of the *Woodrn Sieord.* We republicans think it all the better. I must leave oft" for want of paper and time; and if I do not repeat to you ten thousand times that I love you, it is not from any want of feeling, but from modesty; since I have the presumption to hope, that I have already convinced you of it. The night is far advanced, and the heat dreadful. I am devoured by insects; so, you see, the best countries have their disadvantages. Adieu.

" Lafayette."

All things being in readiness, the party left Charleston and travelled to Philadelphia, with as much expedition as the extreme heat of the weather and the badness of the roads would permit. They visited Governor Caswell in North Carolina, and stopped a short time at Annapolis in Maryland. Here they became acquainted with Major Brice, to whom they had a letter from Carmichael, and who was afterwards Lafayette's aid-de-camp. The vessel had been left at Charleston, where it was loaded with rice for the French market It foundered in going out of the harbour, and both the vessel and cargo were lost.

When Lafayette arrived in Philadelphia he put his letters into the hands of Mr. Lovell, Chairman of the Committee of Foreign Affairs. He called the next day at the Hall of Congress, and Mr. Lovell came out to him and said, that so many foreigners had offered themselves for employment, that Congress was embarrassed with their applications, and he was sorry to inform him there was very little hope of his success. Lafayette suspected his papers had not been read, and he immediately sat down and wrote a note to the President of Congress, in which he desired to be permitted to serve in the American army on two conditions; first, that he should receive no pay; secondly, that he should act as a volunteer. These terms were so different from those demanded by other foreigners, and presented so few obstacles on the ground of an interference with American officers, that they were at once accepted. His rank, zeal, perseverance, and disinterestedness overcame every objection, and he was appointed a major-general in the American army mote than a month before he had reached the age of twenty.

Washington was expected shortly in Philadelphia, and the young general concluded to wait his arrival before he went to head-quarters. The first introduction was at a dinner party, where several members of Congress were present. When they were about to separate, Washington took Lafayette aside, spoke to him very kindly, complimented him upon the noble spirit he had shown and the sacrifices he had made in favor of the American cause, and then told him, that he should be pleased if he would make the quarters of the Commander-in-chief his home, establish himself there whenever he thought proper, and consider himself at all times as one of his family; adding, in a tone of pleasantry, that he could not promise him the luxuries of a court, or even the conveniences, which his former habits might have rendered essential to his comfort, but, since he had become an American soldier, he would doubtless contrive to accommodate himself to the character he had assumed, and submit with a good grace to the custom), manners, and privations of a republican army. If Lafayette was made happy by his success with Congress, his joy was redoubled by this flattering proof of friendship and regard on the part of the Commander-in-chief. His horses and equipage were immediately sent to camp, and ever afterwards, even when he had the command of a division, he

kept up his intimacy at head-quarters, and enjoyed all the advantages of a member of the General's family. The day after the dinner, Washington inspected the fortifications in the Delaware River, and invited Lafayette to accompany him.

Being now in the army, he continued with it as a volunteer, though without any command, till the battle of the Brandy wine. He there' engaged in the hottest part of the action, exposed himself to danger, and exhibited a conspicuous example of coolness and courage. While the troops were retreating in disorder, he dismounted, entered the ranks, and endeavoured to rally them. As he was performing this service a musket-ball passed through his leg; but the wound did not retard his efforts, till his aid told him, that the blood was running from his boot, and then he mounted his horse. He met a surgeon in the rear, who put a slight bandage around his leg, and he rode to Chester. The soldiers, in the mean time, were retreating in a hurried and straggling manner; and, regardless of himself, his first precaution was to place a guard near the bridge, at the entrance of the village, with orders to stop all the retreating soldiers at that place. His wound was then dressed, and the next morning he was taken to Philadelphia. The following letter to his wife was written the day after the action.

" Philadelphia, 12 September, 1777.

" I write you a few words, my dear love, by some French officers, who came over with me, but who, not receiving any appointment in the army, are about returning to France. I begin by telling you, that I am well, because I must end by telling you that we fought yesterday in good earnest, and that we were not the stronger party. The Americans, after a long and brave resistance, were at last routed. As I was attempting to rally them, the English honored me with a musket-ball, which wounded me slightly in the leg; but this is nothing; the ball touched neither bone nor artery, and 1 shall escape without further inconvenience, than having to keep my bed for some time, a thing which puts me much out of humor. I hope you will

not be alarmed; indeed this is a reason why you should be less so than before, since it keeps me from the field for some time as I intend to take good care of myself; be very sure of it.

" I think this affair will lead to unpleasant consequences, which we must try to repair. You must have received many letters from me, unless the English bear the same spite to my letters as to my legs. I have as yet received only one from you, and I long for news. Adieu. I am forbidden to write longer at present. For some days past I have not had time for sleep; the last night was employed in our retreat, and in my journey to this place, where I am very well taken care of. Let my friends know that I am well. Many tender regards to Madame d'Ayen; many compliments to my sister. The officers will depart shortly; they will see you; how happy they are. Good night; I love you more than ever.

" Lafayette."

From Philadelphia he proceeded to Bristol. Mr. Henry Laurens on his way to Yorktown, after the adjournment of Congress, took the route through Bristol, and conveyed Lafayette in his carriage to Bethlehem. This act of kindness was long remembered. When Laurens was a prisoner in the Tower of London, the Marchioness de Lafayette wrote a touching letter in his behalf to the Count de Vergennes, recounting his deeds of humanity and benevolence to the Marquis, and soliciting the aid of the French court to procure his release. Lafayette remained at Bethlehem about two months, till his wound was sufficiently healed to enable him to join the army, and a few days afterwards he was placed at the head of a division.

No. II. p. 60.

BATTLE OF THE BRANDYWINE.

A large part of the ill success of this battle has been ascribed by historians to the mistakes of General Sullivan, in his command of the right wing of the army, and particularly to his want of vigilance in reconnoitring the movements of the enemy in that quarter. The facts of the case, in regard to General Sullivan, do not seem to have been hitherto well understood, as will appear by the extracts, which I am about to make from unpublished papers.

On the 9th of September the American army took post at Chad's Ford, on the east bank of the Brandywine River; and the next day General Sullivan was ordered to take a station higher up the river with the right wing of the army. The left wing, consisting of Pennsylvania militia under General Armstrong, was stationed at a ford two miles below; and General Washington commanded the centre at Chad's Ford, where the main attack was expected. General Howe with the whole British army arrived at Kennet Square, seven miles from Chad's Ford, on the 10th; and the next day, very early in the morning, he commenced his march towards the Brandywine in two columns, one of them under General Knyphausen, proceeding directly to Chad's Ford, and the other under Cornwallis taking a circuitous route by what was called the Lancaster Road, to Trimble's Ford and Jeffrey's Ford above the fork of the Brandywine. Between Chad's Ford and the fork of the river there were several other fords, which General Sullivan was ordered to watch; and he was directed to communicate to the Commander-inchief any intelligence he should obtain, respecting the approach of the enemy towards cither of those fords. It should be kept in mind, however, that, although it was supposed the British would attempt to cross some of these fords, it seems never to have been suspected, that they would make so large a circuit as to cross the two branches of the stream above their junction; whereas the actual plan of Sir William Howe was to make a feigned attack with one column at Chad's Ford, while the other should march by the way of Trimble's Ford and Jeffrey's Ford, two or three miles above the fork, and come upon Washington's army in the rear of the right flank. This scheme was executed with entire success.

As the misfortunes chiefly happened in the quarter where General Sullivan commanded, it was natural perhaps for the public, in the moment of disappoint-

ed hope, to regard them as resulting from his mismanagement. He had enemies in Congress ready to take advantage of these circumstances. Three days after the action Mr. Burke, a delegate from North Carolina, brought against him the following charges.

" 1. That he was several days posted on the right wing of the army, previous to the battle of the Brandywine.

" 2. That he was early in the day cautioned by the Commander-in-chief to be particularly attentive to the enemy's motions, who he supposed would attempt to cross the river, and that he was furnished with light troops for that purpose, and that he suffered the enemy to come upon him by a route he never expected.

" 3. That he conveyed false intelligence to the General, which caused him to alter his position, and brought on a defeat.

" 4. That when his mistake was afterwards discovered, he VOL. V. 58 MM brought up his troops by a circuitous march, and in a disorder from which they never recovered."

Upon the strength of these charges, and some others relating to other particulars, Congress voted that General Sullivan should be recalled from the army till an inquiry should be made into his conduct. The recall was suspended at the request of General Washington, who said the services of General Sullivan were at that critical moment absolutely necessary in the army, as there was already a deficiency of major-generals, Arnold and Lincoln having recently been sent to the northern army.

Meantime General Sullivan took measures to vindicate himself For this purpose he obtained certificates from the Commander-inchief and the other principal officers. In writing to General Washington on the subject, October 24th, he said;

" With respect to the first of these charges, your Excellency knows, that, very late in the day before the action, I was ordered to Brenton's Ford, and to send off a party to a ford a mile and a half above me, the name of which I do not recollect, another to Jones's Ford,

and another to Buffenton's Ford, a mile and a half above Jones's. Upon my asking whether there were no fords higher np, I was informed in presence of your Excellency, that there was none within twelve miles, to cross at which the enemy must make a long circuit through a very bad road, and that all the light horse of the army were ordered to the right to watch the enemy's motions in that quarter. I had no orders to take any care above Buffenton's Ford, nor had I light troops or light horse for the purpose. I have never had any light horse with me since I joined the army. I found four with Major Taylor, when I came to Brenton's Ford, two of whom I sent off with Colonel Hazen to Jones's Ford; nor did I see any till Major Jameson came to me the day of the battle at nine o'clock. On the day J came to that ford, I detached the Delaware regiment to Buffenton's; and as soon as I saw Major Jameson I advised him to send an officer over to the Lancaster road, who returned and said no enemy had passed that way. Major Jameson said he came from the right of the army, and I might depend there was no enemy there. I however sent a captain off, who never returned, till I had the intelligence from another quarter."

The following are the different notes of intelligence, which passed through General Sullivan's hands to General Washington during the day of the action.

" Great Valley Road, Eleven o'clock, A. M. " Dear General, " A large body of the enemy, from every account five thousand, with sixteen or eighteen field-pieces, marched along this road just now. This road leads to Taylor's Ferry and Jeffrey's Ferry, on the Brandywine, and to the Great Valley, at the Sign of the Ship, on the Lancaster Road to Philadelphia. There is also a road from the Brandywine to Chester by Dilworth Town. We arc close in their rear with about seventy men. Captain Simpson lay in ambush with twenty men, and gave them three rounds within a small distance, in which two of his men were wounded, one mortally. I believe General Howe is with this party, as Joseph

Galloway is here known by the inhabitants, with whom he spoke, and told them that General Howe was with him. Yours,

"James Ross, *Lieutenant-Colonel.*"

This intelligence was in the main correct, and General Washington immediately ordered General Sullivan to cross the Brandywine and attack this division of the British army, while he should himself cross at Chad's Ford, and commence a general attack at that place. It was at the same time supposed, however, that the column, which had been seen on the Lancaster Road, would attempt to cross at some of the fords below the fork. While preparations were making to execute the last order from the Commander-inchief, General Sullivan wrote to him the following note.

"Brenton's Ford, 11 September. " Dear General, " Since I sent you the message by Major Moore, I saw Major Spear of the militia, who came this morning from a tavern called Martin's, at the fork of the Brandywine. He came from thence to Welch's Tavern, and heard nothing of the enemy about the fork of the Brandywine, and is confident they are not in that quarter; so that Colonel Hazen's information must be wrong. I have sent to that quarter, to know whether there is any foundation for the report, and shall give your Excellency the earliest information.

" I am, &lc.

"john Scllitan."

This note caused the order for crossing the Brandywine to be suspended, and it had a most important effect on the issue of the action. The next intelligence was from Colonel Bland, who was reconnoitring with a party of light horse.

" A quarter put One o'clock. "Sir, " I have discovered a party of the enemy on the heights, just on the right of the two Widow Davis's, who live close together on the road called the Fork Road, about half a mile to the right of the Meeting-house (Birmingham). There is a higher hill in their front.

" Theodoric Bland."

This note was enclosed to General Washington, with another from General Sullivan.

" Two o'clock, P. M. " Dear General, " Colonel Bland has this moment sent me word, that the enemy are in the rear of my right about two miles, coming down. There are, he says, about two brigades of them. He also says he saw a dust back in the country for above an hour. I am, Ate.

" John Sullivan."

The exact position of the enemy was now ascertained. The column under Lord Cornwallis, after a march of seventeen miles from Kennct Square, had crossed the two branches of the Brandy wine above the fork, and was now marching down the road on the east side of the river towards Dilworth, and had arrived within two miles of Sullivan's right. An extract from a letter written by him to Congress, accompanying the papers intended for his vindication, will add further explanations.

" It was ever my opinion," he says, " that the enemy would come round on our right flank. This opinion I often gave the General. I wrote to him that morning, that it was clearly my opinion. I sent him two messages to the same purpose in the forenoon, and the first intelligence I received, that they were actually coming that way, I instantly communicated to him; after which, the General sent me word to cross the Brandy wine with my division, and attack the enemy's left, while the army crossed below me to attack their right. This I was preparing to do, when Major Spear came to me and informed me, that he was from the upper country, that he had come in the road, where the enemy most have passed to attack our right, and that there was not the least appearance of them in that quarter; and he added, that General Washington had sent him out for the purpose of discovering whether the enemy were in that quarter. The account was confirmed by Sergeant Tucker of the light-horse, sent by me on purpose to make discoveries; and who had passed, as he said, to the Lancaster Road. This intelligence did by no means alter my opinion, which was founded, not upon any knowledge I had of the facts, but upon an apprehension, that General Howe would take that advan-

tage, which any good officer in his situation would have done. I considered, however, that if my opinion, or the intelligence I had sent to the General, should bring him into a plan of attacking the enemy on the advantageous heights of which they were possessed, and a defeat should thence follow, I should be justly censured for withholding from him part of the intelligence I had received, and thereby brought on the defeat of our army. I therefore sat down and wrote Major Spear's account from his own mouth, and forwarded it to his Excellency by a light-horseman, and ordered the Major to follow himself. I never made a comment, or gave any opinion upon the matter.

" Colonel Harrison, a member from Virginia, is possessed of a copy of the letter, as the General's aid-de-camp informed me. I beg Congress to see it, and then judge whether I could have been excused for withholding that intelligence, merely because my opinion did not coincide with the declaration. Had the General crossed over, and left his own advantageous post, and found the whole British army well posted in his front, and his army put to rout, having a river unfordable in his rear, except in one or two places, and most of his troops pushed into it, which must inevitably have been the case, if he was defeated; I say, if this had all happened, which was at least possible, and he had afterwards found out, that I had received and withheld the intelligence, which might have prevented this misfortune, and demanded my reason, I believe I never should have been able to give one, which would be satisfactory to him, to Congress, or to the world. I know it to be part of my duty to give him every intelligence I receive, without withholding any part of it because it does not coincide with my own opinion; and I as well know it is exceedingly hard to be censured for doing my duty, which has been too much the case with me, since I have been in the army."

As to the fourth charge, he observed, " When I received orders to march, I marched in the most direct road to the enemy, and met them a mile from the place where I had before been posted, with my out-guards flying before them. " Lord Cornwallis had ample time to form his men for action. At a quarter past one o'clock Colonel Bland saw his advanced guard about half a mile MM from the Birmingham Meeting-house, very near the spot where the action commenced a little after fonr o'clock. General Howe, in his official account of the battle, says his whole column had passed Jeffrey's Ford at two o'clock, and of course they must all have been on the ground near the Meeting-house at least an hour before the action began. Meantime General Sullivan was waiting for the intelligence of the enemy's approach to reach General Washington at Chad's Ford, and for orders to be sent back in return. This necessary delay enabled Cornwallis to choose his ground and prepare for the engagement, which was done by forming his men in two lines occupying an elevated position, with a brigade in reserve, and a regiment still further in the rear. When General Sullivan came up, therefore, with three divisions of the army, his own, Stephen's, and Stirling's, and began to form them into a line about half a mile in front of the enemy, Cornwallis commenced the action before this manoeuvre could be completed, threw Sullivan's troops into confusion, and caused a precipitate and irregular retreat through the woods in their rear. Many of them were rallied half a mile to the northward of Dilworth, and a second rencounter ensued between this party and the troops of the enemy's left wing, who had followed. The conflict was short and spirited, but a superior force compelled the Americans again to retire. The British right wing got entangled in the woods, and did not come again into the engagement after the first onset at Birmingham Meetinghouse.

As soon as Knyphausen knew by the firing, that Cornwallis was engaged, he pushed across the Brandywine at Chad's Ford, and commenced the attack in earnest on the American intrenchmenta. He was repelled by Wayne at the head of the division lately commanded by Lincoln, and for some time the con-

test was warm and well sustained.

Greene's division, with which was General Washington, advanced towards Dilworth, that it might be in a situation to render aid either to Sullivan or Wayne as occasion might require. The action closed at a position about a mile beyond Dilworth towards Chester, where a detachment from Greene's division took post, and covered the retreat of Sullivan's troops. There was sharp fighting at this place; but night came on, the enemy ceased from their pursuit, and the whole American army found their way to Chester.

After a due investigation, Congress acquitted General Sullivan with honor. Deborre, a French general of thirty-five years' ' commanded in Sullivan's division the brigade, which first broke and gave way. Congress voted an inquiry into his conduct, at which he took umbrage and resigned his commission. In his letter to Congress he complained of hard usage, averring that he did all in his power to rally his men, being wounded in the attempt, and said, if the American troops would run away, it was unjust to censure him for the consequences. There was some truth perhaps in this remonstrance; but Deborre, by his ignorance of the character and habits of the American people, had rendered himself very unpopular in the army, and Congress accepted his resignation without reluctance.

No. III. p. 83.

BATTLE OP GERMANTOWN.

Writers have found much difficulty in attempting to describe this battle in such a manner, as to present a satisfactory explanation of its different parts. This has been chiefly owing to the extreme darkness of the morning, which rendered it impossible for the officers themselves to obtain a knowledge of any other movements, than those in which they were immediately concerned. The following letters of General Sullivan, General Stephen, and Colonel Howard, hitherto unpublished, will afford some additional particulars for elucidating the subject.

GENERAL SULLIVAN TO MESHECH WEARE, PRESIDENT OF

NEW HAMPSHIRE.

" Camp, at White Manh, 25 October, 1777. " Sir, " I hope the constant movements of our army, since the battle of Germantown, will apologize for my not having before given you a particular account of this unsuccessful affair. Upon receiving intelligence, that part of the enemy's force was detached for particular purposes, and that their main army lay encamped with their left wing on the west side of the road leading through Germantown, flanked by the Hessian forces, who were encamped on the Schuylkill, and their right on the east side of the road extending to a wood about one mile from the town, with their light infantry encamped in a line in their front, within less than a quarter of a mile of their picket at Mount Airy, — upon this intelligence it was agreed in council, that we should march the night of the 3d instant and attack the enemy in the following manner.

" My own and Wayne's division were to compose the right wing, which I had the honor to command. This wing was to be sustained by the corps of reserve, composed of Nash's and Maxwell's brigades, commanded by Major-General Lord Stirling. The right wing was to be flanked by Conway's brigade, which led the column. The whole of these marched down the Skippack Road, leading over Chestnut Hill into Germantown. General Annstrong, with about a thousand Pennsylvania militia, was to pass down the road, which runs near the Schuylkill, and attack the Hessians, who covered the enemy's left flank. The led wing was composed of Greene's and Stephen's divisions, commanded by Major General Greene, who were to march down the York Road, and attack the enemy's right, while the troops I had the honor to command attacked their left. General MDougall's brigade was to attack their right flank, and Smallwood's division and Forman's brigade of militia were to make a larger circuit and attack the rear of their right wing. The reason of our sending so many troops to attack their right was, because it was supposed, that, if this wing of the enemy could be forced, their army must be pushed into the Schuylkill, or be compelled to surrender. Therefore two thirds of the army at least were detached to oppose the enemy's right.

" The attack was to begin on all quarters at daybreak. Our army left their encampment at Matuchen Hills at nine in the evening, marched all night, and at daybreak the right wing arrived on Chestnut Hill, when one regiment from Conway's brigade, and one from the second Maryland brigade, were detached to Mount Airy, followed by Conway's brigade to attack the enemy's picket at Allen's House. My own division followed in the rear of Conway's, and Wayne's division in the rear of mine. The picket ws soon attacked, and suddenly reinforced by all their light infantry. This compelled General Conway to form his brigade to sustain the attacking regiments, and to repulse the light infantry. They maintained their ground with great resolution till my division was formed to support them. The enemy endeavouring to flank us on the left, I ordered Colonel Ford's regiment to the other side of the road to repulse them, till General Wayne's division arrived; and upon finding that our left wing, which had near four miles further to march than the right, had not arrived, I was obliged to form General Wayne's division on the east of the road to attack the enemy's right. I then directed General Conway to draw off such part of his brigade as was formed in the road, and in front of our right, and to fall into my rear and file off to the right to flank my division; but, the morning being too dark to discover the enemy's movements, and no evidence being given of General Armstrong's arrival, I was obliged to send a regiment from Wayne's, and another from my own division, to keep the enemy from turning our right. I also detached Colonel Moylan's regiment of lighthorse to watch their motions in that quarter.

" This being done, my division were ordered to advance; which they did with such resolution, that the enemy's light infantry were soon compelled to leave the field, and with it their encampment.

They however made a stand at every fence, wall, and ditch they passed, which were numerous. We were compelled to remove every fence, as we passed, which delayed us much in the pursuit. We were soon after met by the left wing of the British army, when a severe conflict ensued; but, our men being ordered to march up with shouldered arms, they obeyed without hesitation, and the enemy retired. I then detached my aid-de-camp. Major Morris, to inform his Excellency, who was in the main road, that the enemy's left wing had given way, and to desire him to order General Wayne to advance against their right. His Excellency immediately detached part of the residue on my right, and part on the left of the road, and directed Wayne's division to advance, which they did with great bravery and rapidity.

" At Chew's House, a mile and a half from where the attack began, Wayne's division came abreast with mine, and passed Chew's House, while mine were advancing on the other side of the main road. Though the enemy were routed, yet they took advantage of every yard, house, and hedge, in their retreat, which caused an incessant fire through the whole pursuit. At this time, which was near an hour and a quarter after the attack began, General Stephen's division fell in with Wayne's on our left, and, soon after, the firing from General Greene's was heard still farther to the left. The left wing of our army was delayed much by General Greene's being obliged to countermarch one of his divisions, before he could begin the attack, as he found the enemy were in a situation very different from what we had before been told. The enemy had thrown a large body of troops into Chew's House, which caused Maxwell's brigade to halt there with some artillery Vol. v. 59 to reduce them. This was found very difficult, as the house, being stone, was almost impenetrable by cannon and sufficient proof against musketry. The enemy defended themselves with great bravery, and annoyed our troops much by their fire. This unfortunately caused many of our

troops to halt, and brought back General Wayne's division, who had advanced far beyond the house, as they were apprehensive that the firing proceeded from the enemy's having defeated my division on the right. This totally uncovered the left flank of my division, which was still advancing against the enemy's led. The firing of General Greene's division was very heavy for more than a quarter of an hour, but then decreased, and seemed to draw farther from us. I am pot sufficiently acquainted with' the facts to determine with precision what was done in that quarter. A regiment commanded by Colonel Mathews advanced with rapidity near the town; but, not being supported by some other regiments, who were stopped by a breastwork near Lucan's Mills, the brave Colonel, after having performed great feats of bravery, and being dangerously wounded in several places, was obliged with about a hundred of his men to surrender.

" My division, with a regiment of North Carolinians commanded by Colonel Armstrong, and assisted by part of Conway's brigade, having driven the enemy a mile and a half below Chew's House, and finding themselves unsupported by any other troops, their cartridges all expended, the force of the enemy on the right collecting to the left to oppose them, being alarmed by the firing at Chew's House so far in their rear, and by the cry of a light-horseman on the right, that the enemy had got round us, and at the same time discovering some troops flying on our right, retired with as much precipitation as they had before advanced, against every effort of their officers to rally them. When the retreat took place, they had been engaged near three hours, which, with the march of the preceding night, rendered them almost unfit for fighting or retreating. We however made a safe retreat, though not a regular one. We brought off all our cannon and all our wounded. Oar loss in the action amounts to less than seven hundred, mostly wounded. We lost some valuable officers, among whom were the brave General Nash, and my two aids-dc-camp, Majors Sherburne and White, whose singular bravery must ever do honor to their memories. Our army rendezvoused at Paulen's Mills, and seems very.desirous of another action. The misfortunes of this day were principally owing to a thick fog, which, being rendered still more so by the smoke of the cannon and musketry, prevented our troops from discovering the motions of the enemy, or acting in concert with each other. I cannot help observing, that with great concern I saw our brave Commander exposing himself to the hottest fire of the enemy in such a manner, that regard to my country obliged me to ride to him, and beg him to retire. He, to gratify me and some others, withdrew a small distance; but his anxiety for the fate of the day soon brought him up again, where he remained till our troops had retreated. I am, &,c.

" John Sullivan."

General 8tepuen To General Washington.

" Camp, 7 October, 1777. " Sir,

" I understand that many officers of my division are highly disobliged at my saying the troops, whom I commanded in an attack on Saturday last, fled from victory; by which expression I by no means intended to charge them with cowardice; many of them I know to be of experienced bravery. But in order to do justice to these officers as well as myself, I am obliged to entreat your Excellency's patience to hear the circumstances of the action, as far as I was concerned on that occasion.

" The two divisions formed the line of battle at a great distance from the enemy, and marched through marshes, woods, and strong fences, before we came up with the enemy. The first party of them that we discovered was on our left. Against them I detached Colonel Mathews, who was nearest to me, and advancing with spirit. To support him I ordered Major Darke, with part of the eighth regiment, sent an aid-de-camp with him, and charged him to attack the enemy in the rear if possible. I have been informed by my aidde-camp, that our troops behaved gallantly, and drove the enemy after a hot rencounter.

" About this time a body of the enemy appeared in front of the right of General Greene's division, and on the left of mine. I led on the men to the attack. They advanced with great cheerfulness, and the enemy were driven back with their artillery. Upon this a reinforcement to the enemy came in sight on their left, when I sent Mr. Black, who acted as aid-de-camp, to order up a body of troops unemployed on my right, to attack the reinforcement. They marched towards the enemy. I understood they were Colonel Spencer's and Colonel Patton's regiments, that moved towards the enemy; and, upon seeing them advance, the troops, who were formerly engaged, pushed the enemy so closely, that I called to them to give them the bayonet. Upon hearing this, the enemy's officers on horseback rode to their rear out of sight, many of their men running after them, whilst a party ran towards our troops crying for quarter. At this flattering juncture, a large corps dressed in blue, mistaking the enemy, who had surrendered, for a party coming up to charge them, as I suppose. took the start. I called out from the front, that they were running from victory, and hastened to them to stop them, but to no purpose.

" Colonel Lewis and Colonel Russell, of General Greene's division. Colonel Wood with his regiment, and Major Campbell of the eighth of my division, behaved gallantly during the action. Colonel Lewis and Colonel Wood kept the field with their regiments, until they were ordered to retire, when the enemy were advancing against them on all quarters. Several other officers may have distinguished themselves, who escaped my notice in the heat of action. I am, &,c.

" Adam Stephen."

The following extract is taken from a letter, written by Colonel John £. Howard to Colonel Pickering, and dated at Baltimore, January 29th, 1827. It was in answer to inquiries made by Colonel Pickering.

" Sullivan's division was composed of the seven Maryland regiments and Hazen's regiment, formed into two brigades under Smallwood and Gist; but neither of those officers was present, they having command of the Maryland militia under General Greene. I was major of the fourth regiment, commanded by Colonel Hall, which was on the extreme left of the division. Sullivan, on the march, followed closely the advance. As we descended into the valley near Mount Airy, the sun rose, but was soon obscured. The British picket at Allen's House had two six-pounders, which were several times fired at the advance, and killed several persons. Sullivan's division in the valley left the road, and moved to the right through fields, and formed in a lane running from Allen's house towards the Schuylkill; our left about two hundred yards from the house. Soon after being formed, we had orders to move on, and advanced through a field to the encampment of the British light infantry in an orchard, where we found them formed to receive us. A close and sharp action commenced, and continued fifteen or twenty minutes, when the British broke and retreated. In our regiment four officers and upwards of thirty men were wounded; and to the best of my recollection several men were killed. In the advance wc had inclined to the left, until we reached the road; and in the action one company, commanded by Captain Daniel Dorsey, crossed the road. It is certain that no other part of the army was up with us at that time.

" Colonel Hall, who was on foot, ordered me to bring up the company that had crossed the road; but, finding them engaged from behind houses with some of the enemy, who I supposed had belonged to the picket, I judged it not proper to call them off, as it would expose our flank. I reported to Colonel Hall, who then desired me to let him have my horse, and said he would bring them up himself. Riding one way, and looking another, the horse ran with him under a cider-press, and he was so hurt that he was taken from the field. I was then left in command of the regiment, as LieutenantColonel Smith some time before had been detached to Fort Mifflin. The enemy by this time had given way; and I pushed on through their encampment, their tents standing, and in the road, before we came opposite to Chew's House, took two six-pounders, which I supposed were those that had been with the picket; but, as the dragropes had been cut and taken away, we could do nothing with them. I had orders to keep to the right of the road; and, as we passed Chew's House, we were fired at from the upper windows, but received no injury. We passed on to the rear of several stone houses, to an orchard, where we were halted by Colonel Hazen. I speak particularly of the left of Sullivan's division, and can say but little of the right, as it was not within my view after we first formed. But I know that in advancing they fell in with some part of the enemy, and had a sharp action, in which Colonel Stone of the first regiment Major Forrest of the third, and many other officers, were wounded.

" Whilst we were halted, the British army were formed in the School-House Lane, directly in our front, six or seven hundred yards from us; but owing to the denseness of the fog, which had greatly increased after the commencement of the action, we could not see them. About the time of the attack on the house, a part of Muhlenberg's and Scott's brigades, from the left wing, particularly the ninth Virginia regiment, commanded by Colonel Mathews, advanced to the eastward of Chew's House, and penetrated to the Market-House. The British General Grey brought from their left the fourth brigade under Agncw, and three battalions of the third, and made an attack upon them, whilst they were engaged with two regiments brought up from the right wing. Thus assailed in front and on both wings, Mathews defended himself with great bravery, and did not surrender until the most of his officers and men were killed or wounded. He himself received several bayonet wounds. Sullivan had previously VOL. V. N N retreated; for we heard the firing at that place, after we had retired some distance."

The distances mentioned by General Sullivan are not precisely accurate. It is one mile only from Mount Airy to Chew's House, and the same distance from the latter place to School-House Lane, which was the utmost limit to which Sullivan's division penetrated, being the central part of Germantown. In the midst of the fog, and in the confusion of battle, it is not to be supposed, that an exact estimate of distances could be formed. A very interesting letter from Colonel Pickering, respecting the Battle of Germantown, is contained in the *North American Review,* Vol. XXIII. p. 425.

When General Washington's letter to Congress, describing the battle, was read, a resolution was unanimously adopted, " That the thanks of Congress be given to General Washington, for his wise and well-concerted attack upon the enemy's army near Germantown, on the 4th instant, and to the officers and soldiers of the army for their brave exertions on that occasion; Congress being well satisfied, that the best designs and boldest efforts may sometimes fail by unforeseen incidents, trusting that, on future occasions, the valor and virtue of the army will, by the blessing of Heaven, be crowned with complete and deserved success." — *Journals, October 8th.*

Although this battle was a failure in a military view, yet, politically considered, it was eminently important. At the first interview between Count Vergennes and the American Commissioners on the subject of a treaty of alliance, December 12th, 1777, the minister, after complimenting them on the prosperous state of affairs in America, and conversing for some time on the situation of the two armies, said, " that nothing had struck him so much as General Washington's attacking and giving battle to General Howe's army; that to bring an army, raised within a year, to this, promised every thing." — *Life of Arthur Lee,* Vol. I. p. 360. It has been usually supposed, that Burgoyne's defeat was the turning point with the French; but the above fact, related by one of the commissioners who was present, is a proof that the operations of General Washington's army had their due weight in the scale.

No. IV. p. 92.

STORMING OF FORTS MONTGOMERY AND

CLINTON.

GENERAL PUTNAM TO GENERAL WASHINGTON.

Fishkill, 8 October, 17T7. Dear General,

It is with the utmost reluctance I now sit down to inform you, that the enemy, after making a variety of movements up and down the North River, landed on the morning of the 4th instant about three thousand men at Tarrytown; and, after making an excursion about five miles up the country, they returned and reembarked the morning following, advanced up near King's Ferry, and landed on the cast side of the river; but in the evening part of them reembarked, and the morning after landed a little above King's Ferry, on the west side. The morning being so exceedingly foggy concealed their scheme, and prevented us from gaining any idea as to the number of troops they landed. In about three hours we discovered a large fire at the ferry, which we imagined to be the store-houses; upon which it was thought they only landed with a view of destroying the said houses. The picket and scouts, which we had out, could not learn the exact number of the enemy that were remaining on the east side of the river; but, from the best accounts, they were about fifteen hundred. At the same time a number of ships and galleys, with about forty flatboats, made every appearance of their intention to land troops, both at Fort Independence and Peekskill Landing. These circumstances, and my strength, being not more than twelve hundred Continental troops and three hundred militia, prevented me from detaching a party to attack the enemy that day on the east side of the river.

After we had thought it impracticable to quit the heights, which we had then possession of, and attack the enemy, Brigadier-General Parsons and myself went to reconnoitre' the ground near the enemy; and on our return from thence we were alarmed with a very heavy and hot firing, both of small arms and cannon, at Fort Montgomery, which immediately convinced me that the enemy had landed a large body of men in the morning at the time and place before-mentioned. Upon which I immediately detached five hundred men to reinforce the garrison; but, before they could possibly cross the river to their assistance, the enemy, far superior in numbers, had possessed themselves of the fort. Never did men behave with more spirit and activity, than our troops upon this occasion. They repulsed the enemy three times, who were in number at least five to one. Governor Clinton and General James Clinton were both present; bat the engagement continuing till dusk gave them both an opportunity, together with several officers and a number of privates, to make their escape. Governor Clinton arrived at Peekskill the same evening about eleven o'clock, and, with the advice of him, General Parsons, and several other officers, it was thought impossible to maintain the post at Peekskill with the force then present, against one that the enemy might, in a few hours, bring on the heights in our rear. It was therefore agreed, that the stores ought to be immediately removed to some secure place, and the troops take post at Fishkill, until a reinforcement of militia shall come to their aid. I am, Ate.

Israel Putnam.

Governor Clinton To General Washington.

New Windior, 9 October, 1777. Dear General,

I have to inform you, that, in consequence of intelligence received by General Putnam from General Parsons (who lay with his brigade at the White Plains), of the enemy's having received a reinforcement from Europe at New York, and that by their movements there was reason to believe they intended an attack on Peekskill, and to possess themselves of the passes in the Highlands, the General immediately wrote to me these circumstances; and, to prevent if, possible the disagreeable consequences, that might arise if the army at the different posts was not timely reinforced, I ordered that part of the militia of this State, that had not already marched to the northward, to move, and part of them to join General Putnam, and the remainder to reinforce the posts of Fort Montgomery and Fort Clinton; but, it being a critical time with the yeomanry, as they had not yet sown their grain, and there being at that time no appearance of the enemy, they were extremely restless and uneasy. They solicited General Putnam for leave to return, and many of them went home without his permission. Urged by these considerations be thought proper to dismiss a part of them.

As I thought it essentially necessary, that they should remain in the field for some time, in order to check the progress of the enemy, should they attempt to put their designs in execution, I issued another order for one half of them immediately to march, part of them to join General Putnam, and a sufficient number to reinforce the forts and the pass at Sydman's Bridge at the mouth of the Clove; and, in order to induce them to turn out with the greater alacrity, I thought it necessary to fix their time of service to one month, at the expiration of which time they were to be relieved by the other half. While this was in agitation, and before a proper arrangement could possibly be made by the respective officers, as to what part of them could serve for the first month, they were not so expeditious as was absolutely necessary, which the event has fully evinced. A number of the enemy's ships made their appearance on the 3d instant in Tarrytown Bay, where they weighed anchor the next day, being joined by several ships of war and transports from New York. They proceeded up the river as high as King's Ferry, and at daybreak on Sunday the 5th landed a considerable body of men on Verplanck's Point.

As I was apprehensive from many circumstances, that an attack on the forts was intended, I despatched Major Logan, an alert officer, who was well acquainted with the ground, on Sunday evening through the mountains to reconnoitre, and if possible gain intelligence of the enemy's motions. The Major returned about nine o'clock on Monday, informing me that, from the best intelligence he could procure, and the rowing of the boats, he had reason to believe they had landed a considerable force on the west side of the river at King's Ferry, and between that and Dunderberg; but, as the morning was foggy, it was impossible to discern them, so as to form any judgment of their numbers. As soon as I had obtained this intelligence, I immediately despatched Lieutenant Jackson with a small party to discover the enemy's movements; but they had not proceeded more than two miles on the Haverstraw Road, when they were attacked by a party of the enemy, who had formed an ambuscade at a place called Doodletown. They immediately retreated after returning the fire. As soon as the firing was heard, I detached Lieutenant-Colonel Bruyn with fifty Continental troops, and as many of the militia under Lieutenant-Colonel MLaughry, to sustain Lieutenant Jackson; the garrison being at that time so weak, that we could not afford them greater aid on that road, and I imagined it would be necessary to send out a party likewise on the road, which leads to the Forest of Dean. The detachments under Colonels Bruyn and MLaughry were soon engaged, but, being too weak to withstand the enemy's great force, retreated to Fort Clinton, disputing the ground inch by inch. Their gallant opposition, and the roughness of the ground, checked the progress of the enemy for some time. While matters were in this situation in the neighbourhood of Fort VOL. V. 60 NN

Clinton, a large body of the enemy were advancing on the road, which leads from the Forest of Dean to Fort Montgomery. As I had only one field-piece at the above fort, I ordered Colonel Lamb of the artillery to send it off to an advantageous post on that road, with a covering party of sixty men, and another of the same number to sustain them, in order to give the enemy a check, and retard their movements till I could receive a reinforcement from General Putnam, to whom I had sent an express for that purpose. This order being immediately complied with, the piece had hardly reached the place of its destination, and the covering party been posted on strong ground, when the enemy were seen advancing with hasty strides; but being unexpectedly annoyed by discharges of grape-shot from the field-piece, and a well-directed fire from the muskets, which made great havoc among them, as we have since been informed, tbey were repeatedly driven back, till, filing off through the woods upon the right and left with a view of surrounding our men, and the handful of brave fellows being alarmed at their critical situation, they were constrained to abandon the field-piece, after rendering it useless to the enemy by spiking it. In order to cover the men who were retreating, and to check the farther progress of the enemy, I ordered out a twelve-pounder, which, being well served with grapeshot, annoyed them greatly, and gave the men an opportunity of retreating into the garrison with very little loss on our side, except that of Captain Fenno, who commanded the field-piece, and was made a prisoner.

This was about two o'clock in the afternoon; and the enemy approached the works and began the attack, which continued with few intervals till about five o'clock, when an officer appeared with a flag. I ordered Lieutenant-Colonel Livingston to meet him without the works and know his business. Colonel Livingston having demanded his rank and business, he was told by the bearer of the flag, that he was Lieutenant-Colonel Campbell, and that he came to demand the surrender of the fort to prevent the effusion of blood. Colonel Livingston replied that he had no authority to treat with him, but, if they would surrender themselves prisoners of war, they might depend upon being well treated; and if they did not choose to accept of those terms they might renew the attack as soon as he should return within the fort, he being determined to defend it to the last extremity. As soon as Lieutenant-Colonel Livingston returned, the attack was renewed with great violence; and, after as obstinate a

resistance as our situation and the weakness of the garrison would admit, having defended the works from two o'clock till the dusk of the i—ing. the enemy, by the superiority of numbers, forced the works on all sides. The want of men prevented us from sustaining and supporting every part, having received no reinforcement from General Putnam.

Our loss, killed, wounded, and prisoners, is not so great as might have been expected, when the strength of the enemy and our weakness are properly considered. My brother was wounded with 'a bayonet. Many officers and men and myself, having the advantage of the enemy by being well acquainted with the ground, were so fortunate as to effect our escape under cover of the night, after the enemy were possessed of all the works. I was so happy as to get into a boat, crossed the river, and immediately waited on General Putnam, with a view of concerting measures for our future operations, to prevent the designs of General Clinton, and impede his progress in facilitating the movements of Burgoyne from the northward. I can assure your Excellency, that I am well convinced, if night had not approached rather too fast to correspond with our wishes, the enemy would have been disappointed in their expectations; as a reinforcement of five hundred men from General Putnam's army were at the east side of the river, ready to pass for our relief, when the works were forced; and many of the militia were in the mountains on their march to join us, had not the communication between us and them been cut off.

I have to add that by some fatality the two Continental frigates were lost, they having been ordered down by General Putnam for the defence of the chain; but, being badly manned, they could not be got off in time, though I ordered the ship Congress to proceed to Fort Constitution the day before the attack, lest she should meet with a disaster; and the ship Montgomery, which lay near the chain, having neither anchor nor cables to secure her, it being the ebb of tide and the wind failing, fell down so near

the chain, that Captain Hodge was constrained to set her on fire to prevent her from falling into the hands of the enemy. The Congress, unfortunately getting aground on the flat near Fort Constitution, shared the same fate. Fort Constitution, being destitute of troops to defend it, was evacuated, after bringing off part of the stores. I am now about three miles from New Windsor, with Colonel Samuel B. Webb's regiment of Continental troops, the remains of Colonel Dubois', about one hundred of Colonel Lamb's regiment, who escaped from the fort, and some militia; and I intend to collect what force I possibly can to oppose the enemy, should they land on this side of the river.

Sir Henry Clinton commanded in person. Governor Tryon, General Vaughan, and two other general officers, were with him. The army who attacked us, by the lowest account, consisted of three thousand, chiefly British and Hessian troops. The garrison of both our posts did not exceed six hundred men, and many of these unarmed militia. The ordinary garrison was thus reduced by detaching Major Moffat with two hundred men to the post at Sydman's Bridge, and Colonel Malcom's regiment being ordered from thence, and sixty men on Anthony's Nose by General Putnam's orders, received the day before the action. I have only to add, that where great losses are sustained, however unavoidable, public censure is generally the consequence to those who are immediately concerned. If in the present instance this should be the case, I wish, so far as relates to Fort Montgomery and its dependencies, it may fall on me alone; for I should be guilty of the greatest injustice, were I not to declare, that the officers and men under me of the different corps behaved with the greatest spirit and bravery. I am, &c.

George Clinton.
No. V. p. 94.
DUCHY'S LETTER.

The Reverend Jacob Duche was an Episcopal clergyman of Philadelphia, celebrated as an eloquent and popular preacher. He was descended from a most respectable family, and educated at the university in that city. So captivating was his eloquence, aided by a harmonious voice and elegance of person, that he was considered by many to rival Whitefield. At the beginning of the revolution he took an active part on the side of the American whigs, and opened the first Congress with a prayer at the request of that body. He also preached the funeral sermon of Peyton Randolph, the first President, and afterwards a sermon before Congress on the occasion of a public fast. In these performances his sentiments were patriotic, and so highly approved, that Congress invited him to become their chaplain. In this station he continued for several months, and retired from it on account of ill health and his other duties.

A few weeks after Washington was appointed Commander-in-chief, he preached a discourse to Colonel Dickinson's first battalion of city troops, which was printed, and which was dedicated to General Washington. In a letter, accompanying a copy of the discourse, he wrote, " If the manner in which I have treated the subject should have the least good influence upon the hearts and actions of the military freemen of America, or should add one more virtuous motive to those, by which I trust they are already actuated, it will be the best return I can receive from my fellow citizens for this labor of love. I have long been an admirer of your amiable character, and was glad of this opportunity of paying you my little tribute of respect." The whole tenor of his conduct proved the sincerity of these professions, and his devotedness to the American cause.

It was with the greatest surprise, therefore, that, a few days after the British took possession of Philadelphia, General Washington received from him a long letter of a most extraordinary character. It not only contained, in substance, an abjuration of all his former opinions, but severe and illiberal animadversions on Congress, and the leaders in the cause of freedom, censuring alike their motives and conduct. Washington, he said, was the only person

who had power to stop the current, which was fast hurrying the country to inevitable ruin; and on him he called, in the voice of entreaty and almost of admonition, to " represent to Congress the indispensable necessity of rescinding the hasty and ill-advised Declaration of Independency." Washington took no other notice of the letter, than to enclose it in his despatches to Congress. Copies of it were speedily taken and circulated, and it was soon printed in the newspapers. The respectable character of Mr. Duche, and the remarkable tenor of the letter, gave it notoriety at the time, and caused the particulars to be recorded among the events of history.

Mr. Duche had married a sister of Mr. Francis Hopkinson, one of the signers of the Declaration of Independence, who, when the letter was written, was at Bordentown, as a member of the Continental Navy Board. A copy was forwarded to Mr. Hopkinson, and he wrote a letter to Mr. Duche on the subject, which he enclosed to General Washington, that it might be transmitted to him in Philadelphia through the regular conveyance of a flag.

GEORGE WASHINGTON TO FRANCIS HOPKINSON.

" Head-Quartera, 21 NoTemb«r, 1777. " Sir,

" I am favored with yours of the 14th instant, inclosing a letter for the Reverend Mr. Duche. I will endeavour to forward it to him, but I imagine it will never be permitted to reach his hands. I confess to you, that I was not more surprised than concerned, at receiving so extraordinary a letter from Mr. Duche, of whom I had entertained the most favorable opinion, and I am still willing to suppose, that it was rather dictated by his fears than by his real sentiments; but I very much doubt whether the great numbers of respectable characters, in the state and army, on whom he has bestowed the most unprovoked and unmerited abuse, will ever attribute it to the same cause, or forgive the man, who has artfully endeavoured to engage me to sacrifice them to purchase my own safety.

" I never intended to make the letter more public, than by laying it before Congress. I thought this a duty, which I owed to myself; for, had any accident happened to the army entrusted to my command, and it had ever afterwards appeared, that such a letter had been written to and received by me, might it not have been said, that I had betrayed my country? And would not such a correspondence, if kept a secret, have given good grounds for the suspicion? I thank you for the favorable sentiments, which you are pleased to express of me, and I hope no act of mine will ever induce you to alter them. I am, &x.

" George Washington."

Mr. Hopkinson's letter to Duche deserves to be recorded in this place, not more on account of its connexion with the subject, than of the force and feeling with which it is written, and its lofty tone of patriotism and public virtue.

FRAN-CIS HOPKINSON TO JACOB DUCHE.

" Bordentown, 14 November, 1777. " Dear Brother,

" A letter signed with your name, dated at Philadelphia, on the 8th of October, and addressed to his Excellency General Washington, is handed about the country. Many copies are taken, and I doubt not but it will soon get into the press, and become public throughout the continent. Words cannot express the grief and consternation that wounded my soul at the sight of this fatal performance. What infatuation could influence you to offer to his Excellency an address, filled with gross misrepresentation, illiberal abuse, and sentiments unworthy of a man of character? You have endeavoured to screen your own weaknesses by the most artful glosses, and to apologize to the General for the instability of your temper in a manner, that I am sure cannot be satisfactory to your own conscience.

" I could go through this extraordinary letter, and point out to you truth distorted in every leading part. But the world will doubtless do this with a severity, that must be daggers to the sensibilities of your heart. Read that letter over again, and if possible divest yourself of the fears and influence, whatever they were, that induced you to pen it. Consider its contents with an impartial eye, and reflect on the ideas it will naturally raise in the minds of the multitude. You will then find, that by a vain and weak effort you have attempted the integrity of one, whose virtue is impregnable to the assaults of fear or flattery, whose judgment needed not your information, and who, I am sure, would have resigned his charge the moment he found it likely to lead him out of the paths of virtue and honor. You will find that you have drawn upon you the resentment of Congress, the resentment of the army, the resentment of many worthy and noble characters in England, whom you know not, and the resentment of your insulted country. You have ventured to assert many things at large of the affairs of England, France, and America, which are far from being true, and which, from your contracted knowledge in these matters, it is impossible for you to be acquainted with. In the whole of your letter, you have never once recommended yourself to those, whose favor you seem desirous of obtaining, by expatiating on the justice or humanity of their conduct and at the same time have said every thing that can render you odious to those, on whom the happiness of your future life must depend.

" You presumptuously advise our worthy General, on whom millions depend with implicit confidence, to abandon their dearest hopes, and with or without the consent of his constituents to ' *negotiate for America at the head of his army.*' Would not the blood of the slain in battle rise against such perfidy? And with whom would you have him negotiate? Are they not those, who, without the sanction of any civil, moral, or religious right, have come three thousand miles to destroy our peace and property, to lay waste *your* native country with fire and sword, and cruelly murder its inhabitants? Look for their justice and honor in their several proclamations, and look for their humanity in the jails of New York and Philadelphia, and in your own Potter's Field. The whole force of the reasoning contained

in your letter tends to this point; that virtue and honor require us to stand by truth, as long as it can be done with safety, but that her cause may be abandoned on the approach of danger; or, in other words, that the justice of the American cause ought to be squared by the success of her arms.

" On the whole, I find it impossible to reconcile the matter and style of this letter with your general conduct, or with the virtues of your heart. I would fain hope, notwithstanding your assertion to the contrary, that you wrote it with a bayonet held to your breast, by order of the unprincipled usurpers of your native city. But my chief motive for writing to you at this time is to assure you, that I firmly believe that our just defensive war will be crowned with success, and that we shall ere long return to our habitations in Philadelphia. I would, therefore, most earnestly warn you to evade the dismal consequences of your ill-judged address to our beloved General. Do all you can to wipe off, if possible, its unhappy effects. I tremble for you, for my good sister, and her little family. I tremble for your personal safety. Be assured I write this from true brotherly love. Our intimacy has been of a long duration, even from our early youth; long and uninterrupted, without even a rub in the way; and so long have the sweetness of your manners, and the integrity of your heart, fixed my affections.

" I am perfectly disposed to attribute this unfortunate step to the timidity of your temper, the weakness of your nerves, and the undue influence of those about you. But will the world hold you so excused? Will the individuals you have so freely censured and characterized with contempt have this tenderness for you? I fear not. They will only judge of your conduct by its rashness, and proportion their resentment to their sensibility of the wounds you have given. I pray God to inspire you with some means of extricating yourself from this embarrassing difficulty. For my own part, I have well considered the principles on which I took part with my country, and am determined to abide by them

to the last extremity. I beg my love to my good mother, and my affectionate sisters. I often think of them with great pain and anxiety, lest they should suffer from tbe want of those necessary supplies, that are now cut off. May God preserve them and you in this time of trial. I am, dec.

" Francis Hopkinson."

Mr. Duche went to England with bis family, and was appointed a preacher in the Lambeth Asylum, where the fame of his eloquence drew around him a large concourse of hearers. He was respected by the best classes of society, and appears to have received a competent remuneration for his pastoral services, and to have enjoyed all that consideration to which he was entitled by his character and profession. He was ill at ease, however, in a foreign land, and signed to return to his native country. The following letter is creditable to his heart, and shows at least that he was constant in his attachments, and ready to confess an error into which he had been betrayed by a weakness of judgment.

JACOB DUClIE TO GEORGE WASHINGTON.

" Asylum, Lambeth, 2 April, 1733. " Sir,

" Will your Excellency condescend to accept of a few lines from one, who ever was and wishes still to be your sincere friend, who never *intentionally* sought to give you a moment's pain, who entertains for you the highest personal respect, and would be happy to be assured under your own hand, that he does not labor under your displeasure, but that you freely forgive what a weak judgment, but a very affectionate heart, once presumed to advise? Many circumstances, at present unknown to you, conspired to make me deem it my duty to write to you. Ignorance and simplicity saw not the necessity of your divulging the letter. I am convinced, however, that you could not, in your public station, do otherwise. I cannot say a word in vindication of my conduct but this, that I had been for months before distressed with continual apprehensions for you and all my friends without the

British lines. I looked upon all as gone; or that nothing could save you, but rescinding the Declaration of Independency. Upon this ground alone I presumed to speak; not to advise an act of base treachery, my soul would have recoiled from the thought; not to surrender your army, or betray the righteous cause of your country, but, at the head of that army, *supporting and supported by them,* to negotiate with Britain for our constitutional rights.

" Can you then join with my country in pardoning this error of judgment? Will you yet honor me with your great interest and influence, by recommending, at least expressing your approbation of the repeal of an act, that keeps me in a state of banishment from my native country, from the arms of a dear aged father, and the embraces of a numerous circle of valuable and long-loved friends? Your liberal, generous mind, I am persuaded, will nevefexclude me wholly from your regard for a mere political error; especially, as you must have heard, that, since the date of that letter, I have led a life of perfect retirement, and since my arrival in England have devoted myself wholly to the duties of my profession, and confined my acquaintance to a happy circle of literary and religious friends.

" I have written to my father and to many of my friends largely on this subject, requesting them to make such application to the State of Pennsylvania in my behalf, as may be judged necessary and expedient. Should this application be honored with success, I know of nothing that would more effectually satisfy my desires in a mattei VOL. V. 61 0 0 of such importance to myself and my family, as a line or two from your Excellency, expressive of your approbation of my return. Temporal emoluments are not wanting to induce me to remain for life on this side of the Atlantic. I have been most hospitably received and kindly treated by all ranks of people, and I should be ungrateful not to acknowledge in the strongest terms my obligations to those, who have placed me in the easy and comfortable situation I now enjoy. It is not necessity, there-

fore, but unalterable affection to my native country, that urges me to seek a return. With every good wish and prayer for your best felicity, and my most hearty congratulations on the happy event of peace, I have the honor to be your Excellency's most obedient and humble servant,

" Jacor Dlche."

George Washington To Jacor Duche.

" Head-Quarters, 10 August, 1783. "Sot, " I have received your letter of the 2d of April, and, reflecting on Its contents, I cannot but say that I am heartily sorry for the occasion which has produced it. Personal enmity I bear none to any man. So far, therefore, as your return to this country depends on my private voice, it would be given in favor of it with cheerfulness. But, removed as I am from the people and policy of the State in which you formerly resided, and to whose determination your case must be submitted, it is my duty, whatever may be my inclination, to leave its decision to its constitutional judges. Should this be agreeable to your wishes, it cannot fail to meet my entire approbation. I am, &c.

" George. Washington "

The laws of Pennsylvania, excluding the refugees from that State, were not repealed till after the adoption of the Constitution of the United States. Mr. Duchc returned to Philadelphia in the year 1790, much broken in health, having suffered a paralytic affection. Hc died in 1794, being then about sixty years of age.

PARTICULARS RESPECTING THE CABAL WHICH EXISTED AGAINST GENERAL WASHINGTON IN CONGRESS AND IN THE ARMY.

On this subject I shall do little more than bring together such papers relating to it, as have falien into my hands. They will afford, I believe, nearly all the positive testimony that exists, as to the origin, motives, and doings of the faction, commonly known by the name of *Conway's Cabal.* It has received this appellation from the circumstance of its having first bean brought to light through the agency of that officer, and of his having acted a conspicuous part in its

progress. The brief note in the text, from Washington to Conway, is the earliest public record bearing on tho subject. A week afterwards Conway wrote the following letter. Ii would seem, that there had been in the mean time an interview between Washington and Conway, or a written explanation on the part of the latter, which has not been preserved.

THOMAS CONWAY TO GEORGE WASHINGTON.

" *Camp,* 16 *November,* 1777. — Sir; The hopes and appearance of a French war, along with some other reasons, have induced me to send my resignation to Congress. As soon as the trial of General Stephen is over, I hope your Excellency will permit me to depart from the army, in order to return to France as soon as possible. I return thanks to your Excellency for the civilities you have shown me while I had the honor of being under your orders, and beg you will accept of my warm and sincere wishes for the liberty of America and the success of your arms. I am, &c."

The resignation of General Conway was not accepted by Congress. On the contrary, he was a month afterwards elected inspector-general of the army, with the rank of major-general. This was a proof, that a majority of the members of Congress were not friendly to the Commander-in-chicf, since the intrigues of Conway against Washington were perfectly well known in that assembly. General Washington' sentiments had been expressed most unequivocally in a letter to Richard Henry Lee, dated October 17th, in which, after alluding to the report that Conway was about to be appointed major-general, he said, " It will be as unfortunate a measure as ever was adopted; I may add, and I think with truth, that it will give a fatal blow to the existence of the army. " Notwithstanding this opinion thus pointedly declared,' and notwithstanding the insidious conduct of Conway, the appointment was made.

The following letter, the original of which was found among General Gates's papers, is without signature; but there are strong reasons for believing it to have been written by a member of

Congress.

ANONYMOUS LETTER TO HORATIO GATES.

" *Reading,* 17 *November,* 1777. — My dear General Gates; The scenes of your play have been changed so expeditiously, and with such great management, that I am fairly lost in my endeavours to trace my hero through the many great parts of his character. Yon have saved our northern hemisphere, and, in spite of our consummate and repeated blundering, you have changed the constitution of the southern campaign, on the part of the enemy, from offensive to defensive. If you had remained with this army wc might have opposed, but could not have counteracted, the deep-rooted system of favoritism, which began to shoot forth at New York, and which now has arrived at its full growth and maturity. Repeated slights and unjustifiable arrogance combined with other causes to drive from tbc army those, who would not worship the image, and pay an undeserved tribute of praise and flattery to the great and powerful. The list of our disgusted patriots is long and formidable; their resentments keen against the reigning cabal, and their powers of opposition not despicable.

" The campaign here must soon close. If no brilliant action takes place before it ends, if our troops are obliged to retire to Lancaster, Reading, or Bethlehem for winter-quarters, and the country below is left open to the enemy's flying parties, great and very general will be the murmurs; so great and so general, that nothing inferior to a Commander-in-chief will be able to resist the mighty torrent of public clamor and public vengeance. We have had a noble army melted down by ill-judged marches, which disgrace their authors and directors, and which have occasioned the severest and most just sarcasm and contempt of our enemies. How much you are to be envied, my dear General! How different your conduct and your fortune! la short, this army will be totally lost, unless you come down and collect the virtuous band; who wish to fight under your banner, and with their aid save the southern hemisphere. Congress

must send for you. I have ten thousand things to tell. I am, &.c." THOMAS MIFFLIN TO HORATIO GATES.

" *Reading,* 28 *November,* 1777. — My dear General; An extract from General Conway's letter to you has been procured, and sent to head-quarters. The extract was a collection of just sentiments; yet such as should not have been entrusted to any of your family. General Washington enclosed it to General Conway without remarks. It was supported, and the freedom of the sentiment was not apologized for; on the contrary, although some reflections were made on some people, yet the practice was pleaded boldly, and no satisfaction given. My dear General, take care of your sincerity and frank disposition; they cannot injure yourself, but may injure some of your best friends. Affectionately yours." HORATIO GATES TO THOMAS CONWAT.

" *Albany,* 3 *December,* 1777. — Dear General; Your excellent letter has given me pain; for, at the same time that I am indebted to you for a just idea of the cause of our misfortunes, your judicious observations make me sensible of the difficulty there is in remedying the evils, which retard our success. The perfect establishment of military discipline, consistent with the honor and principles, which ought to be cherished amongst a free people, is not only the work of genius, but time. But, dear General, you have sent your resignation; and I assure you, I fondly hope it will not be accepted; it ought not.

" The antipathy, which has long subsisted between the French and English nations, will continue until they cease to be neighbours. Such is the unhappy lot of mankind. The separation occasioned by the declaration of independence has removed the cause of that hatred which the political connexion of the British colonists has implanted in their breasts against the French, and those who wertf attached to their interest. Now that Machiavelism can be no longer attempted to keep up those prejudices in the minds of the unthinking amongst us, the French and the people of the United States will become friends; and I am amazed that men, in the station you

mention, should have been so impolitic, or have possessed so little of the philosophic spirit, as to provoke a gentleman of your acknowledged merits, by illiberal reflections; however, I must declare to you, that I fitmly believe there would be more greatness in continuing to serve the States, notwithstanding the provocation you think you have received from one of their principal members, than in resigning the commission you hold. Capricious or disgraced warriors so often leave the army, that I do not wish to see the name of Conway on the list of officers, who have withdrawn from the service of our republic. I hope the result of your considerations on this subject will retain in our service an excellent officer, who has already exposed his life in our defence; and that you will believe I am with the purest esteem, dear General, your most humble and most obedient servant."

" P. S. This moment I received a letter from our worthy friend, General Mifflin, who informs me, that extracts from your letters to me had been conveyed to General Washington, and that it occasioned an *eclaircissement,* in which you acted with all the dignity of a virtuous soldier. I intreat you, dear General, to let me know which of the letters was copied off. It is of the greatest importance, that I should detect the person, who has been guilty of that act of infidelity. I cannot trace him out unless I have your assistance." HORATIO GATES TO THOMAS MIFFLIN.

" *Albany,* 4 *December,* 1777. — Dear General Mifflin; Yesterday yours of the 28lh of November reached my hands. Its contents have inexpressibly distressed me; for, though to this moment I have been ruminating who could be the villain, that has played me this treacherous trick, yet I can find no clue to a discovery. There is scarcely a man living, who takes greater care of his papers than I do. I never fail to lock them up, and keep the key in my pocket. I assort you, my dear General, I am as cautious to whom I show a private letter, as any of my most sensible and scrupulous friends. Yesterday the original of the enclosed to General Conway was sealed up to be sent, when I received yours, which caused the postscript to be added to it. This untoward affair makes me the more unhappy, as a very valuable and polite officer was thrown into a situation, which most increase his disgust.

" No punishment is too severe for the wretch, who betrayed me; and I doubt not your friendship for me, as well as your zeal for our safety, will bring the name of the miscreant to public light. To enable you to act with all possible propriety, I enclose copies of my letters to the General and to the President of Congress on the same subject. Believe that in any matter, which shall affect your peace of mind, you will find in me that warmth, which your known sincerity convinces me, that I shall experience from you. I am, my dear General, your affectionate friend." HORATIO GATES TO GEORGE WASHINGTON.

" Albany, 8 December, 1777. — Sir; I shall not attempt to describe what, as a private gentleman, I cannot help feeling, on representing to my mind the disagreeable situation in which confidential letters, when exposed to public inspection, may place an unsuspecting correspondent; but, as a public officer, I conjure your Excellency to give me all the assistance you can, in tracing out the author of the infidelity, which put extracts from General Conway's letters to me into your hands. Those letters have been stealingly copied; but which of them, when, and by whom, is to me as yet an unfathomable secret. There is not one officer in my suite, nor amongst those who have free access to me, upon whom I could, with the least justification to myself, fix the suspicion; and yet my uneasiness may deprive me of the usefulness of the worthiest men. It is, I believe, in your Excellency's power to do me and the United States a very important service, by detecting a wretch who may betray me, and capitally injure the very operations under your immediate directions. For this reason, Sir, I beg your Excellency will favor me with the proof you can procure to that effect. But the crime being eventually so important, that the least loss of time may be attended with the worst consequences, and it being unknown to me, whether the letter came to you from a member of Congress or from an officer, I shall have the honor of transmitting a copy of this to the President, that the Congress may, in concert with your Excellency, obtain as soon as possible a discovery, which so deeply affects the safety of the States. Crimes of that magnitude ought not to remain unpunished. I have the honor to be, &c." HORATIO GATES TO THE PRESIDENT OP CONGRESS.

" Albany, 11 December, 1777. — " Sir; The perusal of the enclosed will sufficiently inform your Excellency of the treachery, whicli occasioned my writing to General Washington, that I might discover the wretch who betrayed me. The same anxiety dictates this letter, that, the whole being communicated to Congress, the criminal may be the sooner detected. The reasonable fear of my being deprived of important intelligence from correspondents, rendered diffident, and the danger of my being betrayed to the enemy by the same traitor, or the indiscretion of the persons to whom his confidants may communicate secrets of the greatest importance, must affect your Excellency and every friend to the United States. I cannot believe that the traitorous thief will long escape detection, after the patriotism of the delegates shall have been alarmed. With the most respectful confidence in your care to defend my own honor or prudence, which seem to stand indirectly impeached, I shall wait for the result of your assisting the General in this affair. I am, &c." MARQUIS DE LAFAYETTE TO GEORGE WASHINGTON.

" Camp, 30 December, 1777. — My dear General; I went yesterday morning to head-quarters, with an intention of speaking to your Excellency, but you were too busy, and I shall state in this letter what I wished to say. I need not tell you how sorry I am at what lately happened; it is a necessary result of my tender and respectful friendship for you, which is as true and candid as the other sentiments of my heart, and much stronger than so new an acquaintance might seem to admit. But another reason for my concern is my ardent and perhaps enthusiastic wish for the happiness and liberty of this country. I see plainly that America can defend herself, if proper measures are taken; but I begin to fear that she may be lost by herself and her own sons.

" When I was in Europe, I thought that here almost every man was a lover of liberty, and would rather die free than live a slave. You can conceive my astonishment when I saw, that Toryism was as apparently professed as Whigism itself. There are open dissensions in Congress; parties who hate one another as much as the common enemy; men who, without knowing any thing about war, undertake to judge you, and to make ridiculous comparisons. They are infatuated with Gates, without thinking of the difference of circumstances, and believe that attacking is the only thing necessary to conquer. These ideas are entertained by some jealous men, and perhaps secret friends of the British government, who want to push you, in a moment of ill humor, to some rash enterprise upon the lines, or against a much stronger army.

" I should not take the liberty of mentioning these particulars to you, if I had not received a letter from a young, good-natured gentleman at Yorktown, whom Conway has ruined by his cunning and bad advice, but who entertains the greatest respect for you. I have been surprised to see the poor establishment of the Board of War, the difference made between northern and southern departments, and the orders from Congress about military operations. But the promotion of Conway is beyond all my expectations. I should be glad to have new major-generals, because, as I know that you take some interest in my happiness and reputation, it will perhaps afford an occasion for your Excellency to give me more agreeable commands in some instances. On the other hand, General Conway says he is entirely a man to be disposed of by me, he calls himself my soldier, and the reason of such behaviour towards me is, that he wishes to be well spoken of at the French Court; and his protector, the Marquis de

Castries, is an intimate acquaintance of mine.

" But since the letter of Lord Stirling, I have inquired into his character, and found that he is an ambitious and dangerous man. He has done all in his power to draw off my confidence and affection from you. His desire was to engage me to leave this country. I now see all the general officers of the army against Congress. Such disputes, if known to the enemy, may be attended with the worst consequences. I am very sorry whenever I perceive troubles raised amongst defenders of the.same cause; but my concern is much greater, when I find officers coming from France, officers of some character in my country, to whom a fault of that kind may be imputed. The reason for my fondness for Conway was his being a very brave and very good officer. However, that talent for manoeuvring, which seems so extraordinary to Congress, is not so very difficult a matter for any man of common sense, who applies himself to it. I must render to General Duportail and some other French officers, who have spoken to me, the justice to say, that I found them as I could wish upon this occasion, although it has made a great noise amongst many in the army. I wish your Excellency could let them know how necessary you are to them, and engage them at the same time to keep peace and reinstate love among themselves, till the moment when these little disputes shall not be attended with such inconveniences. It would be too great a pity, that slavery, dishonor, ruin, and the unhappiness of a whole nation, should issue from trifling differences betwixt a few men.

" You will perhaps find this letter very unimportant; but I was desirous of explaining to you some of my ideas, because it will contribute to my satisfaction to be convinced, that you, my dear General, who have been so indulgent as to permit me to look on you as a VOL. V. 62 friend, should know my sentiments. I have the warmest love for my country, and for all good Frenchmen. Their success fills my heart with joy; but, Sir, besides that Conway is an Irishman, I want countrymen, who in every point do honor to their country. That gentleman had engaged me, by entertaining my imagination with ideas of glory and shining projects, and I must confess this was a too certain way of deceiving me. I wished to join to the few theories about war, which I possess, and to the few dispositions which nature has given me, the experience of thirty campaigns, in the hope that I should be able to be more useful in my present sphere. My desire of deserving your approbation is strong; and, whenever you shall employ me, you can be certain of my trying every exertion in my power to succeed. I am now bound to your fate, and I shall follow it and sustain it, as well by my sword as by all the means in my power. You will pardon my importunity. Youth and friendship perhaps make me too warm, but I feel the greatest concern at recent events. With the most tender and profound respect, I have the honor to be, Az-c." GEORGE WASHINGTON TO THE MARQUIS DE LAFAYETTE.

" *Head-Quarters,* 31 *December,* 1777. — My dear Marquis; Your favor of yesterday conveyed to me fresh proof of that friendship and attachment, which I have happily experienced since the first of our acquaintance, and for which I entertain sentiments of the purest affection. It will ever constitute part of my happiness to know, that I stand well in your opinion; because I am satisfied that you can have no views to answer by throwing out false colors, and that you possess a mind too exalted to condescend to low arts and intrigues to acquire a reputation. Happy, thrice happy, would it have been for this army, and the cause we are embarked in, if the same generous spirit had pervaded all the actors in it. But one gentleman. whose name you have mentioned, had, I am confident, far different views. His ambition and great desire of being puffed off, as one of the first officers of the age, could only be equalled by the means which he used to obtain them; but, finding that I was determined not to go beyond the line of my duty to indulge him in the first, nor to exceed the strictest rules of propriety to gratify him in the second, he became my inveterate enemy; and he has, I am persuaded, practised every art to do me an injury, even at the expense of reprobating a measure, which did not succeed, that he himself advised to. How far he may have accomplished his ends, I know not; and, except for considerations of a public nature, I care not; for it is well known, that neither ambitious, nor lucrative motives led me to accept my present appointments; in the discharge of which, I have endeavoured to observe one steady and uniform system of conduct, which I hall invariably pursue, while I have the honor to command, regardless of the tongue of slander or the powers of detraction. The fatal tendency of disunion is so obvious, that I have in earnest terms exhorted such officers, as have expressed their dissatisfaction at General Conway's promotion, to be cool and dispassionate in their decision upon the matter; and I have hopes that they will not suffer any hasty determination to injure the service. At the same time, it must be acknowledged, that officers' feelings upon these occasions are not to be restrained, although you may control their actions.

" The other observations contained in your letter have too much truth in them; and it is much to be lamented, that things are not now as they formerly were; but we must not, in so great a contest, expect to meet with nothing but sunshine. I have no doubt that every thing happens for the best, that we shall triumph over all our misfortunes, and in the end be happy; when, my dear Marquis, if you will give me your company in Virginia, we will laugh at our past difficulties and the folly of others; and I will endeavour, by every civility in my power, to show you how much and how sincerely I am your affectionate and obedient servant." GEORGE WASHINGTON TO THE PRESIDENT OF CONGRESS.

" *Valley Forge,* 4 *January,* 1778. — Sir; Unwilling as I am to add any thing to the multiplicity of business, that necessarily engages the attention of Congress, I am compelled by unavoidable necessity to pass my answer to General Gates through their hands. What could induce General Gates to communicate to that honorable body a copy of his letter to me is beyond the depth of my comprehension, upon any fair ground; but the fact being so, must stand as an apology for the liberty of giving you this trouble, which no other consideration would have induced me to take. With the greatest respect, Sir, I am, &c." GEORGE WASHINGTON TO HORATIO GATE8.

" *Valley Forge,* 4 *January,* 1778. — Sir; Your letter of the 8th ultimo came to my hands a few days ago, and to my great surprise informed me that a copy of it had been sent to Congress, for what reason I find myself unable to account; but as some end doubtless was intended to be answered by it, I am laid under the disagreeable necessity of returning my answer through the same channel, lest any member of that honorable body should harbour an unfavorable suspicion of my having practised some indirect means to come at the contents of the confidential letters between you and General Conway.

" I am to inform you then, that Colonel Wilkinson, on his way to Congress in the month of October last, fell in with Lord Stirling at Reading, and, not in confidence that I ever understood, informed his aid-dc-camp, Major MWilliams, that General Conway had written this to you; ' Heaven has been determined to save your country, or a weak General and bad counsellors would have ruined it.' Lord Stirling, from motives of friendship, transmitted the account with this remark; ' The enclosed was communicated by Colonel Wilkinson to Major M'Williams; such wicked duplicity of conduct I shall always think it my duty to detect.' In consequence of this information, and without having any thing more in view than merely to show that gentleman, that I was not unapprized of his intriguing disposition, I wrote to him a letter in these words;

" Sir; A letter, which I received last night, contained the following paragraph; " In a letter from General Con-

way to General Gates he says, ' *Heaven has been determined to save your country, or a weak General and bad counsellors would have ruined it.* ' I am, Sir, etc. "'

" Neither this letter, nor the information which occasioned it, was ever directly or indirectly communicated by me to a single officer in this army out of my own family, excepting the Marquis de Lafayette, who, having been spoken to on the subject by General Conway, applied for and saw, under injunctions of secrecy, the letter, which contained Wilkinson's information; so desirous was I of concealing every matter that could, in its consequences, give the smallest interruption to the tranquillity of this army, or afford a gleam of hope to the enemy by dissensions therein.

" Thus, Sir, with an openness and candor, which I hope will ever characterize and mark my conduct, have I complied with your request. The only concern I feel upon the occasion, finding how matters stand, is, that in doing this I have necessarily been obliged to name a gentleman, who, I am persuaded, although 1 never exchanged a word with him upon the subject, thought he was rather doing an act of justice, than committing an act of infidelity; and sure I am, that, till Lord Stirling's letter came to my hands, I never knew that General Conway, whom I viewed in the light of a stranger to you, was a correspondent of yours; much less did I suspect that I was the subject of your confidential letters. Pardon me then for adding, that, so far from conceiving that the safety of the States can 'be affected, or in the smallest degree injured, by a discovery of this kind, or that I should be called upon in such solemn terms to point out the author, I considered the information as coming from yourself, and given with a friendly view to forewarn, and consequently to forearm me, against a secret enemy, or in other words a dangerous incendiary; in which character sooner or later this country will know General Conway. But in this, as in other matters of late, I have found myself mistaken. I am, Sir, your most obedient servant." JAMES CBAIK TO GEORGE

WASHINGTON.

" *Port Tobacco, Maryland,* 6 *January,* 1778. — Dear Sir; Notwithstanding your unwearied diligence, and the unparalleled sacrifice of domestic happiness and ease of mind, which you have made for the good of your country, yet you are not wanting in secret enemies, who would rob you of the great and truly deserved esteem your country has for you. Base and villanous men, through chagrin, envy, or ambition, are endeavouring to lessen you in the minds of the people, and taking underhand methods to traduce your character. The morning I led camp, I was informed by a gentleman, whom I believe to be a true friend of yours, that a strong faction was forming against you in the new Board of War and in the Congress. It alarmed me exceedingly, and I wished that he had informed me of it a day or two sooner, that I might have taken an opportunity of mentioning it to you. He begged that I would do it before I went away; but upon consideration I thought I had better defer it until I reached home, as perhaps I might make some further discoveries on ray way. At my arrival in Bethlehem I was told of it there, and was told that I should hear more of it on my way down. I did so, for at Lancaster I was still assured of it. All the way down I heard of it, and I believe it is pretty general over the country. No one would pretend to affix it on particulars, yet all seemed to believe it.

" It was said, that some of the eastern and southern members were at the bottom of it, particularly one, who has been said to be your enemy before, but denied it, Richard Henry Lee; and that General Mifflin, in the new Board of War, was a very active person. This last I am afraid is too true. I have reason to believe he is not your friend from many circumstances. The method they are taking is by holding General Gates up to the people, and making them believe that you have had a number three or four times greater VOL. V. PP.

than the enemy, and have done nothing; that Philadelphia was given up by your management, and that you have had many opportunities of defeating the enemy; and many other things as ungenerous and unjust. These are the low artifices they are making use of. It is said they dare not appear openly as your enemies, but that the new Board of War is composed of such leading men as will throw such obstacles and difficulties in your way, as to force you to resign. Had I not been assured of theee things from such authority, that I cannot doubt them, I should not have troubled you with this. My attachment to your person is such, my friendship is so sincere, that every hint, which has a tendency to hurt your honor, wounds me most sensibly, and I write this that you may be apprized, and have an eye toward those men, and particularly General Mifflin. He is plausible, sensible, popular, and ambitious, takes great pains to draw over every officer he meets with to his own way of thinking, and is very engaging. " The above, I can with sincerity say, I have written from pure motives of friendship, and I have no enmity to any of these men, any further than they are enemies to you. If they are your enemies, every honest man must naturally conclude they are enemies to their country, and the glorious cause in which we are engaged, and will no doubt most strenuously exert every nerve to disappoint their villanous intentions. That God, of his infinite mercy, may protect and defend you from all your open and secret enemies, and continue you in health to finish your glorious undertaking, is the sincere prayer of your most devoted and obliged humble servant. THOMAS CONWAY TO GEORGE WASHINGTON.

" *January* 10A, 1778. — Sir; I remain in a state of inaction until such time as your Excellency will think fit to employ me. I understand that your aversion to me is owing to the letter I wrote to General Gates. I have made you a candid answer upon that subject, and such an answer as must satisfy you and every man of a liberal disposition. There is not a subaltern in Europe but what will write to his friends and acquaintances, and mention freely his opinion of the Generals and of the army; but I never heard that the least notice was taken of these letters. Must such an odious and

tyrannical inquisition begin in this country? Must it be introduced by the Commander-in-chief of this army raised for the defence of liberty? It cannot be, and I am satisfied you never had such thoughts.

" Supposing yon, Sir, to be where I am sure you do not mean nor wish to be, supposing you to be an absolute king, yet it would be more generous, more to your glory and interest, to despise the vile reports of any officious sycophant, than to gratify your resentment against any officer concerned in such reports. I do not pretend, Sir, to be a consummate general; but, as an old sailor knows more of a ship than admirals who have never been at sea, long experience and constant practice made me think, that I could in some measure be a helping hand in putting your army upon a better footing, and in correcting the many abuses of which no one is more sensible than you are.

" I cannot believe, Sir, neither does any officer in your army believe, that the objection to my appointment originates from any body living but from you; for, since three foreign officers, who did not serve here or elsewhere as long as I did, have been promoted without difficulty, I have and every one has reason to conclude, that my promotion would have been acceptable, had you seemed to give it the least countenance. But the two receptions you honored me with, when I paid you my respects, and the dissatisfaction you testified at the resolves of Congress, were more than sufficient to incense the officers, and to encourage them to an opposition. Your dispositions towards me, Sir, have been clear, and the very behaviour of some gentlemen of your family did not permit me nor any one else to entertain the least doubt of them. I have told you, Sir, and have the honor to repeat to you, that I do not wish to give you or any officer in the army the least uneasiness. Since you will not accept of my services, since you cannot bear the sight of me in your camp, I am very ready to go wherever Congress thinks proper, and even to France; and I solemnly declare, that, far from resenting the un-

deserved rebuke I met with from you, I shall do every thing in my power to serve this cause. These are the true sentiments with which I remain, Sir, dtc."
ANONYMOUS LETTER TO PATRICK IIENRY.

" *Yorktown, 12 January,* 1778. — Dear Sir; The common danger of our country first brought you and me together. I recollect with pleasure the influence of your conversation and eloquence upon the opinions of this country in the beginning of the present controversy. You first taught us to shake off our idolatrous attachment to royalty, and to oppose its encroachments upon our liberties, with our very lives. By these means you saved us from ruin. The independence of America is the offspring of that liberal spirit of thinking and acting, which followed the destruction of the sceptres of kings, and the mighty power of Great Britain.

" But, Sir, we have only passed the Red Sea. A dreary wilderness is still before us; and unless a Moses or a Joshua are raised up in our behalf, we must perish before wc reach the promised land. We have nothing to fear from our enemies on the way. General Howe, it is true, has taken Philadelphia; but he has only changed his prison. His dominions are bounded on all sides by his outsentries. America can only be undone by herself. She looks up to her councils and arms for protection; but, alas! what are they *1* Her representation in Congress dwindled to only twenty-one members; ' her Adams, her Wilson, her Henry are no more among them. Her councils weak, and partial remedies applied constantly for universal diseases. Her army, what is it? A major-general belonging to it called it a few days ago, in my hearing, a mob. Discipline unknown or wholly neglected. The quarter-master's and commissary's departments filled with idleness, ignorance, and peculation; our hospitals crowded with six thousand sick, but half provided with necessaries or accommodations, and more dying in them in one month than perished in the field during the whole of the last campaign. The money depreciating, without any effectual measures being taken to raise it; the country distracted with the Don Quixote attempts to regulate the price of provisions; an artificial famine created by it, and a real one dreaded from it; the spirit of the people failing through a more intimate acquaintance with the causes of our misfortunes; many submitting daily to genera Howe; and more wishing to do it, only to avoid the calamities which threaten our country. But is our case desperate? By no means. We have wisdom, virtue, and strength enough to save us, if they could be called into action. The northern army has shown us what Americans are capable of doing, with a General at their head. The spirit of the southern army is no way inferior to the spirit of the northern. A Gates, a Lee, or a Conway, would in a few weeks render them an irresistible body of men. The last of the above officers has accepted of the new office of inspectorgeneral of our army, in order to reform abuses; but the remedy is only a palliative one. In one of his letters to a friend he says, ' A great and good God hath decreed America to be free, or the General and weak counsellors would have ruined her long ago.' You may rest assured of each of the facts related in this letter. The author of it is one of your Philadelphia friends. A hint of his name, if found out by the handwriting, must not be mentioned to your roost intimate friend. Even the letter must be thrown in the fire. Bat some of its contents ought to be made public, in order to awaken, enlighten, and alarm our country. I rely upon your prudence, and am, dear Sir, with my usual attachment to you, and to our beloved independence, yours sincerely."

The following curious paper, dated January 17th, was communicated anonymously to Congress, under a cover directed to Mr. Laurens, the President. Instead of laying it before Congress, or showing it to any other person, Mr. Laurens enclosed it to General Washington. It was entitled *Thoughts of a Freeman.* I have seen no hints, which afford a clue to its author. It must have been drawn up by one of the leaders of the faction, and doubtless

contains a summary of all the topics of complaint, which the opponents to the Commander-in-chief used for effecting their aims.

ANONYMOUS PAPER TRANSMITTED TO CONGRESS.

" / *believe* — that the enemy's leaving their shipping, and marching so many miles by land, and taking possession of the city of Philadelphia, with so little loss and opposition, has been very deceiving and discouraging to many of the true friends of America; that an inquiry into the reasons for not attacking and harassing them in their march from Elk, till their taking possession of Philadelphia, ought to be strictly gone into; that the reasons why the enemy's left wing, at the battle of Chad's Ford, was left without a proper reconnoitring party, ought to be known; that the proper method of attacking, beating, and conquering the enemy has never as yet been adopted by the Commander-in-chief; that more men will die this winter, than it would have cost lives to conquer the enemy last summer and fall; that it is better to die honorably in the field, than in a hospital; that the many fruitless and unaccountable marches have had a great tendency to fill the hospitals with sick; that the baggage has many times been sent away to the great hurt of the health of the army; that, contrary to the good old maxim, raiment has been regarded more than life.

" That the general contempt shown to the militia by the standing forces is a dangerous omen; that, in every victory as yet obtained by the Americans, the militia have had the principal share; that the liberties of America are safe only in the hands of the militia; that the honorable Congress in many cases have been too much led by military men; that such precedents may in time become dangerous; that it is high time for the honorable Congress, as the superior powes Vol. v. 63 p p of America, to exercise their authority with strict justice and impartiality; that the late success to the northward was owing to a change of commanders; that the southern army would have been alike successful, had a similar change taken place; that the en-

emy have been greatly deceived, having no reason to expect so valuable a prize as the city of Philadelphia with so few broken bones; that after they got Philadelphia they might have been destroyed, having exposed themselves several times.

" That had proper supplies been given to the forts on the river. their shipping could not have come up, without which they could not have stayed in the city; that the sending of generals from headquarters to order the erazure and evacuation of Red Bank Fort is very mysterious; that, if they only were fit to judge, they ought to have been sent six weeks sooner, and, if the forts were not suificiem, to have given orders and directions to have them made so; that those judges must be ignorant of General Greene's coming to their relief, or else they would not have ordered the said evacuation; that when members of the same body act, not in conjunction, but in opposition to each other, it argues great weakness in the head; that, if the enemy again come out to forage, which they cannot avoid, the supreme power ought to give orders for their being attacked at all events; that, if there is no general fit and willing to lead on the said attack, the said power ought to send one; that it is a very great reproach to America to say there is only one general in it; that the enemy have not eight thousand effective men in and about the city of Philadelphia; that the increasing of the standing army is not right, except better methods are adopted for supplying the same; that no action has yet been lost for want of men, able, willing, and fit to fight; that the present army, with the militia, are sufficient to conquer the present force of the enemy, at least they were, not long ago; that, if the army is not better managed than heretofore, numbers will avail nothing.

" That the dividing and subdividing the quarter-master's department has been prejudicial to the country as well as to the army; that the army was better supplied, and the country people better satisfied, before than since; that many of the good people of these States have been very ill used, who have supplied the quarter-master's department, who, after many journeys for their money and receiving only the insolence of office, have despaired of ever getting it; that the carriages, horses, and harness, belonging to the army, are in a very bad condition; that the greater part of the horses will be unfit for ervice before spring, if better methods of procuring forage are not speedily adopted; that the present place of encampment is ill chosen on account of forage; that there is too much forage left within reach of the enemy, though even yet a great deal of it might be brought off; that some departments of the army ought to be strictly inspected, and the heads should be bound in large securities, until all demands against said departments are paid off, and their accounts appear fair; that some people have too much interest in the continuance of the war; that the several departments of the army are in a very bad state.

" That the head cannot possibly be sound, when the whole body is disordered; that the people of America have been guilty of idolatry, by making a man their god; and the God of heaven and earth will convince them by woful experience, that he is only a man; that no good may be expected from the standing army, until Baal and his worshippers are banished from the camp.
" JOSEPH JONES TO GEORGE WASHINGTON.

" *Williamsburg, 22 January,* 1778. — Dear Sir; On my return to Congress I found the Speaker's letter, informing me that ray resignation was accepted by the House of Delegates, and that I might as soon as I pleased return home, which I did after staying about a week, to put the business we had been sent upon to camp in a proper train; the issue of which I had then every reason to expect would be according to the wishes of the army, but what the event has been I have not yet been informed. Many reasons pressed me to retire from Congress; and, if I felt a concern, it was only that in case I continued I might possibly be of some use in obstructing, or endeavouring at least to prevent, the mischievous consequences of those

base acts and machinations, that are but too prevalent among some people, and which it is the duty of every good man to resent and suppress. I knew not so much of these matters before I went to camp, as I discovered there, and after my return; for it was on my return only, that I had the first information given me of the conduct and language of a certain popular Pennsylvanian lately appointed to the new Board of War. Of the disposition and temper of another gentleman of that board, whose name the fortunate events of last fall have greatly exalted, I had before heard. But, whatever may be the design of these men, and however artfully conducted, I have no doubt but in the end it will redound to their own disgrace.

" You stand too high in the public opinion to be easily reached by their attempts; and the same equal and disinterested conduct, the same labor and attention, which you have manifested in the public service, from the first of the contest, will shield and protect you from the shafts of envy and malevolence. There may be instances, and these your good sense will point out to you, which require your notice, and the public welfare may be injured if they are passed over in silence; but, in all other respects, such petty-larceny attacks deserve, as they will ever meet with, your contempt. I am, dear Sir, &x.

HORATIO GATES TO GEORGE WASHINGTON.

" *Yorktovm,* 23 *January,* 1778. — Sir; The letter of the 4th instant which I had the honor to receive yesterday from your Excellency, has relieved me from unspeakable uneasiness. I now anticipate the pleasure it will give you, when you discover that what has been conveyed to you for an extract of General Conway's letter to me was not an information, which friendly motives induced a man of honor to give, that injured virtue might be forearmed against secret enemies. The paragraph, which your Excellency has condescended to transcribe, is spurious. It was certainly fabricated to answer the most selfish and wicked purposes. I cannot avoid sketching out to your Excellency the

history of General Conway's letter, from the time that it came to my hands by Lieutenant-Colonel Troup, my aid-de-camp, to whom General Conway delivered it at Reading on the 11th of October, to this time, as far as it has affected me and the officers of my family.

" That letter contained very judicious remarks upon that want of discipline, which has often alarmed your Excellency and, I believe, all observing patriots. The reasons which, in his judgment, deprived us of the success we could reasonably expect, were methodically explained by him; but neither the 'weakness' of any of our generals, nor ' bad counsellors,' were mentioned; and consequently cannot be assigned or imagined as part of those reasons to which General Conway attributed some of our losses. He wrote to roe as a candid observer, as other officers in every service freely write to each other, for obtaining better intelligence than that of newspapers, and that freedom renders such letters thus far confidential in some measure. The judgment of the person who receives them points out to him, according to time and circumstances, the propriety or impropriety attending their being communicated, when no particular injunction of secrecy was requested.

" Particular actions rather than persons were blamed, but with impartiality; and I am convinced that he did not aim at lessening in my opinion the merit of any person. His letter was perfectly harmless; however, now that various reports have been circulated concerning its contents, they ought not to be submitted to the solemn inspection of even those, who stand most high in the public esteem. Anxiety and jealousy would arise in the breast of very respectable officers, who, rendered sensible of faults, which inexperience, and that alone, may have led them into, would be unnecessarily disgusted, if they perceived a probability of such errors being recorded. Honor forbids it, and patriotism demands that I should return the letter into the hands of the writer. I will do it; but at the same time I declare, that the paragraph conveyed to your Excellency as a genuine part of it, was in words as well as in substance a wicked forgery.

" About the beginning of December I was informed that letter had occasioned an explanation between your Excellency and that gentleman. Not knowing whether the whole letter or a part of it had been stealingly copied, but fearing malice had altered its original texture, I own, Sir, that a dread of the mischiefs, which might attend the forgery, I suspected would be made, put me for some time in a most painful situation. When I communicated to the officers in my family the intelligence I had received, they all entreated me to rescue their characters from the suspicions they justly conceived themselves liable to, until the guilty person should be known. To facilitate the discovery, I wrote to your Excellency; but, unable to learn whether General Conway's letter had been transmitted to you by a member of Congress or a gentleman in the army, I was afraid much time would be lost in the course of the inquiry, and that the States might receive some capital injury from the infidelity of the person who I thought had stolen a copy of the obnoxious letter. Was it not probable that the secrets of the army might be obtained and betrayed through the same means to the enemy 1 For this reason, Sir, not doubting the Congress would most cheerfully concur with you in tracing out the criminal, I wrote to the President, and enclosed to him a copy of my letter to your Excellency.

" About the time I was forwarding those letters, Brigadier-General Wilkinson returned to Albany. I informed him of the treachery which had been committed, but I concealed from him the measure I was pursuing to unmask the author. Wilkinson answered, he waa assured it never would come to light, and endeavoured to fix my suspicions on Lieutenant-Colonel Troup, who, said he, might have incautiously conversed on the substance of General Conway's letter with Colonel Hamilton, whom you had sent not long before to Albany. I did not listen to this insinuation against my aid-decamp and mine.

" Would that your Excellency's pre-

diction relative to General Conway had not been inserted in your letter, which came to me unsealed through the channel of Congress. I hope always to find that gentleman a firm and constant friend to America. I never wrote to him in my life, but to satisfy his doubts concerning the exposure of his private letter; nor had any sort of intimacy, nor hardly the smallest acquaintance with him, before our meeting in this town. With great respect, I am, dtc." THOMAS CONWAT TO GEORGE WASHINGTON.

" *Yorlctown,* 27 *January,* 1778. — Sir; General Gates delivered to me the letter, which I had directed to him last October, and of The above letter is printed exactly according to the original. The closing paragraph is essentially different as contained in *Wilkinson's Memoirs,* Vol. L p. 400., and in the *Life of Alexander Hamilton,* Vol. I. p. 134. It is titer printed as follows.

" I did not listen to this insinuation against your aid-de-camp and mine. I considered it even as ungenerous. But the light your Excellency has just assisted me with, exhibiting the many qualifications which are necessarily blended together in the head and heart of General Wilkinson,! would not omit this fact; it will enable your Excellency to judge whether or not he would scruple to make such a forgery as that, which he now stands charged with, and ought to be exemplarily punished. To attempt sowing dissensions among the principal officers of the army, and rendering them odious to each other by talse suggestions and forgeries, is in my opinion a crime of the first magnitude; it involves with it all the consequences of positive treason. That the forgery now in view was machinated for injuring General Conway, and perhaps myself, in your judgment, is now evident to me; and I trust the detection will operate as it ought to operate upon your Excellency, as well as the members of the Congress, before whom your letter necessitates ma to lay this answer. The station of the calumniator seems to justify your Excellency for having believed till now, that the extract was genuine; and yet, Sir, I cannot help wishing you had sent me

a copy of it immediately after your explanation with General Conway. Would that your Excellency's prediction relative to him had not been inserted in your letter, which came to me unsealed through the hands of Congress. I sincerely wish the detection of this forgery may render ns all more cautious, and that to procure a fair and dispassionate explanation, whenever insinuations arc made to the prejudice of respected characters, may become an established rule in society, as well ss in public business, throughout the United States. I am, *&.c.* "

This is altogether gratuitous, not being in the letter received by General Washington. It is probable that Wilkinson published the letter from the first draft, without suspecting it to have been altered before it was sent off.

which I had kept no copy. I find with great satisfaction, that the paragraph so much spoken of does not exist in said letter, nor any thing like it. The letter was communicated before my arrival to several members of Congress, and, as soon as I received it, 1 delivered it to three other members, who have perused it. As this calumny has gained ground, and was spread through the army, I meant to have the letter published with the certificate of General Gates, but was prevented by President Laurens and some other members, whom I had consulted on the subject, and who were of opinion that such a measure would inform the enemy of a misunderstanding prevailing among the generals of the American army. Therefore, Sir, I must depend upon your justice, candor, and generosity, for putting a stop to this forgery.

"lama victim to calumny these two months past, and perhaps longer. I met with a reception from your Excellency such as I never met with before from any general during the course of thirty years in a very respectable army. Your mind has been embittered and prejudiced against me. Now that you are undeceived, I hope that your resentment will fall upon the authors of the forgery. I do not know what prediction you have made concerning me in one of your letters, neither do I desire ever to learn it. If it is a disagreeable one, I wish it may not be accomplished. Although I am no prophet, I can foretell that your virtues will acquire new lustre, and hine with a greater light, if you guard against flattery and calumny, which have so often led astray the best of men. I am with much respect, Sir, Ate."

When making the above request of General Washington, it is singular that Conway should not have enclosed a copy of the obnoxious letter, which he said had been obtained from General Gates, and seen by several members of Congress. This was certainly a very suspicious circumstance, if it was in reality as inoffensive as he represented, especially as it would at once have removed the primary cause of the difficulty. The letter was not made public, nor does it appear that either the original or a copy was ever seen by General Washington, or by any person who made its contents fully known. This is strong presumptive proof, that, although it did not contain the precise words of the quotation, the substance was fairly reported. The allusion to General Washington's " prediction " is explained is the closing part of his first letter to Gates on this subject. It was of course communicated by Gates to Conway.

GEORGE WASHINGTON TO HENRY LAURENS.

" *Valley Forge, 31 January,* 1778. — Sir; I this morning received your favor of the 27th instant. I cannot sufficiently express the obligation I feel to you, for your friendship and politeness upon an occasion in which I am so deeply interested. I was not unapprized, that a malignant faction had been for some time forming to my prejudice; which, conscious as I am of having ever done all in my power to answer the important purposes of the trust reposed in me, could not but give me some pain on a personal account. But my chief concern arises from an apprehension of the dangerous consequences, which intestine dissensions may produce to the common cause.

" As I have no other view than to promote the public good, and am unambi-

tious of honors not founded in the approbation of my country, I would not desire in the least degree to suppress a free spirit of inquiry into any part of my conduct, that even faction itself may deem reprehensible. The anonymous paper handed to yon exhibits many serious charges, and it is my wish that it should be submitted to Congress. This I am the more inclined to, aj the suppression or concealment may possibly involve you in embarrassments hereafter, since it' is uncertain how many or who may be privy to the contents.

" My enemies take an ungenerous advantage of me. They know the delicacy of my situation, and that motives of policy deprive me of the defence I might otherwise make against their insidious attacks. They know I cannot combat their insinuations, however injurious, without disclosing secrets, which it is of the utmost moment to conceal. But why should I expect to be exempt from censure, the unfailing lot of an elevated station *1* Merit and talents, with which I can have no pretensions of rivalship, have ever been subject to it. My heart tells me, that it has been my unremitted aim to do the best that circumstances would permit; yet I may have been very often mistaken in my judgment of the means, and may in many instances deserve the imputation of error. I cannot forbear repeating, that I have a grateful sense of the favorable disposition you have manifested to me in this affair, and beg you will believe me to be, with sentiments of real esteem and regard, Sir, &c." GEORGE WASHINGTON TO HORATIO GATES.

" *Valley Forge, 9 February,* 1778. — Sir; I was duly favored with your letter of the 23d of last month, to which I should have replied sooner, had I not been delayed by business that required my more immediate attention. It is my wish to give implicit credit to the assurances of every gentleman; but, in the subject of our present correspondence, I am sorry to confess, there happen to be some unlucky circumstances, which involuntarily compel me to consider the discovery you mention, not so satisfactory and conclusive, as you seem to

think it. I am so unhappy, as to find no small difficulty in reconciling the spirit and import of your different letters, and sometimes of the different parts of the same letter with each other. It is not unreasonable to presume, that your first information of my having notice of General Conway's letter came from himself; there were very few in the secret, and it is natural to suppose, that he, being immediately concerned, would be most interested to convey the intelligence to you. It is also far from improbable, that he acquainted you with the substance of the passage communicated to me; one would expect this, if he believed it to be spurious, in order to ascertain the imposition and evince his innocence; especially as he seemed to be under some uncertainty as to the precise contents of what he had written, when I signified my knowledge of the matter to him. If he neglected doing it, the omission cannot easily be interpreted into any thing else than a consciousness of the reality of the extract, if not literally, at least substantially. If he did not neglect it, it must appear somewhat strange that the forgery remained so long undetected, and that your first letter to me from Albany, of the 8th of December, should tacitly recognise the genuineness of the paragraph in question; while your only concern at that time seemed to be the tracing out the ' author of the infidelity, which put extracts from General Conway's letter into my hands.'

" Throughout the whole of that letter, the reality of the extracts is by the fairest implication allowed, and your only solicitude is to find out the person that brought them to light. After making the most earnest pursuit of the author of the supposed treachery, without saying a word about the truth or falsehood of the passage, your letter of the 23d ultimo, to my great surprise, proclaims it ' in words, as well as in substance, a wicked forgery.' It is not my intention to contradict this assertion, but only to intimate some considerations, which tend to induce a supposition, that, though none of General Conway's letters to you contained the offensive passage mentioned, there might have been something in them too nearly related to it, that could give such an extraordinary alarm. It may be said, if this were not the case, how easy in the first instance to have declared there was nothing exceptionable in them, and to have produced the letters themselves in VOL. V. 64 Q Q support of it? This may be thought the most proper and effectual way of refuting misrepresentation and removing all suspicion. The propriety of the objections suggested against submitting them to inspection may very well be questioned. ' The various reports circulated concerning their contents' were perhaps so many argument for making them speak for themselves, to place the matter upon the footing of certainty. Concealment in an affair, which had made so much noise, though not by *my* means, will naturally lead men to conjecture the worst; and it will be a subject of speculation even to candor itself. The anxiety and jealousy you apprehended from revealing the letter, will be very apt to be increased by suppressing it.

" It may be asked, Why not submit to inspection a performance perfectly harmless, and of course conceived in terms of proper caution and delicacy? Why suppose, that ' anxiety and jealousy would have arisen in the breasts of very respectable officers, or that they would have been unnecessarily disgusted at being made sensible of their faults, when related with judgment and impartiality by a candid observer'? Surely they could not have been unreasonable enough to take offence at a performance so perfectly inoffensive, ' blaming actions rather than persons,' which have evidently no connexion with one another, and indulgently ' recording the errors of inexperience.'

" You are pleased to consider General Conway's letters as of I confidential nature; observing that 'time and circumstances must point out the propriety or impropriety of communicating such letters.' Permit me to inquire whether, when there is an impropriety in communicating, it is only applicable with respect to the parties, who are the subjects of them. One might be led to imagine this to be the case, from your having admitted others into the secret of your confidential correspondence, at the same lime that you thought it ineligible it should be trusted to those ' officers, whose actions underwent its scrutiny.' Your not knowing whether the letter under consideration ' came to me from a member of Congress-, or from as officer,' plainly indicates that you originally communicated it to at least one of that honorable body; and I learn from General Conway, that before his late arrival at Yorktown, il had been committed to the perusal of several of its members, and was afterwards shown by himself to three more. It is somewhat difficult to conceive a reason, founded in generosity, for imparting the free and confidential strictures of that ingenious censor on the operations of the army under my command, to a member of Congress; but perhaps ' time and circumstances pointed it out.' It must indeed be acknowledged, that the faults of very respectable officers, not less injurious for being the result of inexperience, were not improper topics to engage the attention of members of Congress.

" It is, however, greatly to be lamented, that this adept in military science did not employ his abilities in the progress of the campaign, in pointing out those wise measures, which were calculated to givo us ' that degree of success we could reasonably expect.' The United States have lost much from that unseasonable diffidence, which prevented his embracing the numerous opportunities he had in council of displaying those rich treasures of knowledge and experience he has since so freely laid open to you. I will not do him the injustice to impute the penurious reserve, which ever appeared in him upon such occasions, to any other cause than an excess of modesty;' neither will I suppose, that he possesses no other merit than that after kind of sagacity, which qualifies a man better for profound discoveries of errors that have been committed, and advantages that have been lost, than for the exercise of that foresight and provident discernment, which enable him to avoid tho one and anticipate the Other. But, willing as I am to subscribe to all his pretensions, and to believe that his remarks on the operations of the campaign were very judicious, and that he has sagaciously descanted on many things that might have been done, I cannot help being a little skeptical as to his ability to have found out the means of accomplishing them, or to prove the sufficiency of those in our possession. These minutie, I suspect, he did not think worth his attention, particularly as they might not be within the compass of his *vittcs.* " Notwithstanding the hopeful presages you are pleased to figure to yourself of General Conway's firm and constant friendship to America, I cannot persuade myself to retract the prediction concerning him, which you so emphatically wish had not been inserted in my last. A better acquaintance with him, than I have reason to think you have had, from what you say, and a concurrence of circumstances, oblige me to give him but little credit for the qualifications of his heart; of which, at least, I beg leave to assume the privilege of being a tolerable judge. Were it necessary, more instances than one might be adduced, from his behaviour and conversation, to manifest that he is capable of all the malignity of detraction, and all the meannesses of intrigue, to gratify the absurd resentment of disappointed vanity, or to answer the purposes of personal aggrandizement and promote the interest of faction. I am with respect, Sir, your most obedient servant." ALEXANDER HAMILTON TO GEORGE CLINTON.

" *Head-Quarters, 13 February,* 1778. — Dear Sir; There is a matter, which often obtrudes itself upon my mind, and which requires the attention of every person of sense and influence among us; I mean a degeneracy of representation in the great council of America. It is a melancholy truth, Sir, the effects of which we daily see and feel, that there is not so much wisdom in a certain body as there ought to be, and as the success of our affairs absolutely demands. Many members of it are no doubt men, in every respect, fit for the trust; but this cannot be said of it as a body. Folly, caprice, a want of foresight, comprehension, and dignity, characterize the general tenor of their actions. Of this, I dare say, you are sensible, though you have not perhaps so many opportunities of knowing it as I have. Their conduct, with, respect to the army especially, is feeble, indecisive, and improvident; insomuch that we are reduced to a more terrible situation than you can conceive. False and contracted views of economy have prevented them, though repeatedly urged to it, from making that provision for officers, which was requisite to interest them in the service. This has produced such carelessness and indifference to the service, as is subversive of every officer-like quality. They have disgusted the army by repeated instances of the most whimsical favoritism in their promotions; and by an absurd prodigality of rank to foreigners, and to the meanest staff of the army They have not been able to summon resolution enough to withstand the impudent importunity and vain boasting of foreign pretenders; but have manifested such a ductility and inconstancy in their proceedings, as will warrant the charge of suffering themselves to be bullied by every petty adventurer, who comes armed with ostentatious pretensions of military merit and experience. Would you believe it, Sir? it is become almost proverbial in the mouths of the Frendi officers and other foreigners, that they have nothing more to do, to obtain whatever they please, than to assume a high tone, and assert their own merit with confidence and perseverance. These things wound my feelings as a republican more than I can express, and in some degree make me contemptible in my own eyes.

" America once had a representation, that would do honor to any age or nation. The present falling off is very alarming and dangerous. What is the cause *I* and How is it to be remedied T are questions that the welfare of these States requires should be well attended to. The great men, who composed our first council, — are they dead, have they deserted the cause, or what has become

of them? Very few ate dead, and still fewer have deserted the cause; they are all, except the few who still remain in Congress, either in the field or in the civil offices of their respective States; far the greater part are engaged in the latter. The only remedy then is to take them out of these employments, and return them to the place where their presence is infinitely more important.

" Each State, in order to promote its own internal government and prosperity, has selected its best members to fill the offices within itself, and conduct its own affairs. Men have been fonder of the emoluments and conveniences of being employed at home; and local attachment, falsely operating, has made them more provident for the particular interests of the States to which they belonged, than for the common interests of the confederacy. This is a most pernicious mistake, and must be corrected. However important it is to give form and efficiency to your interior constitutions and police; it is infinitely more important to have a wise general council; otherwise a failure of the measures of the Union will overturn all your labors for the advancement of your particular good, and ruin the common cause. You should not beggar the councils of the United States to enrich the administration of the several members. Realize to yourself the consequences of having a Congress despised at home and abroad. How can the common force be exerted, if the power of collecting it be put in weak, foolish, and unsteady hands? How can we hope for success in our European negotiations, if the nations of Europe have no confidence in the wisdom and vigor of the great Continental government? This is the object on which their eyes are fixed; hence it is, America will derive its importance or insignificance in their estimation.

" You and I had some conversation, when I had the pleasure of seeing you last, with respect to the existence of a certain faction. Since I saw you, I have discovered such convincing traits of the monster, that I cannot doubt its reality in the most extensive sense. I dare say you have seen and heard enough to set-

tle the matter in your own mind. I believe it unmasked its batteries too soon, and begins to hide its head; but, as I imagine it will only change the storm to a sap, all the true and sensible friends to their country, and of course to a certain great man, ought to be upon the watch, to counterplot the secret machinations of his enemies. I am, with great regard and respect, Ate." GEORGE WASHINGTON TO WILLIAM GORDON.

" *Valley Forge,* 15 *February,* 1778. — Dear Sir; Since my last to you about the end of January, I have been favored with your letter of the 12th of that month, which did not reach my hands till within these few days. The question there put was, in some degree, solved in my last. But to be more explicit, I can assure you, that no person ever heard me drop an expression that had a tendency to resignation. The same principles, that led me to embark in toe opposition to the arbitrary claims of Great Britain, operate with additional force at this day; nor is it my desire to withdraw my service?, while they are considered of importance in the present contest; but to report a design of this kind is among the arts, which those, who are endeavouring to effect a change, are practising to bring it to pass. I have said, and I still do say, that there is not an officer in the service of the United States, that would return to the sweets of domestic life with more heartfelt joy than I should. But I would have this declaration accompanied by these sentiments, that, while the public are satisfied with my endeavours, I mean not to shrink from the cause. But the moment her voice, not that of faction, calls upon me to resign, I shall do it with as much pleasure as ever the weary traveller retired to rest. This, my dear Doctor, you are at liberty to assert; but, in doing it, I would have nothing formal. All things will come right again, and soon recover their proper tone, as the design is not only seen through, but reprobated. With sincere esteem and regard, I am, ccc. " JOHN FITZGERALD TO GEORGE WASHINGTON.

" *Yorktoum,* 16 *February,* 1778. — Dear Sir; I make no doubt but you will be surprised to have a letter of this date from me at this place. I was detained nine days on the other side of the Susquehanna for an opportunity of crossing it, and, when I did, it was not without great difficulty and some danger. Upon my arrival here on Saturday afternoon, I waited upon Mr. Laurens, who, then being much engaged, asked me to breakfast next morning, giving me to understand that he had something of consequence to say to me. In the morning he asked me, if you had ever seen the much talked of letter from General Conway to General Gales. I answered, I was certain that you never had, unless since my departure from camp. He then said it was now in the hands of Mr. Roberdeau, who, to his knowledge, showed it to some, and he had reason to believe to a great many, and that, though the paragraph quoted by Colonel Wilkinson was not set down *verbatim,* yet in substance it contained that and ten times more. Upon this I determined to demand it from Mr. Roberdeau in order to let you have a copy of it.

" I waited on him this morning, when, after a short introduction, I let him into the intention of my visit. He assured me he had shown the letter only to two, the President and another, and gave me his honor, that he had delivered it to a French gentleman by an order from General Conway, which was sent back after he had crossed the Susquehanna. He was full of his assurances, that the letter did not contain the paragraph alluded to, which gave him infinite satisfaction, as he entertained the highest respect both for you and General Gates. He added, however, that had the letter remained in his possession, he should not have thought himself at liberty to let a copy be taken, without the consent of the gentleman who intrusted him with it. I told him, that, as he had pledged his honor about the delivery of it, I thought it unnecessary to say any more upon that subject, but that I should have thought it my duty to take the most effectual means of procuring a copy, had the original remained in his hands.

" I then returned to Mr. Laurens, who

gave me an extract, which he had taken from it, which I take the liberty of enclosing to you. The whole of that letter I understand was couched in terms of the most bitter invective, of which this is a small sample. I enclose you this extract rather for your private information, than with an expectation of its answering any other purpose at this time. I am of opinion that the gentlemen, who have been most active in this business, are by this time heartily sick of it, and plainly perceive that the fabric, which they were endeavouring to rear, was likely to fall upon their own heads. Mr. Laurens's sentiments upon the whole of this matter were exceedingly just, and delivered with the greatest candor. I am, die" HORATIO GATES TO GEORGE WASHINGTON.

" *Yorktown, 19 February,* 1778. — Sir; Yesterday I had the honor to receive your Excellency's letter of the 9th instant, and Colonel Fitzgerald was at this time one of General Washington' aids-decamp. The extract taken from Conway's letter by President Laurens was in the following words. " What pity there is bnt one Gates! But the more I see of this army, the leas I think it fit for general action under its actual chiefs and actual discipline. I speak to you sincerely and freely, and wish I could serve under you." earnestly hope no more of that time, so precious to the public, may be lost upon the subject of General Conway's letter. Whether that gentleman does or does not deserve the suspicions you express, would be entirely indifferent to me, did he not possess an office of high rank in the army of the United States; for that reason solely I wish he may answer all the expectations of Congress. As to the gentleman, I have no personal connexion with him, nor had I any correspondence, previous to his writing the letter which has given offence; nor have I since written to him, save to certify what I know to be the contents of the letter. He therefore must be responsible; as I heartily dislike controversy, even upon my own account, and much more in a matter wherein I was only accidentally concerned. In regard to the parts of your Excellency's

letter addressed particularly to me, I solemnly declare that I am of no faction; and if any of my letters taken aggregately or by paragraphs convey any meaning, which in any construction is offensive to your Excellency, that was by no means the intention of the writer. After this, I cannot believe your Excellency will either suffer your suspicions or the prejudices of others to induce you to spend another moment upon this subject. With great respect, I am, Sir, &c." PATRICK HENRY TO GEORGE WASHINGTON.

" *Williamsburg, 20 February,* 1778. — Dear Sir; You will, no doubt, be surprised at seeing the enclosed letter, in which the encomiums bestowed on me are as undeserved, as the censures aimed at you are unjust. I am sorry there should be one man who counts himself my friend, who is not yours.

" Perhaps I give you needless trouble in handing you this paper. The writer of it may be too insignificant to deserve any notice. If I knew this to be the case, I should not have intruded on your lime, which is so precious. But there may possibly be some scheme or party forming to your prejudice. The enclosed leads to such a suspicion. Believe me, Sir, I have too high a sense of the obligations America has to you, to abet or countenance so unworthy a proceeding. The most exalted merit has ever been found to attract envy. But I please myself with the hope, that the same fortitude and greatness of mind, which have hitherto braved all the difficulties and dangers inseparable from your station, will rise superior to every attempt The anonymous letter to Patrick Henry, dated January 12th, and primed above, p. 495.

of the envious partisan. I really cannot tell who is the writer of this letter, which not a little perplexes me. The handwrjting is alto gether strange to me.

" To give you the trouble of this gives me pain. It would suit my inclination better to give you some assistance in the great business of the war. But I will not conceal any thing from you, by which you may be affected; for I really think your personal welfare and the happiness of America are intimately connected. I beg you will be assured of that high regard and esteem, with which I ever am, dear Sir, your affectionate friend and very humble servant." GEORGE WASHINGTON TO HORATIO GATES.

" *Valley Forge, 24 February, 1778.* — Sir; I yesterday received your favor of the 19th instant. I am as averse to controversy as any man; and, had I not been forced into it, you never would have had occasion to impute to me even the shadow of a disposition towards it. Your repeatedly and solemnly disclaiming any offensive views, in those matters which have been the subject of our past correspondence, makes me willing to close with the desire you express, of burying them hereafter in silence-and, as far as future events will permit, oblivion. My temper leads me to peace and harmony with all men; and it is peculiarly my wish to avoid any personal feuds or dissensions with those, who are embarked in the same great national interest with myself, as every difference of this kind must in its consequences be very injurious. I am, Sir, your most obedient servant." PATRICK HENRY TO GEORGE WASHINGTON.

" *Williamsburg, 5 March,* 1778. — Dear Sir; By an express, which Colonel Finnie sent to camp, I enclosed to you an anonymous letter, which I hope got safe to hand. I am anxious to hear something that will serve to explain the strange affair, which I am now informed is taken up respecting you. Mr. Custis has just paid us a visit, and by him I learn sundry particulars concerning General Mifflin, that much surprised me. It is very hard to trace the schemes and windings of the enemies to America. I really thought that man its friend; however, I am too far from him to judge of his present temper.

" While you face the armed enemies of our liberty in the field, and by the favor of God have been kept unhurt, I trust your country will never harbour in her bosom the miscreant, who would ruin her best VOL. V. 65 supporter. I wish not to flatter; but when arts, unworthy honest men, are use/1 to defame and traduce you, I think it not amiss, but a. du-

ty, to assure you of that estimation in which the public hold yon. Not that I thiuk any testimony I can bear is necessary for your support, or private satisfaction; for a bare recollection of what is past must give you sufficient pleasure in every circumstance of life. But I cannot help assuring you, on this occasion, of the high sense of gratitude which all ranks of. men in this your native country bear to you. It will give me sincere pleasure to manifest my regards, and render my best services to you or yours. I do not like to make a parade of these things, and I know you are not fond of it; however, I hope the occasion will plead my excuse. Wishing you all possible felicity, I am, my dear Sir, your ever affectionate friend and very humble servant." GEORGE WASHINGTON TO PATRICK HENRY.

" *Valley Forge, 27 March,* 1778. — Dear Sir; About eight days ago I was honored with your favor of the 20th ultimo. Your friend ship, Sir, in transmitting to me the anonymous letter you had received, lays me under the most grateful obligations, and if my acknowledgments can be due for any thing more, it is for the polite and delicate terms in which you have been pleased to communicate the matter.

" I have ever been happy in supposing that I had a place in your esteem, and the proof you have afforded on this occasion makes me peculiarly so. The favorable light in which you hold me is truly flattering; but I should feel much regret, if I thought the happiness of America so intimately connected with my personal welfare, as you so obligingly seem to consider it. All I can say is, that she has ever had, and I trust she ever will have, my honest exertions to promote her interest. I cannot hope that my services have been the best; but my heart tells me they have been the best that I could render.

" That I may have erred in using the means in my power for accomplishing the objects of the arduous, exalted station with which I am honored, I cannot doubt; nor do I wish my conduct to be exempted from reprehension farther than it may deserve. Error is the portion

of humanity, and to censure it, whether committed by this or that public character, is the prerogative of freemen. However, being intimately acquainted with the man I conceive to be the author of the letter transmitted, and having always received from him the strongest professions of attachment and regard, I am constrained to consider him as not possessing, at least, a great degree of candor and sincerity, though his views in addressing you should have been the result of conviction, and founded in motives of public good. This is not the only secret, insidious attempt, that has been made to wound my reputation. There have been others equally base, cruel, and ungenerous, because conducted with as little frankness, and proceeding from views, perhaps, as personally interested. I am, dear Sir, 'with gTeat esteem and regard, your much obliged friend, Ate" GEORGE WASHINGTON TO PATRICK BENRT.

" *Camp,* 28 *March,* 1778. — Dear Sir; Just as I was about to close my letter of yesterday, your favor of the 5th instant came to hand. I can only thank you again, in the language of the most undissembled gratitude, for your friendship; and assure you, that the indulgent disposition, which Virginia in particular, and the States in general, entertain towards me, gives me the most sensible pleasure. The approbation of my country is what I wish; and, as far as my abilities and opportunities will permit, I hope I shall endeavour to deserve it. It is the highest reward to a feeling mind; and happy are they, who so conduct themselves as to merit it.

" The anonymous letter, with which you were pleased to favor me, was written by Dr. Rush, so far as I can judge from a similitude of hands. This man has been elaborate and studied in his professions of regard for me; and long since the letter to you. My caution to avoid any thing, which could injure the service, prevented me from communicating, but to a very few of my friends, the intrigues of a faction, which I know was formed against me, since it might serve to publish our internal dissensions; but their own restless zeal to advance their views has too clearly betrayed them, and made concealment on my part fruitless. I cannot precisely mark the extent of their views, but it appeared in general, that General Gates was to be exalted on the ruin of my reputation and influence. This I am authorized to say, from undeniable facts in my own possession, from publications, the evident scope of which could not be mistaken, and from private detractions industriously circulated. General Mifflin, it is commonly supposed, bore the second part in the cabal; and General Conway, I know, was a very active and malignant partisan; but I have good reasons to believe, that their machinations have recoiled most sensibly upon themselves. With sentiments of great esteem and regard, I am, dear Sir, your affectionate humble servant." JAMES WILKINSON TO GEORGE WASHINGTON.

" *Reading, 28 March,* 1778. — Sir; I beg you to receiTe the grateful homage of a sensible mind, for your condescension in exposing to me General Gates's letters, which unmask his artifices and efforts to ruin me. The authenticity of the information received through Lord Stirling I cannot confirm; as I solemnly assure your Excellency I do not remember the conversation which passed on" that occasion, nor can I recollect particular passages of that letter, as I had but a cursory view of it at a late hour. However, I so well remember its general tenor, that, although General Gates has pledged his word it is a wicked and malicious forgery, I will stake my reputation, if the genuine letter is produced, that words to the same effect will appear; else how could Conway acknowledge to Colonel Stewart that he had written such a letter, or how could Dr. Hutchinson have heard this identical passage mentioned in Philadelphia before he left that city? I am, &x."

Thus have been brought together such authentic materials, respecting the origin and objects of this faction, as have fallen into my hands. The character of Conway became at length so thoroughly developed, that even the eyes of Congress were opened. While on command at Albany, in the spring of 1778,

he wrote a letter to Congress, impertinent, rude, and complaining, in which he intimated a wish to resign his commission. A motion to accept General Conway's resignation was immediately carried. When he received the intelligence, he expressed great astonishment, said it was not his intention to resign, and that his meaning had been misunderstood. He proceeded immediately to Congress, and claimed to be restored; but the tide had changed, and his explanation and request were equally unavailing.

Being now without employment, he repaired to Philadelphia when that city was evacuated by the British. His freedom of speech and offensive manners involved him in difficulties with the American officers, and on the 4th of July he fought a duel with General Cadwalader. The ball passed through Conway's mouth and the upper part of his neck, and for some time the wound was supposed to be mortal. In this state, after lingering several days, he wrote the following letter..

See an extract from this letter in the preterit volume, p. 372. THOMAS CONWAY TO GEORGE WASHINGTON.

" Philadelphia, 23 July, 1778. " Sir, " I find myself just able to hold the pen during a few minutes, and take this opportunity of expressing my sincere grief for having done, written, or said any thing disagreeable to your Excellency. My career will soon be over; therefore justice and truth prompt me to declare my last sentiments. You are in my eyes the great and good man. May you long enjoy the love, veneration, and esteem of these States, whose liberties you have asserted by your virtues. I am with the greatest respect, &c.

" Thomas Conway."

This voluntary confession of his fault, whether proceeding from the reproaches of conscience, or motives of honor and justice, may perhaps be considered as a reparation for the personal injuries he had done to the Commander-in-chief, but it will not remove the guilt nor efface the memory of his conduct, in attempting to kindle the flame of discord, and sow the seeds of faction,

which threatened the safety and even the national existence of the state, whose cause he was pretending to serve. Contrary to his expectation and that of his surgeon, he recovered from his wound. Deserted by his former friends, deprived of his station in the army by Congress, and censured with indignation by the public voice, nothing was now left for him but to depart from the country in disgrace. He sailed for France before the end of the year. Much has been said by different writers, as to the names of the individuals implicated in this affair, and their ultimate design. That a factious spirit prevailed in Congress and the army, that this spirit was fomented by a few intriguing persons, and that a small party at least entertained views hostile to the Commander-in-chief, cannot be doubted. But in my opinion there is not sufficient evidence to prove, that there was any concerted plan of action, or any fixed design among the leaders. A few aspiring men, like Gates and Mifflin, it may be presumed, flattered themselves with indefinite hopes, and looked forward to a change as promising the best means of aiding their ambitious views; but that they united in any clear or fixed purpose is not probable. Their schemes never arrived at this degree of maturity. Their efforts consisted in secretly encouraging disaffection to Washington, contravening his wishes, and obstructing his plans, till his popularity should thus be gradually undermined, and they might venture to adopt bolder measures. This was soon found to be a vain labor.

VOL. V.. R R

To what extent Congress participated, or what individuals were chiefly concerned, can be decided only by,the tenor of their resolves and their recorded votes. From these it may certainly be inferred, that the faction had a few active partisans in that body. Some writers have laid the charge heavily upon the New England members; but this charge has been ably and conclusively refuted in Mr. Austin's *Life of Gerry,* where several interesting facts on the subject may be found. Others implicate the Southern members, but with no better evidence than conjecture. In truth it cannot be proved, nor is it probable, that any combinations unfavorable to the Commander-in-chief existed, either in the army or in Congress, which partook of local interests, or were sustained by the prejudices of any particular State or district of the Union.

No. VII. pp. 150, 164, 175.

HOWE'S LETTERS.

GENERAL HOWE TO GENERAL WASHINGTON.

Philadelphia, 6 November, 1777. Sir,

I am favored with your letter of the 4th instant. The general exchange of prisoners is so desirable a measure in justice to the officers and men immediately concerned, that I have repeatedly demanded of you a releasement of prisoners equivalent to those yon have received, as far as the numbers in your possession will admit, on which condition I could enter upon a further exchange. The officers I have already permitted to return to their homes, on account of some peculiarity in their situations; and other indulgences, needless to mention, must sufficiently have evinced my desire to relieve the whole; and, when this previous point before mentioned is adjusted by our respective Commissaries, I shall readily agree to make the exchange as general as possible, and to the return of all such officers and men as may afterwards remain unexchanged on either side, under obvious and reasonable conditions.

Those at present prisoners with me are ready to be delivered on the shortest notice, and it rests solely with you to justify me in doing it. In the mean time, as I understand the British, Hessian, and Provincial officers and soldiers in your possession are disposed of in many different places, and very distant from hence, I am to request that you will order the most exact returns of them and their situation to be forwarded to ray head-quarters, that the wants of the officers and soldiers, as to money, credit, clothing, and medicines may be supplied by persons appointed by me, and having from you the-necessary passports.

I cannot conclude this letter without making complaint against Mr. Boudinot, your commissary of prisoners, for his inattention to the wants of both officers and men, and for not affording an opportunity, though solicited, to make them known to me, that they might be supplied. I am also to call upon you to redress the grievances of several among them, who I am well informed are roost injuriously and unjustifiably loaded with irons.

With due respect I am, Sir, your most obedient humble servant,

W. Howr.

Philadelphia, November, 1777.

Sir,

I am averse to altercation, and therefore wish to be explicit and understood in my answer to your letter of the 14th instant, and to your very importunate requisition of the 23d. I shall never agree to a partial exchange of prisoners, until you have on your part fulfilled the cartel agreed upon; but as that matter has already been sufficiently investigated in the course of our correspondence, and by deputies respectively appointed, it is unnecessary to enlarge upon the subject. As liquidating the account, by the delivery of an equal number of prisoners for those received by your agents and commissaries, is the only preliminary, which can be admitted for a further arrangement; of course it rests with you, whether an exchange is to take place or not, and therefore you stand responsible for the inconvenience, which the officers and men of our respective armies must unavoidably be put to in their present state of captivity.

In order to alleviate their distress, and remove the evil as far as depends upon me, I shall permit officers for officers of equal rank to go home upon their paroles. That rule, if you choose to adopt the measure, shall be observed for such officers as you send upon their paroles to this place, New York, or Rhode Island. I could wish there were no grievances on either side, real or imaginary, to be complained of, as every man, in my opinion, who comes fairly under the description of a prisoner of war, without any aggravating circumstances on his part, is undoubtedly enti-

tled to good treatment, and every indulgence, which can in prudence be granted; bat that indulgence can only be regulated by the situation of the place, in which the prisoners happen to reside. If ever any officer or commissary under my command has deviated from the civility, care, and attention due to prisoners of war, under the above description, it is not consistent with my-knowledge, and is contrary to my directions and intention.

The provision issued to the prisoners, who are or have been in my hands, has been uniformly the same, and is agreeable to a regulation, which has long been established for victualling British troops, when they are on board men of war or transports. They surely must receive that allowance, as a field-officer visits them every morning, who has orders to hear their complaints and to report to me. You cannot suppose there could be any intention of deviating from this rule in the case of Joseph Cloyd and William Dewes. I have no objection to your sending a commissary, with a supply of clothing, money, and other necessaries for the prisoners at Philadelphia, who shall be permitted to visit the places where they are confined.

In return, I expect you will send passports for persons, who shall not be above the rank of quartermasters or commissaries, to carry supplies for the prisoners in your hands at Hartford and other places, where they are confined. You can stipulate the places to which it is necessary the quartermasters and commissaries should go. I cannot with any precision ascertain them, and therefore leave it at large for your determination. I cannot enter into the merits of Mr. Boudinot's report to you, as he refers to a correspondence with Commissary Loring, who is at New York. You wish me to particularize the cases I allude to, of prisoners of war being injuriously and unjustifiably loaded with irons. Major Stockton and other officers of the New Jersey Volunteers were put in irons at Princeton. The Major and a captain of that regiment were marched out of that place under a guard, and handcuffed together.

I am with due respect, Sir, your most obedient servant.

W. Howe.

Philadelphia, 21 December, 1777. Sir, I have deferred answering your letter of the 28th of November, daily expecting to receive the promised list of prisoners in your possession, which I was sorry to find Mr. Boudinot had no knowledge of, when he met my commissary on the 2d instant; but, having directed a letter to be written to him on that subject, I trust he will no longer delay so necessary a communication, more particularly when I am given to understand you will have pleasure in affording them every degree of relief their unfortunate situation will admit. I shall be ready to return your officers in proportion upon their parole, as soon as I receive mine from you.

I hope you will excuse my compliance with your request of the 14th instant, for granting passports to vessels carrying provisions and fuel for the troops under the articles of the convention, conceiving it would not be possible to prevent the passports from being improperly used, and being hopeful that the troops may be.permitted to embark at Rhode Island, agreeably to General Burgoyne's request, which will make such provision unnecessary. The transports designed for that service sailed from hence some time ago. In consequence of a former letter from you, a vessel was ordered to be laden at New York, and to proceed with flour to Boston for the troops. This want being supplied, I trust that fuel may be procured without any great inconvenience, or a necessity for passports from me, even though the troops should not embark so soon as I expect.

With due respect I am, Sir, your most obedient servant.

W. Howe.

No. VIII. p. 190.

GENERAL BURUOYNE TO GENERAL WASHINGTON.

Cambridge, 25 November, 1777. Sir,

Your Excellency will have observed by the despatch from Sir William Howe to me, which passed through your hands, that it was matter of great doubt whether the transports destined to carry the troops to England, according to the convention, would be able to make the port of Boston in this advanced season of the year; and, therefore, that it might be advisable to send them to Rhode Island, upon the supposition that a mere change of place, which made no alteration in the intent and meaning of the convention, would-be readily agreed to.

That no time may be lost in an embarkation, which I conceive willbo equally desirable to the troops and to this country in point of conveniency, I take the earliest occasion to apply to your Excellency, or through your means, if you judge necessary, to the Continental Con VOL. V. 66 R R gress, for consent to march the troops to Providence, or such otheT place as may be commodious to pass them by small craft to Newport; this march to take place whenever advice shall be received of the arrival of the transports. Should any objection be against Rhode Island, any convenient port in the Sound would equally answer the purpose.

Should any considerations arise, which I do not foresee, to make the whole proposal objectionable to yourself or the Congress, and the troops should be obliged to wait the passage of the transports round Cape Cod, I in that case request passports for myself and my suite to Rhode Island, in order to embark on board a separate frigate; not only matters of great private concern in business, but also my state of health, requiring my speedy return to England. I have no scruple, Sir, in asking this favor at your hands, nor shall I have any in acknowledging it, confident that no duty is impaired by an intercourse of personal civilities in matters where the public cause cannot possibly be committed or affected. The packet directed to Sir William Howe, enclosed herewith, contains recommendations in which the preferment of many meritorious individuals is deeply interested. I am persuaded, Sir, that description will be a full apology for troubling you to pass it by a trumpet. I have the honor to be, Sir, &c.

J. Burgotnb.

No. IX. p. 196.

ENCAMPMENT AT VALLEY FORGE.

A wide difference of opinion prevailed among the officers, in regard to the manner of cantoning the troops in the winter after the campaign of 1777. A council of war was held, on the 30th of November, in which the subject was largely discussed. It was found that the views of the officers were divided upon three different plans; first, to quarter the troops at Wilmington; secondly, to canton them in huts in the valley of Tredyfrin, a few miles west of the Schuylkill; thirdly, to station them in a line from Reading to Lancaster. Each of these plans had its advocates. Washington requested all the general officers to communicate their sentiments in writing. This was done by the most of them in a detailed manner, each giving his reasons for the plan he approved, and his objections to the others. Opinions and counsels were so various and contradictory, as to take away all hope of unanimity, and to make it necessary for the Commander-inchief to act according to his own judgment, and upon his own responsibility. He at length decided to form an encampment at Valley Forge. The ground was covered with wood. It was now the beginning of winter, and huts were to be built to cover the troops from the weather, and intrenchments dug for the defence of the camp.

From the Orderly Book, December 17th, 1777, *near Valley Forge.* — " The Commander-in-chief with the highest satisfaction expresses his thanks to the officers and soldiers, for the fortitude and patience with which they have sustained the fatigues of the campaign. Although in some instances we unfortunately failed, yet, upon the whole, Heaven has smiled on our arms and crowned them with signal success; and we may upon the best grounds conclude, that, by a spirited continuance of the measures necessary for our defence, we shall finally obtain the end of our warfare, *independence, liberty,* and *peace.* These are blessings worth contending for at every hazard. But we hazard nothing. The power of America alone, duly exerted, would have nothing to dread from the force of Britain. Yet we stand not wholly upon our own ground. France yields us every aid we ask, and there are reasons to believe the period is not very distant, when she will take a more active part, by declaring war against the British crown. Every motive, therefore, irresistibly urges us, nay, commands us, to a firm and manly perseverance in our opposition to our oppressors; to disregard difficulties, endure hardships, and contemn every danger.

" The General ardently wishes it were now in his power to conduct the troops into the best winter-quarters. But where are these to be found? Should we retire to the interior parts of the State, we should find them crowded with virtuous citizens, who, sacrificing their all, have left Philadelphia, and fled thither for protection. To their distresses, humanity forbids ns to add. This is not all; we should leave a large extent of fertile country to be despoiled and ravaged by the enemy, from which they would draw vast supplies, and where many of our firm friends would be exposed to all the miseries of the most insulting and wanton depredation. A train of evils might be enumerated, but these will suffice. These considerations make it indispensably necessary for the army to take such a position, as will enable it most effectually to prevent distress, and to give the most extensive security; and in that position we must make ourselves the best shelter in our power. With activity and diligence, huts may be erected that will be warm and dry. In these the troops will be compact, more secure against surprises than if in a divided state, and at hand to protect the country. These cogent reasons have determined the General to take post in the neighbourhood of this camp; and, influenced by them, he persuades himself that the officers and soldiers, with one heart and one mind, will resolve to surmount every difficulty, with a fortitude and patience becoming their profession, and the sacred cause in which they are engaged. He himself will share in the hardships and partake of every inconvenience.

" To-morrow being the day set apart by the honorable Congress for public thanksgiving and praise, and duty calling us devoutly to express our grateful acknowledgments to God for the manifold blessings he has granted us, the General directs that the army remain in its present quarters, and that the chaplains perform divine service with their several corps and brigades; and earnestly exhorts all officers and soldiers, whose absence is not indispensably necessary, to attend with reverence the solemnities of the day." *From the Orderly Book, December 18th.* — " The major-generals, and officers commanding divisions, are to appoint an active field-officer in and for each of their respective brigades to superintend the business of hutting, agreeably to the directions they shall receive; and, in addition to these, the commanding officer of each regiment is to appoint an officer to-oversee the building of huts for each regiment; which officer is to take his orders from the field-officer of the brigade he belongs to, who is to mark out the precise spot, in which every hut for officers and soldiers is to be placed, that uniformity and order may be observed.

" An exact return of all the tools, now in the hands of every regiment, is to be made immediately to the quartermaster-general, who, with the adjutant-general, is to see that they, together with those in store, are duly and justly allotted to the regimental overseers of the work, who are to keep an account of the men's names, in whose hands they are placed, that they may be accountable for them. The superintendents and overseers are to be exempt from all other duty, and will moreover have an allowance for their trouble.

" The colonels, or commanding officers of regiments, with their captains, arc immediately to cause their men to be divided into parties of twelve, and see that each party has its proportion of tools, and commences a hut for that number; and, as an encouragement to industry and art, the general promises to reward the party in each regiment, which finishes its hut in the quickest and most workmanlike manner, with

twelve dollars. And as there is reason to believe, that boards for covering the huts may be found scarce and difficult to be got, he offers one hundred dollars to any officer or soldier, who, in the opinion of three gentlemen that he shall appoint as judges, shall substitute some other covering, that may be cheaper and more quickly made, and will in every respect answer the end.

" The soldiers' huts are to be of the following dimensions, namely, fourteen feet by sixteen each; the sides, ends, and roofs to be made with logs; and the roof made tight with split slabs, or in some other way; the sides made tight with clay; a fireplace made of wood, and secured with clay on the inside eighteen inches thick; this fireplace to be in the rear of the hut; the door to be in the end next the street; the doors to be made of split oak slabs, unless boards can be procured; the side walls to be six feet and a half high. The officers' huts are to form a line in the rear of the troops, one hut to be allowed to each general officer; one to the staff of each brigade; one to the field-officers of each regiment; one to the staff of each regiment; one to the commissioned officers of two companies; and one to every twelve non-commissioned officers and soldiers."

Before the encampment was completed, General Washington began to turn his attention to a subject, which he considered of the greatest importance, and of the most pressing necessity. The experience of three campaigns had proved, that radical and extensive changes must speedily take place in the organization and management of the different departments of the army, both in regard to its military constitution and discipline, and the methods of obtaining supplies, or its dissolution was seriously to be apprehended. To this task he applied himself, therefore, with unremitted assiduity. According to his custom he obtained the views of each of the general officers in writing. Several of these communications were elaborate essays, in which were discussed at large the entire system of the army, the modes of its establishment, its internal and external regulations, its imperfections and wants, and the remedies that ought to be provided. From these papers, and the results of his own observation and reflections, a long report was drawn up, containing the outlines of a new and improved system, which was adopted in all its essential parts by a committee of Congress, who visited the camp soon afterwards for the purpose of consulting the Commander-in-chief on the affairs of the army; and it was ultimately approved by Congress.

In the *Life of Mezandtr Hamilton,* Vol. I. p. 174, it ia Mid of this piper, that " it U manifestly the work of Colonel Hamilton." This inference is

No. X. p. 214.

BARON STEUBEN.

After serving with distinction in the army of the King of Prussia for several years, Baron Steuben retired to an estate in Swabia soon after the peace of 1763. He obtained honorable stations at the courts of some of the sovereign princes of Germany, particularly at that of the reigning prince of Hohenzollern, where he held the post of grand marshal of the court. In April, 1777, he went to Paris on his way to England, intending to spend the summer with some of his acquaintances in that country, who had invited him to make them a visit.

A desire to see his old friend and companion in arms, the Count de St. Germain, who had recently been elevated to the place of minister of war, caused him to stop in Paris. Having given notice of his arrival to the Count, that minister requested him not to come to Versailles till they should have a private interview on a subject of ' importance. The interview took place, and the Count de St. tierdrawn from the circumstance, that a draft exists in his handwriting. Bat it was in fact the work of many hands. There are few points in the paper itself which are not contained or intimated in some of the communications of the general officers. As one of General Washington's aids, it was natural that Colonel Hamilton should be employed to arrange and condense the materials into the proper form of a report, especially as no one connected with the General's family was better qualified to execute the task, both from his knowledge of the subject and his ability. This is the only tense in which it can be considered as his work. Indeed, whoever is accustomed to consult the manuscripts of public documents will often be led into error, if he ascribes the *authorship* of every paper to the person in whose handwriting it may be found. This remark has particular force, when applied to the important papers to which Washington affiled his name. Tbey were always the results of patient thought and investigation on his own part, aided by such light as he could collect from others, in whose intelligence and judgment he could confide. Whatever pen he may have employed to embody these results, it may be laid down aa a rule, to which there is no exception, that the writer aimed to express as clearly and compactly as he could what he knew to be the sentiments of Washington. This fact alone can account for the extraordinary uniformity in style, modes of expression, and turns of thought, which prevails throughout the immense body of Washington's letters, from his earliest youth to the end of his life. It will seldom be accurate to say, in regard to any of his papers, that the person, in whose handwriting they may be found, was their *author;* nor indeed is it believed that there is in history an instance of a public man, who was in the genuine sense of the term more emphatically the author of the papers, which received the sanction of his name.

main proposed to the Baron to go over to America, and enter into the service of the United States, explaining at the same time the situation and wants of the American army, its deficiency in discipline, and the great advantages it could not fail to derive from an officer of his rank, knowledge, and experience in military regulations and tactics. He represented in favorable terms the political prospects of the Americans, and said they had already declared their Independence, which there was the strongest probability of their being able to maintain; that France and Spain were inclined to render them indirect support; and that an alliance between the United States and the House of Bourbon might ultimately be expected. The same suggestion and reasons were afterwards urged upon the Baron by the Spanish ambassador in Paris, by the Prince de Montbarry, and the Count de Vergennes. He was introduced by Silas Deane to Dr. Franklin, with whom he conversed on the subject. He inquired whether the American commissioners were authorized to confirm any stipulations with him, to which Dr. Franklin replied in the negative, and added, that, so far from having this power, Congress had refused to ratify a contract, which the commissioners had made with Ducoudray and the officers of his suite. Upon this information the Baron abandoned the project, as he was unwilling to sacrifice a post of honor and profit, which he held in Germany, without some security of an equivalent if he went to America.

The Baron returned to Germany, and a few days after his arrival at Rastadt he received a letter from Beaumarchais, pressing anew the proposal of the ministers, and informing him that a vessel was about to depart from Marseilles, in which he could have a passage to America. At the same time a letter came from the Count de St. Germain, urging his immediate return to Paris, and assuring him that satisfactory arrangements should be made. Relying on this pledge, he hastened back to Paris; and at an interview with Count de Vergennes, the minister told him that it was not necessary to insist on any stipulations with the American commissioners, that Dr. Franklin would give him letters to the President of Congress and to some of the principal members, that there could be no doubt of the readiness of Congress to employ an officer of his character and abilities on such terms as would be agreeable to him, and that, should he be disappointed in this expectation, the French government would indemnify him for the losses or injuries he might sustain in his affairs. On this basis the plan was settled. Beaumarchais supplied him with as much money as his immediate necessities required. The Baron embarked at Marseilles, September 26th, 1777, and after a rough and dangerous voyage he landed at Portsmouth, in New Hampshire, on the 1st of December.

It is to be recollected, that at this time the French government bad taken no part openly in favor of the American cause, and consequently could hold no direct communication with Congress concerning a matter of this kind.

From, Portsmouth Baron Steuben wrote the following letter to General Washington, accompanied by copies of his letters of recommendation to Congress.

" Sir,

" The enclosed copy of a letter, whose original I shall have the honor to present to your Excellency, will inform you of the motives, that brought me over to this land. I shall only add to it, that the object of my greatest ambition is to render your country all the services in my power, and to deserve the title of a citizen of America by fighting for the cause of your liberty. If the distinguished ranks in which I have served in Europe should be an obstacle, I had rather serve under your Excellency as a volunteer, than to be an oBject of discontent to such deserving officers, as have already distinguished themselves amongst you.

" Such being the sentiments I have always professed, I dare hope that the respectable Congress of the United States of America will accept my services. I could say, moreover, were it not for the fear of offending your modesty, that your Excellency is the only person under whom, after having served under the King of Prussia, I could wish to pursue an art, to which I have wholly given up myself. I intend to go to Boston in a few days, where I shall present my letters to Mr. Hancock, member of Congress, and there I shall wait for your Excellency's orders, according to which I shall take convenient measures. I have the honor to be, &c.

" Steuren."

Renjamin Franklin To George Washington.

" Passy, 4 September, 1777. " Sir, " The gentleman, who will have the honor

of waiting upon you with this letter, is the Baron de Steuben, Lieutenant-General in the King of Prussia's service, whom he attended in all his campaigns, being his aid-de-camp, quartermaster-general, &c. He goes to America with a true zeal for our cause, and a view of engaging in it, and rendering it all the service in his power. He is recommended to us by two of the best judges of military merit in this country, M. Is Comte de Vergennes, and M. le Comte de St. Germain, who have long been personally acquainted with him, and interest themselves in promoting his voyage, from the full persuasion that the knowledge and experience he has acquired by twenty years' study and practice in the Prussian school may be of great use in our armies. I therefore cannot but recommend him Warmly to your Excellency, wishing that our service may be made agreeable to him. I have the honor to be, &c.

" B. Franklin."

Baron Steuben repaired without delay to Congress; and, when his papers had been read, it was resolved, that the thanks of Congress should be presented to him " for the zeal he had shown for the American cause, and the disinterested tender he had been pleased to make of his military talents," and that his services should be accepted. He joined the army at Valley Forge as a volunteer, and was appointed, May 5th, 1778, inspector-general of the army, with the rank of major-general, his pay to commence at the time of his joining the army.

Lafayette was in correspondence with the Baron on his first arrival in America. The following extract from a letter, written to him by Lafayette, affords a gratifying testimony of the warm attachment, which that young nobleman had already contracted for the Commander-in-chief.

" Permit me," said Lafayette, " to express my satisfaction at your having seen General Washington. No enemies to that great man can be found, except among the enemies to his country; nor is it possible for any man of a noble spirit to refrain from loving the excel-

lent qualities of his heart. I think I know him as well as any person, and such is the idea which I have formed of him. His honesty, his frankness, his sensibility, his virtue, to the full extent in which this word can be understood, are above all praise. It is not for me to judge of his military talents; but according to my imperfect knowledge of these matters, his advice in council has always appeared to me the best, although his modesty prevents him sometimes from sustaining it; and his predictions have generally been fulfilled. I am the more happy in giving you this opinion of my friend, with all the sincerity which I feel, because some persons may perhaps attempt to deceive you on this point." — *MS. Letter, Albany, March 12th.*

No. XI. pp. 228,264.

PROPOSED ENTERPRISE AGAINST CANADA UNDER THE MARQUIS DE LAFAYETTE.

After General Gates returned from the northern department, as president of the Board of War, a project of an irruption into Canada, supposed to have originated with him, was adopted by Congress. An army of two or three thousand men was to proceed from Albany, cross Lake Champlain on the ice, burn the enemy's shipping at St. John's, press forward if possible to Montreal, and effect any other enterprise, which circumstances would permit. The plan was conceived and matured by the Board of War, and approved by Congress, without consulting General Washington; and the first knowledge he had of it was communicated in a letter from General Gates, enclosing another to the Marquis de Lafayette, informing the Marquis that he was appointed to the command of the expedition.. This was near the end of January, 1778. Perceiving the neglect and disrespect shown to the Commander-in-chief, by this mode of proceeding, Lafayette at first hesitated what course to pursue; more especially as the prospect of the success of such an enterprise in the midst of winter, without any obvious preparation, was very doubtful. General Washington, however, advised him to comply with the wishes of Congress, and accept the appointment, since, in any event, this high testimony of their confidence would be honorable to him, and his own prudence would be a sufficient guard to his reputation, in whatever manner the expedition might terminate.

Thus encouraged, Lafayette hastened to Yorktown to ascertain the views of Congress and the details of the plan. Every thing was promised, that he could desire, and General Gates assured him, that there would be no deficiency of supplies either as to men or means. It was a suspicious circumstance, however, that Conway was to be his second in command. The known hostility of that officer, as well as of General Gates, to the Commander-in-chief, raised very natural suspicions in the mind of Lafayette, that a scheme was laid for detaching him from the friend, to whom he was devoted by the strongest motives of principle and affection, and whose interests he was resolved at all hazards to support. This induced him at the outset, both by his conversation and arrangements, to give the most unequivocal proof of his sentiments and resolutions on that head. He succeeded in having the Baron de Kalb appointed to the expedition, who, being older in rank than Conway, would of course be the second in command. This request was not readily granted, but he insisted on it so strenuously, that it was finally conceded. The following letters will explain the sequel of the affair.

MARQUIS DE LAFAYETTE TO GENERAL WASHINGTON.

" Albany, 19 Februuy, 1778. " Dear General,

" Why am I so far from you? And why did the Board of War hurry me through the ice and snow, without knowing what I should do, or what they were doing themselves? You have thought, perhaps, that their project would be attended with difficulty, that some means had been neglected, and that I could not obtain all the success which they had promised me; but your Excellency cannot conceive what I have seen since I left the place where I waa quiet and near my friend, to run myself through all the blunders of madness, or

treachery, or God knows what. Let me begin the journal of my glorious campaign 1

" According to Lord Stirling's advice I went by Coryell's Ferry. Thence I proceeded to the State of New York, and had the pleasure of seeing the friends of America as warm in their love for the Commander-in-chief, as his best friends could wish. I spoke to Governor Clinton, and was much pleased with that gentleman. At length I got to Albany on the 17th, though I was not expected before the 25th. General Conway had been here only three days, and I must confess I found him very active, and looking as if he had good intentions; but we know a great deal upon that subject. His first words were, that the expedition was quite impossible. I was at first very distrustful of this report, but have found that he was right. Such is at least the idea I have formed of this ill-concerted expedition, during these two days past.

" General Schuyler, General Lincoln, and General Arnold had written before my arrival to General Conway, in the most decided terms, that in our present circumstances there was no possibility of beginning an enterprise into Canada. The quartermaster-general, commissary-general, and clothier-general, of what they call the northern department, are entirely of the same opinion. Colonel Hazen, who has been appointed to a place, which interferes with those above mentioned, was the most desirous of going. The reason of such an ardor I think I may attribute to other motives. However, the same Colonel Hazen confesses we are not strong enough to think of the expedition at this moment. As to the troops, they are disgusted, and, if you except some of Hazen's Canadians, reluctant to the utmost degree to begin a winter's incursion into so cold a country. I hare consulted every body, and every body answers, it would be madness. I have been deceived by the Board of War. They have, by the strongest expressions, promised me three thousand men. Now, Sir, I do not believe I can find in all twelve hundred fit for duty, and the greatest part of these are naked, even for a summer campaign. I was to

find General Stark with a large body, and indeed General Gates told me, ' *General Stark will have burnt the fleet before your arrival.*' Well, the first letter I receive in Albany is from General Stark, who wishes to know ' what number of men, from where, for what time, and for what rendezvous, *I desire him to raise.*' Colonel Biddle, who was also to raise men, would have done something, *had he received money.* One asks what encouragement his people will have, the other has no clothes, not one of them has received a dollar of what was due to them. I have applied to every body, I have begged at every door I could for two days, and I find that I could do something, were the expedition to be begun five weeks hence. But you know we have not an hour to lose, and indeed it is now rather too late, had we every thing in readiness.

" There is a spirit of dissatisfaction prevailing among the soldiers, and even the officers,-which is owing to their not having been paid for a long time. This department is much in arrears, and as near as I can ascertain, there are about eight hundred thousand dollars due to the Continental troops, militia, the quartermaster's, and other departments. It was with four hundred thousand dollars, only the half of which is arrived to-day, that I was to undertake the expedition, and satisfy the men under my command. I have sent to Congress the account of these debts. Some clothes, by Colonel Hazen's activity, are arrived from Boston, but not enough.

" We have had intelligence from a deserter, who makes the enemy stronger than I thought. I have sent to Congress a full account of the matter. I hope it will open their eyes. What they will resolve upon, I do not know.; but I think I must wait here for their answer. I have enclosed to the President copies of the most important letters I have received. It would be tedious to your Excellency, were I to enter into minute details. It will be sufficient to say, that the want of men, clothes, money, and the want of time, deprive me of all hopes as to this incursion.

" Your Excellency may judge, that I

am very much distressed by the disappointment. My being appointed to the command of the expedition is known through the continent; it will soon be known in Europe, as I have been desired by members of Congress to write to my friends. The people will be in great expectation, and what shall I answer? I am afraid it will reflect on my reputation, and that I shall be laughed at. My fears upon this subject are so strong, that I would choose to act hereafter only as a volunteer, unless Congress offer me the means of mending this disagreeable business. But I am very far from giving them the least hint upon that matter. General Arnold seems very fond of a diversion against New York, but lie is too unwell to take the field within four or five months. I should be happy if something was proposed to me in that way, but I will never ask, nor even seem desirous of any thing, directly from Congress. I think your Excellency will approve of my staying here till further orders, and of my taking the liberty of sending my despatches to Congress by a very quick conveyance, without their going through the hands of my general. I was anxious to acquaint them soon with my disagreeable and ridiculous situation. With the greatest affection and respect, I have the honor to be, &c.

" Lafayette."

James Duane To Governor Clinton.

" Albany, 19 February, 1778. " Dear Sir, " The day I despatched my last letter to your Excellency, I was honored with a visit from the Marquis de Lafayette, on his route to this city. It was his request and the wish of Congress, that I should attend him, and give him any information in my power. The Marquis is very assiduous and active, and examines and will judge for himself. It is plain that he finds neither the troops nor the preparations in the condition he expected; nor has he met with any person, I believe, civil or military, in this quarter, who approves of the enterprise; though from this part of the State he will receive every thing he asks, which they can grant. His zeal for this country, of which he has given marks even to enthusiasm, and his ar-

dent desire of glory, lead him to wish the expedition practicable; but he is too considerate to pursue it rashly, or without probable grounds of a successful issue. I must mention to your Excellency a circumstance, which shows the liberality of his disposition. He determined, on his entering into Canada, to supply his army through his own private bills on France, to the amount of five or six thousand guineas, and to present that sum to Congress, as a proof of his love to America, and the rights of human nature. With great respect and esteem, I have he honor to be, &c.

" James Dcane."

Marquis De Lafayette To General Washington.

" Albany, 23 February, 1778. " Dear General,

" I have an opportunity of writing to your Excellency, which I could not miss, even should I become tedious and troublesome. If they have sent me far from you, I know not for what purpose, I must at least make some little use of my pen, that all communication between your Excellency and myself may not be cut off. I have lately informed you of my distressing and ridiculous situation. I am sent, with a great noise, at the head of an army, to do great things. The whole continent, France, and, what is the worst, the British army will be in expectation. How far they will be deceived, how far we shall be ridiculed, you may judge by the candid account you have got of the state of our affairs. There are things, I dare say, in which I am deceived. A certain Colonel is not here for nothing. One other gentleman became very popular before I came to this place. Arnold himself is very fond of him. I am sure a cloud is drawn before my eyes. However, there are points I cannot be deceived in. The want of money, the dissatisfaction of the soldiers, the disinclination of every one (except the Canadians, who mean to stay at home) for this expedition, are as conspicuous as possible. *My expedition will be as famous as the secret expedition* against Rhode Island.

" I confess, my dear General, that I find myself of very quick feelings,

whenever my reputation and glory are concerned. My desire of doing something is such, that I have thought of doing it by surprise with a detachment; but it seems to me rash and impossible. I should be very happy if you were here to give me advice, but 1 have not any body to consult. They have sent to me more than twenty French officers. I do not know what to do with them. I beg you will give me the line of conduct, which you advise me to follow on every point. I am at a loss how to act, and indeed I do not know for what I am here myself. However, being the eldest officer, I think it is my duty to mind the business of this part of America as well as I can. General Gates yet holds the title and power of Commander-in-chief of the northern department; but, as two hundred thousand dollars are arrived, I have taken upon myself to pay the most necessary part of the debts we are involved in. I am about sending provisions to Fort Schuyler. I will go and see the fort. I will try to get some clothes for the troops, and buy these articles for the next campaign. I have directed some money to be borrowed upon my credit, to satisfy the troops, who are much discontented. I endeavour to do all for the best, though I have no particular instructions, and I will come as near as I can to General Gates's intentions.

" I fancy the actual scheme is to have me out of this part of the continent, and General Conway as chief under the immediate direction of General Gates. How they will bring it about I do not know, but be certain something of that kind will appear. You are nearer than myself, and every honest man in Congress is your friend; therefore you may foresee and prevent the evil a hundred times better than I can. I would only give that idea to your Excellency. After having written to Europe, by the desire of the members of Congress, so many fine things about my commanding an army, I shall be ashamed if nothing can be done by me in that way. Will you be so good as to present my respects to your lady. With the most tender affection and the highest respect, I am, &c.

" Lafayette."

Similar representations were at the same time made to Congress, and it was resolved to instruct the Marquis dc Lafayette to suspend the irruption into Canada, and at the same time to assure him, " that Congress entertain a high sense o'f his prudence, activity, and zeal, and that they are fully persuaded nothing has or would have been wanting on his part, or on the part of the officers who accompanied him, to give the expedition the utmost possible effect." — *Secret Journal, March 2d.* The Marquis returned to General Washington's camp the first week in April.

No. XII. p. 234.

SIR WILLIAM HOWE TO GENERAL WASHINGTON.

Philadelphia, 5 February, 1778. Sir, By advices received from Rhode Island, transmitting to me a copy oi a letter from General Heath to Lieutenant-General Burgoyne, a copy of which is enclosed, I am informed that it is determined to detain General Burgoyne's troops in New England until all demands for their provisions and other necessaries are satisfied, and that this determination is grounded, not only upon a requisition of mine for provisions to be sent in for the subsistence of the prisoners in my possession, and for the purchase of other necessaries, but upon a forgery by my agents, emissaries, and abettors, of what are called continental bills of credit. This last allegation is too illiberal to deserve a serious answer.

With regard to the other, I know not from what expression, in any of my letters to you, it has been understood, that I made the requisition alluded to. You know that the allowance of provisions to prisoners, from the beginning of my command, has been equal in quantity and quality to what is given to our own troops not on service. If you had thought this insufficient, you might have directed a farther supply from the markets, and were likewise at liberty to send in whatever articles you thought proper from the country. The allowance of fuel has been also regulated, as well as our means would admit, and a similar permission of purchase or supply from

you has never been refused. My letter of the 21st of April last explained to you what was afforded to the prisoners; clothing, and some other necessaries, they had a right to expect from those, who had been the occasion of their being exposed to the chance of captivity, and that idea I have ever understood to be mutual. But notwithstanding the remonstrances I made to you upon that point, finding that supplies were not sent in, my humanity interposed in behalf of the unfortunate men in our possession; and, on a late representation of their distress, I permitted in this city the purchase of blanketing, and such other necessaries as the severity of the winter required, and without which they must absolutely have perished.

Confident as I am, that you will acknowledge this to be a just recital of facts, I cannot but think it unnecessary to say any thing farther, either upon the cruelty falsely alleged to have been exercised against the prisoners, or the unjust reflections you have been so often induced to transmit to me upon that head. In consideration, however, of the real and unavoidable distresses of the prisoners on both sides, as well as to put an end to all fruitless altercation on the subject, I shall consent to an immediate exchange of all prisoners now in our possession, as well officers as private men, so far as the number of the latter, and parity of the rank of the former, will admit. In the mean time, I shall wait the arrival here of the British officers, whom you have released upon their paroles, and shall, without delay, send an equal number to you in return.

With regard to the account for provisions and other necessaries, which I find by General Heath's letter is become a pretext for infringing, if it is not intended as an absolute breach of, the convention of Saratoga, I do readily agree to the immediate appointment of commissioners, on your part and on mine, to settle that account, together with all other accounts for provisions, dec. furnished the prisoners on either side, and to make payment of the balance.

You have only to name your commissioners (two will, I think, be sufficient);

and appoint a convenient place and time for their meeting two gentlemen on my part, to terminate the business. The exchange of prisoners, and the accommodation of the difference that has so long subsisted between us upon that score, may be adjusted at the same time by the same commissioners, upon an equitable plan as formerly proposed by yourself.

These propositions, founded, as they in great measure are, upon your own suggestions, I consider as now mutually agreed upon between us; and therefore I must hope to find that you are capable of carrying them finally into execution, without permitting any set of men to interfere, at their pleasure, with such authority as has been vested in you, for the exchange of prisoners, and for the decision of all matters relating to them. As I have no objection to the earliest meeting of the commissioners for completing the exchange and liquidating the accounts, I trust there will be no new impediment to the release of General Burgoyne's troops, but that you will give immediately such orders for their embarkation upon the arrival of the transports at Boston, as will remove every difficulty. With due respect, I am, dec

W. Howe.

Philadelphia, 14 February, 1778. Sir, I have received the favor of your letter of the 10th instant, in consequence of which I shall send two commissioners to meet those on your part at Germantown, on the day appointed. The distresses,' which from too good authority I understand the lower class of prisoners labor under, induce me to request you will give such directions as may expedite the exchange of the non-commissioned officers and private men, in the mode you have proposed; and as the foreigners and-British must be equally desirous of their liberty, and equally considered in the general release, I trust you will direct that the prisoners sent in are proportioned as nearly as the numbers of each in your possession and their situation will admit.

VOL. V. 68

With respect to the exchange of commissioned officers, you will permit me to premise, that this must be governed by the release of the Hessian field-officers taken at Trenton, and Lieutenant-Colonel Archibald Campbell of the seventy-first regiment, who have not only been longest confined, but have hitherto been the objects of particular exception; the exchange for those gentlemen, as well as for the other officers, will then take place as is agreed upon. This will explain the meaning of the paragraph in my letter quoted by you, with respect to the release of officers upon parole prior to the arrival of LieutenantColonel Campbell and the Hessian field-officers. I desire to be understood, that in this general exchange the officers and soldiers belonging to the army commanded by Lieutenant-General Burgoyne, who were taken prior to the convention of Saratoga, are to be considered within the description of prisoners, equally with those of the army more immediately under my command.

It seems necessary, with regard to citizens, to postpone the exchange of them until the meeting of the commissioners, who, by a personal discussion, may finally ascertain the distinctions and equality of the persons to be exchanged. With due respect, I am, etc

W. Howx.

No. XIII. p. 272.
GENERAL HOWE TO GENERAL WASHINGTON.

Philadelphia, 10 March, 1778. Sir,

I cannot refrain from expressing my surprise, upon the receipt of your letter dated on the 9th instant, desiring that the meeting of the commissioners, appointed by yourself to be on the day following, should be deferred, and to so remote a period as the last of the month, when you must be sensible how essential this meeting is to the relief of the prisoners on both sides, and particularly of those with you, whose sufferings are extreme from the want of the necessaries lately intended for them, which by the most unjustifiable means they were prevented from receiving. Upon these considerations I am to request you will propose some day in the ensuing week far entering upon the business of the commission.

My order for sending General Lee to

Philadelphia by sea was prior to my knowledge of General Prescott's arrival at New York; I have since signified my permission for him to come hither by land, accompanied by Major Williams, of the British artillery, agreeably to the General's own request. When the agreement was concluded upon to appoint commissioners to settle a general exchange, I expected there would have been as much expedition used in returning LieutenantColonel Campbell, and the Hessian field-officers, as in returning Major-General Prescott, and that the cartel might have been finished by the time of the arrival of General Lee. If, however, there should be any objection to General Prescott's remaining at New York, until the aforementioned officers are sent in, he shall, to avoid altercation, be returned upon requisition. With due respect, I am, Sir, &c.

W. Howe.

GENERAL HOWE TO GENERAL WASHINGTON.

Philadelphia, 15 Much, 1778. Sir, 1 have received your letter of the 12th instant, wherein I observe you still persevere in the procrastination of the meeting of the commissioners. That a measure urged by yourself as confessedly interesting to the unhappy prisoners on both sides, and in which I cannot conceive you to be controlled, should Iks thus peremptorily suspended without any reason assigned, carries with it the appearance of something disingenuous. My last letter was, in my opinion, clear and explicit on the subject of Genera! Lee; and my proposition concerning General Prescott might, I think, have obviated any suspicion of ambiguity on my part.

On the arrival of Lieutenant-Colonel Campbell, any officer of yours of the same rank, whom you may be pleased to name, shall be immediately released. Mr. Ethan Allen, I understand, bears the rank of a colonel. With due respeot, I am, Sir, &c.

W. Howb.

No. XIV. p. 310.
THE PRESIDENT OF CONGRESS TO GEORGE WASHINGTON.

Torktown, 14 April, 1T7& Sir, In obe-

dience to the directions of Congress, I am to acknowledge the receipt of your letter of the 4th instant. Congress with great concern perceive, that your sensibility is wounded by their resolu tions. Placing the firmest confidence in your prudence, abilities, and integrity, they wish to preserve that harmony with you, which is essential to the general weal. You may rest assured, that, far from any intention to give you pain, their resolutions have no other motives or end but the public good. They therefore hope, that you will not in future be distressed by apprehensions, as injurious to their honor as they are to your own feelings.

However different the views of Congress may seem to you now from what you supposed them to be, when you entered into your late engagements with General Howe, Congress certainly had nothing in view but a proper respect to the dignity, safety, and independence of these States. The duplicity of General Howe, and authentic information, that the gentlemen appointed by you to negotiate the cartel held opinions repugnant to the sense of Congress, constrained them in a matter of such high moment, as forming a general cartel, to express their sentiments in an explicit manner, lest they might have only to lament, when it was out of their power to remedy, a misapprehension on points deeply affecting, in their judgment, the safety and honor of these States.

Congress expected that you would consider their resolutions of the 30th ultimo in the light of private instructions, calculated to show their sense with respect to the general outlines of the proposed cartel; a practice usual with the supreme power of every Slate in similar cases. You observe that a strict adherence to all the resolutions of Congress must of necessity destroy all idea of a cartel; but, as a distinction can easily be made betwixt such of the resolutions of Congress as flow from general principles of policy, and those which arise from circumstances which have rendered a variation from time to time necessary, it is conceived that an attention to this discrimination will rid you of those embarrassments, which you may, at first view, think yourself entangled with.

The resolution of Congress, of the 19th of December, respecting the mode of settlement for supplies to the enemy's prisoners, seems not to have been sufficiently attended to. It is left at the option of the enemy to pay either in coin, dollar for dollar, or in provisions equal in quantity and kind to what is furnished. Whatever objections may be made against the first mode, there surely cannot be a more just and equal ratio than the latter. General Burgoyne lately made the same objections on this point, which occurred to you; but, on being reminded of the alternative offered by the resolution, he acquiesced, and the victualling ships are now actually delivering provisions in payment for what they received. The commissaries of prisoners on each side may pass receipts for the rations received, expressing the *quantum* of each article received for the subsistence of the prisoners in the power of the contracting parties, and the balance may be paid in provisions, or in coin, at the option of either party. The mode suggested by you is liable to this strong objection, that it would lay us under the necessity of furnishing the enemy's prisoners with us, as well as ours with them, with provisions; which certainly would be a capital advantage to them, if wo consider the distance whence they must derive their supplies.

The resolution of the 30th December was a measure jiaturally Sowing from the Treason Acts, which the respective States have passed in consequence of the express recommendation of Congress. On a mature deliberation, they are convinced, that a deviation from it would be subversive of our character as an independent people, and inconsistent with sound policy. No act of Congress can suspend the operation of the laws of the different States, and therefore they cannot consent that any measure should be adopted in the proposed cartel, which may contravene this resolution. It does not however appear to Congress, that any embarrassment will arise in this matter, unless the enemy should insist upon an article in the

cartel, that Americans taken in arms shall be entitled to the benefit of an exchange. Under the terms of " officer for officer, soldier for soldier, &c." which are generally used in cartels, traitors would no more bo included by the laws of nations than deserters. The carrying of this resolution into practice can depend only on the will of the several States, who in this respect must be presumed to be governed by principles of policy, of which they must necessarily be competent judges.

With respect to the resolution concerning General Lee, at his request Congress are willing that you should wave his exchange for Major-General Prescott as a preliminary article. It is, however, their intention, that no cartel be acceded to, unless it be expressly admitted therein, that General Lee be exchanged for General Prescott.

By order of Congress,

Henry Laurens, *President.* VOL. T. T T

No. XV. p. 361.

BRITISH FORCES IN AMERICA.

As many of General Washington's movements and plans depended on what he supposed to be the strength of the enemy, a view of the genera state of the British army at different stages of the war win contribute much to a just understanding of various parts of bis correspondence. The following summaries have been copied from the original returns in the State Paper Office. The numbers represent *effective* troops.

State of the Army, June 3d, 1777.
Jersey. JVew York.
13799 *Stolen Island. Rhode Island.*
British Infantry. 515 British Infantry. 1064
" Artillery. 11 Hessian ".. 14S6
Waldeck Infantry. 330 British Artillery. 71 856 3631 *PavivaHook.*
British Infantry. 360 Total of the Army, 20957.

Foreign Troops in America, June 24th, 1777.
Hessian. 12777
Anspach. 1293
Waldeck. 679
Total, 14749.
State of the Army, March 26th, 1778.

Philadelphia..w York. Rhode Island.
British. 13078 British. 3486 British. 1610
German. 5202 German. 3689 German. 2116
Provincial 1250 Provincial 3281 Provincial 44 19530 10456 3770
Total of the Army, 33756.

The diminution since the preceding return was occasioned by detachments sent to the West Indies, Florida, and Halifax.

On the 21st of January, 1779, the following regulations were adopted for the Provincials in the King's service. 1. An allowance to every regiment of forty pounds a year contingent money. 2. Three guineas for every recruit approved of and mustered by the inspector. 3. One guinea for each deserter apprehended.

February 15th, 1779.
New York
Long Island
Staten Island
Paulus Hook
Rhode Island
7821
New York and its
Dependencies.
22814
December 1st, 1779.
'British. 13848
German 10836
' Provincial 4072 28756
Total, 3345a
Total, 38569.
Halifax and
Penobscot. 3460 Georgia. 3930
West Florida 1787
Bermuda and
Providence Island (vW
9813

The whole number *of Provincial Forces* at this time in the British army was 8954.

The instructions from the Commander-in-chief to the Marquis de Lafayette (p. 368) will explain the objects for which he was detached from the main army. On the 18th of May he marched

from camp at the head of two thousand four hundred men, with fire cannon, and took post at Barren Hill, on the east side of the Schuylkill, eleven miles from Philadelphia, and about the same distance from Valley Forge. Prompt intelligence of this movement was communicated to General Clinton in Philadelphia by his spies. He immediately formed a plan for attacking Lafayette; and, in the night of the 19th, General Grant marched up the Delaware towards Frankford, at the head of five thousand men, with orders to diverge to the led through Whitemarsh, and come upon the rear of the American detachment. At the same time a strong body of troops under General Grey crossed the Schuylkill, marched up its western bank, and took a station two or three miles below Barren Hill; and another corps, said to have been commanded by General Clinton in person, proceeded along the direct road from Philadelphia, and halted at Chestnut Hill.

Lafayette's position was skilfully chosen. His troops were encamped on a commanding eminence, flanked by the Schuylkill and rocky precipices on the right, and by woods and several strong stone houses on his left. His cannon were in front. A few hundred yards in advance of his left wing were Captain MLane's company and about fifty Indians. Videttes and pickets were stationed on the roada leading to Philadelphia, and those towards Whitemarsh he had ordered to be watched by sis hundred Pennsylvania militia. At a short distance from his left stood a church, where two roads united, one of which led to Matson's Ford across the Schuylkill, and the other to Valley Forge by the way of Swedes' Ford.

Early in the morning of the 20th, while Lafayette was conversing with a girl, who was preparing to go into Philadelphia for intelligence under the pretence of visiting her relations, news came that a body of cavalry had been seen at Whitemarsh,' dressed in red. As Lafayette was expecting a detachment of dragoons to join him in that direction, he at first supposed they were his own men, and felt no concern. He sent out an officer, however, to reconnoitre, who soon returned with the report, that a column of the enemy was in full march

along the road from Whitemarsh to Swedes' Ford, a little more than a mile from his encampment, and that the front of the column had actually gained the road, which led from Barren Hill to Valley Forge. This was General Grant's division, and as another was approaching on the Philadelphia road, the situation of Lafayette's detachment was now alarming and critical, being nearly surrounded by the enemy.

Comprehending in a moment the full extent of the danger, Lafaÿette, with great presence of mind, assumed an air of composure and unconcern, which calmed the fears of his officers. He changed his front without disorder, stationed a party in a churchyard surrounded by a wall, and drew up the remainder in such a manner, that they were protected by the woods and the stone houses. It was now ascertained, that the only road by which he could proceed to Swedes' Ford, was in possession of the enemy. He immediately resolved to retreat to Matson's Ford. The road was concealed from the enemy by an intervening hill covered with wood. General Poor led the advanced guard, and Lafayette brought up the rear. In the mean time he despatched several small parties through the wood, with orders to show themselves at different points as heads of columns, that the enemy might be deceived into a belief of his marching to an attack. The manoeuvre was entirely successful. When General Grant saw these heads of columns, he supposed the army was in their rear, halted his troops, and prepared for action, to prevent his line from being attacked in its flank. Lafayette employed the time thus consumed, in marching quickly to Matson's Ford, and his heads of columns gradually fell back and joined in the retreat. The whole army arrived safely at the ford, crossed it, look possession of the high grounds on the west side of the river, and formed in the order of battle. While the artillery was crossing.the river, there was skirmishing with the enemy's advanced parties, in which the Ameficans lost nine men killed and taken. Two of the enemy's lighthorse were killed, and others

wounded. Seldom has a military manoeuvre been executed with more skill and success.

General Grant marched down the road to the church at Barren Hill, where he met the other division, supposed to be under General Clinton. It was too late to overtake the retreating army. They pushed forward to the ford, but finding Lafayette strongly posted on the opposite side of the river, they made no attempt to cross. All the British troops retired immediately to Philadelphia.

The surprise was owing to the negligence of the militia, who, in disobedience of orders, had removed from their station at Whitemarsh without the General's knowledge. An amusing adventure occurred during the retreat. A body of British light-horse came suddenly upon the Indians, who were posted in a wood at a considerable distance from the main army. The Indians fired their muskets, and set up a hideous yell according to their custom in battle. Both parties ran off, equally frightened at the unexpected and terrific appearance of their antagonists.

No. XVII. p. 395.

INSTRUCTIONS TO SIR HENRT CLINTON.

When Lord North's conciliatory bills were passing through parliament, there seems to have been some' hope on the part of the ministers, that they would be favorably received by the Americans. Preparations were at the same time made, however, for carrying on the war in case the negotiation should fail. The following is the *substance* of the instructions from Lord George Germain to Sir Henry Clinton, as transcribed from the original despatches in the *State Paper Office..*

On the 8th of March, Lord George Germain wrote to General Clinton, that the resignation of General Howe had been accepted by the King, and that General Clinton was appointed as his successor. In the same letter he gave notice, that commissioners would shortly go out with proposed terms of conciliation, which there was reason to believe would bring about.a settlement of the difficulties, and lead to a peace.

" But should the attempt not succeed," said Lord George Germain, " the King is determined, in conformity with the general voice of the nation, to prosecute the war with vigor, and the means will be provided. The following are the intentions of the government respecting the next campaign. Every possible effort will be made to send out reinforcements. Several new corps have been voted by parliament, and, as there is great activity in recruiting, it is hoped that in the course of thesummer ten or twelve thousand British soldiers will be ready, and also a regiment or two of Germans. The war must be pursued on a different plan from that on which it has hitherto been conducted. Care must be taken to provide for the security of the King's possessions in America. An additional force must be sent from England to Canada, as well to secure that province, as to annoy the colonies on that side, and oblige the enemy to keep a boJr of troops in that quarter. Newfoundland, Nova Scotia, and the Florida must be strengthened. A British regiment, and two German regiments, making about three thousand men, are to be sent to Canada; a detachment of artillery to Newfoundland, where a corps is likewise to be raised for the defence of the Island; three regiments to Halifax; two to St. Augustine and Pensacola. When these detachments are made, seven Scotch regiments, of one thousand men each, will remain in the army under your command.

" Should you not succeed in bringing Washington to a general and decisive action early in the season, it is recommended not to pursue an offensive warfare against the interior, but leave men enough to defend the posts, and embark a detachment on board the King's ships, and attack the harbours along the coast between New York and Halifax. Meantime the troops at Rhode Island may be employed in destroying the shipping in Providence River, and other inlets and creeks in that vicinity. If this service cannot be executed, without detaching so many men from Philadelphia as to leave that place insecure, then such a post may be taken on the Delaware River and fortified, as may be defended by a small number of men, the shipping thereby protected, and the navigation of the river obstructed. Philadelphia may then be evacuated, leaving only a garrison at the above post, and taking the remaining troops to New York, except such as are wanted for the expedition against the northern sea-ports. Not that the retaining of Philadelphia is not thought a very important object, and it is to be abandoned only on the condition, that the northern service cannot be effected without it.

" This maritime expedition against the northern sea-ports will probably be completed by the month of October, and it is the King's intention, that an attack shall be made on the southern colonies in the winter, with a view to the conquest and possession of Georgia and South Carolina. The various accounts received from those provinces concur in representing the people generally disposed to return to their allegiance. Arms will therefore be sent out for the well affected. Georgia should be first taken, and the passage into South Carolina will then be comparatively easy. A communication may also be opened with the loyal inhabitants of North Carolina. While these operations are going on, every opportunity should be embraced for making diversions in Virginia and Maryland. Such are the genera views of the ministers, but these hints are not meant as *positive orders;* on the contrary, it is expected the Commander will exercise his discretion according to circumstances."

Five days after the date of the above despatch, that is, on the 13th of March, the Marquis de Noailles communicated an official paper to the English government, stating that a treaty of amity and commerce with the United States had been signed by the King of France. This intelligence caused the ministry immediately to change the plan of conducting the war, which had previously been concerted. On the 21st of March, positive instructions to the following purport were sent to Sir Henry Clinton.

" The French ambassador having given notice, that his King has signed a treaty with the agents of the revolted colonies, it is resolved to make a prompt attack upon the Island of St. Lucia in the West Indies. You will send with the greatest secrecy and despatch an armament of five thousand men, with a proper corps of artillery, ordnance, provisions, and stores, on board transports, and under convoy of a suitable number of ships of war, to make a descent upon St. Lucia. If the attack proves successful, such a number of the troops is to be left there as may be necessary for the defence of the Island, and the remainder to be distributed among the British West India Islands at such places, as the commander of the expedition shall deem expedient. It is essential to the success of the expedition, that it should be carried into immediate effect. The departure of the fleet should be urged by every effort.

" Another division of three thousand men is to be detached to Florida, with provisions, ordnance, and stores. These troops are to proceed in two divisions under a convoy; the first division to consist of such a part of the three thousand men, as it shall be thought advisable to send to St. Augustine; the other division to consist of the remainder and be sent to Pensacola. With this latter division the officer is to go out, who takes the command of all the forces in Florida.

" When these detachments shall have been made, or while they are making, Philadelphia is to be evacuated; all the troops to be embarked, with every thing belonging to the army, and to proceed thence to New York, where they will wait the issue of the negotiation, which the commissioners have been authorized to propose to the Congress.

" Should the negotiation fail, and should you be in danger of being overpowered in New York by the superior force of the enemy, you are to evacuate that place, embark all the troops, and proceed under convoy to Rhode Island. If that post can be maintained, leave a sufficient force for its defence, and proceed with the remainder of the army to Halifax. Let all the force necessary for the defence of Nova Scotia be retained there, and detach what can be spared to Canada, with a due proportion of artillery and stores."

The most remarkable feature in the above instructions is, that they would seem to furnish an almost demonstrative proof, that the British government on the 8th of March was not informed of the signature of the American treaty in Paris, which took place a month before, and was known to Mr. Fox and several other members of Parliament in the opposition, it having been openly proclaimed by them on the floor of the house. If the ministers were acquainted with the fact when they first wrote, it is extraordinary that they should, between the 8th and 21st of March, decide on so radical a change in their plan for conducting the war. In any view, it is not easy to account for their wavering counsels to the commander-in-chief of the British forces in America. They must have had very strong suspicions of the treaty, if not a positive knowledge, before the communication of the Marquis de Noailles, and in either case more consistency of design would be expected.

A few days after the above despatches, Lord George Germain wrote to Sir Henry Clinton; " I have the satisfaction to acquaint you, that the treaty made by the French court with the agents of the rebel colonies appears to have been done without the participation of Spain, as hitherto that court has shown no hostile intentions against Great Britain; and it is probable, that France has been induced to take, that precipitate step through the apprehension, that the distresses of the rebels would oblige them to accommodate with Great Britain without trying the fortune of another campaign. I trust, however, that the people in general have not so entirely lost all affection for this country, and regard for their own interests and future happiness, as to prefer an alliance with France to a renewal of their connexion with Great Britain upon terms so very advantageous to them, as those which the commissioners are authorized to offer, and that peace will be restored without the infliction of further severities." — *3fS. Letter, April 12th.*

Again; " I have sent to Lord and Sir William Howe the acts, which have been passed the last session, as the ground of accommodation with the colonies; and, as they were at the same time directed to transmit them to the Congress, we expect with great impatience an account of their reception and effect, and flatter ourselves it will be favorable, as we understand several of the general officers in Mr. Washington's army, and the people of the country, were disposed to peace." — *July 1st.*

Such were the views of the ministers, even at this stage of the war; but the sequel proved, that their knowledge of the feelings, opinions, and condition of the American people was extremely limited, and biassed by their prejudices and wishes.

No. XVIII. p. 429.

BATTLE OF MONMOUTH.

Soon after General Lee rejoined the army at Valley Forge, a curious incident occurred. By an order of Congress, General Washington was required to administer the oath of allegiance to the general officers. The major-generals stood around Washington, and took hold of a Bible together according to the usual custom; but, just as he began to administer the oath, Lee deliberately withdrew his hand twice. This movement was so singular, and was performed in so odd a manner, that the officers smiled, and Washington inquired the meaning of his hesitancy. Lee replied, " As to King George, I am ready enough to absolve myself from all allegiance to him, but I have some scruples about the Prince of Wales." The strangeness of. this reply was such, that the officers burst into a broad laugh, and even Washington could not refrain from a smile. The ceremony was of course interrupted. It was renewed as soon as a composure was restored proper for the solemnity of the occasion, and Lee took the oath with the other officers. Connected with the subsequent conduct of General Lee, this incident was thought by some, who were acquainted with it, to have a deeper meaning than at first appeared, and to indicate a less ardent and fixed patriotism towards the United

States, than was consistent with the rank and professions of the second officer in the command of the American forces.

The army having crossed the Delaware in pursuit of the British retreating from Philadelphia, a council of war was held at Hopewell, June 24th, in which, after stating the relative strength and position of the two armies, the Commander-in-chief proposed the following questions.

" Will it be advisable for us, of choice, to hazard a general action *1* If it is, should we do it by immediately making a general attack upon the enemy, by attempting a partial one, or by taking such a position, if it can be done, as may oblige them to attack us? If it is not, what measures can be taken, with safety to this army, to annoy the enemy in their march? In fine, what precise line of conduct will it be advisable for us to pursue?"

Lee was strenuously opposed to a general action. Being the highest in rank, and an officer of great experience, the younger officer were much influenced by his arguments and opinions. The council finally decided that a general action was not advisable, but that " a detachment of fifteen hundred men be immediately sent to act, as occasion may serve, on the enemy's left flank and rear, in conjunction with the other Continental troops and militia, who are already hanging about them, and that the main body preserve a relative position, so as to be able to act as circumstances may require." This decision was signed by all the officers except Wayne. It appeared, however, that there was a wide difference of opinion as to the number of men, that ought to be sent against the enemy, although the council ultimately agreed on fifteen hundred. Lee, Stirling, Woodford, Scott, Knox, and Poor were for this number; but Steuben, Duportail, Wayne, Paterson, Greene, and Lafayette were for twenty-five hundred, or at least two thousand. It was the idea of some of the officers, also, that the detachment ought to attack the enemy, though not to bring on a general action; while others believed, that nothing more should be done, than to skirmish with the out-guards, and thus harass the retreating enemy, as circumstances would permit.

After the council was dissolved, Greene, Lafayette, and Wayne wrote separately to the Commander-in-chief, explaining more fully their views. They were not for pushing the enemy to a general action at all events; but they were decidedly of opinion, that a large detachment should be sent forward to attack their rear, and that the main army should be drawn into such a position as to commence an engagement, should the prospects be favorable. These views accorded with those of the Commander-in-chief, and he promptly determined to act in conformity with them.

From General Lee's rank the advanced detachment fell under his command, although he was totally opposed to the measure adopted. Lafayette went to Washington, reminded him of this embarrassment, and offered to take command of the attacking division. Washington said, that such an arrangement would be entirely agreeable to him, but that it could not be effected without the previous consent of General Lee. When Lafayette applied to Lee, he very readily assented, saying that he disapproved of the plans of the Commander-in-chief, that he wis sure they would fail, and that he was willing to be relieved from any responsibility in carrying them into execution. Lafayette immediately took command of his division, and marched towards the enemy. After reflecting upon the matter, Lee wrote to General Washington as follows.

GENERAL LEE TO GENERAL WASHINGTON. " Camp, at Kingston, 2o June, 1778. " Dear General, " When I first assented to the Marquis de Lafayette's taking the command of the present detachment, I confess I viewed it in a very different light from that in which I view it at present. I considered it as a more proper business of a young, volunteering general, than of the second in command in the army; but I find it is considered in a different manner. They say that a corps consisting of six thousand men, the greater part chosen, is un-

doubtedly the most honorable command next to the Commander-in-chief; that my ceding it would of course have an odd appearance. I must entreat, therefore, after making a thousand apologies for the trouble my rash assent has occasioned you, that, if this detachment does march, I may have the command of it. So far personally; but, to speak as an officer, I do not think that this detachment ought to march at all, until at least the head of the enemy's right column has passed Cranberry; then, if it is necessary to march the whole army, I cannot see any impropriety in the Marquis's commanding this detachment, or a greater, as an advanced guard of the army; but if this detachment, with Maxwell's corps, Scott's, Morgan's, and Jackson's, is to be considered at a separate, chosen, active corps, and put under the Marquis's command until the enemy leave the Jerseys, both myself and Lord Stirling will be disgraced. I am, dear General, yours, etc.
" Charles Lee."

As Washington had already given the command to the Marquis, it could not with propriety be withdrawn without his consent. Lee applied to him for the purpose, but the Marquis said he could not without great reluctance give up the command; that it had been yielded to him freely, and he was particularly desirous of retaining it This was on the second day before the battle, and there was a prospect that the enemy would be overtaken during the day. After Lee had urged the point, and appealed to the generosity and magnanimity of the Marquis, the latter at length agreed that iT he did not come up with the enemy so as to make an attack that day, he would then resign the command. Lee had already been detached with a smaller division, but was instructed not to interfere with the Marquis, if he had concerted any definite plan of attacking the enemy. The day passed over without coming to an action, and late at night Lafayette wrote a note to Lee resigning the command. The result, in regard to General Lee, is well known. The battle took place the next day, in the midst of which Lee retreated, contrary to the ex-

pectations of the Commander-in-chief, and in such a manner as to threaten the most serious consequences to the army. He was met by Washington while retreating, and was addressed by him in a tone of reprimand and censure, which wounded the pride of Lee, and gave rise to the following correspondence.

GENERAL LEE TO GENERAL WASHINGTON. Camp, English Town, 1 July 29 Jane?, 1778. " Sir,
" From the knowledge I have of your Excellency's character, I must conclude that nothing but the misinformation of some very stupid, or misrepresentation of some very wicked person, could have occasioned your making use of so very singular expressions as you did on my coming up to the ground where you had taken post. They implied that I was guilty either of disobedience of orders, want of conduct, or want of courage. Your Excellency will therefore infinitely oblige me, by letting me know on which of these three articles you ground your charge, that I may prepare for my justification, which I have the happiness to be confident I can do to the army, to the Congress, to America, and to the world in general. Your Excellency must give me leave to observe, that neither yourself, nor those about your person, could from your situation be in the least judges of the merits or demerits of our manoeuvres; and, to speak with a becoming pride, I can assert that to these manoeuvres the success of the day was entirely owing. I can boldly say, that had we remained on the first ground, or had we advanced, or had the retreat been conducted in a manner different from what it was, this whole army and the interests of America would have risked being sacrificed. I ever had, and hope ever shall have, the greatest respect and veneration for General Washington. I think him endowed with many great and good qualities; but in this instance I must pronounce, that he has been guilty of an act of cruel injustice towards a man, who certainly has some pretensions to the regard of every servant of this country. And I think, Sir, I have a right to demand some reparation for the injury committed; and, un-

less I can obtain it, I must in justice to myself, when this campaign is closed, which 1 believe will close the war, retire from a service at the head of which is placed a man capable of offering such injuries. But at the same time, in justice to you, I must repeat that I from my soul believe, that it was not a motion of your own breast, but instigated by some of those dirty earwigs, who will for ever insinuate themselves near persons in high office; for I really am convinced, that when General Washington acts from himself, no man in his army will have reason to complain of injustice or indecorum. I am, Sir, and hope I ever shall have reason to continue, your most sincerely devoted humble servant. "Charles Lee."

General Washington To General Lee.

" Head-Quarters, English Town, 30 Jane, 1778. " Sir, " I received your letter (dated through mistake the 1st of July), expressed as I conceive in terms highly improper. I am not con scious of having made use of any very singular expressions at the time of meeting you, as you intimate. What I recollect to have said was dictated by duty, and warranted by the occasion. As soon as circumstances will permit, you shall have an opportunity of justifying yourself to the army, to Congress, to America, and to the world in general, or of convincing them that you were guilty of a breach of orders, and of misbehaviour before the enemy, on the 28th instant, in not attacking them as you had been directed, and in making an unnecessary, disorderly, and shameful retreat. I am, Sir, your most obedient servant.

" George Washington."

General Lee To General Washington.

" Camp, 28 30? Jane, 1778." " Sir, " I beg your Excellency's pardon for the inaccuracy in misdating my letter. You cannot afford me greater pleasure, than in giving me the opportunity of showing to America the sufficiency of her respective servants. I trust that temporary power of office, and the tinsel dignity attending it, will not be able, by all the mists they can raise, to offuscate the bright rays of truth. In the mean time your Excellency can have no objection to my retiring from the army. I am, Sir, your most obedient humble servant.

" Charles Lee." This letter in the original is dated Jane 28th, which is evidently « nu«take, because that waa the day of the battle; and moreover it mast have been written after the preceding one from General Washington, to which it *it* an answer. Hence both of General Lee's offensive letters wen erroneotssly dated.

GENERAL LEE TO GENERAL WASHINGTON.

" Camp, 30 June, 1778. " Sir, " Since I had the honor of addressing my letter by Colonel Fitzgerald to your Excellency, I have reflected on both your situation and mine, and beg leave to observe, that it will be for our mutual convenience that a court of inquiry should be immediately ordered; but I could wish that it might be a court-martial; for, if the affair is drawn into length, it may be difficult to collect the necessary evidences, and perhaps might bring on a paper war betwixt the adherents to both parties, which may occasion some disagreeable feuds on the continent; for all are not my friends, nor all your admirers. I must entreat therefore, from your love of justice, that you will immediately exhibit your charge, and that on the first halt I may be brought to a trial; and am, Sir, your most obedient humble servant.

" Charles Lee."

General Washington To General Lee.

" Read-Quarters, English Town, 30 Jane, 1778. " SIE,

" Your letter by Colonel Fitzgerald and also one of this date have been duly received. I have sent Colonel Scammell, the AdjutantGeneral, to put you in arrest, who will deliver you a copy of the charges on which you will be tried. I am, Sir, your most obedient servant.

" George Washington."

Charges Against General Lee.

" *First;* Disobedience of orders in not attacking the enemy on the 28th of June, agreeably to repeated instructions.

" *Secondly*; Misbehaviour before the enemy on the same day, by making an unnecessary, disorderly, and shameful retreat.

" *Thirdly*; Disrespect to the Commander-in-chief, in two letters dated the 1st of July and the 28th of June."

The court-martial was convened on the 4th of July, consisting of one major-general, four brigadiers, and eight colonels. Lord Stirling was president. The court sat from time to time till the 12th of August, when they declared their opinion, that General Lee was guilty of all the charges, and sentenced him to be suspended from any command in the armies of the United States for the term of twelve VOL. V. VV months. The testimony at the trial was extremely full, and it exhibits a minute detail of the operations in the battle of Monmouth. Congress approved the sentence of the court-martial, by a vote of thirteen in the affirmative and seven in the negative, and ordered the *Proceedings* of the court to be published.

END OP VOL. V